To Sam Nunn
Whom I hope will
one day be our Commander in Chief
with thanks.
Pete McCloskey
June 8, 1992

TABLE OF CONTENTS

DEDICATION

The essays that make up this book have been written, off and on over the past five years, following a brief visit back to the mountains of Central Korea in 1987. Their motivation stems from re-reading my favorite books, *Lee's Lieutenants* by Douglas Southall Freeman. It struck me that I had been privileged, when young, to be exposed to a number of men who measured up in every way to the best of Lee's officers. By happenstance, all were Marines.

Like Lee himself, most of my friends had gone on in civil life to lead and inspire others in good causes. Each of them had that rarest of qualities, the ability to motivate others to follow them with confidence. Each passed a little of that quality on to a host of others, in particular to the young Marine reservists I watched in action in Korea during the first half of 1951 and about whom these essays are largely written.

Unfortunately a country law practice with a fair amount of court work doesn't leave much time for writing. These essays are rough at best, and are intended to be no more than a small tribute to some good friends who exemplified, in their time, the best of a demanding ethic, that of the U. S. Marine Corps.

The recent deaths of two of the men I wanted to honor most, Max Merritt and Harvey Nolan, have finally impelled me to call a halt to research and cross-checking and publish something now, rough though it may be, lest there be nobody left alive who will understand. In reviewing the individual essays, I find little cohesion, and considerable duplication. I suspect they will be read by few people other than those rare individuals who study obscure military history, but they at least tell a little about a by-gone time and may be of interest to fellow Marines.

That they appear in print at all is due to (1) a four-week jury trial postponed for 30 days, (2) a fine editor and photographer, my wife, Helen Hooper McCloskey, (3) an indefatigable secretary, Muriel Marelich, (4) the leadership, both in war and civil life, of a friend, John C. Wallace, who talked me into enlisting in the Marine Corps in 1948, and finally (5) the inspiration of two individuals who every person mentioned in these pages will agree stand among the greatest living Marines of our time, Captain Jack R. Jones, and First Lieutenant Spike Schening, Company Commander and Executive Officer, respectively, of Charlie Company, First Battalion, Fifth Marine Regiment, during the winter and spring of 1950-51.

As one former rifle platoon leader in their battalion commented about Jones and Schening: "We were privileged to walk with giants."

Like Robert E. Lee, they had worthy lieutenants of the regular Marine Corps, but Jones and Schening stand alone in the respect and affection of all who knew them.

Supreme Court Justice Oliver Wendell Holmes, Jr., three times wounded as a line company officer in that fiercest of wars, our Civil War, remarked in later life that he had been privileged to be "touched with fire" in his youth. Every Marine who served with Jack Jones and Spike Schening, from Guadalcanal, Pelelieu and Iwo Jima to the Chosin Reservoir and the final assault on The Punch Bowl in June of 1951, had that same privilege.

To them this book is dedicated.

Woodside, California
Ground Hog's Day, 1992

The Taking Of Hill 610

And Other Essays on Friendship

By Paul N. "Pete" McCloskey, Jr.

Edited by Helen Hooper McCloskey

The Cover
This watercolor painting "Assault on Hill 610" was found in a junk store years later by Colonel Charles Bunnell, who as a lieutenant had participated in the assault on 610 on June 2, l951. The artist, "Towey," has never been found. The radio operator is Frenchy Robichaud who made it to the top only to be wounded ten days later in the Soyang Valley southeast of the Punch Bowl.

First Edition
Published by Eaglet Books
580 Mountain Home Road
Woodside, CA 94062
(415) 851-0218

Library of Congress Catalog Card No. pending

Printed in the United States of America

A number of historic documents including reports and letters that appear in this book have been retypeset to improve their legibility; no changes in content have been made.

Jack R. Jones, Company Commander, Charlie Company, First Battalion Fifth Marines, November 10, 1950 to May 7, 1951.

Second Lieutenant John C. Wallace, First Platoon, Charlie Company, 1st Tank Battalion.

Second Lieutenant Max Merritt, USMC Platoon Leader, 3rd Platoon, Charlie Company, Fifth Marines, just before Inchon.

Charlie Company's officers, Masan, Korea, January, 1951. Left to right, kneeling: Bill Kerrigan, 2nd Plt.; Spike Schening, X.O.; standing: Dale Brown, 1st Plt.; Bob Richter, MGs; Walter "The Snow Fox" Godenius, C.O., Able Company; Jack Jones, C.O. Max Merritt, 3rd Plt., is not in the picture as he was still in the hospital in Japan, convalescing from wounds received at the Chosin Reservoir, Nov. 28, 1950.

Jack Jones and Max Merritt, 1988.

John C. Wallace, President, Petrolane, Inc.

Second Lieutenant Charles U. Daly, Captain Jack R. Jones, First Lieutenant Spike Schening, 1988.

Chapter 1

The Taking of Hill 610

This is a story for and about some friends.

It's time, 40 years after the fact, to permanently record a little-noticed achievement by two quiet Americans who have become a legend in their time amongst a group of friends who respect them above all others.

Both are modest men. Neither would claim credit for the success described in this story, nor even for having contributed to that success. One was able to watch the results of his handiwork only from a distance. The other wasn't around to watch, having been removed from the scene a few days earlier by a competent North Korean mortar gunner.

Yet these two men accomplished what most men hope for in their lifetimes but rarely achieve. By their leadership, patient instruction and example, they fashioned from unlikely material a creature of excellence which, for a few short weeks at least, was a living monument to their skills.

The two men were infantry officers of the regular Marine Corps. Each was a seasoned veteran of more than one of the bitter Pacific island assaults of World War II. One had been a rifle platoon leader on Iwo Jima, the other a squad leader on Guadalcanal who had been awarded a battlefield commission on Peleliu. Between them they held several Purple Hearts, two Silver Stars and two Navy Crosses.

Their creation in the winter and spring of 1951, its brief period of excellence a translation of their own professional skills, was a Marine rifle company made up mostly of reservists, some 230 young men previously unknown to combat save for a handful of veteran sergeants.

The two men were Captain Jack Jones and First Lieutenant Richard "Spike" Schening, USMC. In the early months of 1951, they served as Company Commander and Executive Officer, respectively, of Charlie Company, 1st Battalion, Fifth Marines, known amongst its peers as C/1/5.

Charlie Company had come into existence in August, 1950, made up of regular Marines, drawn from posts and stations around the world and rushed to flesh out the hastily-assembled First Marine Division which would land at Inchon, Korea, on September 15, 1950. The Division captured Seoul in two short weeks and broke the back of the first attempted communist expansion since World War II, a sudden North Korean attack which had almost driven the South Koreans and their U.N. allies into the sea only a few weeks earlier. That attack had been halted in part by the superb performance of the understrength Fifth Marine Regiment, operating in August, 1950 around the Pusan Perimeter with only two companies for each of its three infantry battalions. This force, with various supporting artillery and tank units, would ever after be proudly known as "The Brigade." Initially, the Brigade's First Battalion's two veteran rifle companies, Able and Baker, understandably looked on Charlie Company as unreliable. Bloodied in three grueling battles with the North Koreans in the searing heat of August at various key points around the Pusan Perimeter, Able and Baker had pride in themselves but were skeptical of inexperienced newcomers. Charlie Company had been hastily assembled at Camp Pendleton in August, along with Fox Company for the 2nd Battalion and Item Company for the 3rd. The three new companies, each over 200 strong, had joined the Brigade veterans at Pusan in early September, just in time to ship out for the landing at Inchon.

In the two weeks it took to capture Seoul, the First Battalion's Commander understandably relied on his two veteran companies, and Charlie Company, following some confusion on the beach after a mishap by its landing craft commanders, received less than its share of the action on the road to Seoul. At one point one of its rifle platoons did manage to take the objective assigned to the First Marine Regiment on its flank. The First Marines were led by the redoubtable Chesty Puller, and Puller's wrath, expressed to Charlie Company's 2d Lieutenant Max Merritt, was a good deal worse than the North Korean resistance had been.

After Seoul, the Division was shipped to the east coast of Korea to start the long advance north to the Yalu. It was at Yudam-ni, southwest of the Chosin Reservoir in the early morning hours of November 28, 1950, that Charlie Company finally earned the full respect of the veterans of the Brigade. Jack Jones, fresh from a desk job in Washington, had taken command of the company on November 10, after the Division's move to the Korean eastern coast. His leadership at the Chosin Reservoir in late November and in early December was awesome, battling both mass attacks of the Chinese and paralyzing cold. Charlie Company's record at the Reservoir has been the subject of comment in two books, *The New Breed* and *Retreat, Hell!*.

In *Retreat, Hell!*, (Morrow & Co.) published in 1988, there is a chapter appropriately entitled *"Charlie Arrives,"* chronicling the Company's successful dawn counterattack on November 28 against the Chinese on Hill 1282, rescuing the remnants of Easy Company of the 7th Marines.

The Chinese had attacked the 5th and 7th Regiments with overwhelming strength on the night of November 27th, overrunning Easy Company's mountaintop position on Hill 1282, and from it, threatening the headquarters and artillery units in the valley below.

Hill 1282 was the key to the fate of both regiments, now surrounded by over 100,000 Chinese.

With Easy Company overrun, at 1:00 a.m., Jones was ordered to try to regain the position with Charlie Company, less one platoon sent to assist another beleaguered company of the 7th Marines. A few words from "Charlie Arrives" sum up the story:

"It took Charlie Company more than two hours just to get within 200 yards of the top."

"Jones and Smith led the men over the top as the Marines shot, clubbed and bayoneted the Chinese and drove the 3rd Company, 1st Battalion, 235th Chinese Communist Forces Regiment, from their holes."

"Fighting was so heavy and casualties so high that Jones' men couldn't do anything for the wounded."

"Then the Chinese struck again, violently, furiously. They wanted the hilltop back in the worst way and were willing to pay any price. Jones heard the bugles first, then the shouting. Then the Chinese attacked in waves. Grenades and small-arms fire cut them down."

"Six times Jones ran forward to help bring back wounded. Grenade fragments hit him in a leg. A squad of Chinese charged into one of his machine gun positions, and all were killed."

"The Chinese paid dearly for trying to take Hill 1282. In addition to the more than 400 dead who covered its slopes, there were many hundreds of dead and wounded on top. Captured Chinese documents indicated that only six survived Jones' assault against the 3rd Company, 1st Battalion, 235th CCF Regiment. Of 116 officers and men in the 2nd Company, 94 were killed."

"The price for holding the hill was high, too. Easy Company was reduced to less than 30 men, some wounded, most suffering from frostbite. Jones' Charlie Company suffered 15 dead and 67 wounded."

"After eighteen hours of fighting as savage as any in the history of small unit warfare, Hill 1282 belonged to the Marines."[1]

Thirteen days of bitter fighting followed as the Division battled the encircling Chinese and sub-zero temperatures, finally reaching the safety of a perimeter around the port of Hungnam on December 10.

Jones led what was left of the Company back from Yudam-ni and Hagaru-ri over Toktong and Funchilin Passes and down to Hungnam, bringing its dead, wounded and equipment. Evacuated by ship, the Company rested and retrained in a peaceful rural area known as "the bean patch" near Masan at the southern tip of Korea, and Jones was able to talk the battalion commander into liberating Spike Schening from an unwanted staff job to be his Executive Officer.

Schening, a seasoned veteran of Guadalcanal and Peleliu, had been the Executive Officer of Charlie Company at Inchon, but was later assigned as the Battalion's Assistant S-3 (Operations) officer. He was delighted to get out of a staff job and back with a rifle company.

In January the Division moved north to begin a painstaking, small-unit search for North Korean guerrillas in the hills and valleys around Pohang on Korea's southeastern coast.

By that time, even the Brigade veterans in 1/5 recognized Jones as the best of company commanders and Schening as the ablest of executive officers.

Still not fully recovered from horrendous casualties at the Reservoir, the First Division was finally brought up to strength on February 16 with the arrival of 1900 men and 65 officers of the 5th Replacement Draft, landed at Pohang from the troopship, the U.S.S. General J. C. Breckinridge.

Nine young reserve lieutenants and over 200 enlisted men reported to the First Battalion of the Fifth Regiment after darkness had set in. Unaware of the privilege it carried, one lieutenant was sent to Charlie Company, where he was immediately assigned to the 19 man 60mm mortar section, a place where relatively little harm could be done by even the most inexperienced of new second lieutenants.

Two friends, Buzz Lubka and Bill Heer, went to Able Company; two others, both of World War II experience, Carey Cowart and Jim Ables went to Baker; four others, Les Proctor, Ralph "Parson" Baylock, Chuck Daly and John Baker went to either Weapons Company or Headquarters Company. Daly was assigned command of the native Koreans who made up the Battalion's Labor Company, known with some affection as "The Chiggy Bears." The Chiggy Bears' appearance was nondescript, their clothing tattered, but the number of cans of water, C-Rations and ammunition they could carry up steep ridge lines on home-made A-frames was prodigious, and more than once would save the rifle companies they supported.

The arrival of the Fifth Replacement Draft was timely; the following morning, February 17, the Battalion was up at dawn, loaded aboard "6x6" trucks and headed north for the first of four days of a "motor march" to the small country town of Wonju in central Korea.

The Chinese advance south of the 38th Parallel had slowed in January and 8th Army Commander General Matthew Ridgeway determined that a counter attack was in order, if only to restore the morale of his forces, disheartened by three months of steady withdrawal. The 187th Airborne Brigade was able to stop the last serious Chinese attack at Wonju.

Thus, on the morning of February 21, 1951, Charlie Company found itself at full strength with

---

[1]See Appendix A for the Unit Diary of 1/5 for the Reservoir Campaign, together with excerpts from *The New Breed, Retreat Hell!* and an eyewitness account by a Charlie Company rifleman.

back-to-duty veterans and new reservists, chosen, probably because of Jones' proven abilities, to be the leading company in the first counter-offensive against the Chinese, attacking north and east from Wonju. Six of its seven officers, and all of its rifle platoon leaders had been at the Reservoir. To them the fresh snowfall and relatively low hills around Wonju were no problem.

General Douglas MacArthur came over from Tokyo to stand in the rain at a slushy roadside, khaki uniform, familiar gold braided cap and all, to salute the heavily-laden Marines as they slogged through the Airborne's lines in a double column north towards the equally-battered town of Hoeng'song.

In Korea only five days, Charlie Company's newest second lieutenant was already suffering from dysentery, no doubt from an improperly-washed mess kit. He was 50 yards past MacArthur before it sunk in by whom he had just been saluted, no more than a dozen feet away.

More impressive to the lieutenant were the ribald manual salutes from the paratroopers standing alongside their muddy foxholes, deriding the length of time the Marines had spent in the rear area while the Airborne had been doing the fighting.

For the next several weeks, as the U.N. forces moved cautiously northwards, the Chinese slowly withdrew. There was lots of patrolling, an occasional night probe by the Chinese and rare sporadic exchanges of long-range rifle and machine gun fire, but few casualties on either side, at least in the First Battalion's zone of action. Carey Cowart, serving as Baker Company's mortar observer, was the only officer killed in action (KIA). As winter changed into spring, Jones and Schening worried about the continuing attrition each month through the rotation of their veteran platoon leaders, with their replacements, untried and only briefly-trained reserve lieutenants from unwar-like places like Stanford and Yale. Nevertheless, Jones and Schening were patient with the newcomers, trying, if not always successfully, to instruct them in fields of fire, where and how foxholes should be dug and camouflaged on military crests, night security and a hundred other of the basic but vital lessons of survival in the mountainous terrain of central Korea against hardy Chinese and North Korean infantrymen. New lieutenants were carefully paired with veteran platoon sergeants who could break them in slowly to the daily challenges of leadership.

After the heavy casualties at the Chosin Reservoir, the Company was lucky during the winter and early spring of 1951. It missed the heaviest skirmishing in February and March in the mountains between Hoeng'song and Chun'chon, and when the first Chinese spring counter-offensive hit on April 22nd, was fortunate to be holding a ridgeline west of the Hwachon Reservoir which was bypassed by the massive numbers of Chinese who successfully broke through the 6th ROK Division on the Marine Division's left flank. Only Baker Company, led by First Lieutenant Jim Cronin, took heavy casualties. One Baker platoon, led by Lt. Harvey Nolan and a new replacement, Pat McGahn, fought a desperate night battle on Hill 313 overlooking the town of Hwachon, and by morning had persevered against a determined Chinese attack, losing 7 KIA and 23 WIA, over half the platoon and its attached machine gun section. Nolan and McGahn would ultimately be awarded the Navy Cross for their work. In a tragic accident during the withdrawal, Jim Ables became the Battalion's second officer KIA.

Another regiment, the First Marines, contained the initial Chinese breakthrough in desperate night battles atop rugged ridgelines, and the Fifth Regiment was able to withdraw without serious incident to a new defense position west of Hong'chon, a nearly-demolished city near the 38th Parallel which the Marines had moved through on the way north only a few weeks earlier.

In early May, the inexorable Marine Corps promotion process occurred. Captain Jones was selected for Major and thereby forced upwards into a staff position, that of the S-3 Battalion Operations Officer. Schening was promoted to Captain and became Charlie Company's commander.

The Marines of the First Battalion breathed a sigh of relief at Jones' assignment. The Battalion was unique in that its commanding officer was a rarity in the regular Marine Corps, a social lion referred to with some irreverence by the Battalion's junior officers as "Idiot Six." A number of ladies in

Japan and elsewhere were accustomed to send him tins of British cookies, jigger-sized bottles of liquor and jars of hard candies. When in a good mood he would occasionally pass these out from his headquarters tent or his cavernous pockets to passing lieutenants and riflemen.

There had been more than one occasion where the Battalion had grumbled at what were perceived to be unnecessary discomforts suffered due to the Colonel's idiosyncrasies. On one occasion, in the battle for Hill 313 in late April, he had ordered a tank commander, over the latter's objection, to fire at people of unknown identity on top of 313. The resulting round wounded several of Baker Company's machine gunners. Baker's Executive Officer had to be forcefully restrained from doing damage to the Colonel's person. Word of the incident spread through the Battalion with considerable speed.

The Battalion felt a quiet envy for the professional leadership of 2/5, Lt. Col. Glen Martin, a reserve officer who had won the Navy Cross and served as a platoon leader and Company Commander during World War II. Martin had served as 2/5's Weapons Company Commander at the Reservoir. His S-3 operations officer, a former paratrooper named Gerry Averill, had been the object of veneration by the 71 officers and 1900 enlisted men who had come over on the Breckinridge as members of the Fifth Replacement Draft in February, 1951. Averill was the only regular officer aboard and commanded considerable respect as a veteran of Choiseul, Iwo Jima and the famous First Parachute Regiment.

Averill had rather forcefully demanded daily calisthenics during the two and one-half weeks aboard ship, pointing out that the average life expectancy of a second lieutenant in combat was six minutes and that everyone had damn well better get in shape if they were to have any hope of survival. He was right.

The Marine replacement drafts which arrived early each month were ill-prepared enough for the Korean winter and steep mountains. Without Averill's rigorous insistence, a lot of the 5th Draft might well have been too late in the early weeks in Korea getting up to the high ground positions which were the safest of all places in Korea.

The Battalion's operation officer (S-3) made the plans for the rifle companies' movements each day. A good S-3 could make up a great deal for a bad battalion commander.

With Martin as C.O. and Averill as S-3 of the 2nd Battalion, it was appreciated that 2/5 was in good hands. On one occasion, a Charlie Company platoon leader, moving cautiously with his platoon into enemy-controlled territory after the Chinese second spring offensive in late May, had run into Colonel Martin, all alone, well out in front of the rest of his battalion. He had merely said "Keep a good eye out, lieutenant," and indeed they had captured a Chinese prisoner within the next quarter of a mile. No one had ever seen the First Battalion's C.O. anywhere but "in the rear with the gear," a common phrase of the day.

Averill and Jones, friends from the paratroops and Iwo Jima, were two of a kind, and in the minds of Charlie Company's junior officers at least, as spring began, only Jones' common sense and battle experience stood between them and potentially unreasonable and dangerous directions from the Battalion Commander. The Regimental Commander, Colonel Richard Hayward, was a famous veteran of "the Old Corps" dating back to Nicaragua in 1928 and highly respected, but regimental headquarters was a far off place, visited by the rifle companies only when the whole regiment got together in Division Reserve. Division Headquarters was an even further place, and never visited. There people were rumored to wear clean uniforms and have hot showers and good meals.

The war in Korea in the spring of 1951 was really a rifle platoon's war. The ridgelines were usually too narrow and steep to permit more than two or three men abreast in an attack, and at night the riflemen in two-man foxholes perhaps ten yards apart on the military crests of the highest mountain tops that could be found in the area knew only that there were other Marines from their own platoon a few yards away when a stealthy probe or sudden attack occurred, usually at midnight or the early morning hours.

A rifle platoon had three squads of 13 men each; the platoon leader had a radioman, runner, two Navy hospital corpsmen and a Korean interpreter, as well as a platoon sergeant and platoon guide.

Platoon leadership mattered a great deal. A platoon leader's minor mistake in map reading could mean hours of unnecessary climbing of the wrong ridgelines or potential disaster from misdirected artillery fire. Mistakes were easy to make. Captain William Godenius, commanding Able Company during the midwinter guerrilla hunt, was affectionately known as "The Snow Fox" for an occasion when his company became lost in the tangled mountains around Pohang.

With overwhelming air and artillery superiority, the days belonged to the Marines advancing north against key terrain features in increasingly-rugged mountains. At night, however, the world was a perilous place of tense watchfulness on hilltop perimeters against the ever-possible assault by canny groups of enemy who could creep silently into position and then attack with a sudden rush, trying to overwhelm a few foxholes with overwhelming numbers.

Such an attack was not the only worry. On one stormy winter night, a drowsy Charlie Company Marine, sitting in a forward foxhole had been snatched away by a Chinese patrol, leaving his companion sleeping at the bottom of the hole. This had left an indelible impression of the need for constant watchfulness through the long night hours. Every night represented a *potential* danger, and the slightest noise a possible infiltrating enemy to the Marines in the forward foxholes, usually standing a 50% watch in times of close proximity to the enemy.

The Brigade veterans had all been rotated home by March, and with the arrival of the Eighth Replacement Draft in early May, nearly all of the Seoul to Chosin veterans had been rotated home as well. Charlie Company, like the Division's other rifle companies, was now composed almost entirely of new reservists.

The loss of Captain Jones was no real problem because Spike Schening held the affection of the troops in a measure almost equal to that of the legendary Jones. Captain Jones had been the father of the company, Schening its good uncle. Spike had served as Executive Officer through a lot of tough situations. With supreme self-confidence and ever-present good humor, he was thoroughly trusted and respected for his professional experience and sound judgment. His morning shout, "Up and roll your gear" and his insistence on taut, squared-away horseshoe packs and policing of the company area upon departure came to be regarded as special company rituals.

Unfortunately, Spike's tenure didn't last long. Arriving on a ridgetop in late May where the Second Battalion of the 7th Marines had taken heavy casualties in two days of unsuccessful frontal attacks on a Hill known only as "566" (for its elevation in meters) Schening ordered one of his platoons to take it from the flank the following morning. By the grace of God, preoccupation of the defenders with a frontal assault by a platoon of the 7th Marines, and the good fortune of an early morning fog around the crest of the hill, the platoon was successful, killing 40 and capturing 22 of the defenders. In a simultaneous frontal attack, the 7th Marines' platoon leader, Bob Buchmann, one of the young lieutenants who had come over on the Breckinridge was killed and his platoon decimated.

It was Schening's day, but his enjoyment of it was limited to a few brief minutes. He stalked forward with his gnarled walking cane to the leading fire team of the assault platoon some 200 yards north of 566 to congratulate its men. Returning to the newly-captured hilltop he found it being converged upon by dozens of Marines from both battalions. Spike was roaring out his gentle commands to "spread out . . . take cover . . . get off the God-damned skyline . . ." when North Korean gunners put three undoubtedly pre-registered 122 mortar rounds in on top of the hill, severely wounding Spike and a number of others from Charlie Company's headquarters group and mortar section, as well as from the unlucky 7th Marines. The eight men of one of the assaulting machine gun squads, going back over the top of the hill to get their packs from the morning's jump-off point, were also badly hit.

Charlie Company continued on fairly well that day in Spike's absence: one Charles U. Daly led the Second Platoon in a continuing assault which overran both the offending mortar position and the Korean regimental headquarters further up the ridgeline. Confronted by a surly and uncooperative North Korean major on the captured hilltop, Daly, his black Irish heart grieving over the loss of some of his best Marines, was reported by one of his enlisted men to have personally pushed the offender over a steep precipice.[2]

With Schening gone and Jones back at battalion head-quarters, however, the Company was now entirely in the hands of reserve officers, all new, all scholarly and none of warrior-like demeanor.

The few remaining veteran NCOs and enlisted men had reason to shudder. The newly-designated company commander and executive officer were of unknown experience and judgment. The three rifle platoon leaders, the machine gun officer and the mortar officer were likewise all young reservists, no more than a few months out of college. The oldest officer in point of time with the company had arrived only in February, 3-1/2 months earlier. The regular lieutenants who had led the three rifle platoons in the February advance from Wonju, veterans of the Chosin Reservoir battles, Gene Brown, Bill Kerrigan and Max Merritt, had all been rotated home or promoted to other commands, but not before being generous to their successors with their counsel. The other lieutenants who had done so well at the Reservoir, Byron Magness, Robert Corbett, Harold Dawe and Bob Richter, were also gone.

There was understandably a considerable concern as to whether the Company could measure up to its unexpected success on 566 with Schening gone and Jones having all he could do to keep an unreliable battalion commander under reasonable control.

Thus dawned the day of June 2, 1951, the day that the professionalism of Jones and Schening and their patience, training and example of the previous six months was to bear fruit.

Probably no one in the Battalion knew that lovely spring morning that it was exactly thirty-three years to the day that their forebears of the First Battalion, Fifth Marines, on June 2, 1918, had gone into the lines near Chateau Thierry, a few days later stopping the advancing grey-clad shock troops of the German Army with accurate aimed rifle fire at 500 yards in the wheat fields around Belleau Wood. The 5th and 6th Marine Regiments at Belleau Wood had established the first military reputation in this century for American foot soldiers. The Marines attached to the Second Army Division in France in 1918 had engaged in a succession of hard battles at Chateau Thierry/Belleau Woods, Soissons and Blanc Mont which were to set the standard for the Marines of Guadalcanal, Tarawa, Iwo Jima, Okinawa and other challenging places to seek to emulate a generation later.

Perhaps in 1951 Marine Commandant Clifton Cates and Fleet Marine Force Pacific (FMF Pac) Commander Lemuel Shepherd still remembered June 2, 1917. They had been young lieutenants in those wheat fields and at Belleau Woods. With them had been another young officer, Carl Wallace of Minnesota. All were wounded, Wallace severely so. A higher-ranking Marine, John C. Breckinridge, would later have a U.S. Navy transport named in his honor, the same ship which transported the 1900 men and 71 officers of the Fifth Replacement Draft to Korea.

Shepherd, Breckinridge and Wallace sired sons of uncommon leadership ability who were to distinguish themselves in Korea.

---

[2]Daly's words, as recalled in 1989:

First I thought the grenades were incoming mortar rounds then suddenly we were among them. At first it was hard to get the Marines to fire, to react to the flashes of incoming small arms fire and the darting, confusing figures. Just as we got to the top, Warner radioed for us to pull back. We said no. The first group of Marines charged beyond the crest. I was in a rage because of our casualties. Our second-wind charge carried us into the midst of what appeared to be a collection of NCO's and officers. We shot several but there were more of them left alive then there were available Marines, so I ordered the prisoners to strip. They did. One ran for the cliff. He was shot as he made his leap. One of the prisoners was badly wounded. I'm not proud of the fact that when a rifleman asked "should I do him a favor?" I replied "yes." I should have shot the guy myself rather than telling another Marine to do the job for me.

When they came of military age, the Shepherd, Breckinridge and Wallace boys enlisted in the Marine Corps, talking their best friends into joining them. Aboard the Breckinridge nearing the Korean coast, in February, 1951, when asked which rifle regiment he preferred to join, one lieutenant chose the 5th Marines solely in the belief that that had been his friend John Wallace's father's regiment in 1918.

By 1951, Cates and Shepherd had become the Marine Corps' leading generals, in Washington and Hawaii, respectively, trying to expedite the return to strength of a Marine Corps which President Truman had reduced to the point of extinction and threatened to abolish only a few months earlier. Truman had been an Army artillery captain with the American Expeditionary Force (A.E.F.) in France in 1917 and thought, perhaps with some justification, that the Army had done at least as much of the fighting in two wars, but that the Marines had gotten most of the glory. Former A.E.F. Veteran Truman at the outset of the Korean War once characterized the Marine Corps as "the Navy's police force," having a publicity capacity "second only to Stalin's."

Survivors of battles far more dangerous than those of 1951, Cates and Shepherd nevertheless would have recognized Jones and Schening as worthy trustees for the traditions they had helped create.

They would have been far less impressed, however, with the collection of reservists now leading Charlie Company, with most of the seasoned NCOs gone and only the memories of the principles so recently installed by Jones and Schening to serve as guideposts.

June 2, 1951

It was a beautiful spring morning. For a week the Company had been moving north by day, digging into ridge-top perimeters at night. A second Chinese spring offensive had shattered the Army's Second Division front in a massive night attack in the mountains of eastern Korea in late May, but under heavy air attack, had run out of momentum. The Fifth Regiment's 2nd and 3rd Battalions had helped stop the Chinese and the whole Regiment, along with the First and Seventh, was now counter attacking against a screen of determined North Korean units defending every ridgeline and mountaintop as the battered Chinese withdrew behind them.

In one of the wide Korean valleys running northeast from Yanggu, the valley, at the northern end, narrowed to a defile no more than 100 yards wide between low-lying hills. The defile was perhaps 500 yards long, and in addition to a shallow stream, was occupied by the main road north from Yanggu to Chorwon, one of the hubs of what the newspapers referred to as "The Iron Triangle," the ostensible anchor of the enemy's defenses in North Korea above the 38th Parallel.

The defile was dominated at its northern end by a massive mountain complex, the crowning crest of which was shown on Marine maps simply as "610." Hill 610, however, was perhaps 1800 yards distant from the northern end of the defile. The path to it led up a steep 45° slope which rose abruptly from the rice paddies 200 yards from the end of the defile onto a wooded ridge crowned by a small bare hill which dominated the defile, but was in turn dominated by a second ridge above it which, after a deep ravine, rose to 610 itself. In the distance, beyond 610 to the north, stretched ever-higher and even more rugged mountains, culminating in names which were to later gain fame, Taeam-san, the Punch Bowl and Heartbreak Ridge.

Those designations were unknown to any of the Marines on June 1st, however, as the point rifle platoon and an accompanying tank platoon of five tanks proceeding cautiously through the defile began to take fire from the ridgeline leading to 610.

Baker Company and the 2nd Battalion were in the ridges to the right; the 7th Marines somewhere across the valley on the left.

The tanks moved out and stopped in a column along the small valley on the right side of 610, with the riflemen well spread out alongside and behind.

At the southern base of the ridgeline, across the streambed, there was a small terraced rice paddy area, perhaps 100 yards across, where a few stone foundations were all that remained of what must have once been a peaceful rural village. The ridgeline rose abruptly from the paddies 200 yards or so upwards to where it leveled off for perhaps another 200 yards, to be crowned by the small round hill at its northern end. Because of the flattening out at the top of the first steep slope, the small hill at the northern end of the ridge could command the valley on both sides below as well as the 200 yard level ridgeline to its immediate front but could not cover the forward 45° slope as it dropped away to the valley. The small hill, perhaps 30 yards in diameter, was devoid of growth and ringed by bunkers. This hill was in turn dominated by the second ridge to its north, perhaps 300 feet or so higher in elevation. This second ridge-line was heavily wooded with a series of hillocks and broken terrain; it then dropped steeply into a ravine before the final steep slope up another 300 feet in elevation to the curving sugar-loaf ridge of 610 itself.

From 610 there was yet another and wider ravine, from which a knife-like ridge ascended sharply off to the northwest to a bald peak designated as "680" with a narrow, conical top perhaps 600 yards away. While 680 appeared to have a fortified observation post of some kind, 610 was the really dominant terrain feature, 200 yards in length, curving slightly, heavily wooded, and from what the Marines in the valley below could see of it, obviously the heart of the enemy's position.

On the afternoon of June 1, the platoon leaders of the 1st and 2nd Platoons from the valley below had been able to see the fortifications on the first and second ridgelines, although they lost sight of the far side of 610 once entering into the valley from the defile.

They had noted with some interest that the North Koreans sporadically, every 15 or 20 minutes or so, would drop 30 or 40 rounds of mortar fire on the first 45° slope which could not be seen and covered with direct fire from their hilltop positions. The two platoons spent much of the afternoon just north of the defile, lying behind the tanks on the right side of the valley, watching the occasional mortar barrages which could not be predicted as to timing but apparently reflected a serious worry of the Koreans that someone could be moving up the slope to attack the first key hilltop. The Koreans and Chinese were not prone to waste mortar ammunition.

A tank lieutenant from the Fifth Replacement Draft, Wally Barrett, commanded the five M-46 tanks of the 1st Platoon, Charlie Company of the First Tank Battalion. The tanks occasionally exchanged machine gun and 90 mm fire with the bunkers along the ridgeline. During the long afternoon, although the tank platoon lost its veteran platoon sergeant to machine gun fire, Charlie Company's only casualties were several of the packs which the infantrymen had been glad to leave on the tanks as they moved up, set on fire by Korean tracers. This was no small loss. The spring nights were cold and the riflemen had had occasion to rue the order during a warm spell some weeks earlier to turn in their down winter sleeping bags in return for a single blanket. Without a blanket the only recourse was to sleep "spoon-style" with other Marines, something no one relished. Warmth at night was always a major goal. Whenever a Marine got sick or was hit and sent to the rear, his blanket was immediately appropriated.

The new Company Commander, a reserve First Lieutenant, had taken over three days earlier when Spike Schening was hit. The Company had also gotten two new lieutenants, Charlie Bunnell the former Battalion Historical Officer, (Was Truman right?) and a new replacement, Doug Dacy. Dacy and Daly were old friends. Bunnell, Daly and John Goodrich, the new executive officer, were all Yale graduates. Bunnell, after several weeks as platoon leader of the 3rd Platoon, had moved up to be the Machine Gun Platoon leader, and Dacy took over the 3rd Platoon from Bunnell.

That night the company moved up into the low hills to the right of the valley, forming a tight defense perimeter. At the evening company officers' meeting word was passed that Hill 610 was the Regiment's final objective, and that if the Company could take it, the Regiment was scheduled to go into reserve for a welcome few days' rest.

The Battalion Commander and his command post were some distance to the rear, but it was said that the next day the Company would have air strikes available and all the supporting fire needed.

Of particular significance, a new forward observer replacement from the artillery battery supporting the Battalion had earned the company officers' respect by sharing a bottle of whiskey he had brought over from the States and giving his solemn promise that they could always count on his "being in the forward fox holes with you" to make sure that the 11th Marines' fire support was accurate and plentiful.

The plan of action for the following morning was for the 1st Platoon to jump off early, cross the creek and move up the 45° slope to take the first hill, with Daly then taking the 2nd Platoon around the right side to move up and attack the intermediate ridge. Dacy's 3rd Platoon would then move up on the 2nd Platoon's right onto the main ridgeline and assault 610 with covering fire from the 2nd Platoon.

The new company commander had a penchant for wanting all three of the platoons to get their share of the action and through luck, good or bad, the 3rd Platoon had suffered relatively minor casualties compared to those that the 1st and 2nd had taken in the preceding several days. Amongst those newly-hardened veterans, it was known as "the Candy Ass 3rd."

The 1st and 2nd platoons, exclusive of their attached machine gun sections, were now down to 30 to 35 men from their regular strength of 45 as June 2 dawned, with the 3rd Platoon at practically full strength. The three machine gun sections, one attached to each rifle platoon, were also at nearly full strength except for the squad which had lost several men on 566. The final wooded crest of 610 looked worthy of a full company's best efforts from the Company's jump off point across the valley.

As the 1st Platoon moved out to a point where it could drop down to the valley floor to the left, even the first objective looked fairly forbidding. As the Marines crossed over the crest of a little saddle before starting to move down to the valley below, the radioman, an "old-timer" of perhaps 20 who had survived the Inchon landing and the Reservoir and was scheduled to go home on rotation a few days later, slipped and claimed that he had sprained an ankle and couldn't walk. His companions thought at the time that he was going home in three days and just didn't want to make the assault, but there was a certain understanding of his position. His SCR 300 radio was put on the back of the platoon runner, Rocky Bruder, an 18 year old from the University of Colorado. Rocky was particularly well-liked by everyone in the platoon for his cheerful disposition and willingness to do whatever he was asked.

The previous night, the platoon leaders of the 1st and 2nd Platoons had told the new C.O. about the periodic mortar barrages they had observed on the front slope of the first hill and urged, with some force, that it was imperative that once started up the hill, the assault shouldn't delay en route. The key to the 1st Platoon's part of the assault was to get across to the base of the ridgeline where it couldn't be observed from the top, then move up the 45° slope as quickly as possible. Once on the top of the ridge they hoped to get overhead supporting fire for the final assault on the hill at the northern end from the tanks echeloned along the right side of the valley. From the tanks' position their gunners could see the top of the ridge except for the far left side of 610 itself and could bring direct fire to bear on the bunkers at least on the right side of the first two ridge tops.

The tanks clanked up into position as the 1st Platoon went down the trail to the valley floor, with their 90 mm guns trained on the bunkers at the crests of the ridgeline, not more than 1,200 yards above them, a comforting sight indeed to the plodding rifleman. The platoon got across the streambed and the rice paddies without attracting fire and formed up at to the base of the hill where they were screened from view from above.

As a guide to the tanks for their location as they climbed the hill, the platoon leader and two leading squad leaders put air panels on their backs. These were brightly colored rectangles of orange, red or purple, perhaps 1 foot by 2 feet in size, with metal snaps which clipped together to hold them around the neck.

The platoon started up the hill, Bruder with the lieutenant, the two squad leaders abreast and probably 20 yards to their left and right with their squads spread out behind them. The two machine squads and the third squad were spread out in the rice paddy below, taking cover where they could find it along the rice paddy dikes, but steering clear of the rock foundations of the destroyed houses because of considerable experience with what happened to shrapnel when it glanced off rock in razor-sharp slivers. When the platoon leader was perhaps 40 yards up the steep slope, with perhaps a dozen men on the hill and another 30 to 35 below, an astonishing message came over the radio on Bruder's back. The unmistakable voice of the Battalion Commander, old Idiot Six himself, was ordering the Company Commander to hold up the assault so the Colonel, at his observation post in the rear, could bring an air strike to bear on the hill above! The platoon's leading echelon was then precisely in the position where ten or twelve mortar barrages had fallen the day before at intervals of from 15 minutes to a half hour apart. The lieutenant grabbed the radio and yelled at the Company Commander to tell him to forget the airstrike, that he was in the killing zone of the mortar barrages of the day before and that it was imperative that the attack be continued. He was ordered to stay where he was, however, and looking up, could see the four fighter bombers coming into the area.

Unfortunately, at their elevation, the pilots could not tell which hilltop was being attacked. The artillery liaison officer was back with the Colonel and the forward air controller in the rear. The pilots were apparently asking for target designation from their controller back at the battalion command post, but while the rifle platoon leader could hear the Battalion Commander's transmissions, neither the artillery forward observer nor the air controller were able to hear the platoon leader. The latter could transmit only to the Company Commander and to Wally Barrett, the tank commander, who was in plain view across the valley. Barrett could hear the others on the battalion radio net, but could apparently transmit only by line-of-sight to the rifle platoon leader clinging precariously to the steep hill above him. Before any action could be taken to bring the air strike on target, the Koreans, as feared, commenced one of their sporadic mortar barrages. It may have been that there were only 30 or 40 rounds, but they seemed like hundreds to the 1st Platoon. They also seemed to be coming down at almost the exact angle of the hill slope, with perhaps half of them falling on the hill where the lead Marines were and the other half whistling by a few feet over their shoulders to detonate in the rice paddy below. The lieutenant put his carbine on safe after one particularly close burst and watched helplessly as the rounds were going off among the Marines in the paddies below. Luckily only two or three Marines were wounded, one, as it turned out, extremely seriously. He had taken cover at the edge of a rice paddy dike perhaps eight inches high. One round literally fell right on top of him, leaving him sprawled across a crater perhaps three feet wide. It seemed impossible that he could have lived, but he did. His name was Bob Aylmer, a BAR man who, although seriously disabled in both legs and one arm was able, in the early 1960s, through Chuck Daly, then working for Jack Kennedy in the White House, to get a job as a security officer at the State Department in Washington.

When the barrage ended the lieutenant worked his way around to the right of the hill from where he could see the hill top, and asked the tank commander to put white phosphorous rounds into the bunkers commanding the top of the ridge. When the white phosphorous shells exploded, the smoke lasted perhaps 30 to 40 seconds, just long enough for the platoon leader to radio to the Company Commander who in turn radioed to battalion to tell the aircraft where the targets were with respect to the smoke, by then almost gone. The planes came in in successive attacks, unloading first their 500 pound bombs, then their napalm tanks and rockets and making several strafing runs with their 50 caliber machine guns. The platoon leader used that time to get up to the top of the ridge as fast as he could with Bruder, their packs making the going slow. As the last strafing run was made, the two squad leaders and platoon leader had just reached the top of the ridge where it flattened out, with perhaps 200 yards of open ground stretching in front of them to the bunkers on the small hill at the northern end. Aside from Bruder and the two squad leaders, the rest of the platoon were scattered down the hillside, laboriously climbing up the steep slope with the nearest man perhaps 30 yards from the top. The lieutenant asked Wally Barrett to give him full fire cover with his 90s and machine guns and he opened up with everything he had. Still only the platoon leader, Bruder and the two squad leaders had reached the plateau. The plan was to fix bayonets and assault as soon as the riflemen and machine gunners, still toiling up the slope, were in position.

At this point, however, over the radio came a second disastrous message.

Again, the Battalion Commander could be heard literally shrieking at the tank commander to lift the overhead fire of his 90 mm guns and machine guns which were ranging back and forth across the bunker line on the hilltop and on the higher ridge, effectively keeping the North Koreans pinned down.

The 1st Platoon was in absolutely no danger from Barrett's tank fire and, with the air panels, wouldn't be until the lead Marines were within 10 yards or so of the first bunker on the hill's military crest some 200 yards away. Through the Colonel's field glasses, however, it must have looked as if the tank fire was endangering the continued attack. Again the lieutenant raged and stormed over the radio to the Company Commander, describing the situation, but the tank fire suddenly ceased. The lieutenant yelled at the squad leaders to get moving and without thinking he and Bruder took off at a dead run towards the first bunker where they could see a machine gun pointing at them, but with no enemy in sight. They got as far as the gun and the first trench line, still with no enemy in view but with the crest of the small hill still some 20 yards or so in front of them.

At this point, over the hilltop came a single Korean soldier, apparently unarmed, and obviously on his way to man the machine gun. He and the two Marines stopped short of each other with about 10 yards intervening. The lieutenant pointed his carbine at him, saying "Tow Shong," the words the Chinese guidebook said meant "surrender." It wasn't known at that time that it was a North Korean unit on the hill, but in any event there was no response. Bruder, who ordinarily carried an M-1 rifle, had taken his predecessor's 45 pistol in exchange for his rifle, but couldn't get it out of the holster while dealing with the unfamiliar radio harness. To their mutual horror, they then saw that the Korean soldier they had thought unarmed was holding a grenade at his belt, with a silver percussion cap protruding which he seemed to be trying to tap on his belt buckle to arm. The lieutenant pulled the trigger of his carbine, forgetting that he had put it on safe back during the mortar barrage. That was the second time he had made that same mistake in four days and this time it was again nearly fatal. The Korean rolled his grenade at the two Marines' feet. They tried to jump away and the lieutenant finally got his carbine off safe and put three or four rounds at point blank range into the unlucky soldier. Luckily, the grenade didn't explode. In his nervousness, the young machine gunner probably hadn't tapped the percussion cap hard enough, just as in the lieutenant's negligence, he had forgotten to take his carbine off safe.

The squad leaders were still 50 to 100 yards back, trying to bring up their people, so Bruder and the lieutenant ran the few yards to the top of the hill, to see an incredible sight.

Perhaps 30 North Koreans were standing or sitting around the backside of the hill, about 30 yards in diameter, either buckling up their gear or moving out of the bunkers which ringed the hill. The Marines and their opponents looked at each other in a brief moment of mutual amazement; Bruder emptied his 45 and the lieutenant the remaining rounds in his 30-round carbine magazine. Instead of returning their fire, most of the North Koreans took off down the hill. The lieutenant fired off his entire remaining magazine and he and Bruder with empty weapons took three prisoners who were apparently too frightened to run away.

By this time the squad leaders and several Marines had gotten up and for a few seconds had a turkey shoot at the fast-disappearing Koreans. All were frustrated that the laboring machine gunners didn't quite make it in time to finish the job.

It was still relatively early on a sunny morning.

The platoon set up the prescribed "hasty defense" but it was obvious there wasn't going to be any serious counterattack from the steep ravine to their front. They took some long range fire from the higher ridge across the ravine, but the Marines' two machine guns and the tanks below quickly silenced the enemy machine gun emplacements in view on the forward slope and crest.

The lieutenant sent back word to the Company Commander to ask the artillery forward observer to put some 105 fire on the ridge ahead. Within a few minutes the 105s came in all right, but on the Marines rather than the higher ridge. It was later learned that the new observer had mistakenly fired the same concentration which he had fired on the hill as the Marines had moved to attack it earlier that morning. Perhaps with some good fortune the supposed "forward" observer was wounded and evacuated before he had to face his colleagues.

For the third time that day the lieutenant yelled and raged over the radio to the Company Commander and the barrage finally stopped, to be followed by the correct concentration of fire on the ridgeline to their front. The platoon had lost several more Marines to wounds, however, luckily, none of them fatal.

By this time the Korean mortars had also found the range and the Marines began to take incoming 120 millimeter mortar fire, a fairly scary experience, in part because of the whistle of air through the perforated tail assemblies, the pitch of which gave a very accurate forecast of how close each round would land. The Marines took all the cover they could in the Korean bunkers, but found that of the 33 men now left in the platoon and attached machine gun section, there was room for only 30 in the small emplacements the Koreans had dug. The 20 year old platoon sergeant, E. J. "Goodbastard" Clark, pushed the three prisoners, now clad only in loincloths, out onto the shell-ravaged hilltop, and he and the platoon leader tried to back into two bunkers already filled to capacity by other Marines. They ended up sitting six feet or so apart facing each other, Clark's rifle and the lieutenant's carbine held on the three shaking North Koreans.

Then came one particularly loud whistle. The Marines ducked as far as they could back into the bunkers. There was a huge thud and cloud of dust but no explosion. When the dust cleared, sticking out of the ground exactly between Clark and the lieutenant, almost between their respective boots, was the tail assembly of a 120 mm mortar round—thanks to some quirk of fate, a dud. Clark and the lieutenant looked at each other through the dust with some relief.

The Korean bunkers sheltered the platoon from all but two or three casualties, again all wounded and no KIAs. The three barrages, however, only two of them enemy, had reduced the platoon and machine gun squads to no more than half strength, perhaps 20 rifle-men in total from the three original 13-man squads, and 10 or so machine gunners from the original 17-man section.

Another tragedy occurred. Chuck Daly's radio became unworkable; the only recourse was to send him the 1st Platoon's radioman, Rocky Bruder. He joined Daly's platoon as it started its assault up the intermediate wooded ridge. Daly cleared the enemy from the ridge with his usual dispatch, but as he was standing at Rocky's side to report that he had gained the ridge line, a burst of automatic fire severed Rocky's jugular vein, killing him instantly and showering his blood all over Chuck. This hurt Chuck several ways, knowing how much the 1st Platoon thought of Rocky.[3]

Chuck's platoon had taken their portion of the hill by noon, and it was now up to the 3rd Pla-

---

[3]Daly's recollections:

I remember the evening we were behind a little dike watching the gook mortars registering in on the path the 1st Platoon had to take next morning and agreeing that to stop anywhere on the way up the hill would be fatal. The next day the 1st Platoon moved through that fire and up the hill. When my German-born corporal, Dohse and I came across the paddy to pick up the wounded we found Bob Alymer badly hit with one eye gone, two bad legs and a ripped arm. He said he'd been left to guard a prisoner. After the 1st Platoon had left him to make the charge out of that trap and on up the hill he felt dizzy so he shot the prisoner in the legs to prevent possible escape. We dragged him and the prisoner by their collars out of the mortar fire and across the paddy.

After the 1st Platoon's charge, my platoon took an intermediate objective. My radio was busted. The 1st Platoon's radioman came to us to help. He asked if he could rest a minute and I said no because I'd been out of touch. He reached out to hand me the phone when a burst of machine-gun fire came from behind and below us.

It must have killed him instantly even though he groaned "corpsman" as he fell. The enemy gunner must have gone over one click and up one click because the next burst which came almost instantly killed a Marine just on the other side of me and a couple of feet up the hill.

toon to assault up a side finger ridge ahead of the 2nd Platoon's position and once on the main ridge, assault 610 itself.

This was by far the hardest task yet. A full company would have had a hard time.

The 3rd Platoon's first attempt ran into heavily-defended bunkers and considerable mortar fire. Dacy revealed years later that they also took some 50 caliber machine gun rounds. He incurred the Colonel's wrath by suggesting over the radio that they were coming from the rear where Weapons Company had moved up into the valley below.

In any event, the attack stalled in the wooded ravine just short of the steep slope to 610 itself, and either the Colonel or the Company Commander told Dacy's radioman, Frenchy Robichaud, to tell Dacy he was relieved. Doug declined to leave, however, and after being pitched off the hill on one occasion, remained with the platoon in an unofficial capacity as an extra rifleman in the final assault. He later returned to command a platoon, did so for nearly a year distinguishing himself with his troops as a fine platoon leader, with perhaps the longest continuous service of Charlie Company's succession of platoon leaders.

It was a long afternoon for the 1st Platoon, waiting for the 3rd platoon trying to work their way up the steep slope to 610, their efforts blocked from view by the wooded ridge Chuck Daly was hanging on to through what seemed heavy mortar fire every few minutes or so.

At one point, Sergeant Clark and the lieutenant had moved back to the back of the slope they had come up that morning, lying on their backs, enjoying the sunshine and looking down at the ravine they had traversed the previous day and the wide valley in the distance. Through the ravine slowly came a column of 6x6 trucks, heavily loaded with what must have been the Battalion's Headquarters and Service (H&S) and Weapons Companies. On the front fender of the lead truck a Marine was sitting. As it dipped down to ford the shallow stream which came down the valley to the west, there was an explosion causing the front end of the truck to rise up before the truck turned over on its side. The Marine on the fender was projected upwards in a lazy somersault and fell back on the stream bed. The truck had hit a mine the tanks had missed. The Marines in the trucks jumped out and ran to take cover in the same area the 1st Platoon had formed up in for the assault earlier that morning. Some Korean observer up on 610 or 680, however, immediately called in another 120mm barrage. Clark and the lieutenant watched as H&S and Weapons Company men—those people, who unlike rifle company Marines, usually had hot chow and safe bivouacs in the rear, started to yell "Corpsman" down in the valley below them. The two were actually laughing for a moment over the fact that Weapons Company was finally getting a taste of what they had come to believe was only a rifle company's way of life.[4]

At that moment, the lieutenant had one of only three philosophical thoughts he could remember 40 years later from 10 months in Korea. He briefly wondered what kind of an animal he had become, only a few months out of Stanford Law School, to find humor in the predicament of other Marines.

It was later said that the man on the front fender had been the Battalion's chaplain, Father Quirk.

With no officer, the 3rd Platoon, under its platoon guide, Sgt. Chet Hanson, age 22, had gotten a firm foothold in the wooded ravine at the base of 610 with perhaps 400 yards or so still to get up the steep, broken, heavily bunkered slope ascending to the final steep climb to 610 itself.

The 2nd Platoon had been badly punished by heavy mortar fire once it gained its objective on the intermediate ridge hours earlier and was also down to half its strength or less, with both Navy

---

[4]This was totally unfair. At the Chosin Reservoir, Weapons 1/5 with 6 officers and 166 enlisted had 9 KIA and 25 WIA. That very night of June 2, a heavy machine gun squad from Weapons Company was brought up to cover the primary route of approach to the rifle companies' defense perimeter and lost several killed and wounded, more than the rifle squads of Able Company on either side of them.

corpsmen wounded and only a single sergeant, the platoon guide, remaining unhit. The 3rd Platoon had taken similar casualties, its platoon leader relieved and its platoon sergeant back at company head-quarters, but its riflemen clung firmly to their position on the intermediate ridge and eastern side of 610, only yards away, in some cases, from the system of mutually-supporting North Korean foxholes and bunkers checkered up the wooded slope.

Around four in the afternoon the Company Commander sent up an order for the 1st Platoon to move up through the 2nd Platoon's area, collect as much machine gun ammunition as they could and then move through the 2nd Platoon to make the final assault on 610, with fire support to be provided by the 3rd Platoon.

The troops were not entirely happy with the word that they were to make another assault to bail out the 3rd Platoon, but saddled up, moved down into the ravine single file and up onto the 2nd Platoon's position as it came under yet another 120 mm barrage.

As the lieutenant reached a point just below the crest, his platoon strung out behind him, down the ridge came the 2nd Platoon's guide running to the rear. The lieutenant held his carbine on him and told him he would shoot him on the spot if he didn't get back with his platoon, but the sergeant was crying and started to go past him down the hill. Afraid that the sergeant's fear would shake up his own platoon, the lieutenant hit him as hard as he could with the butt of his carbine, probably knocking him cold. The lieutenant didn't wait to see but moved his platoon up through the 2nd Platoon's position, with the 2nd Platoon's runner, a marvelous small-size 18 year old named R. V. Lee, Corporal Dohse[5] and Daly himself collecting several cans of ammunition for the machine guns. Up ahead they came to a sort of rocky crow's nest where Chet Hanson and another young sergeant, Phil Elson, the 3rd machine gun section's leader, had set up a command post with the 3rd Platoon strung out in front of them in the wooded ravine running to the base of 610. Both Hanson and Elson had previously been in the 1st Platoon and were highly respected.

The two lieutenants and two sergeants could now see parts of the rocky 200 yard curving crest of 610 through the trees above them, perhaps 600 yards away. Many of the trees on the crest had been knocked down or defoliated by artillery fire and air strikes. The 3rd Platoon controlled the right side of the wooded ravine to the base of 610, exchanging occasional fire with the Koreans who, in addition to their cliffside bunkers, occupied a well-defined trenchline and bunker system perhaps 5 yards below the crest of 610. There were a lot of gullies in between, and unfortunately, all but the Korean positions on the extreme right were shielded from the tanks by the forested ridgeline the Marines now occupied. The lieutenant told Hanson and Elson about the C.O.'s order for them to give him covering fire while he attacked. The two sergeants reacted with righteous anger, telling the lieutenant in blunt language that 610 was the 3rd Platoon's objective and for him to back off and give them covering fire. It was really their pride that was involved . . . proving to the rest of the Company that they were as good as anyone else.

The lieutenant, shaken by the long day's events, was only too happy to give them the chance. Hanson and Elson marshalled their troops and took off with a yell, assaulting the steep side of 610 with a vengeance. The 1st Platoon's machine guns gave them overhead fire until they got up onto 610 itself. At this point, Chet Hanson came hopping back on one leg with a big grin; he had been shot in the foot,

---

[5] A word about Corporal Gunther Dohse, USMC, Charlie Company's most respected enlisted man. He had been a private in the German Army in 1945, immigrated to the U.S. and enlisted in the Marine Corps. At the Reservoir, he saved the Company by bringing a tank into Charlie Company's position just in time to prevent the Marines, most of their BARs not functioning because of the cold, from being overrun. When his own foxhole was overrun and his fellow occupant killed, Dohse had played dead for several freezing hours at the bottom of his hole, with two Chinese soldiers sitting on him. When dawn came and a counterattack flushed out the enemy, Dohse got up, threw a grenade after them and killed them both. In April, he had been awarded a Silver Star in a ceremony when the Battalion was in reserve. Dohse was held in awe by the men of Charlie Company, officers and men alike. (See Appendix A) There was a general concensus that it was a lucky thing we didn't have Germans on the other side in Korea.

but the 3rd Platoon had thrown the Koreans off at least the right half of 610 and the term "Candy-Ass" had been banished forever. Their radio operator, "Frenchy" Robichaud, perhaps Charlie Company's most irrepressible and colorful Pfc, radioed that the 3rd Platoon held the key right crest of 610 but couldn't go any farther. What the lieutenants of the 1st and 2nd Platoons didn't know at the time was that both John Goodrich and Charlie Bunnell, independently seeing the 3rd Platoon's plight, had come over with Sergeant Bartlett from the company command post across the valley to help. Goodrich had successfully brought counter-battery fire to bear on the Korean mortars and both he and Bunnell assaulted with Dacy and the 3rd platoon in the final surge from different sides to the top of 610.[6] At one crucial moment, Bunnell and Goodrich, past the main peak of 610 and sheltered in a small ravine between it and the long curving crest of the crest ridge to the west, ran out of ammunition. They were saved from counterattacking burp gunners by a burst of supporting fire from one of the 3rd Platoon's machine guns operated by Sergeant Thompson on the peak a few yards behind them. It was reported in the Yale paper several weeks later that two Yale men had attacked a hill in Korea singing "Boola, Boola" as they climbed. Yale men have always been a bit peculiar. The third Yale lieutenant in the Company, Chuck Daly, deserves special mention in this regard, but that awaits another story.

From Robichaud's call, with Hanson a casualty and half of the ridge still in enemy hands, it was clear the 3rd Platoon needed help, so the 1st Platoon fixed bayonets, moved up and swung around on

---

[6]Goodrich described his own experience in these words:

"As we attacked up the mountain, we took a lot of burp gun fire and a constant rain of grenades fell on us. Those of us in the forward attack elements could see the grenades coming and take evasive action by moving a few steps to the side and curling up into as small a target as possible until the grenade exploded. Unfortunately, if the Marines behind us were not observant they would often receive the full blasts of the grenades.

We in turn would throw our grenades up hill into the foxholes of the defenders. The battle for Hill 610 continued foxhole by foxhole.

It was necessary to clear one defensive position at a time. I would advance a few feet so that I could then concentrate on the next foxhole behind the one we had taken. In the meantime my men were picking off as many North Koreans as they could with their highly accurate M-1 fire. The defenders were brave and determined but they were no match for the Marines. There were many, many individual encounters that day between an attacking Marine and a defending North Korean. Fortunately for us most of them were won by the attacking Marines. As we concentrated on the grenades that were being rolled down on us by the North Koreans we kept an eye out for low spots in the ground, rocks, tree root, or rock outcroppings and any natural object that might offer some cover when we saw a grenade coming or came up against a foxhole defender with a burp gun. We would rise to a crouch and quickly move forward to another position from which we would engage the nearest defender. This process was repeated over and over as we pressed our attack up the side of Hill 610.

As I finally came over the top of my side of the crest I came face to face with a North Korean soldier at a distance of about 40 feet. Both of us fired our final few rounds of ammunition at each other as we hit the ground for cover. After firing his last few rounds, the North Korean lost no time exiting to the rear while I searched my pockets for just one more clip of 45 caliber ammunition. I had just realized that I was completely out of ammunition and grenades when I saw Charlie Bunnell who had come over the top of the other side of the mountain. As we came within speaking range, we learned that both of us, together with Sergeant Bartlett who had also made the top of the mountain, were out of ammunition. The three of us took cover beneath a very steep hill which actually divided the top of Hill 610 into two levels, the one we were on and the one occupied by the last of the North Korean defenders.

The North Koreans mounted a counter attack, proceeding cautiously down the ridgeline behind a screen of burp gun fire. As each individual's ammunition gave out, his place in the front line would be taken by another North Korean soldier who had reloaded his weapon.

Out of ammunition, Charlie and I shouted orders to imaginary platoons to attempt to fool the attackers. We collected stones to use as a last resort.

The three of us were well hidden at the bottom of our steep little hill and as I heard the muzzle blasts of the North Koreans coming closer a new sound was heard from the crest of the mountain behind us. The new sound came from Sergeant Thompson's air cooled 30 caliber machine gun. The whole front line of counterattacking North Koreans fell before Sergeant Thompson's fire. This broke the back of the counterattack and the North Koreans who were still able retreated back into the woods. Then the 1st Platoon came up and we had the hill."

their left, moving up onto the middle part of 610. There they ran out of gas themselves just below the crest, perhaps 5 yards from the top, and got engaged in a grenade rolling contest with the Koreans who had retired to just below the crest on the other side.

The lieutenant was lying beside a young 19 year old Indian machine gunner called "Chief" Zamora, his gun trained on the crest just above them. A grenade fragment caught Zamora in the throat and he couldn't breathe. The lieutenant yelled for a corpsman and Doc Burchick, all 130 pounds of him, came up, turned Zamora over on his back, pulled out his sheath knife and literally poked a hole in Zamora's throat, putting some sort of tube or twig in it and making Zamora, who had been turning black, hold it with his hand so that he could breathe through the hole. Burchick then taped his hand to his chest and went on to attend others along the skirmish line just below the crest.

It later turned out that this was a tracheotomy operation the 19 year old Burchick had read about but never seen. In a few minutes Zamora was able to sit up and walk back down the hill for treatment. Burchick's operation, certainly no more than 10 yards away from enemy riflemen, with grenades going off every few seconds, may have been the closest surgery ever performed to an enemy in combat. He was put up for the Navy Cross and it was awarded to him. To the Marines of the 1st Platoon, it should have been the Congressional Medal of Honor.

By this time, the Koreans seemed to be running low on grenades, so the 1st Platoon went over the top, securing the ridge, then moving along it for a final assault on its last bunker at the left end. The lieutenant dropped a white phosphorous grenade in the bunker and as he looked around found that the only people with him were John Goodrich and Charlie Bunnell. The Executive Officer had an empty 45 and the Machine Gun Officer an empty BAR. Had there been any enemy left to counterattack the three would have been easy prey.

What was left of Charlie Company now found itself in a precarious predicament. It was close to dark. The three rifle platoons held 610 all right but there were precious few of them left, with a heavily wooded hilly terrain stretching out before them, the bare, evil-looking cone of 680 serving as the perfect enemy observation post and dominating the area a few hundred yards away. The Company was obviously vulnerable to a successful night counter attack, as there were a lot of wooded areas down to the front and left flank which could screen massing troops. There was some indication that at least some enemy had reoccupied the ridge the 2nd Platoon had held earlier in the day. At this time, the Company's fighting strength was around 60 men and the five lieutenants. Except for Clark, Elson, Thompson and Bartlett, all of the sergeants had become casualties or were somewhere else. The company headquarters and mortar section had not yet come up.

Even behind there was now occasional firing in the wooded area across which the Company had attacked. The supply chief, Sergeant Scheidt, was seriously wounded by an ambush there as he tried to bring up relief supplies with Chiggy Bears. There were enough men to cover only the left portion of the crescent ridge, with perhaps 30 two-man foxholes in a U-shaped formation a few yards below the crest. The perimeter was no more than 15 yards in width and perhaps 100 yards long. The 1st Platoon had sixteen men left, plus four stretcher cases. They set up their two machine guns in the old Korean foxholes and manned eight adjoining foxholes on the nose leading to Hill 680 as dusk came on. The last hilltop bunker, about 10 yards above the center of the 1st Platoon's 50 yards of front, was appropriated as a command post, still smoking from the white phosphorous. Sometime later the company commander, with the 60mm mortars and his radio man, came up. His first words to Goodrich and Bunnell were that they "ought to be courtmartialed" for leaving the company command post. He probably felt badly over having missed the fight. In any event, no charges were ever brought. Bunnell was later decorated for his day's work, with good reason; Goodrich should have been but the company commander for some reason never recognized his contribution.

The Company wasn't looking forward to nightfall, but just before dark, a wonderful thing happened.

Up from the rear came a long, heavily-armed column, Able Company, clean uniforms and an exceedingly healthy-looking group of what looked like almost a full strength company.

Buzz Lubka's platoon was at the head of the line.

They had come to relieve Charlie at the forward part of 610 and as they waited along the top of the ridgeline, still fairly well covered with Korean bodies and the rack and ruin of shell holes and splintered trees, Charlie Company moved back down their line, each of the sixteen of the 1st Platoon who could walk carrying one corner of the stretchers that had been rigged up out of branches and ponchos for their four non-walking wounded. The 2nd and 3rd Platoons were in similar shape. No 8th and I Corps sunset parade in Washington, D.C. could ever evoke more pride in the marchers as they passed down the silent line of Able Company Marines waiting to take over their hard-earned position. Hill 610 was a Charlie Company achievement and while the Company looked like a group of Mauldin's WW II dogfaces, there was a certain quiet pride involved.

The Company dug into the rear 1/4th of the ridge, with the wounded inside the perimeter. The front 3/4ths of 610 was taken over by Able Company, with a heavy machine gun section from Weapons Company occupying the 1st Platoon's old position at the front end facing north and west towards the dangerous wooded areas and 680.

Around midnight, the North Koreans attacked as expected. The Able Company men later advised that their first wave hit the 1st Platoon's old position with men carrying bamboo poles. Buzz Lubka wouldn't let his men fire and disclose their positions and the battle was waged largely with grenades. The attached heavy machine gun from Weapons Company opened up, however, and was lost. The fighting in the Able Company sector went on for some time, but at Charlie Company's end of the hill there were only a few probes and the Company's line was not penetrated.

Able Company's wakeful night was followed by a frustrating day. It started with an almost-miraculously-successful assault of 680 along a ridgeline so steep and narrow that only one man could walk along it at a time. Able's platoons leap frogged each other knoll by knoll. Bill "The Pube" Heer led his platoon in single file, plodding right up and through the foxholes and bunkers on 680's crest. At every step the Marines watching from 610 thought Heer would get it between the eyes but the defending Koreans were apparently too shell-shocked by the preliminary artillery bombardment to offer serious resistance.

Able Company's platoons continued to leap-frog each other, driving the defenders out of successively higher ridgetop positions towards Hill 692 with flank supporting fire from Baker Company's machine gun platoon, now commanded by Harvey Nolan, the hero of Hill 313.[7] Baker was now commanded by former Charlie Company platoon leader, Bill Kerrigan.

At the peak of their success, however, a terrible thing happened. An aerial observer in a small spotter plane, seeing people moving up the ridgeline well in advance of where he thought Marines could possibly be, called in an airstrike. Four Marine Corsairs roared in, dropping napalm, 500-pound bombs and rockets, then strafing with their .50 calibres. Miraculously, no one was killed, but the Colonel ordered Able Company back from the ground they had so painfully taken. When several of their wounded filed back through Charlie Company's lines on 610 that night, some Marines were crying and all were bitterly disappointed. A classic success had been turned into a disaster through no

---

[7] A Baker Company lieutenant's recollections:

I watched most of Hill 610 from an adjacent ridgeline. I almost got blown away myself that day. A North Korean soldier jumped out on the path in front of me and pulled the trigger on his burp-gun. Click, then bang; one dead enemy and a slightly shaken Charlie Cooper; my time hadn't quite arrived. Also the next day Harvey Nolan had the one opportunity I've ever seen, except in Basic School, to employ a reinforced machinegun platoon in direct support, firing across Buzz Lubka's front, leading him by about 10 meters. It worked like a charm. Light and heavy .30's plus 4 .50 cals!

That air strike when Marine Corsairs put everything they had into A Company was a horrible sight.

fault of their own. They took heavy casualties from 120mm mortar fire during their withdrawal, including their C.O., Captain Hap Spuhler.

The next day, June 4th, the Battalion was withdrawn into reserve, with a 15 mile lateral hike to the southeast to a peaceful river valley near the destroyed town of Inje.

Back in reserve, Charlie Company finally felt it had achieved, at least for a brief time, a small part of the cohesion and skill which had marked its predecessors and its more-famous companion rifle companies, Able and Baker. The lieutenants recognized they could never hope to match the performance of the Brigade regulars who had fought so well at the Pusan Perimeter nor those who had survived the overwhelming Chinese mass attacks at the Reservoir. The reserve lieutenants felt, though, that they were at long last part of a seasoned, competent Marine rifle company in the tradition of the Corps. They knew that it wasn't to their own credit; that the Company's successes had been due primarily to the training and example of Jones and Schening who probably in turn owed their own superb abilities to those who had led them in the far more difficult actions of World War II.

This, I believe, is the basic ingredient of the Marine Corps ethic; young untried men, forever trying to live up to the fabled men who have gone before—fully recognizing they could never undergo the hardships or dangers their predecessors had faced and overcome, but wanting to try, purely as a matter of pride, not to let them down.

The best of the regular Marine officers, men like Jones and Schening and reserves like Colonel Martin, were gentle and kind human beings. They might be superb combat commanders but they took no lasting pleasure from the casualties they inflicted.

The Marines in the Charlie Company of the spring of 1951 were generally not large, strong manly specimens; they were ordinary people who probably joined the Marines as their lieutenants had, wanting to test themselves against the Corps' tradition of excellence. No one could accuse them of undue heroism or good sense. The Company's various assaults were motivated most of all by the concern that other Marines might feel that Charlie Company was letting them down or see that their leaders were inept or afraid, as indeed there was a recurring temptation to be.

Strange to say, although the platoon leaders felt the *Company* had performed superbly, they were now even more afraid of the propensities of Idiot Six to endanger their newly-precious good health. With Spike Schening gone, only Major Jones, the Company's former company commander and now the Battalion S-3, was trustworthy in the new "old salt" judgment of the junior officers. The newly-proud veterans of Hills 566 and 610 had a strong desire to stay alive and well. This joy of living was a new phenomenon. No longer were they untried "90 day wonders" of dubious experience and abilities. They felt some respect from their surviving troops, a new respect more than matched by their own faith in the young Pfc's. They knew that as officers they also had been suspect in the enlisted Marines' eyes until the shared successes of the previous few days. Even today there are no doubt survivors of the three rifle platoons who consider their lieutenants in the same category as the Battalion Commander, being officers, thereby by definition to be distrusted as potential glory-seekers or bumblers at their possible expense.

Nevertheless, the 1st Platoon's only surviving sergeants, E.J. Clark and Jimmy Nichols, the three new squad leaders, a Corporal and two Pfcs, average age probably 19, were convinced that Charlie Company had become the finest rifle company in the Marine Corps. Who else had routed a Korean regiment which had held up a battalion of the 7th Marines for two days, and who else had taken 610, the designated objective of the whole 5th Marine Regiment? Able and Baker Companies were highly respected but they didn't have the privilege of a Jones or Schening to lead them.

The new pride was tempered by a new fear as well, however, a fear that would continue and grow in the weeks ahead as the drive north to the Punch Bowl resumed. The Company would badly miss those who had trained and shaped it, and it was an open question whether its new officers could collectively pass on to the group of innocent replacements who joined the Company three days later the principles and inspiration instilled by Jones and Schening.

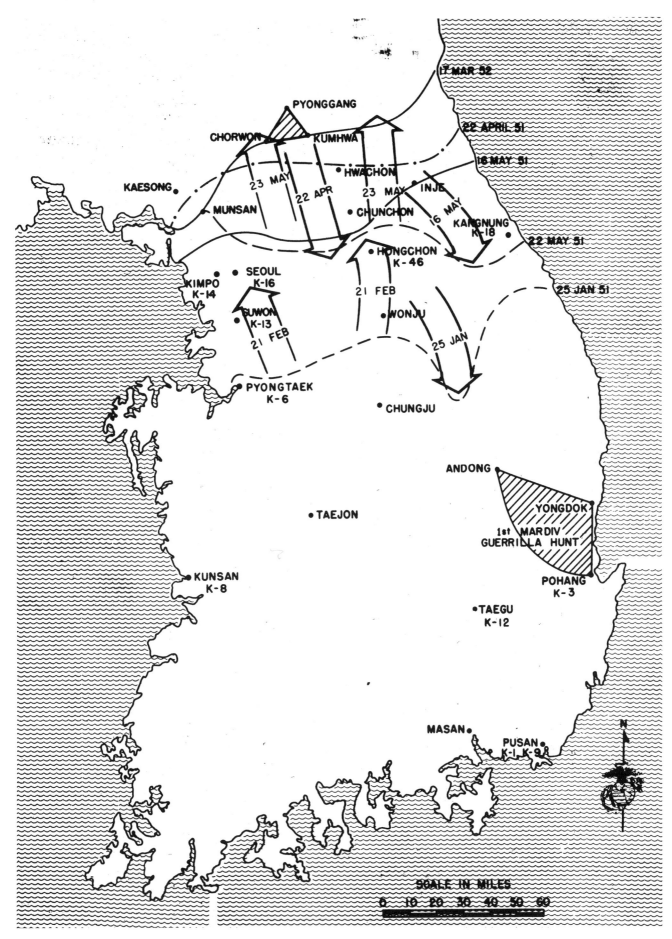

This map shows the three Chinese Offensives of 1951, in January, April and May, as well as the two U.N. Offensives, in February/April and May/June. (Taken from U.S. Marine Operations in Korea, Vol IV, back inside cover.)

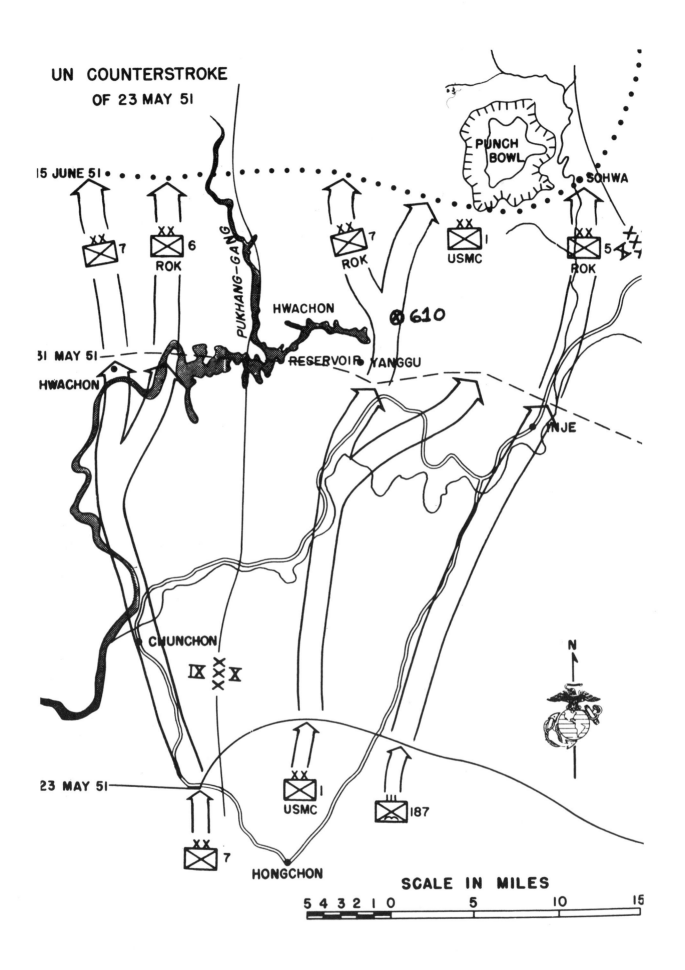

UN COUNTERSTROKE
OF 23 MAY 51

15 JUNE 51

PUKHANG-GANG

PUNCH BOWL

SOHWA

XX 7   XX 6
ROK

XX 7
ROK

XX 1
USMC

XX 5
ROK   7

HWACHON

⊗ 610

31 MAY 51

HWACHON   RESERVOIR   YANGGU

INJE

CHUNCHON

IX XXX

23 MAY 51

XX 1
USMC

III 187

N

XX 7

HONGCHON

SCALE IN MILES

5 4 3 2 1 0   5   10   15

This map shows the Drive to the Punch Bowl May 23-June 19, 1951, with Hill 610 located northeast of Yanggu. (Taken from U.S. Marine Operations in Korea, Vol IV, last page.)

Hill 610 as seen from the position of the tanks. This photograph was taken in March 1987. 610 is the top peak right of center. The 1st Platoon's objective is on the left, the 2nd Platoon's in the middle. The peak at the far right is Hill 680, taken by Able Company on June 3.

The 1st hill en route to Hill 610, as seen from the floor of the valley to the east. This hill was taken by the 1st Platoon on the morning of June 2, coming up the ridgeline from the left side of the picture.

Hill 610 as seen from the base of the 1st Platoon's hill.

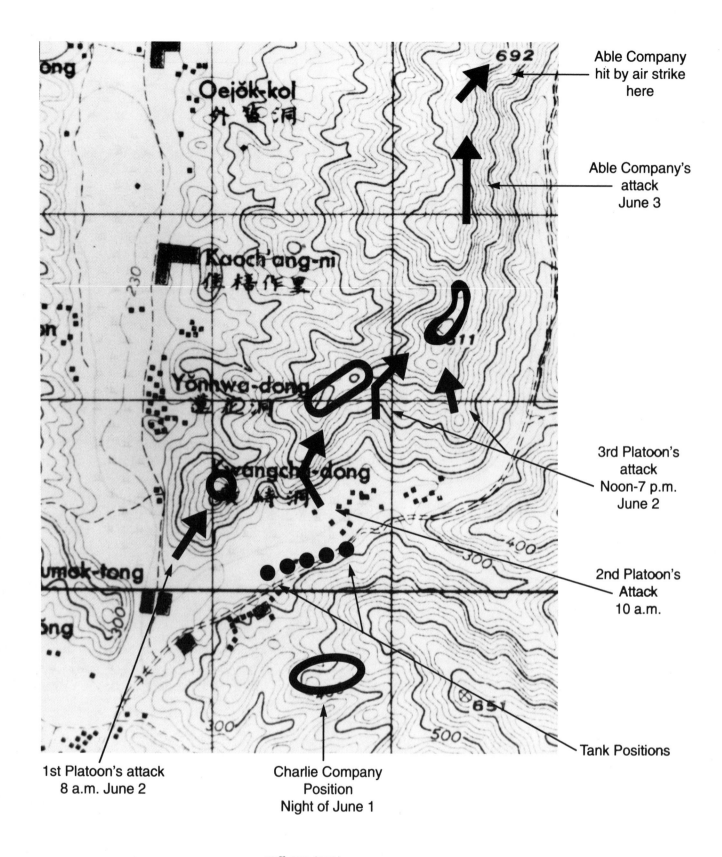

Able Company hit by air strike here

Able Company's attack June 3

3rd Platoon's attack Noon-7 p.m. June 2

2nd Platoon's Attack 10 a.m.

Tank Positions

1st Platoon's attack 8 a.m. June 2

Charlie Company Position Night of June 1

Hill 610 (611)

The maps of 1951 were taken from Imperial Japanese surveys made in 1918. The hilltop elevations could be up to a full meter off. This later map designates the former Hill 610 as "611."

One square is 1000 meters. The contour intervals are 20 meters.

The attacks of the Charlie Comany Platoons on June 2 and the Able Company Platoons on June 3 are shown by the arrows.

The last 600 yards to 610 as seen from the crows' nest where the 1st and 2nd Platoon's machine guns supported the 3rd Platoon's assault around 6 p.m., June 2.

The last 300 yards to 610. It was more wooded in June, 1951. The ridge on the left could not be seen from the tanks' position in the valley below. It contained an interlocking trench system 5 yards on this side of the 200 yard long ridge. There were also a number of individual fox holes and bunkers extending down the slope at the center and right. Helen McCloskey, foreground.

Yanggu

The tanks' position, June 1 and 2. (Where farm building now stands)

The ravine through which C/1/5 and tanks approached June 1.

Looking South towards Yanggu from 1st Platoon's hill, taken on morning of June 2.

1st Platoon position 9 a.m.-4 p.m. June 2, 1951.

2nd Platoon position 10 a.m.-7 p.m. June 2, 1951

Looking south from the Crest of 610. The 2nd Platoon's wooded ridge is in the foreground. The 1st Platoon's hill behind it.

The author at the west end of 610 in March, 1987; 680 in the background. Weapons Company's 30 caliber heavy machine gun opened up and was lost at this point around midnight, June 2, 1951.

Hill 680
"PUBE HILL"

The photograph below, taken in March 1987 from the west end of 620, reflects no real change from Hill 680's appearance on June 3, 1951, except that the trees were in foliage then. The ridge in the foreground was the route followed by the leapfrogging platoons of Buzz Lubka and Bill Heer, "The Pube," of Able Company on June 3rd, with the final ascent to the crest led by Heer. To understand "The Pube's" nickname one need only note that in 1951 his round cherubic face was topped with a bald pate fringed by golden curls. Heer, of German origin, is pronounced "Hair."

This photograph shows "The Pube's" joyous face when being transferred out of a platoon leader's billet on June 20, 1951.

The North Koreans used these 76mm mountain guns with great skill. (Taken from The Pusan Perimeter, *by Edwin P. Hoyt.)*

Catching a ride to the front, May 26, 1951. Lt. Wally Barrett in the turret.

The author with 1st Lt. Black Jack McCaffrey (artillery) and 1st Lt. Wally Barrett (tanks) Division school on the new Code of Military Justice spring, 1951. Barrett's tanks, later commanded by John Wallace, were the primary fire support for the assault on Hill 610, June 2, 1951.

"How can the foxholes still be there 36 years later?"

Platoon Sgt. E.J. "Good Bastard" Clark. Atop the first knoll on the ridge line to Hill 610, with prisoners between 120 mm mortar barrages, morning of June 2, 1951.

In 1987 this 74-year-old Korean still remembered the fight for 610, the base of which is at the left. Note the steepness of the slope which the 3rd Platoon had to climb.

The thatched roofs have changed to tin, but the A-Frame goes on forever.

Company officers' meeting, Charlie Company advance patrol base southwest of Chun'chon, late April, 1951. Spike Schening at far left.

Part of the 1st Platoon, Charlie Company. Doc Burchick is second from the right.

1st platoon Command Group, May, 1951.

Chapter 2

The Historical Reports

The preceding narrative of Hill 610 is a highly personalized account, seen through the eyes of only one low-level participant whose memory, and that of others who were present is somewhat dimmed these many years after the fact. In cross-checking facts with the survivors 35 to 40 years later, it quickly became clear that memories could differ widely. From 100 yards, or even 10 yards away, an incident in combat could appear much different to a participant.

In 1989 I sent a draft of the story to Buzz Lubka of Able Company, who had taken over the west end of the Charlie Company perimeter on 610 on the evening of June 2.

Buzz's recollections of June 2 and June 3, 1951 follow:

"17 Truxton Road
Dix Hills, New York 11746

Dear Pete,

I appreciated the opportunity to look over your tribute to Jack and Spike. It was a very emotional experience. We were privileged to walk with giants.

The following are my recollections of the evening/night of 2 June and 3 June, in narrative form:

Able moved through Charlie. (Although we might have looked like 250 Marines we were running with platoons down to 25 to 30 per platoon.). I (3rd Platoon) was in the lead. I occupied the forward part of 610, Bill Heer was in back of me. I dug in my platoon around the nose on the forward part of the position. The first thing we did after setting up a hasty defense was to clean up the position. I told my platoon sergeant "Let's clean up this mess. You know I like a neat battlefield." So we rolled the enemy dead off the position. There was a trail leading from the nose along the ridge line towards 680. I reconned the trail with my platoon sergeant. I told him I wanted the trail wired with trip flares, feeling they would come back this way. The trips were placed about 30 yards in front of the nose of the position. Then we started to dig in and also occupied the 8 holes your platoon had used earlier that night. I set up the platoon CP in the large crater in the back of the bunker on 610. We set a 50% watch.

Just as we were refining the night defense position up came a section of heavy machine guns (Browning A-1 water cooled from Weapons Company). So we had to adjust the line.

Finally I got my squad leaders together and told them we had trip flares out. I didn't want any machine guns firing unless the enemy was marching lock step up the trail. I wanted to fight with hand grenades so as not to reveal our position from muzzle blasts until absolutely necessary. No digging in for me that night. I felt we'd be hit. My platoon sergeant and my machine gun section leader bunked in the shell hole, with the sound power telephone back to the company CP. The CO was Hap Spuhler, USMC and the ExO Captain Crosby, USMCR (What a waste). We really had a Captain CO and Captain ExO. The company gunnery sergeant was Manning, a tower of strength for young brass bar cadets.

Sure enough about 2300 the flares were tripped and the enemy started popping grenades. I elbowed the two Marines on either side of me and hollered, "Here they come". I tried to get out of the shell hole and struggled because I had a charley horse in my leg and couldn't move. I finally clawed my way out of the hole to the side of the bunker. In clawing my way out of the hole I left the sound power phone. I wasn't about to go back for it and I hollered, "Pancho (my radio operator) come up on the radio and tell the Six we have lots of company." My platoon hadn't fired any weapons. They were using grenades. In front of us one of the enemy started shouting, "Marine tonight you die!" They were goading us to respond and stand up and fire our weapons. We didn't take the bait. Then one of the enemy hollered, "Marine, I know you, I was room boy for you in Tientsin, China." That ran chills up my spine. I was in the First Marine Division in Tientsin, China from October 1, 1945 to May 1947. I was enlisted at that time and we sure as hell had room boys then. (I wonder if there were some Chinese with the North Koreans)

So we fought them off with grenades. One heavy machine gun opened up and we lost the gun because the attackers zeroed in on it. They never penetrated our line, and so they started to slip around the side of the forward nose. I called Bill on the radio and told him that he was going to have company because the enemy was slipping down towards his position.

In the morning we had 10 to 15 enemy dead in front of us. There were some vials among the enemy equipment and we decided that the attacking force must have taken drugs before the attack.

On the morning of 3 June Able moved off 610 down the trail to the next commanding piece of ground. On this ground Hap Spuhler, at noon, ordered Cam Johnson (football Honorable Mention All American from Purdue) to jump off. He had only 25 men in his platoon, so I got the call. I had about 26 men in my platoon. I asked whether or not we would get air. Negative. I went to the artillery FO (forward observer) and pointed to the next commanding piece of ground and told him I wanted prep fires. I told him we would move under it and he was to lift fires when the rounds would endanger us, since he had excellent observation. We jumped off and drove the enemy off. I had BAR men with bipods firing off hand at the fleeing enemy. Then on to the next knoll. We were pinned down. I turned around and found Spuhler coming up on my position. When he arrived he asked what was going on. I told him we were pinned down and I was going to set up a base of fire and envelop. He asked what he could do. (Very unusual because COs liked telling platoon leaders how to do it.) I told him just to give me time, and then he disappeared. After a fire fight we gained the knoll. I was consolidating the position when Bill Heer closed on me. In front of us and before 680 were a series of knobs and hillocks. I told Bill that I could support him when he went after the next knob. So for the rest of the afternoon Bill and I were leap frogging each other, providing each other a base of fire. Every piece of ground was contested. In retrospect, our supporting each other was an outstanding example of small unit tactics, right out of the book. On one of the moves I received a call from Creamy Baker Six (Bill Kerrigan, who had been the ExO of Able before he moved to Baker). He told me he could support my movement with his machine guns. I told him that I would put air panels on my forward elements, could he observe? Affirmative. I suggested he better be sure he remembered the gunner's and leader's rule. Baker machine guns provided supporting fire for us. By about 1700 I was going after a knob, 692, when Spuhler called on the radio and said, "Three, you had better hurry up because they are racing you for it." The enemy that we were driving off all afternoon apparently was trying to counter attack. We formed a skirmish line at the crest. I ordered grenades to be thrown followed by a rush over the top. I also directed that when throwing grenades we shout "Fire In The Hole" (Bill Kerrigan taught us this when he was ExO of Able). Over the top we went. Bill closed on us. I looked at the next significant terrain feature which now I guess was 692. It went right down to the valley and then straight up again. I called the Six and told him that this was about all we could do for the day. We couldn't take 692 without a concerted preparation, and we would need more than our significantly understrength company. I told him we could hold what we had. I told Bill we could hold this ground and suggested he tie in with me and that Johnson could tie in the rear of the company perimeter. I thought all we needed were beans, bullets and bandages and we could hold. The ground was big enough to hold the company and small enough to defend effectively. I told Bill we should run fire teams down to clean out the fingers.

I turned around and saw a Corsair making a pass over us. He didn't drop any ordnance. I ordered "Display air panels." Then four aircraft started the daisy chain, delivering ordnance. They were so close we could see the pilots. We tried to wave them off, to no avail. We all hit the deck. I got inside my helmet and thought, "I wonder what Lorraine and the baby are doing now." I saw the napalm tanks falling and thought, "I wonder how it feels to burn to death." Then I said to myself. "You dumb son of a bitch, you'll find out soon enough."

Air did their thing. 500 pound bombs, napalm, Tiny Tim rockets and to add insult to injury they strafed us. I later learned the planes were from VMF-214, which in WWII was Pappy Boyington's Black Sheep squadron. I also learned that the air strike was controlled by an OE (small spotter aircraft) from VMO-6. No casualties from the air strike but we all had dirty skivvies.

Somehow the word got out that Able Company had taken an air attack and had been wiped out. Idiot Six ordered what he thought was left of Able back to the position we occupied at noon. I went nuts screaming that it was crazy to pull back, we took all that ground, bled for it and now we're abandoning it for no reason. We will only have to go back after it the following day and bleed some more. But we turned tail and started the move back. It was dark and foggy and starting to rain by this time. As we moved back we came under fire from the 120's that had been plaguing you. I remember there were five tubes. They were so close that we could hear the rounds going into the tubes. They had the trail zeroed in. We moved and waited for the first round to hit, hit the deck and waited for the other four to detonate. Then we'd get up and move again. During this time Spuhler was hit, and out of action. I was told later that Manning, the company gunnery sergeant kept telling him he had to turn the company over to Mr. Lubka. It of course didn't happen. Crosby took over. As we moved we were getting a lot of incoming. Finally we reached the position we left at noon. It was occupied by Korean Marines who had a Marine Corps Lieutenant advisor. I told him "we need some help with our dead and wounded." He said, "KMCs are not stretcher bearers." I raised hell to no avail. We brought in our dead and wounded and our weapons. The last three Marines in the position that night were Manning, Heer and Lubka. We were lugging whatever weapons we could carry.

By 2230 we had set up night defensive positions in the rear of the KMCs. I grounded my gear and told my platoon sergeant to set up the platoon CP in a certain spot. It was raining hard by now. I told them to use my gear to rig some shelter from the rain if they needed it. Then I proceeded to troop leading, head count, redistributing ammunition, checking the wounded including Spuhler, etc. Bill came up and asked if he could bunk with me. I told him that I was a guest in the "House" and he would have to check with my NCOs. He bunked with us. Crosby came up and asked if he could bunk with me. I gave him the same answer I gave Bill. He stayed. I then asked him what watch he wanted stood. He said he wanted a 100% watch. I told him it couldn't happen. We had been fighting all day, taken an air attack and been mauled by 120mm mortars. Furthermore we were an interior unit (KMCs in front of us) and a 25% watch was adequate. I asked him if he had run wire (telephone) back to battalion. He said he hadn't. I told him he had better come up on the radio. I asked him if he wanted me to set the radio watch for the night. "You don't expect me to sleep tonight with Hap Spuhler in this condition do you? I'll man the radio tonight." I tried to explain that Hap was happy as a clam. He was shot through with morphine and did not have a life threatening wound. Further his runner, Fithian (who in 1955 joined my Rifle Company in Kaneohe in the 4th Marines) had dug in and was covered, out of the rain. So finally we settled down by 2330. Rations and ammo came up about midnight. I saw to them. After midnight Crosby decided he could sleep, so I had to set the radio watch for the rest of the night.

This is my testament to 2-3 June.

"Buzz"

I can attest to the accuracy of Buzz Lubka's account. Buzz went on to a fine career, integrating into the regular Marine Corps and later commanding an infantry battalion in Viet Nam. He was perhaps the most professional of the reserve lieutenants. As a former enlisted man, he had been deeply impressed by the professionalism of Gerry Averill. Buzz was and is, incapable of exaggeration or embellishment.

His radio operator, "Pancho," paid him the highest compliment a Marine officer can receive, far higher than any medal, Navy Cross or otherwise.

Private First Class, later Master Gunnery Sergeant Ralph A. Vasquez, USMC, wrote a simple note to Buzz in 1989:

"You took care of your troops. I'm probably here now (alive) because of you and I believe there are others somewhere alive also because of you and because of me following what you taught me."

No higher praise can be given a Marine officer.

It may therefore be worthwhile for students of military history to ponder the difference in the recollections of rifle platoon leaders and those who write official histories of modern warfare.

In the Korean War, each infantry battalion was required to keep a "Unit Diary."

The Unit Diary was a document prepared each evening under the Battalion Commander's direction by some unfortunate staff officer assigned the duty of "Battalion Historical Officer." The daily accounts were summarized at the end of each month and forwarded to higher headquarters for permanent recording in the archives of the Marine Corps.

A comparison of 1/5's Unit Diary with Lubka's narrative demonstrates fairly vividly that the war as seen by platoon leaders was an entirely different series of events from those observed (or listened to over the radio) by headquarters people.

Unlike earlier wars, in the Korean War, during the spring of 1951 at least, battalion command posts were generally several hundred yards, sometimes a mile or more behind the rifle company positions. The rifle companies nearly always dug in each night into tight perimeters with two- man foxholes on the military crests of the highest ridgelines or mountain tops that could be found in the battalion's tactical area of responsibility (TAOR). On many occasions, in order that each defense position have 360° protection, the individual rifle platoons had separate perimeters on hilltops or knolls several hundred yards apart. The other rifle companies could be on parallel ridge lines across wide valleys with no contact at all between companies for days at a time.

The battalion command post (CP) was usually in a sheltered ravine in the rear, with tents to house the commander and his executive officer, the S-3 and S-2 (operations and intelligence, respectively) center, as well as communications, supply and other headquarters functions. There were jeeps available (to communicate with Regiment) and field desks with typewriters to record casualties and make daily reports.

A good S-3 or S-2 might go forward to study the terrain facing the rifle companies, but during the entire time I served with C-1-5, I never saw our battalion commander anywhere near a position which was in the process of being attacked or defended. This was understandable; the C.O.'s job was to coordinate supporting arms, re-supply, and communications, not to lead assaults or direct defenses.

Thus, he usually had ample time each evening to compose or review the daily diary of the Battalion's activities.

Nevertheless the commander's distance from the front, could and often did, lead to a certain distortion of unit diaries, with bias towards map locations, CP displacements, types of rations eaten, and the whereabouts of the Regimental Commander. There were also the numerous errors staff officers could be expected to make in piecing together what information came back to them from sporadic radio transmissions about events and terrain features they did not see. In the case of 1/5, much of what appears in the Unit Diary about what the rifle companies were doing was just plain untrue.

To the rifle companies, the Battalion CP was "in the rear with the gear," a place where no one was expected to understand whatever problems or terrain the rifle companies were facing. This is where the importance of Jack Jones became so paramount. The rifle companies knew that Jones as S-3, unlike the Battalion Commander, would *personally* look at key terrain features before any orders were issued affecting the well-being of the men asked to attack them.

By way of example of the difference in views from the platoon and battalion levels, some pages from 1/5's Unit Diary of June, 1951 follow:

3/HAC/hw
Ser 003
10 July, 1951

~~SECRET~~

From: Commanding Officer
To: Commandant of the Marine Corps
Via: (1) Commanding Officer, 5th Marines
        (2) Commanding General, 1st Marine Division
        (3) Commanding General, Fleet Marine Force, Pacific

Subj: Historical Diary for the month of June, 1951

Ref: (a) Paragraph 11401, Marine Corps Manual

Map: AMS L751 KOREA, 1:50,000. SHEETS: 6828/III/IV

SUMMARY

The month of June opened with the 1st Battalion, 5th Marines, in defensive positions, with the rifle companies forward of the battalion C.P., preparing to continue the attack which had been in progress since 28 May. "A" and "B" Companies, utilizing supporting mortars, artillery and air, attacked throughout the day and secured Regimental Objective #3, TA1918, where they consolidated for the night. "C" Company, using supporting arms and a platoon of tanks as well, advanced against stiff resistance toward Regimental Objective #5, TA1919-S. The objective was secured on 2 June against persistently stubborn resistance from a firmly entrenched enemy. The other companies secured their assigned objectives through furious assaults against the enemy positions and with the aid of all available supporting arms. Besides being well dug-in and camouflaged, the enemy launched an unusually large amount of mortar and artillery barrages, frequently in the battalion C.P. area. This, as well as the difficult terrain which was in their favor, caused a considerable amount of friendly casualties and added to the difficulty of the 1st Battalion attacks. Most of the enemy retaliatory counterattacks were at night. The attack continued through 3 June until the commanding terrain feature was secured. The rifle companies were directed to consolidate positions for the night on hill #680, TA1821, on the ridge line south of the key terrain feature. An air strike had been requested earlier but the aircraft failed to arrive. As the forward elements of "A" Company were re-

~~SECRET~~

turning to hill #680, the aircraft appeared, and, due to failure
of the TACP radio, the strike was directed by an OY aircraft.
Before the strike could be called off these elements of "A" Company
were subjected to strafing and napalming. Fortunately no
friendly casualties were suffered as a result of the strike.
The next morning the 1st Battalion was ordered to move to a new
assembly area at TA3220, after being relieved on position by
the 1st Battalion, KMC Regiment. The battalion arrived at the
new area early in the evening after a long, all day march
through a light rain. The 1st Battalion remained there until
7 June, when it moved forward to relieve the 2nd Battalion, 5th
Marines on position. The attack was continued on 8 June, with
the companies first sending strong combat patrols forward. During the day, the C.P. was subjected to intermittent enemy mortar
and artillery fire. Eight officers and one hundred and fifty-
nine enlisted men joined the battalion on that date. The next
day the enemy used heavy counter mortar and artillery fire and
resisted stubbornly against the 1st battalion attack. On 10 June
"A" Company initiated the attack in the left portion of the
battalion zone toward hill #721, TA2828. "B" and "C" Companies
also advanced and secured their intermediate objectives. "A"
Company, advancing against stiff resistance, was unable to secure it's objective due to approaching darkness, and it, as well
as the other companies, set up defensive positions for the night
on the best defensible ground. On 11 June, "A" Company secured
hill #721 after launching four concerted attacks against approximately two hundred firmly entrenched and bitterly determined
enemy. Supporting artillery fires were devastating, but the enemy countered with harrassing artillery fires, some of which
were directed against the attached tanks, which were working
their way up the valley floor. During the darkness of early
morning on the 12th, the enemy launched one of its strongest
night attacks against "B" Company, but they were driven off before day-break. "B" Company initiated the attack for Regimental
Objective #3, TA2829-O; the other companies continued their advance. Resistance was heavy throughout the day, and all supporting arms were used to best advantage. On 13 June, "B" Company
initiated the attack, seized its objective, TA2829-M, and dispatched patrols to its front and flanks. "A" and "C" Companies
then advanced and secured their objectives against heavy resistance. On 14 June, "B" and "C" Companies began a coordinated
attack on Division Objective "B". As they neared the objective,
"A" Company passed through them and secured hill #573, TA2832.
"B" Company held up for the night at TA2831-T; "C" Company, on
hill #808, TA 2731-Q. This put the companies in positions facing
the high ridge which was Regimental Objectives #6 and #7, on the

Kansas Line. The objectives were observed to be covered with
enemy, apparently digging in. Heavy artillery barrages were
called down throughout the late afternoon and night with good
results. One 15 June "A" Company seized hill #578, TA2933,
utilizing supporting fires from "B" and "C" Companies. During
the night "A" Company, in its defensive positions on the objective, was attacked by a skillful and cleverly camouflaged enemy.
"A" Company suffered three KIA, 12 WIA, and lost two machine guns.
One 16 June "B" Company moved to consolidate positions with "A"
Company, and all three companies dispatched security patrols to
their front and flanks.   The attack was discontinued, awaiting
relief of 1/5 by 2/5 on 18 June. On 17 June the Battalion Commander requested permission to continue the attack onto Regimental Objective #7. This was approved and, under artillery and
air cover. "B" Company jumped off in the attack for hill #907.
Upon reaching the crest of the hill, "B" Company met with a
murderous volumn of automatic weapons fire from firmly entrenched
enemy. The company suffered numerous casualties, including two
platoon leaders, and was forced to withdraw. "B" Company then
consolidated positions on hill #578, TA2933, with "A" Company.
LtCol. W. P. ALSTON, who was to take command of the battalion
after LtCol. John L. HOPKINS left, arrived at the combat C.P.
On 18 June "C" Company was attached to 2/5 when it relieved
1/5 on position. The 1st Battalion then proceeded by motor convoy to an assembly area at TA3026. The galley had been brought
up from the rear and went into operation, serving a hot evening
meal to the battalion after they had squared away in the new area.
At 0001 on 21 June, LtCol. ALSTON officially assumed command
of the 1st Battalion, 5th Marines. The battalion remained in this
assembly area for the remainder of the month. A training
schedule and organized athletics were set up after the men had
had a few days of complete rest. On the 21st Memorial Services
were held in honor of the members of the 1st Battalion, and
Korean cargo-dores, who were killed in the recent operation.
The total number of combat casualties for the 1st Battalion for
the month of June were: 28 KIA; 201 WIA. The total number of
casualties for the operation beginning on 25 May and ending on
18 June were: 33 KIA; 237 WIA. During the last week in the
month the battalion dispatched daily reconnaissance patrols to
various points where the battalion would most likely be committed, and patrols for local security. The month of June closed
with the 1st Battalion in the assembly area on standby to move
to a forward assembly area.

NARRATIVE

1 June:

The month of June opened with the 1st battalion, 5th Marines in defensive positions; "A" and "B" Companies at TA 1918-N, "C" Company at TA 1717-B, and the Battalion C.P. at TA 1817-O. The battalion was preparing to continue the attack which had been in progress since 28 May. The Regimental Commander and his advance command party, having arrived at the Battalion C.P. the previous evening, remained overnight to discuss attack plans and to observe the progress of the operation. The attack continued at 0820 in the morning with "B" Company jumping off to seize the commanding terrain at TA 1919-S, after this terrain had been softened up by an air strike and an artillery barrage. In coordination with "B" Company's attack, "G" Company, attached to 2nd Battalion, 5th Marines, launched an attack on the right flank from hill #902, TA 2019, to relieve the pressure on "B" Company's front. At 1000 "C" Company made contact at TA 1618-W with a tank platoon of "C" Company, 1st Tank Battalion, whose support it used to commence an attack toward Regimental Objective #5. At 1000, "C" Company and its attached tanks were subjected to heavy enemy 105 artillery and 120mm mortar fire at TA 1618-O. No casualties resulted from this fire. "B" Company, in the meantime, continued a cautious and determined advance against ever-increasing enemy resistance. The Company's intermediate objectives had to be gained by hard fighting, assaulting the enemy with hand grenades and close-range rifle fire. The enemy were firmly entrenched in deep, camouflaged, and solidly constructed bunkers. Hill #700, TA 1819, was secured at 1400; positions there were consolidated, and the company reorganized to prepare to continue the attack onto hill #651, TA 1918. At 1415 "G" Company returned to the 2nd Battalion after having effectively relieved some of the pressure on "B" Company. "C" Company, throughout its all-day attack received sporadic artillery and mortar fire. At one point the tank platoon was held up temporarily while enemy mines were removed from the valley floor ahead of them. At 1500 "C" Company called artillery preparatory fire on Regimental Objective #5. "B" Company called an air strike, heavy artillery, 4.2" and 81mm mortar fire on hill #651 prior to and after attacking. They encountered light resistance and secured the hill at 1620. "A" Company, which had followed "B" Company, moved on forward and secured Regimental Objective #3, where both companies consolidated positions for the night as ordered. "C" Company and attached tanks, at TA 1720-L, received intense automatic, small arms,

105 artillery, 82mm and 120mm mortar fire at 1700, from objective #5. Air strikes were conducted on this and Division Objective "Z" with excellent results. Due to approaching darkness, "C" Company was ordered at 1800 to establish its defense perimeter for the night on the high ground at TA 1719. At 1805 a section of the 81mm mortars from Weapons Company, displacing forward by vehicle, received six rounds of enemy 105 artillery which wounded four men. The Battalion C.P. had not displaced. The Regimental Commander and party departed at 1825 to return to the Regimental C.P. Upon reaching their positions for the night, the companies received ammunition and supplies by cargo-dore transport. Fifteen POWs and five civilian refugees had been taken during the day. The S-1 turned them over to regiment. The battalion suffered seventeen WIAs, of which twelve had to be evacuated. There was no enemy contact by the battalion during the night.

2 June:

At 0900 a patrol of Korean National Police, attached to the battalion, departed from the C.P. with the mission to search out the valley floor at TA 1718 and TA 1818. They completed this without contacting enemy. "C" Company, supported by "C" Company tanks, and "A" Company in rear of them, jumped off in the attack at 0915 to seize Regimental Objective #5, after first pulverizing it with air strikes, artillery, and rocket fire. Fifteen minutes later "C" Company reported it was receiving heavy 82 mm mortar fire at TA 1619-E. At 1000 "B" Company began to move out along the ridge line running parallel to the 1st Batallion's right boundry just inside the 2nd Battalion's zone of action. At 1030 "C" Company secured the high ground at TA 1620-0 against stubborn enemy resistance and continued the attack along the prominent ridge line running northeast to hill #610. Hill#610 was the commanding terrain feature and provided an excellent observation point. The enemy resisted tenaciously, throwing heavy automatic, small arms, mortar fire, fragmentation, and concussion grenades as the Marines closed in. "C" Company advanced slowly and deliberately, utilizing all available supporting arms - air, artillery, rockets, 4.2 and 81 mm mortars, and seized the intermediate objectives, several knolls along the ridge, leading up to hill #610. The tanks in the valley floor provided excellent overhead fire from their 50 Cal. machine guns, and their 90mm cannon proved extremely effective in destroying bunkers. The attack continued all day. By 1600 "C" Company had reached hill #610 and, after a heavy supporting artillery barrage, had begun to fight its way up the slope. An estimated two hundred to two hundred and fifty enemy were firmly entrenched atop the hill, employing small arms, automatic weapons, grenades, and mortars.

Nevertheless, the hill was secured by 1945. "A" Company, which had followed "C" Company, moved up onto the hill, and the two companies consolidated positions for the night. "B" Company was ordered to establish a defense at TA 2021-O and E to TA 2122-V. Earlier in the afternoon, at 1445, the battalion area was cleared, and the C.P. displaced to TA 1718-M. At 1545 Weapons Company, in the vicinity of TA 1619-Y, received four rounds of enemy 105 artillery and suffered five killed and two wounded. The new C.P. opened at 1730 at TA 1718-O. Supply trains with ammunition, rations, and water were immediately dispatched to the companies. At 1900 two hundred to three hundred enemy troops in column formation were sighted at TA 1721-K to P. Aircraft were on station, and within five minutes an air strike dispersed them. Later, at 2030, "C" Company reported it was receiving sporadic 82mm mortar fire from TA 1621-K. Artillery was called, and the enemy fire ceased. At 2200 the supply train returning from "C" Company was ambushed in the vicinity of TA 1721-X by approximately a squad of enemy using burp guns, rifles, and hand grenades. Two Marines were wounded before the enemy were driven off. Eight POWs and forty-five civilians were apprehended and turned over to Regiment during the day. The battalion suffered thirty-two casualties; six were KIA, twenty-six were WIA. One hundred med reported in to sick bay, and a total of forty-one, including the WIAs, were evacuated.

3 June:

Between 0150 and 0400, "A" Company was attacked by an estimated sixty enemy. The attack was repulsed with no friendly casualties. From 0730 to 0815 an air strike was conducted on hill #680, TA 1821, and the ridge line running north to hill #738, TA 1823. Upon termination of the strike, an artillery barrage was brought down on hill #680, followed by a rocket barrage on hills #692 and #738. At 0915 "A" Company, with the 2nd platoon, "C" Company tanks, 1st Tank Battalion attached, plus a section of 75mm recoilless rifles from the 5th Marines A-T Company, jumped off in the attack to seize hill #680, under cover of still another artillery barrage. The company advanced steadily against stubborn resistance until direct fire from the tanks' 90mm cannon could destroy the bunkers atop the hill. At 1125 the objective was secured. At 1200 "C" Company was ordered to patrol extensively 1000 yards northwest from hill #610. The patrol which had been dispatched, returned at 1415 with negative enemy contact. At 1400 "A" Company continued the attack to hill #692 against intense enemy small arms, automatic weapons, and AT gun fire from an estimated three enemy companies defending the high ground. "B" Company supported the attack by providing flanking fire from TA 1922. Elements of the 2nd Battalion also supported the attack by fire. Between 1500 and 1515 an air strike was conducted on hill #692, with excellent results. By 1600 "A" Company had reached TA 1822-H and was advancing against intense automatic weapons and heavy 120mm mortar fire. "B" Company received moderate mortar fire at TA 1922-M. Friendly mortar and artillery fire was called to neutralize it. The Battalion C.P., in the meantime, had commenced its displacement at 1610 to the vicinity of TA 1820. The old area was cleared at 1630. The new Battalion C.P. at TA 1830-M was opened at 1730. At 1700 "A" Company was held up at TA 18220H by intense enemy small arms, automatic weapons and 120mm mortar fire. At 1825 the company was subjected to an unusually heavy concentration of enemy 120mm mortar at TA 1825-G. The Company Commander, Captain Spuhler, suffered a severe wound but refused to be evacuated and continued to direct the attack. An air strike had been requested several hours earlier, but no aircraft had been available. The assault continued, and at 1845 the aircraft appeared. Radio communications from the TACP failed, and the strike began under direction from an OY aircraft of VMO-6. The airplanes made six to eight runs, strafing and napalming the ridge in the area specified earlier. Forward elements of "A" Company by this time had moved into the target area and were subjected to the friendly strike for some minutes until it could be called off by radio relay through Regiment. Fortunately no casualties were incurred. Immediately following the air strike, the enemy launched another mortar barrage. The Battalion Commander ordered the attack to be discontinued and for "A" and "C" Companies to consolidate positions for the night on hill #680, TA 1821. "B" Company established its perimeter at TA 1922. At 1930 a truck loaded with Korean CTC stretcher bearers, enroute to evacuate the "A" Company casualties, hit a mine at TA 1821-X. Three Marines and thirty cargo-dores were wounded, as well as the Catholic Chaplain, Father Quirk, who was severely hurt. However, all of the "A" Company casualties, except four stretcher cases, were evacuated by 2300. Due to a heavy downpour of rain, darkness, and treacherous mountain trails which turned to seas of mud, these stretcher cases could not be evacuated until the following morning. 5th Marines Fragmentary Order #55-51, received verbally at 2330, advised the Battalion Commander that the 1st Battalion, KMC Regiment could relieve the 1st Battalion, 5th Marines on position at 0800, 4 June, 1951. The Battalion was ordered to prepare to move to an assembly area at TA 3220. During the day eight POWs and eight refugees were taken and turned over to Regiment. Eighty-one men turned in for sick call. Forty-six,

all WIAs, were evacuated. Thirteen WIAs returned to duty.
There were eight KIAs. There was no enemy contact during the
night in the 1st Battalion area.

4 June:

Liaison was established with the 1st Battalion, KMC Regiment at 0600. The advance party, consisting of a representative
of each staff section and the company executive officers, departed the Battalion C.P. at 0800 for the new assembly area in
the vicinity of TA 3220, several miles northeast of Inje. At
0803 "A" Company sent a strong combat patrol of reinforced platoon strength to search out hill #692. This patrol returned
at 1200 with negative enemy contact. The relief of the 1st
Battalion on position by the 1st Battalion, Korean Marine Corps
Regiment, was completed at 1130, and the 1st Battalion, 5th
Marines commenced its displacement to the new assembly area in
the vicinity of TA 3220 at 1230. The order of movement was
"B", "C", Weapons, H&S, and "A" Company. The Battalion Commander led the troops in the march which was a distance of about
14,000 meters. The advance party and vehicle convoy left at
0800. They had to take a long route back south by Division
Headquarters and Inje. The troops followed a more direct route
eastward to the new area. The old area was cleared by 1300.
The motor convoy arrived at TA 3220 and opened the C.P. at 1625.
The troops, having marched through intermittent showers throughout the day, arrived at the area at 2030 and set up in bivouac
for the night. A total of twenty-one patients were treated
at sick-bay prior to the departure in the morning, and after
arrival in the new location in the evening. Nine were WIA;
eighteen were evacuated. One WIA returned to duty.

In addition to the contemporaneous accounts kept by battalion headquarters folk, it was common for after-action analyses and reports to be prepared, generally by Marine historians who tried to interview individual participants months or years after the fact, as well as review the battle maps and such other records as might have survived an infantry battalion's various moves and perils.

Higher-ranking officers were easier to locate for interviews than were enlisted men and lieutenants. Most of the latter had become casualties or had gone back to civilian life. Consequently the reports tend to reflect the battalion unit diaries and the recollection of headquarters officers rather than the experiences of the troops who participated.

A single statement in 1/5's Unit Diary sums it all up: "The total number of casualties for the operation beginning on 25 May and ending on 18 June were 33 KIA, 237 WIA."[1] Most of these casualties were in the three rifle companies, so total casualties in the three companies were only about one-third. At the Chosin Reservoir, in Charlie Company alone, there were 23 KIA and 81 WIA, with 88 others evacuated, mostly for frostbite. The numbers are deceptive since a number of replacements joined the Company each month, and quite often the new men were the first casualties.

Some years after the Korean War, in 1961, an "Official" five volume summary was printed entitled *U.S. Marine Operations in Korea.* In Volume IV, "The East-Central Front," appears the following official version of the taking of Hill 610:

"FIGHT OF THE 5TH MARINES FOR HILL 610

During the heyday of the battleship, every midshipman dreamed of some glorious future day when he would be on the bridge, directing the naval maneuver known as crossing the T. In other words, his ships would be in line of battle, firing converging broadsides on an enemy approaching in column. Obviously, the enemy would be at a disadvantage until he executed a 90° turn under fire to bring his battered ships into line to deliver broadsides of their own.

It was a mountain warfare variation of crossing the T that the Korean Reds were using against the Marines. Whenever possible, the enemy made a stand on a hill flanked by transverse ridgelines. He emplaced hidden machine guns or mortars on these ridgelines to pour a converging fire into attackers limited by the terrain to a single approach. It meant that the Marines had to advance through this crossfire before they could get in position for the final assault on the enemy's main position.

There were two tactical antidotes. One was well-directed close air support. The other was the support of tanks advancing parallel to enemy-held ridgelines and scorching them with the

---

[1] The ratio of killed to wounded was far lower in the early Korean War than in earlier wars, probably because of the poor quality of the Chinese and North Korean small arms and lack of artillery. Burp gun, rifle and machine gun bullets were not always lethal; Chinese grenades had high explosive power, but the shrapnel fragments were often very small. Only in mortars, particularly the fearsome 120 millimeter, were the Chinese and North Korean weapons equal to American arms in their impact and effect. In World War I, for example, against German weapons, including poison gas, the First Battalion, Fifth Marines with a T/O strength of around 1000 men (close to 1/5's T/O strength in Korea) had the following ratio of casualties:

Chateau Thierry/			
Belleau Wood	June 6-19	142 KIA	405 lesser casualties
Soissons	July 19-25	18	216
Mt. Mihiel	Sept. 12-16	4	202
Blanc Mont	Oct. 3-9	53	402
Exermont-Meuse	Nov. 1-11	45	448
		263	1673

Our predecessors of 33 years earlier obviously had a much tougher time of it. See Appendix A for an account of Charlie Company at the Reservoir, Appendix B for the history of 1/5 in World War I, Appendix C for the Brigade's actions at the Pusan Perimeter, and Appendix D for the Battalion's part in the Inchon-Seoul Campaign.

direct fire of 90mm rifles and 50 caliber machine guns.

On June 1 the two regiments in assault, the 5th and 7th Marines, found the resistance growing stiffer as they slugged their way forward toward **Line Kansas** (Map 15). Within an hour after jumping off, 2/5 was heavily engaged with an estimated 200 enemy defending Hill 651 tenaciously. At noon, after ground assaults had failed, a request was put in for air support. Four VMF-214 planes led by Captain William T. Kopas bombed and strafed the target. This attack broke the back of NKPA opposition, and 2/5 moved in to seize the objective.

Early on the morning of the 2d, Lieutenant Colonel Hopkins' 1/5 moved out to secure the southwest end of the long ridgeline that stretched northeast from Yanggu (Map 15) and afforded a natural avenue of approach to Taem-san and the **Kansas** line on the southern rim of the Punch Bowl. The Marine advance got under way at 0915. After two four-plane strikes by VMF-214 and a "preparation" by 1/11 and the 1st Rocket Battery, the Battalion attacked across a valley with Baker company (First Lieutenant William E. Kerrigan) on the right and Charlie Company (First Lieutenant Robert E. Warner) on the left to seize the terminal point on the ridge leading to Hill 610 (Map 15). Able Company (Captain John L. Kelly) followed Charlie as Company C (Captain Richard M. Taylor) of the 1st Tank Battalion moved into supporting position.

Converging fire from transverse ridges had the Marine riflemen pinned down until the tankers moved along the valley road running parallel. Direct 90mm fire into NKPA bunkers enabled C/1/5 to advance to the forward slope of Hill 610. The enemy fought back with machine guns and grenades while directing long-range rifle fire against 2/5, attacking along a parallel ridge across the valley.

By 1945 the last bunker on Hill 610 had been overrun. Meanwhile, 2/5 had pushed ahead some 5,000 yards to the northeast.

The capture of Hill 610 will never have its glorious page in history. It was all in a day's work for Marines who could expect a succession of such nameless battles as they clawed their way forward. That night the weary men of 1/5 were not astonished to receive a counter-attack in the darkness. It was all part of the job, too. After driving off the unseen enemy, the new tenants of Hill 610 snatched a few hours of sleep. They were on their feet again at dawn, ready to go up against the next key terrain feature in a rocky area that seemed to be composed entirely of Hill 610s.

The next knob along the ridge happened to be Hill 680, about 1,000 yards to the northwest. VMF-214 planes from K-46 napalmed and strafed the enemy, and Able Company led the 1/5 attack. During the air strike the Koreans had taken to cover in their holes on the reverse slope.

They were back in previously selected forward slope firing positions by the time the Marines came in sight. Close-in artillery support enabled the attackers to get within grenade range and seize the last NKPA bunker by 1400. Able Company pushed on.

Midway from 680 to the next knob, Hill 692, the advance was stopped by enemy small-arms and mortar fire. An air strike was requested on the bunkers holding up the assault, but fog closed in and the planes were delayed more than two hours.

At 1600, after Able Company had renewed the assault without air support, four VMF-214 Corsairs started a target run controlled by a liaison plane from VMO-6. The foremost Marines, almost at the summit by this time, had to beat a hasty retreat to escape the napalm and 500-pound bombs being dumped on Hill 692. Fortunately, there were no friendly casualties. Some were caused indirectly, however, when hostile mortar fire caught Marines withdrawing along a connecting saddle to the comparatively safe reverse slope of Hill 680. When the danger passed, Able Company returned to the attack on 692 and routed the remaining defenders.

The 1st Marine Division made it a policy thereafter that only the forward air controllers on the ground were to direct close air support along the front. Control of air strikes farther behind the enemy lines was reserved for the OYs."

Comment:

Obviously both the 1/5 Unit Diary and the "official" history were dead wrong on a number of key points. The official histories read well but simply aren't true. Able Company didn't return to the attack on Hill 692. The following day it walked 15 miles back into a reserve area. The Korean Marines continued the attack.[2] Over its leaders' objections the company was recalled back to behind its original positions. Buzz Lubka's memory is clear and precise. Nobody on that knife-like ridge to 680 and 692 could ever forget that day of June 3.

The errors apparently stem from the interviewing historians' talking to rear echelon commanders instead of participants.

However inaccurate "official" military histories may be, it is true that neither 610 nor 680 were much different from other hills attacked by the various rifle companies of the First Marine Division during the winter and spring of 1951 en route to the truce line in Central Korea. Each of the Division's 81 rifle platoons had its special numbered and otherwise-unknown hills to remember, and I suspect that most assaults were, of necessity, led by platoon leaders. It was not considered honorable to ask one's squad leaders to be the first man up the ridge line or over a hilltop in an assault. On a patrol, yes, but not an assault.

Buzz Lubka, Bill Heer, Charlie Cooper, Pat McGahn and Chuck Daly led their platoons. Bill Heer's last 200 yards to the top of 680 was in single file and it is a miracle that there wasn't one North Korean rifleman to raise his head and gun him down as he plodded up that ridge. 680 has always thereafter been called "Pube Hill."

The platoon leaders' assaults, however, were not entirely their own. They reflected a desire to live up to Jones and Schening and Cronin and a continuity in inspiration from Cates and Shepherd and Wallace in 1917 and 1918 to their sons and a whole host of young men a generation later who would try to live up to their fathers and uncles and brothers at Guadalcanal, Peleliu, Iwo Jima, Tarawa and Okinawa. The survivors in the regular Corps who held the line at the Pusan Perimeter and the Chosin Reservoir passed the tradition on to the reserves who succeeded them in early 1951. On February 15, 1951, the First Battalion, Fifth Marines, had 41 regular officers and 2 reserves; four months later, the numbers were exactly reversed, 2 regulars and 41 reserves.

There will always be a sufficiency of young men wanting to be Marine reserve officers; the real need is for quality career Marine officers, both commissioned and non-commissioned, who will put up with the frustrations and boredom of peacetime, slow promotions and an uncaring public and be around to train the reserves when the need arises. Those few are the true heroes of our time.

The Marine Corps history of one typical career Marine officer is found in Appendix F.

That the relatively few regular Marines in time of crisis can both absorb, and given enough time, train the reserves to try to serve in their image, is perhaps the most enduring character of the Corps. As long as that quality is preserved, it guarantees a continuity of excellence for both regulars

---

[2]There is an historical note about the Korean Marine Corps (KMC) that doesn't appear in the "official" histories. When we were about to leave Hill 610 on the morning of June 4th, we got a little glimpse into the different culture of our allies. We were relieved on position by a KMC platoon, its commander perhaps 19, 5'3" and with an innocent face.

I was kneeling, making sure my pack was rolled tight, when there was a deafening explosion beside me. I hit the deck and after a few seconds stopped shaking enough to be able to look up to see the Korean lieutenant putting his .45 back in its holster. He had just shot one of his Marines behind the right ear.

The explanation, through our interpreter: There was still some North Korean gear lying around the hilltop. The Korean Marine had violated a rule of the KMCs that no enemy equipment was to be rifled. In the following two weeks, the KMC's took "Taem-San" the highest peak in the First Division's zone of action. We never had any worries when they were on our flank, but we could never bring ourselves to adopt their disciplinary methods.

and reserves.

That continuity, going back to the Bon Homme Richard, stays on today with young Marines who have never heard a shot fired in anger, but who, should they face combat will try to live up to the legends of Khe Sanh, Con Thien and Elephant Valley as well as Iwo, Tarawa, Peleliu and Belleau Wood.

That continuity was demonstrated by Marines of 1/5 in retaking Hue City after Tet in 1968 with over half of their riflemen killed or wounded in the process. It was demonstrated again in 1991 when 1/5 helped retake Kuwait City in Operation Desert Storm with only 1 WIA. It will undoubtedly be demonstrated again in some unlikely place and time before this century ends.

On 610, that continuity was exemplified by two rare men, Jones and Schening of the regular Marine Corps, who passed it on to the men they led and trained, Hanson, Elson, Daly, Dacy, Goodrich, Bunnell, Dohse, Clark, Bruder, Burchick, Robichaud and Lee. 610 was **their** hill, but only through the bequest of the Jones-Schening legacy.

Survivors of Able Company, in reserve after the taking of the south rim of the Punch Bowl, late June, 1951. Pfc. Ralph "Poncho" Vasquez (second row, second from right.)

Chapter 3

The Aftermath

After a purely delightful several days in reserve on the rocky riverbed of the Soyang River near Inje, alongside the Army Second Division's 9th Regiment, the Regiment geared up and on June 7th resumed the attack northwards along the ridgelines running northwest from the Soyang River towards the Punch Bowl. The south rim of the Punch Bowl was the designated "final objective," and part of a diagonal line slanting across the Korean Peninsula called "The Kansas Line."

A number of veterans had been rotated home on June 5, but the Battalion was bolstered by 8 new officers and 159 enlisted men from the Ninth Replacement Draft. The troops were divided up fairly equally amongst the three rifle companies. Two weeks later, most of them had become casualties.

On June 11th and 12th, working with tank patrols in the winding Soyang River valley, all three of Charlie Company's platoon leaders were wounded, Daly and Bunnell grievously so.[1] The next day,

---

[1]Daly's account:

"I was evacuated in the bubble of a helicopter which had a bumper sticker: "JOIN THE U.S. MARINES." When I was in the surgical tent after being evacuated by helicopter they put my stretcher to one side after doing some preliminary work to try to keep my arm attached. Some other stretcher bearers carried Bunnell in. I called out "where did they get you Beau?" "They got the family jewels" he responded. There was absolute silence in the tent. The silence was broken by the sound of a chunk of shrapnel being dropped onto the enamel operating table after it had been removed from Beau's groin. Then he said "let me keep that piece, Doc. I want to bring it home so my woman can wheel it around in a baby carriage."

I remember lying on the dock in Pusan waiting to be hoisted aboard the hospital ship by crane. My bladder was bursting so I asked for a "duck." A corpsman yelled up and one was thrown down from an upper deck. It was a challenge to relieve myself in front of 500 pairs of eyes, but pressure won.

When I was on the hospital ship Jack Jones came to my bunk. His wounds were fresh, too, but he was used to these matters. He persuaded me to get up so we could go to the ship's officers' mess to watch a western mystery movie (a "who crapped in the saddlebags?" as he put it).

When we were at Tripler Hospital in Japan, Jones who had been there before, led us AWOL into the town. At some fancy hotel I was trying to persuade a nurse to ease my various ailments. Jack interrupted the proceedings by having the hotel band play a tune "in honor of 1st Lt. Charles U. Daly on his first wedding anniversary."

Jones told us that to control us when we got to Hawaii the hospital staff would take our trousers. We all put them underneath the blankets which were between us and our stretchers. We arranged with a nurse on the plane to have a car meet us

Jones moving up the ridges to observe the three advancing rifle companies, was wounded by a grenade booby-trap, losing two fingers. Burchick and Robichaud had also been seriously wounded the previous day and evacuated. The heart of the Company was being cut away.

In Charlie Company there were now left only one lieutenant, one sergeant and a handful of the 235 enlisted men who had attacked north out of Wonju four months earlier.

With Jones gone, there was a certain dread each day as to what the Colonel might order to be done from his far-back command post.

Reaching the last series of north-south ridges leading up to the massive east-west rim of the Punch Bowl, it was Able and Baker's turn to take fearsome casualties, including Baker's last surviving platoon leader, Charlie Cooper. In Able Company, Bill Heer and Buzz Lubka led two days of successive assaults up almost impossible ridgelines, blanketed by fire from both sides of the higher rim of the Punch Bowl. Heer lost 55 of 63 men, killed or wounded; Lubka almost as many.[2] Johnson's platoon had two machine guns lost during a fierce North Korean counterattack. On June 17, it was Baker's turn. Charlie Cooper, a regular who had joined Baker just in time for Hill 313 on April 22, had been wounded twice earlier in seven straight weeks of the heaviest combat since the Reservoir, but was given the assault honor, with Idiot Six personally directing his attack by radio from some hilltop well to the rear. At one point, the Colonel shook his fist at the forbidding ridgeline of the Punch Bowl some 2,000 yards away and shouted some unforgettable words over the entire battalion radio net: "Get off the hill, you fucking gooks! The napalm is coming; We'll have roast pork tonight!" To the rifle platoon leaders listening in on the battalion radio net, these words were more terrifying than inspirational. The Colonel actually asked permission for his battalion to be allowed to assault Hill 907, the key peak at the south rim of the Punch Bowl. At the end of a long day trying to take 907, Charlie got his 3rd and near-fatal wound. Evacuated to the battalion aid station and almost-unconscious, he was unable to speak as Idiot Six stood at his side and commented: "Too bad, he was a fine young officer." The Battalion was taken off line but Charlie Company remained. Temporarily assigned to the Second Battalion, Charlie Company received orders to assault the south rim of the Punch Bowl where Baker Company had taken such heavy losses. The First Platoon was again designated as the attack platoon. When, with some trepidation its platoon leader and lead fire team reached the jump-off point, still 500 yards below the crest, a fortuitous event came to pass, one to be forever remembered by its beneficiaries.

From left to right, charging along the fearsome ridge above them, came a singing, bayonet-wielding group of Marines, flushing the North Koreans from their bunkers. It was George Company of the Third Battalion which had gained a foothold to the west and completely flanked the enemy position.

Charlie Company had held a dim view of George 3/5 from an occasion two months earlier when

---

at a particular hospital gate Jack knew about. Soon after arriving at the hospital those of us who were able to maneuver made a dash for that gate and had a great night on the town. When we returned to the hospital some army colonel said that the hospital was just as much a military organization as the front lines, we had deserted our posts and we were going to remain in the hospital until we rotted. A day or two later a Marine general came by to pass out various citations. He pinned one on one of our number who had lost his arm, and commented how happy the wounded fellow must be, knowing that he would be home soon. The lieutenant advised him that none of us were going home because we were going to rot in the hospital on the colonel's orders. We were on the plane to California the next day.

I recall that on the hospital plane I was showered by papers floating down from McGahn's stretcher which was above mine in the tier of three. I asked him what the hell he was doing. He said he was writing his speech for the Rotary Club.

---

[2]The unlucky 9th Replacement Draft men were particularly hard-hit. Every replacement but one who joined the 1st Platoon of Charlie Company became a casualty. Of 32 men who joined Able Company, all became casualties. The attrition rate among the "old" men was much lower. Experience, or perhaps a dearly-earned sense of caution, materially increased the chances of survival.

on a warm April day resting in reserve along the Pukhan River, one of George Company's zealous platoon leaders, John L. "Tex" Downes, had run a poop-and-snoop training exercise through the Company's peaceful, sleeping camp, knocking painfully-washed clean underwear off tent ropes and into the dust in the process.

All was forgiven at the Punch Bowl, however, as Downes' men, now under Jim Daugherty, and the platoons of Bo Marache, and Tom Johnston cleared out the bunkers Charlie Company had feared meant its sure demise. Downs, Daugherty and Marache had all been in the First Special Basic Class at Quantico and George company had literally saved the day. There was no way Hill 907 could be taken by the frontal assault ordered by 1/5's intrepid leader.[3]

From 500 yards away it was hard for the Charlie Company men to believe what they were hearing . . . a spirited and raucous singing of the Marine Corps Hymn as George Company ran through the Korean bunkers and trench lines. Charlie Company happily retired to a peaceful ravine at the foot of the ridge. It was the last heavy combat exposure for the Battalion in 1951.

A few days later the Chinese and North Koreans asked for a truce, and a casualty-conscious UN Command accepted with some caution.

Most of the survivors who had been with the Battalion since Wonju were sent to safe jobs in the rear, several all the way back to Masan on Korea's south coast, to serve as personnel and supply officers or in other jobs less honored but far safer than that of a rifle platoon leader. After a fierce battle in late August and September for the northeast ridges of the Punch Bowl during which 1/5 was held in reserve, the war changed into ridgetop trench warfare with minefields, barbed wire and a series of nasty fights for heavily-fortified positions which were to last for nearly two long years. The war of movement had ended at the Punch Bowl.[4]

Wonju, Charlie Company's starting point in February, 1951, later became the sister city of Roanoke, Virginia, the city from whence had come one of the 138 Marine reserve units which filled out the Division just in time for the Inchon landing. That unit's C.O., Bill Hopkins, after surviving the hard battles for Seoul and at the Reservoir, had been wounded near Pohang. He would later become a famous lawyer and Majority Leader in the Virginia State Legislature.

Generals Cates and Shepherd successfully persuaded the Congress, not only to preserve the Marine Corps from President Truman's axe, but to see its strength increased to 200,000.

General Shepherd succeeded General Cates as Commandant of the Marine Corps. He lived

---

[3]Charlie Cooper's recollections:

He (Idiot Six) gave me a lot of fire support on my 17 June assault on Hill 907. He wouldn't even let Bill Kerrigan talk on the net; one platoon assaulting a regimental objective, the Command Post of the 10th Korean Division; with the Battalion CO coordinating the fire support. He must have been two miles from the gunfire! We kicked off at 0800 that day; I was wounded on top at 1700. What a day that was! I landed on top of that very hill in 1983, during my first visit as CG, FMF-PAC. What memories!

---

[4]A fine book on the trench warfare after the September, 1951 battles at the Punch Bowl is Jim Brady's *The Coldest Winter*, Orion Books, (1990). Brady served in Dog Company, 2nd Battalion, 7th Marines, and was lucky enough to have another Yale graduate, now Senator John Chafee of Rhode Island as his company commander. Brady's tour in Korea covered both the winter of 1951-52 against the North Koreans northeast of the Punch Bowl, as well as the spring of 1952 against the Chinese in the lower hills on the west coast near Panmunjom.

An equally good book reflecting an enlisted Marine's irreverent view of the last seven months of the war is *The Last Parallel* by Martin Russ, Rinehart & Company, Inc. (1957).

Those of us who were relieved from the lines by June of 1951 were ever thankful that we never had to worry about the extensive minefields that were the worry of every Marine during the last two years of the war.

into his 90s, revered as one of the greatest and most effective Marine Corps Commandants. One of his sons, Dee Dee, served as a platoon leader and Exec of A/1/5 and another, Bo, as C.O. of George Company, 3/5, the same outfit which had saved Charlie Company from its potentially-disastrous attack on Hill 907 at the Punch Bowl. General Breckinridge's sons, John and Jim, both came to 1/5's rifle companies as lieutenants; John was killed in a Chinese ambush in November, 1951.

John and Jim Wallace graduated from tank school and took over tank platoons. In Korea, John was given command of the same tank platoon which had saved his friend's life on 610.

One of the friends John had talked into enlisting in the Platoon Leaders Class from Stanford in 1948, Bill "Stub" Geary, came to command an Amphibious Tractor Platoon on the Han River. On one black January night in 1952 with artillery ammunition strictly rationed, he fired off the entire 75 mm ammunition allowance for the Division at what may or may not have been a massive Chinese small boat attack across the Han. In the morning there was some debris floating in the river and an outraged ordnance officer back at the Division CP.

The 5th Marines' Regimental commander, Colonel Richard Hayward, a Pfc in the 5th Marines in Nicaragua in 1928, went on to prestigious assignments including the Navy War College and ultimately retired as a Brigadier General, dying in 1988 after two great celebrations sponsored by his former lieutenants, one in Washington, D.C. and one in Atlantic City. Two of his battalion commanders and nearly 20 of his former company-grade officers toasted Hayward's revered status as the grand old man of the 5th Marines. Naval Academy graduate Charlie Cooper, thrice wounded in his seven weeks with Baker Company, continued on to make a truly-distinguished name for himself in Viet Nam, ultimately retiring as a Lieutenant General, the second-highest rank in the Marine Corps. His friends thought he should have made Commandant, but only the President can make that choice.

Upon Hayward's honest belief, back at regimental headquarters, that Idiot Six had played a leading role in 1/5's advance to the Punch Bowl, he was nominated from above for the Navy Cross.[5] The only event which could remotely be connected to this rare honor was the Colonel's "bold and skillful management" of the supporting fires on June 2 and 3 which had permitted Charlie Company to take Hill 610 and Able Company to take 680 and the ridgeline to the north. It took the great man several months of searching through the hospitals in Japan before he could persuade the necessary three eyewitnesses, all headquarters officers, to corroborate his alleged fire control brilliance on June 2. No Charlie, Able or Baker Company officer or enlisted man would sign the papers. The Colonel, charming and debonair in peacetime circumstances, retired several years later after a pleasant tour of recruiting duty in Los Angeles, successfully evading an assignment to the Cold Weather Training School at Pickel Meadows, California, far from the comforts of headquarters life he had enjoyed so much, even from his tent in Korea. His passing was noted without rancor by those who had survived his leadership. Jones made Lieutenant Colonel before retiring with heart problems, becoming a respected lay leader of the Mormon Church in Southern California, looking after hundreds of people in his community with the same thoughtful care he had given his troops in Korea.

Spike Schening stayed in the Corps, and got his fourth Purple Heart years later as a Battalion Commander in Viet Nam, hit by incoming artillery fire on a hill apparently not unlike 566. No doubt he was roaring out commands to "Spread out, take cover" as he had 15 years earlier. Retired as a full Colonel, he immediately volunteered for hazardous rescue duty with the Red Cross, most recently in the retaking of Kuwait City where 1/5 was one of the assault battalions.

After a long hospital convalescence, Daly went on to serve on President Kennedy's staff in the White House and later as Vice President of both Harvard and the University of Chicago. Charlie Bun-

---

[5]Lubka in 1989: "At breakfast last year Charlie Bunnell and I unloaded on General Hayward on what we thought of Idiot Six. His comment was "I didn't know how bad it was."

nell, after an equally-long convalescence, integrated into the regular Marine Corps, retiring after 25 years as a full Colonel. Bill Kerrigan and Buzz Lubka earned distinguished records in the regular Marine Corps, retiring as Colonels, while Pat McGahn became Atlantic City's most prominent lawyer, the personal attorney for entrepreneur Donald Trump. McGahn successfully organized the statewide ballot measure legalizing gambling in Atlantic City, thereby resuscitating that ancient and colorful playground city in time for one last great reunion honoring General Hayward. It was only fitting that McGahn and Harvey Nolan were together for that reunion, 39 years after their baptism of fire on Hill 313, for which both received the Navy Cross. Harvey Nolan passed away a few months later, as did Max Merritt who had done so well on the road to Seoul and on Hill 1292 at the Reservoir.

For the rest of the reserve lieutenants of 1951, I suspect most of us occasionally give a private prayer each June 2 for the regulars like Jones and Schening and Averill and the hope that the Marine Corps ethic they passed on to us will stay alive and well in today's less-dangerous world.

Supreme Court Justice Oliver Wendell Holmes Jr., a young lieutenant of the 20th Massachusetts Regiment in the Civil War, wounded three times, at Ball's Bluff, Antietam and Fredericksburg, perhaps best summed up that ethic over 100 years ago.

> "As life is action and passion, a man should share the action and passion of his time at peril of being judged not to have lived."

> "I do not know the meaning of the universe, but in the midst of doubt, in the collapse of creeds, there is one thing I do not doubt and that is that the faith is true and adorable which leads a soldier to throw away his life in obedience to a blindly accepted duty, in a cause which he little understands, in a plan of campaign of which he has no notion, under tactics of which he does not see the use."

> "War, when you are at it, is horrible and dull. It is only when time has passed that you see that its message was divine. I hope it may be long before we are called again to sit at that master's feet . . ."

> "The joy of life is living; is to put out all one's powers as far as they will go . . . to ride boldly at what is in front of you, be it fence or enemy . . . to keep the soldier's faith against the doubts of civil life, more besetting and harder to overcome than all the misgivings of the battlefield . . . to know that one's final judge and only rival is oneself. . ."

> "When we meet thus, (Memorial Day, 1884) when we do honor to the dead in terms that must sometimes embrace the living, we do not deceive ourselves. We attribute no special merit to a man for having served when all were serving. We know that if the armies of our war did anything worth remembering, the credit belongs not mainly to the individuals who did it, but to average human nature. We also know very well that we cannot live in associations with the past alone, and we admit that, if we would be worthy of the past, we must find new fields of action or thought, and make for ourselves new careers."

> "There is one who on this day is always present to my mind. He entered the army at 19, a second lieutenant . . . his few surviving companions will never forget the awful spectacle of his advance alone with his company in the streets of Fredericksburg. In less than sixty seconds he would become the focus of a hidden and annihilating fire from a semicircle of houses. His first platoon had vanished under it in an instant; ten men falling dead by his side. He had quietly turned back to where the other half of his company was waiting, had given the order, 'second platoon forward!' and was again moving on, in obedience to superior command, when the order he was obeying was countermanded. The end was distant only a few seconds . . . his death seemed to end a portion of our life also."

"It is not well for soldiers to think much about wounds. Sooner or later we shall fall: but mean-time it is for us to fix our eyes upon the point to be stormed, and to get there if we can."

The streets of Fredericksburg, 25 miles south of Quantico, are peaceful now, but these words from the last century sum up, to me at least, the Marine Corps ethic which Jones and Schening have so honorably pursued in their lifetimes of public service.

Woodside, California
Christmas, 1991

At the left and right: Pat McGahn and Harvey Nolan, awarded the Navy Cross for holding Hill 313 west of the Hwochon Reservoir on the night of April 22, 1951; in the middle: Dick McCue, 2/5, and General Hayward enlisted USMC 1927, retired 1958.

McGahn, Kerrigan and Cooper with The Old Man Himself, March, 1988.

Chuck McAtee, Harry Steinmeyer and Paul McWilliams, 1988. McAtee and McWilliams were platoon leaders in 3/7; Steinmeyer an Amtrak platoon leader in World War II and company commander in Korea. McWilliams is holding a copy of Gerry Averill's book, Mustang.

General Hayward with two platoon leaders. At right: Elliot Richardson, Second Lieutenant, U.S. Army, D-Day, 1944 and hero of the Saturday Night Massacre, 1973. Middle: the author.

Captain Gerry Averill and Mrs. Averill, March 1988. The one regular Marine officer aboard the General J.C. Breckinridge. His insistence on daily calisthenics for 2½ weeks aboard ship undoubtedly saved lives during the 1st weeks in Korea for the 70 officers and 1900 enlisted men of the Fifth Replacement Draft who landed at Pohang, February 16, 1951.

Front Row: McCue, Merritt, Jones, Schening and Kerrigan. Back Row: McGahn, McCloskey, Waldo, Lubka and Daly. (Atlantic City, New Jersey, 1988.)

Left to right, Bill Heer, Bill Kerrigan, Pat McGahn, Basile Lubka and Charlie Cooper, the heart of Able and Baker Companies, 1/5. There were at least eight Purple Hearts awarded to this group, luckily non-posthumously through no fault of their own.

The Skipper and Mrs. Jones, (with the author), March 1988, Washington, D.C.

Joe Reisler and Mike Rogers, Platoon Leaders, First Marines, when that regiment held the 40th Chinese Field Army at Hill 902 on April 23-24, 1951.

Captain Harry Steinmeyer, WW II and Korea.

Captain Lewis Puller IV, Vietnam.

Second Lieutenant John Gearhart, WIA at The Punch Bowl, September 1951. (Volunteered himself and 2nd Lt. Pat Robertson for combat duty in June, 1951. Robertson went on to become the Division Rear Echelon Liquor Officer.)

2nd Lt. Nick Arundel of The Plains, Virginia. He handled "line crossers" in Korea, and later blew up the electric power station in Hanoi in 1954.

Mr. and Mrs. Tex Downes, G/3/5. 1951.

Two fine lawyers: George Lehner of Washington, D.C. whose painstaking search for Marines of 1951 finally forced dismissal of the Robertson case and Pat McGahn, holder of 4 Purple Hearts and a Navy Cross from 3 months with B/1/5.

Black Jack McCaffrey and bride, 1988. 1st Lieutenant, 11th Marines, 1951.

Lts. Bunnell and Daly about to be evacuated by heli-copter, morning of June 12, 1951.

Former 2nd Lt. Chuck Daly, Fifth Replacement Draft, 1951, reading an alleged telegram from a famous shipmate: "Sorry I can't be with you tonight, but I missed the fucking boat again." (The Rev. Pat Robertson, Republican Candidate for the Presidency, March, 1988.)

Charlie Company 1/5 Survivors of the U.S. Hospital Ship Repose: Bunnell, WIA June 12 1951; Daly, WIA June 12, 1951; Jones, WIA June 13, 1951; Schening, WIA May 29, 1951.

OBITUARIES

Richard W. Hayward Dies; Brigadier General in Marines

Richard Wright Hayward, 83, a retired Marine Corps brigadier general who was a highly decorated combat veteran of World War II and the Korean War, died Feb. 2 at Fairfax Hospital. He had a heart ailment.

During World War II, he commanded the 2nd Marine Parachute Battalion and the 1st battalion of the 8th Marine regiment. He saw duty in the Pacific Theater from Guadalcanal to Saipan, Tinian and Okinawa.

In February 1951, he took command in Korea of the 5th Marine Regiment of the 1st Marine Division. He led his regiment north from the embattled Pusan Perimeter. In May and June 1951, he led his marines over harsh terrain while escorting vital supplies.

It was during this trek, near Mundong, that he directed a pitched battle from the fighting front, saving his marines and the supplies while defeating the enemy. For this action, he was awarded the Army's Distinguished Service Cross, its highest award for heroism, except for the Medal of Honor.

In addition to the Distinguished Service Cross, his combat awards included the Legion of Merit, the Bronze Star, two Purple Hearts and three Air Medals.

Gen. Hayward was a native of New York City and attended Cornell University. He enlisted in the Marine Corps as a private in 1926 and was commissioned while serving in Nicaragua in the 1930s. Before World War II, he served ashore in China and the Philippines and commanded Marine Corps detachments aboard ships of the Asiatic and Pacific fleets.

After World War II, he graduated from the Army Command and Staff College at Fort Leavenworth, Kan., where he later served on the faculty and staff. He also was an analyst with the Office of Naval Intelligence and was a special assistant and senior Marine aided to the secretary of the Navy before going to Korea.

After Korea, he served as deputy chief of staff of the Pacific Fleet Marine Force, then went to the Naval War College, where he graduated and served on special study groups. He then went to Norfolk, where he became a strategic analyst with the office of the Supreme Allied Commander Atlantic, the senior NATO naval command. He then served in the office of the Joint Chiefs of Staff before retiring from active duty in 1958.

After that, he worked for Aerojet General Corp. and the McLaughlin Research Corp. here before retiring a second time about 1970.

A resident of Arlington, he had lived in the Washington area since 1958. He was a member of St. Agnes Catholic Church in Arlington and the Washington Golf and Country Club.

Survivors include his wife, the former Elizabeth MacKeown, of Arlington; a son, Richard VI, of Key West, Fla.; two daughters, Elizabeth H. Bray of Boston and Cynthia H. Davis of New York City; a brother, retired Navy Vice Adm. John T. Hayward of Jacksonville, Fla.; two sisters, Elinor Pollock of McClean and Marjorie Madey of Baton Rouge, La., and three grandchildren.

Chapter 4

The Pacifist Warrior

On the occasion of his 60th birthday, May 29, 1987, a few close friends of Charles Ulickdeburgh Daly gathered at his Cape Cod home to share their collective wonder that he had survived so long.

The friends, nearly all of them frauds of considerable notoriety in their respective walks of life, shared a unanimous conviction that Daly was the greatest fraud of them all.

For over 35 years Daly had somehow been able to posture himself in public and private life as an advocate of peace and love for his fellow man, especially the downtrodden peasantry of the third world, while surviving countless bar room brawls and concealing a history in his youth of having ventured 10,000 miles from his own native land to personally extinguish not less than a hundred poor peasants in their's.

In this same 35 years, while constantly advocating government assistance for the weak and homeless, particularly minorities, Daly had managed to amass a small fortune in real estate, generally in white-only areas and rented through white-only agencies to the rich and famous.

No scholar at Yale, where despairing parents had sent him in the vain hope he might become a gentleman, Daly had somehow been able in later life to have himself appointed to the Vice Presidencies of two of America's most prestigious academic institutions, Harvard University and the University of Chicago. Although frugal if not miserly with his own charitable contributions, Daly also rose, almost by default, to the chairmanship of a noted eleemosynary foundation based in Chicago, personally seeing to the distribution of its $10 million annual income to an assortment of charlatans and idealists, indeed anyone who could come up with some far-fetched scheme to restore America's midwest heartland to a measure of competitiveness with the beaches of Florida and the fleshpots of New York, those same beaches and fleshpots where Daly was wont to spend most of his leisure time.

His nefarious career spanned the worlds of the arts, business and politics as well as academia and well-paid philanthropy.

For a time he wandered bemusedly in the steps of Ernest Hemingway in Spain; for a time he dabbled in control of the international molasses market; for several years he was at the side of our first Irish-American President, John F. Kennedy, and for a brief time he succeeded Bobby Baker in the inner circle and dependency of Lyndon B. Johnson.

Unable to articulate more than three words at a time without use of a four-letter Anglo-Saxon expletive, perhaps Daly's greatest achievement was in beguiling the sweet and compassionate daughter of a Canadian Episcopal Bishop, a lady who gave him 40 years of total love and adoration. Equally impressively, through some form of chicanery and deceit, Daly managed to obtain and preserve the grudging respect of the Bishop himself, who went to his grave unknowing of Daly's true character.

But this story is not of the more well-known ambiguities in the Daly reputation. It is intended as an accurate story of that single brief period in his youth, when Daly truly earned the respect of a warrior constituency, a respect he has chosen to hide from his latter-day associates since its source is so out of keeping with the role he has chosen to play in later life, that of a humanitarian man of peace. Daly's success in this great fraud is not unlike that of a man he secretly admires, that other great Irishman of our time, the Gipper, Conqueror of mighty Grenada and director of 16 inch naval gunfire at Lebanese mountain villages. Like the Gipper, Daly too has had his military side.

Unknown to many, Daly was the only son of an Irish capitalist who fought the British in 1916 with Eamon de Valera and spent his later years exploiting the cheap native labor of the Caribbean.

From his earliest childhood, Daly wanted to follow in his father's footsteps. He therefore quite understandably stole away from Yale one summer and enlisted in the United States Marine Corps, the same organization which, since the sinking of the Maine in 1898, has done so much to preserve most of Central America for Anaconda Copper, the United Fruit Company and other capitalist titans whose primary interest lies in stable government and good dividends.

Alas, Daly was not to be privileged to subdue the peasants of Nicaragua, El Salvador or the Dominican Republic. By happenstance his generation of Marines had another worthy opponent, the peasant armies of China and North Korea.

Since, as a noted Irishman once observed of an earlier counterpart of Daly's, "the truth is not in him," and in the absence of any credible account from Daly himself, the brief story that follows is intended to preserve for Daly's heirs and posterity an accurate account of a four month period dating from the arrival of 23 year old Second Lieutenant Charles U. Daly in Yokesuka, Japan, on February 10, 1951 to his subsequent return to the U.S. Naval Hospital in Yokosuka four months later, nursing a shattered elbow, the result of an accurate round from a percipient North Korean sharpshooter.

The Korean War was well into its eighth month, the near- disasters of the Naktong Perimeter and the Chosin Reservoir behind it, and the Chinese advance finally halted near Wonju in the mountains of Central Korea south of the 38th Parallel, when Daly, fresh out of Quantico's special infantry officers' training school arrived at Yokosuka, 13 1/2 days out of San Diego aboard the U.S.S. General J.C. Breckinridge.

When the Breckinridge warped up alongside the dock on that late February afternoon, carrying some 71 Marine Officers and 1,900 enlisted, collectively known as the Fifth Replacement Draft, it was a fairly routine occasion.

No so 8 hours later.

The Breckinridge was the last troop ship to have its passengers granted liberty in Yokosuka.

Why? Primarily because of the lifelong and passionate insistence of the Irish—exemplified to an inordinate degree in Daly—that there be equal justice for all.

The 71 officers were granted liberty to visit Yokosuka's famous geisha houses. The less trustworthy enlisted men, however, were limited to the PX and sterile confines of the Yokosuka Naval Base, surrounded shoreside by an 8' barbed wire fence.

Strolling down an alley in the red-light district outside the fence, Daly and two other second lieutenants of Irish descent discovered an obscure gate in that fence, which, with some little effort, could be wedged open from the outside to allow one Marine at a time to edge through. Sensitive to the physical needs and desires of the mass of frustrated Marines prowling the inside of the fence, Daly and one Dick McCue took the necessary action, stepping aside to watch over 1,000 young and lustful Marines rush through the gate before an undermanned and unprepared Navy Shore patrol could stem the tide.

It was a famous night in Yokosuka, involving no small damage to its internationally-known geisha industry. Every Marine but one got back safely to the ship, however, and the one who missed took a train to Kobe to rejoin the Breckinridge on its brief stop there two days later.

One aged veteran of the 5th Replacement Draft has had the years erase his entire memory of those several days in Japan save for one.

He recalls with clarity Daly's determined search for the ancient culture of Japan in the bath and geisha houses of Yokosuka and Kobe and some memorable words Daly uttered in his last hours in peaceful surroundings. That veteran, Angus Deming, now an internationally-known correspondent for one of the world's premier periodicals, recalls going with Daly to a Japanese-operated transoceanic telephone installation to receive a tearful query from the heavily-pregnant Mrs. Daly 8,000 miles away as to whether her hero still loved her on Valentine's Day, 1951.

Daly's response, shouted in the shocked presence of several dozen Marines:

"You bet your sweet ass I love you, baby."

Two nights later, Daly and eight other second lieutenants reported to the lst Battalion, 5th Marine Regiment in a rice paddy outside of Pohang, Korea. The following morning at dawn the battalion, now some 1,100 strong, loaded aboard trucks for a four day move north to Wonju to lead the first counter attack against the Chinese who had crossed the 38th Parallel several weeks earlier in a cautious advance into South Korea.

The lst Battalion was a seasoned and proud organization. It had been one of the bulwarks of the lst Marine Brigade's stemming of the North Korean drive at the Naktong Perimeter in August and had distinguished itself at the Inchon Landing in September and again in the desperate fighting withdrawal from the Chosin Reservoir in late November and early December, 1950.

Of the nine new lieutenants, two each were assigned to Able, Baker, Weapons and Headquarters Companies, and one to Charlie Company. Daly would have much preferred Baker Company, a historically-all-Irish officered unit with famous names like Tobin, Fenton, Cronin and Nolan, and later McGahn and Kerrigan. The luck of the draw, however, sent Daly to Headquarters Company where his demonstrated management skills were recognized at the outset. He was given one of the battalion's most unenviable commands, 100-odd nondescript, tattered, gaunt and bearded native Korean laborers, who were required nearly every evening to carry ammunition, water, rations and supplies up to the rifle companies, by then usually digging in in two-man foxhole perimeters around the highest ridge lines in the area. The Koreans were officially called cargodores but were known universally as "Chiggy Bears," respected for an incredible ability to carry huge loads on A-frames up steep mountain slopes, but otherwise unnoted and forgotten.

No one cared about the Chiggy Bears. If it rained or snowed, whether they had food or tents, it didn't mean much to anybody, and particularly to the lst Battalion's patrician Lieutenant Colonel and Commander, a man dedicated to his own creature comforts, those being a warm tent, a large supply of tinned English biscuits from lady admirers, and absolute obeisance from the unfortunate officers on his staff.

To Daly, however, from birth an idealistic advocate of social justice and human dignity, the Chiggy Bears were his very own, representing all the injustices done the Irish through history.

Daly begged, cheated and stole to keep his charges alive and in reasonable comfort when they weren't carrying impossible A- frame loads of food and communication up to the rifle companies.

Daly was a benevolent protector of his charges. Whatever prerogatives a second lieutenant had, he exercised on their behalf.

On a day late in April one of his troopers came to him with a desperate and tearful plea. Through an interpreter, with many halts and misunderstandings, he managed to convey the message to Daly that one of his parents back in Wonju had died, that his children and wife were in dire straits, and that he needed a week to straighten out his family affairs.

The Battalion was then many miles north of Wonju, camped in reserve at Chun'chon with no enemy near. After stern threats to the unfortunate one, Daly composed the following message in English, to be carried as a Safe Conduct Pass by the non-English speaking Korean. Its language was conveyed by the interpreter to the miscreant in unmistakable terms and read roughly as follows:

"To any American or Korean M.P., Greetings:

The bearer of this pass, Kim Won Suk, is entitled to travel to Wonju via Hoengsong and back to the 1st Battalion, 5th Marines HQ at Chun'chon solely along the MSR (Main Supply Route) during the period 25 March-April 1, 1951.

If he is found more than one mile from this route during this period, or found *anywhere* after April 1, please shoot him immediately.

Charles U. Daly
2nd Lt., Commander, Labor Company
1st Battalion, Fifth Marine Regiment

Precisely one week later, a smiling, bowing Kim Won Suk reported back to his commander, to be received with surprise and astonishment.

What might have befallen the loyal and true Mr. Suk had the battalion moved, from Chun'chon, say 10 miles north during the week, as it was to do a few days later, is too painful to contemplate.

As winter turned into spring, Daly's love and efforts for his scraggly men doubled and redoubled. Their impoverished plight moved him deeply.

He badgered his superiors for help. To his every plea, however, for blankets, tents, a bigger ration of rice, the Colonel turned a deaf ear. As the Battalion Commander's impatience rose, so also did Daly's black Irish rage.

He came to view the Colonel as a greater enemy than the gradually-withdrawing Chinese. The Colonel was not beloved by anyone in the Battalion, but he was a particular anathema to Daly.

Finally came an event which was to change Daly's life, and to end the lives of perhaps 100 others.

Pulled back into a relatively-safe reserve area for a few days, with the spring flowers in bloom, someone found a volley ball and net. The Colonel proclaimed that a sporting event would be held, a volleyball game between his staff officers of Headquarters Company and the officers of Charlie Company, Charlie having had the misfortune to be billeted closest to the Colonel's well-stocked headquarters tent. Even in reserve, none of the rifle companies wanted to be near the Colonel. (On one occasion he had sacrificed a significant part of Baker Company to protect his headquarters tent from a Chinese breakthrough and was almost shot by Baker's Executive Officer after he ordered a tank commander to shell Baker Company's position above his tent in a moment of panic.)

For some reason Charlie Company had only 5 officers available, but Daly quickly volunteered to be the 6th.

At 6'3" and perhaps 150 pounds, the lean and lanky Colonel had fancied himself a volleyball player since his days at Stanford. As the game began, he clearly was enjoying himself hugely, his height and reach being greater than those of anyone on either side.

Daly had apparently recently suffered a particularly grievous humiliation from the Colonel with respect to his Chiggy Bears and their needs. Brooding darkly, he bided his time until he was rotated to center court immediately across the net from his esteemed leader. A ball was set to him.

As the ball went high in the air above the center of the net, the Colonel stretched gracefully skyward to block a shot from Daly's side, his eyes on the descending ball and his arms outstretched to the heavens. From the rear line some of us watched with a mixture of horror and delight as Commander Daly of the Chiggy Bears, all 5'11" of him, went up with the Colonel, but instead of going for the ball, smashed a full right jab *through* the net, catching the Colonel somewhere in the vicinity of the jaw. The Colonel went over backwards like a falling log, and of course was immediately surrounded by solicitous headquarters company officers who did their best to restrain their mirth.

Joy reigned supreme on the Charlie side of the net. Daly had endeared himself forever to the men of the lst Battalion to whom word was speedily spread that the Colonel had finally been dealt his just desserts. Of equal importance, the Charlie Company officers determined to a man that one such as Daly was too good to be allowed to stay in Headquarters Company where it was clear the Colonel would, sooner or later, have him court-martialed for insubordination.

It is not clear that the Colonel ever fully understood who or what had done him in. He was slow in recovering consciousness, and the Code of Silence is not unknown in the Marine Corps.

It shortly came to pass, however, that upon the next rotation home of one of Charlie Company's veteran lieutenants, Daly, by mutual consent and pleasure, was assigned to Charlie Company.

It was an auspicious time. With a sudden attack in late April, the slowly withdrawing Chinese had stunned the United Nations forces, breaking through the Republic of Korea's Sixth Division one night and forcing the lst Marine Division on its right flank to fight a rear-guard blocking action for several days.

In mid-May a second Chinese offensive shattered the Second Army Division in the mountains to the east.

The Marines were ordered to lead the counter-attack. On the evening before his 24th birthday, Daly got his opportunity, at last, to follow in his father's footsteps; he was assigned command of Charlie Company's 2nd Platoon, 44 riflemen with a 17-man machine gun section attached.

The Company was at nearly full strength on that evening as it prepared on the morrow to assist a battalion of the 7th Marines who had been held up for two days on a rugged north-south ridgeline, held stubbornly by a North Korean regiment in a series of machine gun bunkers on successive knolls, flanked by steep cliffs.

Daly's career as a rifle platoon leader was brief but spectacular.

The first morning following his ascension to the exalted position of Platoon Leader, 2nd Platoon, on May 29, 1951, Daly led his platoon in a classic bayonet assault on the North Korean position.

It was both Daly's birthday and the start of a significant reputation amongst fellow Marines. He may have been the first and last Marine rifle platoon leader to actually overrun an enemy regimental command post. By the day's end, Charlie Company had lost its company commander and three other officers wounded, but Daly had partially evened the score. He has never admitted this, but at least one enlisted participant in his final assault on the Korean regimental headquarters has reported that Daly personally pushed the captured and surly Korean commander off a 1,000 foot cliff.

The Colonel, his wounded pride and face by now repaired, was gracious enough to nominate his nemesis for the Silver Star.

Three days later, it appeared it might be a posthumous award. Daly spent the afternoon of the lst of June behind five M-46 tanks which were putting direct 90 millimeter cannon fire into a line of bunkers along a series of knife-like ridges leading up to a commanding height designated on the maps on Hill 610. 610 was the regimental objective; supposedly when taken, the lst Battalion was slated to go into reserve for a few days. 610 *looked* like it would take the whole battalion's effort. There were bunkers and trench lines capable of protecting a defending regiment. Each of the steep ridge lines leading to the crest was barely wide enough for one or two men abreast, and each ridge line was covered by fire from higher positions.

But if 610 looked difficult to attack, it was equally difficult to defend from those bunkers and trench lines on the forward military crests when the defenders were looking into the muzzles of 90 millimeter cannon and coaxial machine guns on tanks 1,000 yards below in the valley.

The North Koreans could not stay in their forward holes against such firepower, but as Daly watched that afternoon, he noted with some trepidation that the defenders had conceived a way to deter movement up the ridgelines by dropping 50 to 100 mortar rounds on the forward ridge lines at intervals of 20 minutes or so. The impact zones were areas to get through quickly, if at all.

Charlie Company was ordered to attack on the morning of June 2nd, with the 1st Platoon to take the first ridge line, perhaps 400 meters high, Daly's 2nd Platoon to swing past on the flank and take the main second ridge line, another 100 meters higher, and finally the 3rd Platoon under Doug Dacy to move past Daly's position and assault Hill 610 itself.

The 3rd Platoon had missed the action on May 29th and was still at full strength, but even then there was some concern that it might take more than one platoon for the final assault on the awesome mass of 610, an arc-shaped sugar loaf ridge perhaps 250 yards long, dropping sharply on all sides.

The 1st Platoon's initial attack went fairly well, except that halfway up the forward slope it was halted by an order of the Colonel so that His Lordship could exercise what for a battalion commander was rare good sport: the coordination of an air strike by four circling fighter bombers. To the Colonel, a mile to the rear in a safe observation post, this was a happy training exercise in fire control. To the 1st Platoon of Charlie Company, toiling up the 45 degree slope with the comforting explosions of the tanks' fire keeping the North Koreans out of their forward bunkers, it was disaster.

The Colonel had stopped them in the middle of one of the mortar impact areas of the day before, and with their usual competence, the Koreans put fifty or so 120 millimeter rounds right on top of the 1st platoon, seriously wounding a number of Marines and enraging the survivors.

Finally, despite the Colonel, the first ridge was secured and it was Daly's turn. As he had done on May 29th, he personally let the bayonet assault, driving the enemy back up towards 610. By noon he held his assigned objective, 600 yards of ridgeline, still 1,000 yards below 610 with a deep ravine in between.

His casualties had not been overwhelming in the initial assault, but as the afternoon wore on his troops spread out in the Korean bunkers were subjected to almost continuous and accurate mortar fire, causing heavy casualties, including both Navy hospital corpsmen.

The 3rd Platoon got close to the crest of 610 from the flank, but couldn't get up the last 200 yards against a series of bunkers which were concealed and in defilade from the tanks in the valley below. The new company commander, impatient with the 3rd Platoon's commander, relieved him of command and ordered the 1st Platoon to move through Daly's position and attack 610, with the 3rd Platoon to give covering fire from its precarious hold on the flank ridge.

As the 1st Platoon moved up to Daly's position, Daly's platoon guide, a veteran of the Inchon landing and finally scheduled for rotation home 2 days later, cracked psychologically and fled down the hill. It had been a bad day. The company commander, with perhaps half of his company casualties by late afternoon, was not heard from for a time. Daly and the 1st Platoon leader met the two young sergeants now in charge of the 3rd Platoon at a rocky crow's nest at the northern end of Daly's ridge, looked at 610, an awesome sight, and relayed to the two 20 year olds, Chet Hanson and Phil Elson, the company commander's last order that the 3rd Platoon was to give the 1st Platoon covering fire instead of resuming their own attack.

This was too much for the sergeants' pride. They said "Hell, No, Lieutenant, you give us covering fire and *we'll* attack." The 1st Platoon leader, by now the Marine Corp's biggest coward, was happy to oblige, and in a whooping, howling attack, the non-officer-led 3rd Platoon rushed the final mountaintop, with covering fire from the machine guns of the 1st and 2nd Platoons and joined by the Company's Executive and Machine Gun Officers. The 3rd Platoon gained the summit of the right half of 610 and was jointed by the 1st Platoon in a final assault. By dusk, Charlie Company, now down to perhaps 60 effectives out of its original strength of 235, held 610.

The Koreans were pushed off the crest, but continued to harass the Charlie Company position, seriously wounding the company's supply sergeant as he tried to bring up additional ammo from the valley below.

Only the arrival of Able Company, 200 strong and healthy, prevented the loss of 610 to a determined North Korean banzai attack that night. Able Company had taken over the forward 2/3rds of 610 and bore the brunt of an assault which overran its forward machine gun position.

The next day gave no rest for the wicked. Able Company moved north in the attack and Daly's battered platoon was selected for a patrol. Daly, fearing a raid on his packs by the 1st and 3rd Platoons in his absence, left his newest replacement back to guard the packs.

In midday, that poor soul became Charlie Company's only casualty of the day. In a commendable desire not to befoul the 2nd Platoon's pristine line of foxholes 4 or 5 yards on the forward slope of 610 (the reverse slope for Charlie Company's attack the previous evening,) the newest arrival crossed 10 yards back over the ridgeline into the 1st Platoon's area where most of the 1st Platoon were sleeping amongst the fallen trees and debris of the Korean defenders' fighting holes. Dropping his trousers to relieve himself, he managed to trigger an unexploded grenade and was painfully wounded in the feet and lower legs. The explosion woke up the 1st Platoon's Marines, who were torn between sympathy, anger and humor over the intruder's obvious goal and unfortunate posture.

Upon his weary return from a long and arduous patrol, Daly's comments about his latest casualty were unworthy of permanent recording.

The following day, the Battalion was relieved by a Korean Marine unit and hiked a long 15 miles east to Inje where it was to bivouac in a rather pleasant valley along the Soyang River. The Army's 9th Regiment of the 2nd Infantry Division had gotten there a day or so before, however, and had set up tents in the soft rice paddy ground north of the road, leaving Charlie Company a small grassy, tree-lined area south of the road and a wide expanse of rocky dry river bed.

Daly's 2nd Platoon had the luck to draw the tree-lined grassy bank, and with it, several hundred neatly-stacked boxes of 120 millimeter mortar shells the retreating Chinese had left behind.

There was a lot of grousing about the 2nd Platoon's good luck amongst the rest of the Company as they spread their blankets out in the rocks for a pleasant June evening, but who cared ... for the first time in weeks there was no need to dig foxholes.

And wonder of wonders, word filtered across the road that the 9th Infantry was going to have a USO Show that evening, with two real live women, the first anyone had seen since Japan, at least between 8 and 70, the Chinese having taken every able bodied man and woman between those ages north with them as they withdrew.

Even more intriguing was the rumor that one of the women was Irish!

This was too much for Daly. He bathed in the river, shaved, and gathered up another Irish lieutenant for a major foray. As the Marines of the 1st Battalion were taking seats for the show on the rice paddies behind the 9th's soldiers, Daly led his friend stealthily to the rear of the squad tent, whose many Army officers at the front indicated was being used by the two U.S.O. ladies as a dressing room. With his trusty bayonet knife and accustomed charm Daly sliced a hole and crawled into the tent from the rear, striking up a conversation with the two amazed ladies, one of whom indeed was Irish. The gist of the conversation was why didn't these two lovelies come over and share C-rations with the Marines that evening? The invitation was entirely acceptable to the two ladies, but as a deal was being struck, in came an Army Major with fire in his eyes, ordering the Marine Lieutenants to be gone post haste. They watched the show from the far rear, and at its conclusion, an obviously-outraged Army officer ordered all Marines to get to their side of the road and stay there.

The C-rations were eaten bitterly by the Marines that night to the happy sounds of hot chow and music on the Army side of the road, but all was forgiven around midnight when the Chinese managed to move a long-range artillery battery into position and shelled *only* the Army's side of the road.

There was a good deal of glee out in the rocks of the river bed, and some secret hope perhaps that a round or two might set off some of those neatly-stacked mortar shells around which Daly's platoon was bivouacked on the soft grass.

A few days later the company was back in the attack northwards towards a scenic landmark known as "The Punchbowl," now with *three* lieutenants from Yale, including Daly's friend, Charlie Bunnell, formerly limited to staff duty because of his unusual erudition and intelligence. On June 11, the Colonel conceived his finest plan yet to learn about the enemy at maximum risk to his own troops—a coordinated tank-infantry patrol 3 miles north up the narrow valley of the Soyang to the Punch Bowl, the ridges on both sides populated with numerous competent Chinese and Korean mortarmen.

By the end of the day the 1st and 2nd Platoons had all they could do to protect the tanks with rapidly-diminishing numbers, and in a few short hours on the evening of the 11th and the morning of the 12th, Charlie Company had all three of its platoon leaders wounded, Daly and Bunnell seriously. Daly and Bunnell were loaded aboard a MASH helicopter for transportation back to a field hospital and thence home. Daly's elbow was shattered badly enough to put him in the amputation ward for weeks but he badgered the doctors and nurses so unmercifully that they finally let him keep the arm.

In later years that arm was used in a number of athletic contests, fair and foul, and on one famous occasion, to throw a student protestor out of the office of the Vice President of the University of Chicago.

Thus ends what until now has been the largely-unknown Marine Corps saga of Charles U. Daly, pacifist warrior and monumental fraud. In later years, it is believed his conscience over the two weeks of havoc he had wrought amongst the peasant soldiers of China and North Korea bothered him a good deal more than he would admit, enough so as to cause him, like other famous robber barons, to become involved in various schemes which passed for public service and assistance to the poor and downtrodden, but in the end, enriched his pocketbook greatly.

By the time he reached 60, Daly was known to be the owner of palatial mansions in not less than 10 of America's more important metropolises and to be the slumlord of run down tenements in a dozen more ghetto areas between Atlantic City and Washington, D.C., Northeast.

He remains unrepentant, and with the lovely Bishop's daughter still at his side is well known in most of the Irish pubs in the western world.

Chatham, Massachusetts
May 29, 1987

1991 Postscript

Shortly after the marvelous party she gave for her husband at Chatham on the Cape in May, 1987, Mary Daly passed away from cancer.

Keeping busy with his friend Tip O'Neill in an effort to finally end 300 years of Catholic-Protestant warfare in Northern Ireland, Daly was lucky enough to ultimately befriend Tip's legislative assistant, the beautiful Christine O'Sullivan, half his age but twice as intelligent.

Celibacy is no easier than truth for the likes of Daly, so in due course the pair were married by that born-again Irish priest, Father Dick McCue, the same former Marine platoon leader who forty years earlier had helped Daly perpetrate the ravaging of Yokesuka's geisha houses.

Like Ibn Saud, Daly has since been adding a new child to his family each year and shows no sign of stopping. He has become the Curator of the John F. Kennedy Library at Dorchester, Massachusetts, and like other librarians and academics, gives little outward evidence of his decadent and lascivious past.

Commander Daly of the Chiggy Bears and the author. In reserve southwest of Honq'chon after 1st Chinese Spring Counteroffensive, late April, 1951. The bulges at the belt are grenades. Not too chic, but a lot safer than clipped to the shirt pocket as worn by various Generals.

The Irish Brigade: Daly, Dacy, McCloskey and McGahn, May 29, 1987—36 years after Daly overran a North Korean Regimental C.P. on his 24th birthday.

The Pacifist Warrior. Obviously as evil in old age as he was when trying to inveigle nurses in the amputee wards of various hospitals in Japan, Hawaii and California in 1951.

Chapter 5

Hospital Corpsman Third Class Thomas Burchick

As jobs in the U. S. Armed Services go, that of a Navy Hospital Corpsman generally provides a fairly easy life.

U.S. Navy hospitals are usually in or close to large cities. Most Navy bases have recreational benefits, and even sea duty involves living and working in a relatively comfortable environment.

There is one exception.

In time of war, Marine Corps rifle companies are assigned eight young corpsmen, two per rifle platoon and two with the company headquarters.

These corpsmen have to be in superb physical condition. They carry packs on long marches with riflemen, patrol with riflemen, eat C rations with riflemen and at night dig deep foxholes with riflemen.

A Marine is taught from his day of enlistment that Marines are the elite fighting men of the world and that only riflemen are truly in God's image. It is not easy during training and peacetime for a Marine to accept corpsmen as equals.

Combat, however, changes everything.

In combat, when Marines are taking cover from machine gun, mortar and artillery fire, the corpsman alone may have to be up and running to wounded men, kneeling at their side to apply bandages, administer morphine and occasionally act as a stretcher bearer in life or death situations. To a Marine rifleman the corpsman who does all these things under fire becomes an object of veneration.

The Marine knows that the 19 or 20 year old Navy corpsman has **volunteered** to share the combat rifleman's own rigorous hardships. When the first cry of "Corpsman" goes up under incoming fire, the rifleman finally understands that a corpsman is a very special human being.

Whether trembling in a foxhole or trying to dig a hole with his nose in a rice paddy, the rifleman respects any person willing to move around and help others when shrapnel and bullets are in the air.

Most young Navy corpsmen, knowing this, are anxious to preserve this rare respect, and anxious indeed to show Marines that they too are worthy of the Corps' fabled traditions. Consequently they commonly perform uncommon acts of courage on a daily basis during the tensest times of infantry combat. Their casualty rate can be far higher than that of the Marines they serve.

Among Navy corpsmen, Thomas "Doc" Burchick was an extraordinary individual. To the

Marines of Charlie Company, First Battalion, Fifth Marines, led by Captain Jack Jones and XO Spike Schening, Burchick was respected above all others.

On three occasions in less than three weeks, Burchick's conduct was so outstanding as to deserve permanent recording in naval archives.

May 29, 1951

At dawn on the morning of May 29, the 1st Platoon of Charlie Company was ordered to assault the flank of a strongly-held North Korean ridgeline position listed on our maps as Hill 566.

For the preceding two days, the 2nd Battalion of the 7th Marines had been trying in a series of frontal assaults to take 566, a sugar-loaf shaped hill perhaps 100 yards long, which sat squarely astride and perpendicular to the main north-south ridge-line which divided the zones of action of the 5th and 7th Regiments. The west side of this ridgeline was a cliff which defied any flank envelopment, but on the east side there were finger ridges every 500 or 1000 yards or so stretching down to the valley below. Terraced rice paddies occupied the ravines between these ridgelines which were somewhat wooded except for the areas where fortifications had been cut into their hilltops by the defenders. Log bunkers were connected by deep trenches along the military crests. On 566 there were three separate machine gun bunkers commanding the ridgeline and ravine to the south and one down the finger ridge to the east. The position was invulnerable from the west because of the cliff.

The 2nd Battalion, 7th Marines had taken a hilltop on the ridgeline some 600 yards south of Hill 566 on May 27, but had been badly hit on the 27th and 28th in unsuccessful attacks to cross the intervening ridge to 566. On the late afternoon of May 28, Charlie and Baker Companies of the 1st Battalion had been ordered up from the valley to the east to assist 2/7. Just before dusk on the 28th, the 2nd platoon of Charlie Company had gotten on the finger ridge leading directly up to 566 only to be turned back by the direct fire of the machine gun which blanketed the last 200 yards of the approach. Baker Company had gotten close to the top in the ensuing darkness, but had likewise been forced to withdraw back to the low ground below.

The finger ridge was not more than 10 yards wide and the last climb to the North Korean emplacements was devoid of cover save for scattered stumps and debris. An estimated 200 enemy occupied the bunkers and connecting trenches along the military crest, the last of which was at the apex of the finger-ridge, perhaps 50 yards below the top of the sugar-loaf shaped hill. The main north-south ridgeline was also only about ten yards wide at its widest and joined the western ends of both 2/7's hill and 566, thereafter proceeding north in a series of ever-higher knolls.

Spike Schening, Charlie Company's commander, selected Burchick's platoon to make the initial assault the following morning.

Augmented by the battalion S-2 scout, Whit Moreland, and a corporal named Harris[1] from the regimental PIO section, the platoon moved out before dawn, and at first light had reached the finger-ridge leading up to 566 undetected.

Luckily, morning fog surrounded the hilltop. The last 200 yards to the top was fairly steep. The platoon leader was in the center, with the squad leaders of the 1st and 2nd squads a few feet to his left and right, their men strung out behind them. Neither squad was at full strength, but the gunners of the two attached machine gun squads were carrying their light machine guns with hand-rigged wire handles, tripods attached, immediately behind the squad leaders. The machine gun ammo carriers and the 3rd squad brought up the rear.

---

[1] It was known that Harris, a ski instructor from Sun Valley, Idaho, had been ordered by his boss at the regimental CP never to be up with a rifle company, that his place was behind a typewriter and well behind the front lines. He was wounded twice while violating this order with Charlie Company in two different assaults, and rumor had it that he was court martialed after the second occasion by an outraged regimental PIO officer.

By reason of the fog, the lead Marines were able to quietly move up the ridge undetected and were perhaps 60 yards below the enemy's position when suddenly the fog cleared a little and the lieutenant found himself looking uphill at a surprised North Korean gunner squatting beside a Japanese Nambu machine gun, eating rice with chopsticks out of a silver bowl. The lieutenant threw a grenade in a high arc as hard and far as he could throw it and hit the deck as the Korean jumped behind the Nambu. He got off only a short burst, luckily over the heads of the Marines, before the grenade went off and looking up, they saw that the machine gun was canted to one side and several surprised Korean heads were popping up along the trenchline on either side of the Nambu.

The riflemen and BAR men went into action immediately, and the Marines moved up by fire and maneuver until perhaps four or five men were within thirty yards of the enemy trenchline. Heads no longer kept appearing, but a steady hail of grenades came bouncing and rolling down the hillside. The men in the front rank were able to dodge them but behind them there were several casualties, one of whom was Harris and another, an Irish BAR man from New York, Arthur McHugh. McHugh's great grandfather had fought in that most famous of Irish brigades in the Civil War, "The Fighting 69th." About the time the platoon leader gave the order to fix bayonets and assault, McHugh was being bandaged for a severe arm wound by Burchick. Burchick had been present during a number of training school instruction periods when the Company was in reserve and had repeatedly heard the standard Marine Corps word that BARs were to be kept in action at all costs. Thus after bandaging McHugh, he picked up McHugh's 19 lb. Browning automatic-rifle and lugged it up the hill behind the front rank of advancing riflemen.

The lieutenant, on the ridge crest where the going was easiest, was the first to arrive at the machine gun, and found perhaps a dozen North Korean soldiers squatting in the bottom of the trench on either side, taking grenades out of wicker baskets at their feet, tapping them on a helmet or rock and lobbing them over the side of the trench. There was some quick bayonet work and the lieutenant emptied all thirty rounds of his carbine into this group. One of Baker Company's platoon leaders, (later Lieutenant General) Charlie Cooper, observing from across the ravine reported that the platoon leader then gave the unmemorable yell, "we've got 'em by the balls, let's squeeze 'em," and ran up the hill. The left squad charged up the trenchline to the left, ultimately rolling up all of the machine gun bunkers and their occupants, while the right hand squad moved around the hill to the right flushing out the occupants still sleeping in the bunkers on the reverse slope.

Unintentionally, therefore, (and somewhat foolishly) when the platoon leader reached the top where the hill leveled off, he found himself alone, looking at perhaps thirty or forty surprised North Korean soldiers on the reverse northern slope who were buckling on their gear and checking their weapons, getting ready to move out to the forward slope but apparently caught by the suddenness of the attack. The lieutenant fired his second and last thirty round magazine into this group, who unaccountably decided to take off running. About that time, he heard a shout, "Look out, Lieutenant," and turned to see four Korean soldiers emerging from a sleeping bunker below him on the right which he had missed. The lead man was just bringing his burp gun into position to cut him down when there was a burst of automatic rifle fire. The four North Koreans went down in a bloody heap, and the lieutenant turned to see Tom Burchick, all 130 lbs of him, with McHugh's 19 pound BAR pointed skyward. The recoil of the twenty rounds fired at full automatic had almost knocked him down. He had saved the lieutenant's life, while outrageously violating the Geneva Convention's rule that hospital corpsmen shall not carry or fire weapons.

There were still 20 or 30 North Koreans in view fleeing north in front of them and on the ridgeline to their right and the lieutenant was shouting wildly at his machine gunners and 2nd and 3rd squads to get up and into firing position when there occurred one of the great humorous moments of that year in Korea.

From a thatched-covered bunker on the rear slope of 566, some fifty yards up ahead and to the right, suddenly emerged a Mongolian pony with a Korean infantryman almost as big as the pony. He was clad in a padded jacket with both arms and legs wrapped around the pony's neck and back. The pony's mane and tail were long and bushy and this apparition from the days of Genghis Khan galloped past the stunned Marines some 10 yards down the side of the finger-ridge they had just come up, in full view of at least fifteen or twenty surprised infantrymen toiling up the hill. To a man, they dropped to one knee or fired from the shoulder at the speeding pony, the first anyone had ever seen in Korea. That pony may be running yet, because there was no visible sign that any of the alleged expert riflemen for which the Corps is famous even came close to hitting either him or his rider.

With Burchick, Moreland and a few Marines who had now caught up, the platoon kept on, swept the top and north side of the hill and tried to continue the assault up the north-south ridgeline. The left squad, under a young sergeant named Jimmy Nichols and fire team leaders, Rich Saccomanno and Ray Pace, were the heroes of the attack, with less than ten men charging through the Korean bunkers and trench lines which had held up the 7th Marines for two days. It was later said the platoon had killed 40 and captured 22, with most of the heavy work being done by the 1st squad. The names of those men, as best remembered 37 years later, were Steinbeck, Slate, Smith, Jankuska, Bruder, Boyle, Pilkington and Brill. The platoon was finally stopped by the next knoll north of 566, with some determined Korean defenders just over the crest. In a grenade contest with the North Koreans, probably no more than five yards over the crest, Moreland was killed rolling over on a grenade which otherwise would have probably taken out both the platoon leader and platoon sergeant. The platoon sergeant, Delbert Klein of San Francisco, was seriously wounded. Moreland's parents in Austin, Texas ultimately received their son's Congressional Medal of Honor. Later in the morning, the 2nd platoon, led by Chuck Daly, took this knoll and several further up the ridgeline, ultimately overrunning what was reputed to be the headquarters of a North Korean regiment.

June 2, 1951

Burchick's second act of unusual heroism occurred only three days later, when Charlie Company was assigned the assault of a particularly difficult regimental objective, Hill 610, a massive mountain complex which dominated the key road to Chorwon (of the famous "Iron Triangle") as well as the southwesterly approaches to Taeam-San, the mountain which commanded the route to the 1st Division's final objective, the Punch Bowl itself.

The North Koreans had established a strong bunker position around the crest of Hill 610, a knife-like, arc-shaped ridge some 200 yards in length, the only approach to which was from a ridge-line and series of wooded knolls and ravines, all of which were defended by strong dug-in positions.

It took all three platoons most of the day to fight their way up the ridge to the base of 610 itself, still some 400 yards above us. There the 3rd Platoon, augmented by two officers from the company headquarters, made a truly classic bayonet assault, getting a solid hold on the right hand side of 610.

The 1st Platoon then moved up alongside the 3rd platoon, getting almost to the crest of the middle part of 610 only to be held up by some tenacious grenade throwers just over the crest. Neither they nor the Marines were anxious to be the first to look over the top, so for what seemed like an hour, but was probably only a few minutes, a grenade war took place between the opposing riflemen, only a few yards below the crest on each side.

The 1st Platoon was strung out for perhaps 50 yards and it was here that Doc Burchick performed the historic feat that earned him the Navy Cross.

The lieutenant was lying next to a machine gunner, an Indian called "Chief" Zamora, a fine, quiet, modest boy from New Mexico. Zamora was lying with his gun sighted at the crest above, no more than five yards away, when a grenade fragment caught him in the throat in some way that blocked his breathing. He seemed to be choking to death and turning black when Burchick came up, the grenades going off all around, turned Zamora on his back, whipped out his 3" sheath knife, and poked a hole at the base of Zamora's throat. He then cut a stick from one of the shattered branches lying around, stuck it in the hole and taped Zamora's hand to hold it in place, with Zamora obviously drawing breath and new life from the hole in his throat. Finally Zamora was able to get up and move to the rear. The grenades slacked off and the platoon finally rolled over the crest, the occupants of the final bunker at the far end being neutralized by dropping in a white phosphorous grenade.

With the last of the Koreans disappearing down through the woods in the distance, the lieutenant looked around and found two first lieutenants, Charlie Bunnell, and John Goodrich, one with an empty BAR and one with an empty .45. They had come up to help the 3rd platoon in its great hour of challenge.

It was only then that his companions could reflect a little on Burchick's feat. He had performed a surgical operation, a tracheotomy, an operation he had read about but never seen, on a Marine who would otherwise have died. Besides saving Zamora's life, Burchick had done the operation no more than 10 yards from a determined enemy of unknown size, amidst rolling and exploding grenades. From inquiries years later at the Navy Historical Museum in Washington, the lieutenant learned that Burchick's operation was the closest-to-the-enemy surgery ever performed in the annals of U.S. naval history.

Burchick's day was a busy one. By nightfall, when Able Company came up to take over the front 2/3rds of 610 in a two-company perimeter, Charlie Company was probably down to perhaps 60 men in its rifle platoons and attached machine gun section. It was a proud group of men though. It was worth the whole long day when the 1st Platoon turned over its eight foxholes at the left crest of 610 and moved past the silent length of Able Company which had come up to relieve them, 16 men walking, Burchick one of them, four to each corner of a stretcher with the platoon four non-walking wounded. The 2nd and 3rd platoons were in about the same shape. Only the mortar section was relatively unscathed. No words were said nor needed to be. The final blow was having the Company's Supply Sergeant seriously wounded in an ambush late in the day while bringing up rations and ammo through the same ravine from which the 3rd Platoon had attacked 610's final crest.

At least the Charlie Company folks *hoped* that Able Company was impressed at an achievement which on a number of occasions during the day had seemed unattainable.

From that day on, Charlie Company carried a certain pride in itself, and no man held respect higher than Doc Burchick. In the ten days that remained before he was himself severely and almost fatally wounded, and ever since in the minds and hearts of those who saw him on Hills 566 and 610, he and perhaps Chet Hanson, the young sergeant who had led the 3rd Platoon to its amazing success on 610, remain, next to Captain Jones and Spike Schening, the most famous and beloved of the Charlie Company Marines of the spring of 1951.

June 11, 1951

Burchick's final day in combat was typical. On June 11, the 1st platoon was assigned to accompany a tank platoon up the narrow valley of the Soyang River, 3 miles to the base of the famous Punch Bowl. The valley marked the extreme right flank of the Division. A ROK division held the far ridge. In those days the ROKs were not always reliable. They held a great fear of the Chinese, particularly in night attacks, and if they were not well led they could be on one's flank one night, but several miles to the rear the next morning if they were hit hard. The ridges on either side of the valley, after the first 500 yards at least, seemed to be manned by particularly-skilled Korean mortar observers. The orders from the Battalion Commander were simple: "Go up the valley three miles to where it bends and report back to me what's around the bend."

This turned out to be easier said than done.

By coincidence, the tank platoon that came up to escort Burchick's platoon up the valley of the meandering Soyang River was the same one that had saved the Company in the assault on 610. Its commander was Wally Barrett, a wonderfully-humorous veteran of World War II.

From the moment the platoon moved out that morning, spread out at intervals of not less than twenty yards in front of and around Barrett's tanks, it took incoming 120mm mortar fire every few minutes. It seemed as if the enemy uncharacteristically had an unlimited ammunition supply and couldn't stand letting the tanks move up the valley. It wasn't that the mortar rounds were excessively dangerous; even a direct hit only shook up the tank crews, and the near misses tended to bury themselves in the soft ground of the rice paddies. The individual rice furrows and low dikes gave surprisingly good cover unless a round hit right on top of you. On a number of occasions, the riflemen would hear Wally Barrett's cheerful "See you in a while, Marines" as the first round whistled in and he dropped down into his tank, pulling the hatch cover shut behind him.

The platoon had four men wounded during the morning, each of them in the same painful way, fragments of shrapnel slicing into their buttocks as they tried to flatten every other part of their anatomy into the rice paddies.

In each case Burchick, or the platoon's other corpsman, Tom Kristapovich, would run through the incoming fire to the wounded man's side, bandage his hind end as best he could, and send the unfortunate one hobbling back to the battalion aid station.

The platoon didn't come close to making the three miles the Colonel had wanted.

As late afternoon came, it withdrew back down the valley. The Koreans became bolder and started to move down the slopes and snipe long-range from the sides of the hills. They weren't so bold, however, as to want to attract the return fire of the tanks' 90 mm guns and machine guns, so it was more of an annoyance than a danger. Both the infantrymen and tankers were anxious to get back to their lines before dark, however.

When the platoon reached a loop of the Soyang it had waded that morning, probably fifty yards wide and four feet deep, they were nearly back to where the Battalion held the left-hand ridge and the ROK's the right. With blankets having replaced the Marines' warm down sleeping bags several weeks earlier, the lieutenant made the decision that his troops would ride the tanks across the river so as not to be wet, cold and miserable all night.

The tanks echeloned across the valley to hold off the cautiously pursuing North Koreans, and one at a time would ford the river with eight or so Marines aboard, then turning on the far bank to give covering fire for the Marines still on the other side.

With the last group on Wally Barrett's command tank as it nosed down into the river, the lieutenant was riding on the left front next to the driver. Suddenly there was a huge explosion. The lieutenant's thoughts as he flew through the air and the cold waters of the Soyang closed over his head were that he was the dumbest man alive, that he had violated the cardinal rule of Jones and Schening, bunching up his men in one place where a single artillery round could wipe them all out.

The "no bunch up" rule kept a lot of Marines alive in Korea. The enemy would rarely shoot at one or two men alone in daylight because of the massive return fire that could be brought to bear. Getting eight or ten Marines clustered together on a hilltop or a tank, however, was too tempting not to draw fire, and it was an unforgivable mistake on the lieutenant's part.

It turned out that it wasn't artillery, but a buried mine the tank had hit, blowing off the tank's left tread as well as blowing the wooden escape hatch cover up against the driver's legs, nearly severing them.

Burchick not only quickly put tourniquets on the terribly- injured Marine tank driver, but bandaged his legs securely and then served as one of four stretcher bearers carrying him across the chest-deep and swift-flowing Soyang.

Wally Barrett rather sadly set off a thermite grenade in the barrel of his tank's 90mm gun and crossed the river, where the 1st Platoon was ordered to dig in to give night protection to another platoon of tanks which came up to replace Barrett's.

As the Marines started to dig their foxholes, they had a first-of-a-kind experience. There was a sudden thunderclap and explosion of dirt, then another every 30 seconds or so. Unlike the warning whistle of incoming mortars and howitzer fire, there was no warning. The Chinese or North Koreans had apparently mounted some sort of direct fire artillery piece on a wooded knoll up the valley and bore-sighted it down at the tanks around which the Marines were digging their foxholes. A second after the noise of the breech block clanging shut was heard from the knoll, the round hit.

The lieutenant was sharing his hole that night with Doc Burchick, but when the first round hit he was standing next to Sergeant Jimmy Nichols of Oklahoma, who, with Klein hit and Clark rotated home, was now acting as platoon sergeant. Nichols and the lieutenant hit the deck and stayed there.

For the first time since the lieutenant had been in Korea there was nothing to do—no fire to return, no people to deploy, no command presence to exercise— just lie there and hope for luck.

His face in the dirt was right next to Nichols' hand, and as the rounds kept coming in he saw Nichols' hand begin to shake. He began to shake as well.

The tanks couldn't locate the enemy artillery piece to return fire, but after awhile it seemed to have gotten dark enough to hamper the enemy observer's view. No rounds came in for several minutes and the lieutenant finally gave the order for everyone to get up and start digging again. A midnight probe, if not a counterattack, was highly probable, and the 2nd Platoon was sent down from the ridges to help out.

Burchick and the lieutenant were standing alongside each other in the dark, chopping away at the rice paddy with their entrenching tools, perhaps a foot deep into their hole, when there came one last explosion. The lieutenant felt a burning sensation in the front and back of his right leg and looked down to see that the shrapnel had neatly torn the pantleg off at mid-thigh level, but that Burchick had taken the full blast of the shell, with shrapnel in his right side from his head to his ankle.

The shell must have hit directly on line with his 130 lb. frame, since he had taken most of what would have leveled the lieutenant, and his wounds looked fatal. For the second time in two weeks, he had saved the lieutenant's life, this time at a terrible cost.

The platoon's other corpsman, Doc Kristapovich, and two others including Nichols were badly hurt by the same blast, and three slightly wounded. Without any right to do so, the lieutenant ordered the tank commander, a first lieutenant who outranked him, to ferry his four badly hurt people back to the aid station, and he did so.

The men of each of the 81 rifle platoons in the First Marine Division can tell similar stories about the performance and heroism of their Navy Corpsmen, but there can't have been anyone better than Tom Burchick. Every man in the 1st Platoon would say he was the best Marine in the outfit. His conduct should be enshrined at the Naval Academy and in Navy annals along with those of John Paul Jones, Admirals Farragut and Dewey and Colin Kelly. Burchick's actions were truly in the highest traditions of the U.S. Naval Service.

When it comes time to finally unveil the new Korean War Memorial in the nation's Capitol, I hope he will be in the front rank of honored guests with his fellow Navy combat veteran, George Bush.

1st Marine Division Drive To Yanggu
23-31 May
Showing Regimental Routes

MAP 13

Hwachon Reservoir

Yanggu
31

31

Inje

1 M ×2

31

30

30

29

27-9

28

Hill 566

29-30

27

26

Koritwi-gol

Soyang R.

28

26

1 M ×2

26

27

25

24-5

26

25

Kari-san

25-6

24

25

1051

KEY

- - - - - -	Rt. of 1st Mar.
— — —	" " KMC
• • • • •	" " 5th Mar.
—————	" " 7th Mar.

Numbers inside circles
represent dates in May '51

1

7

KMC

Hangye

Hongchon

SCALE

0   500   1000 Yds.

This map shows the U.S. Marine attack from May 23 to 31 following the Chinese Second Spring Counteroffensive against the Second Army Division. Note the daily advances of the First, Fifth, Seventh and KMC regiments save for the two-day holdup of the Seventh Marines, May 27-29. On the morning of May 29, Spike Schening's Charlie Company took Hill 566 which had held up the Seventh's advance. (Taken from U.S. Marine Operations in Korea, Vol IV, page 129.)

E.J. "Goodbastard" Clark, Platoon Sergeant, the author and Hospitalman 3/c Tom "Doc" Burchick, in reserve near Inje, June 5, 1951. Clark was rotated home that day. The 1st Platoon's perimeter was entirely in the rocky river bed of the Soyang River. The 2nd Platoon enjoyed the grassy bank and grove of trees in the background . . . along with several hundred neatly stacked boxes of 122mm mortar rounds, which escaped detonation from a Chinese artillery barrage the night before.

This photograph appears to show Hospital Corpsman 3rd Class Thomas Burdick administering assistance to 5 Marines of the 1st Platoon of Charlie Company 1/5 around May 26, 1951. (Taken from Department of the Army booklet, Korea 1951-53, page 144.)

McCloskey, Boyle & Elson bathing in the Hong'chon River, May 21, 1951.

1st Platoon Runners Bruder and Boyle. Bruder was KIA on the way up 610 on June 21, 1951. He had volunteered to carry the radio for the 2nd platoon's assault after surviving the 1st Platoon's attack.

Hill 566 as seen from Spike Schening's OP, late afternoon, May 28, 1951.

Looking back south at Hill 566 from the knoll where Whit Moreland was killed on May 29, 1951. Spike Schening and Hank Straub were wounded on top of this hill shortly after this picture was taken. Doc Burchick killed four North Korean burp gunners with a BAR at 10 yards at the left edge of the picture just below the crest.

The Mongolian horseman came out of the woods at right and galloped down the diagonal trail to the left, passing at least 40 Marines of the 2nd and 3rd squads as they assaulted up the ridge from the left. All of these alleged-expert riflemen emptied their M-1s at the horse and rider. The latter is presumably alive and well today somewhere in North Korea.

Chapter 6

The Sergeant Who Was Asked Too Much

Among the branches of the U. S. Armed Forces, the Marine Corps is unique in one respect. Its most honored rank is not that of General or Colonel or Captain. It is that of Sergeant.

While most officers may be respected, nearly all sergeants are respected.

Behind this is an ancient faith, that the individual Marine rifleman, not his commander, is the most important ingredient of the Corps; that Marine enlisted men can do anything and overcome any obstacle in small infantry unit operations if only they are properly led. A Marine's most important leader is his sergeant.

From boot camp to the end of his enlistment, a Marine is taught to follow that leader closest to him. The enlisted Marine properly expects his sergeants to protect him from that most dangerous of risks, an inexperienced second lieutenant.

While an officer is accepted as having a high I.Q., and probably a college degree, neither of these achievements insures that common sense or good judgment required of a sergeant by his fellow Marines.

A fair number of Marines have turned down chances to become officers in order to remain in the ranks. Indiana Congressman, then Private First Class Andrew Jacobs, at age 17, turned down an appointment to West Point in 1950 in order to go to Korea with his reserve unit. That he survived the First Chinese Spring offensive in 1951 and was later elected to the Congress caused equal amazement to those who knew him. To this day, however, Congressman Jacobs reserves his praise for enlisted Marines. Only his own platoon leader, killed in action at the Punch Bowl in September, 1951, earned Jacobs' respect.[1]

While a sergeant controls a Marine's daily existence, and can make his life miserable in training, an officer's mistake in combat or desire to earn a medal can imperil a Marine's health, comfort and life itself. The most minor mistake in map reading by his platoon leader can be fatal to a rifleman. Beyond lieutenants and captains, the risk of error by officers of higher rank increases exponentially.

America's most famous general, Robert E. Lee, may have worried in later years about his decision to order Pickett's charge and 11,000 casualties on the third day at Gettysburg. Sir Winston

---

[1] An editorial comment by Jacobs appears in the final chapter in this book.

Churchill was not honored for his decision to attack the Turks at Gallipoli.

Marines in combat generally regard all but the best of officers with some suspicion until they prove themselves, particularly those staff or desk officers who do not dig their own foxholes and who are instinctively understood by rifleman to be somewhat ignorant, if not insensitive, to a rifleman's needs or worries.

Not so, the sergeant. He digs his own foxhole, eats what the troops eat and is expected to be the leader in any assault. The sergeant starts with the presumption that he has earned his stripes through the demonstration of competence to that most exclusive of fraternities, staff sergeants, gunnery sergeants and master sergeants, known as "Staff NCOs."

A friend of mine who graduated from San Diego Boot Camp in 1944 tells a story which illustrates this point better than any editorial comment can express.

Six foot four, in good health and filled with the desire to succeed, my friend rose to the head of his training platoon, and on graduation day was named its honor man, designated to stand in the final parade formation at the platoon's head, the platoon's red and gold guidon in his proud custody.

For illustration's sake, he will be called Janssen.

During the nine weeks of pure hell which his drill instructor (D.I.), a corporal, had put him through in order to instill confidence in Janssen that his miserable self might *possibly* be permitted one day to join the world's greatest fighting force, Janssen had heard about officers but had rarely seen one, and then only at a great distance.

He knew that the Training Regiment had a Lieutenant Colonel in command, and he knew that somewhere there were captains and majors with some sort of authority. In the few brief class-room hours devoted to subjects other than the rifle and its care and cleaning, he had heard of lieutenants and Guadalcanal, but his 16-hour day began, ended and was completely occupied with the snarling corporal, his D.I., who hourly demonstrated his contempt for Janssen and his fellow sufferers, using, in the parlance of his time, a single contemptuous word as the only designation of which Janssen and his ilk were worthy. There was one individual, however, whom even the D.I. held in respect, the veteran Gunnery Sergeant who was the company's First Sergeant, and before whom each member of the training company occasionally had to appear for administrative matters such as the naming of insurance beneficiaries, medical shots and the like. The Gunnery Sergeant, unlike Janssen, was *always* neat, his uniform *always* sharply pressed, his shoes *always* spit-shined, . . . *and* he wore numerous ribbons including the Silver Star and Purple Heart and had been at Guadalcanal.

To the D.I., the Master Sergeant was a great Marine; to Janssen, he was God.

When graduation day came at last, and Janssen received his first word of grudging approval from the D.I., he was in euphoria. Even long, hot hours standing in formation in the Southern California sun for the final inspection and parade were bearable. The inspecting party trooped the lines of the assembled companies and finally reached Janssen's platoon. Into Janssen's painful, straight-ahead vision came the hawklike face of his D.I. "This is honor man Janssen, Sir," the Corporal said to the Lieutenant. A new, boyish, pink-cheeked face appeared. "Congratulations Janssen; Colonel, this is Honor Man Janssen, Sir," squeaked the Lieutenant. "Congratulations, Private Janssen," came the deeper voice of the Colonel as he passed into Janssen's field of vision and pinned the honor man's medal on Janssen's chest.

Neither the Lieutenant, the Colonel nor their congratulations moved Janssen. Their words came from a different world.

But then into his view came the grizzled face of the Gunnery Sergeant, who, as he leaned forward to rip the medal from Janssen's thrust-out chest, growled, "Remember Janssen, you're still a shit-bird," and passed on.

Only then was Janssen impressed. The great man had spoken, and unlike the words of the officers, Janssen knew the truth had been told.

During the Korean War, a Marine rifle company had three 45-man platoons, each with three 13-man squads. A sergeant squad leader had three four-man fire teams, each built around the Browning automatic rifle (BAR) carried by the BAR man, and led by a fire team leader entitled to the rank of corporal. The platoon leader, a second lieutenant, had a platoon sergeant, platoon guide usually a buck sergeant, a runner, a radioman and, in combat, two Navy medical corpsmen.

The quality of its five sergeants, not its single officer, usually marked the rifle platoon's reputation, reliability and combat-readiness. The troops expected their sergeants to protect them from the inexperience, peculiarities and potentially-life threatening decisions of new lieutenants, particularly those who showed any desire to become a hero. Keeping the Lieutenant squared away was a job expected of the platoon's sergeants.

In addition to the three rifle platoons, the Marine rifle company also had a machine gun platoon with three 17-man sections of two squads each. The machine gun squad had a squad leader, a gunner (who carried the tripod), an assistant gunner who carried the gun itself, the 1919-A4 light, air-cooled machine gun, and five ammo carriers. In the attack, one section was generally attached to each of the rifle platoons. Their skill and speed in getting their guns into action could make or break a rifle platoon's attack across open ground.

There was also a 19-man mortar section with three 6-man squads, a sergeant as section chief, and a lieutenant as mortar section leader. Each squad, section and platoon was led by a sergeant; the platoon guide in the rifle platoons was also a sergeant under the Table of Organization (T/O).

The company commander had his own radio man, his executive officer, first sergeant, gunnery sergeant, supply sergeant, several runners and an anti-tank rocket section. When the machine gun platoon was assigned out to the rifle platoons in the attack, the machine gun officer was an extra hand. Radio call signs were elementary. The company commander of A Company in the 1st Battalion might be "Creamy Able Six", the Executive Officer "Able Five", the platoon leaders "Able One", "Able Two", and "Able Three". The battalion commander was simply Creamy Six. To his troops, depending on his abilities, the commander might be known as "El Supremo Six," or "Idiot Six." Of a rifle company's 235-plus strength, the Table of Organization provided for 7 officers and 29 sergeants. The sergeants, their experience and abilities, furnished the heart and soul of the company's fighting competence. With good sergeants, the officers' tasks were easy, the good morale of the troops generally assured.

After the heavy fighting at the Chosin Reservoir, the First Marine Division's twenty-seven rifle companies would customarily rotate as many as 30 or 35 of their combat veterans home each month, even in non-combat periods. New replacements generally arrived in the same trucks that were to take the veterans to the rear. From early 1951 on, nearly all the new arrivals, officers and enlisted alike, were reserves fresh out of a brief few weeks of training school, Quantico for the officers, Camp Pendleton for the enlisted men.

During periods of heavy combat, casualties could increase replacement numbers enormously.

Company commanders were thus constantly shifting a seasoned NCO to a different platoon to pair off with a brand new second lieutenant; platoon leaders were constantly shifting fire team leaders and squad leaders as vacancies occurred.

The 1st Platoon of Charlie Company, First Battalion, Fifth Marines (C/1/5), in four short weeks in the spring of 1951 went from five sergeants, (a platoon sergeant, platoon guide and three squad leaders), to *no* sergeants. In the same period, entitled to nine corporals as fire team leaders, the platoon ended up with a corporal as platoon sergeant and three PFCs as squad leaders. Of a T.O. (Table of Organization) strength of 45, plus its attached 17 man machine gun section, the 1st Platoon had 58 killed or wounded in a single six-week period. Most of the rifle platoons in the three rifle regiments had similar experiences.

This didn't necessarily mean a lessening in leadership ability. A great many Marine PFCs have the leadership talent to be officers or they wouldn't have enlisted in the Corps in the first place.

It wasn't conducive to longevity in command in Korea to be a platoon, squad or fire team leader. By the nature of their job and the terrain, whether on patrol or in the assault, leaders were usually the first to ascend ridge lines and cross over hilltops.

A leader was *expected* to lead.

Only when one reached company commander status with a primary responsibility for coordinating supporting mortar, artillery and tank fire, was a Marine officer entitled to command rather than lead. Even then, in crucial situations, a Marine company commander might occasionally be found leading his troops, as did Captain Jack R. Jones in the crucial counterattack to retake Hill 1282 in the early morning of November 28, 1950. Jones held two Navy Crosses, the first earned on Iwo Jima, the second on Hill 1282.

In the Korea of 1950-1951, sergeants and corporals tended to have a particularly high turn-over rate. They earned their stripes, although promotions never quite caught up with responsibilities, and it was not uncommon after periods of heavy combat to see PFCs leading squads which sergeants were supposed to command.

Against this background, it is worthwhile to mention the story of the rise and fall of one sergeant, if only to illustrate one of the basic unfairnesses of the rotation system used in the Korean War.

For the purposes of this story, we'll call him White. Sergeant White was a regular Marine who had earned the three stripes of a buck sergeant before he came to combat in Korea. He was one of hundreds of regulars pulled hastily out of embassies, ships, posts and stations around the world in July and August, 1950, to create the First Marine Division that landed at Inchon on September 15, 1950, breaking the back of the North Korean invasion which had nearly united Korea under Communist rule.

White was assigned to Charlie Company, 1st Battalion, 5th Marines, and saw hard fighting at the Chosin Reservoir in November and early December.

When the Division managed to extricate itself from Chinese encirclement at the Reservoir and ship out of Hungnam for rest and rehabilitation at "The Bean Patch" near Masan at Korea's southernmost tip, Sergeant White had handled himself well and had more than the usual complement of cockiness. He had been nominated by his Company Commander, Captain Jack Jones, for a Bronze Star for bravery in action. One December night, celebrating the Christmas season with 15 or 16 others in a crowded squad tent by lantern light, White was cleaning his .45 pistol. The other Marines were lying and sitting around drinking beer, sharing the warmth of an oil-burning stove.

One of the company's best-known jokers poked his head through the tent flap and said something to the effect, "Hey you guys, knock it off, I can't sleep with all the noise you're making."

Told to bug off, he returned a few minutes later, reached an arm into the tent holding a hand grenade and inquired, "What'll you do if I drop this grenade?"

White sighted down the barrel of his .45 and said, "And what'll you do if I shoot your ass off?" With that, the hand dropped the grenade, the spoon whirring off with its unmistakable "ping." A group of thrashing Marines, well aware of the 4.6-second fuse, tried to cut or flail their way out of the tent. The lantern was knocked over and out and a gun went off, sending a round through the shoulder of the grenade- dropper and slightly nicking a passing Marine in the company street outside as well.

When nothing happened after a few seconds, it was slowly realized that the grenade was only a joke, that the powder had been extracted and that it was White's pistol which had gone off. No one was really hurt save the grenade prankster, for whom no sympathy was felt of any kind. The U.S. issue grenades of 1950-51 were powerful levelers and the 4.6 seconds of pure fear experienced by the otherwise-relaxed Marines was not easily forgiven.

There was one individual, however, who blamed Sergeant White. The new battalion commander, known by those in his command by the unflattering title of "Idiot Six," had promulgated a "No-round-in- the-Chamber" rule for the Battalion in bivouac. The rule made unquestionably good sense. Too many Marines had been hurt by accidental discharges. The Colonel had not known of White's valor in battle and wanted him court-martialed as an example to the troops. A special court-martial was ordered, but before the necessary papers could be assembled and filled out, the Battalion was ordered north and dispersed in small units to chase North Korean guerrillas in the snowy mountains around Pohang. While in this frustrating effort, orders came in mid-February, 1951, for the Battalion to load aboard trucks and move north to Wonju to lead the first counter attack against the Chinese.

It wasn't until weeks later in April that the Battalion had a few days in reserve along the banks of the Pukhan River, and sufficient time to convene the three-officer special courtmartial which the Colonel was still determined should demonstrate his terrible swift wrath when his rules were disobeyed.

Somehow it had become known that as the Company's newest replacement, I had had two years of law school. Captain Jones asked me to defend White. Just in time, because the Colonel forcefully demanded that I serve as prosecutor. I was able to beg off only by pleading a conflict of interest, having already discussed the matter with White.

It turned out there was another would-be lawyer in the Battalion, First Lieutenant Les Proctor, later to become a prominent District Attorney in Austin, Texas.

Neither Les nor anyone else in the battalion wanted to see White punished, but on the Colonel's orders, trial was set for the following afternoon with Proctor acting as prosecutor.

Captain Jones was no admirer of the Colonel, but he was too much of a professional Marine to show it, or to allow the Colonel to be criticized in his presence. Nevertheless, he made it clear to me that White was one of the best sergeants in the Company, and he wanted every possible effort made in his behalf. It was hard to argue that there hadn't been a round in the chamber while White was cleaning his .45. If not, he would have had to have been the world's fastest trigger man to pull back the bolt, put a round in the chamber and then squeeze off a round in the sudden chaos and blackness of the squad tent when the grenade's spoon flew off.

The testimony of those present seemed to confirm that the .45 had gone off almost simultaneously with the dropping of the grenade.

But then again, who could say? In the confusion of 16 Marines in a panic trying to forcibly remove themselves from a crowded and darkened tent, nobody was counting seconds.

A primary principle of U. S. criminal law is that any reasonable doubt entitles an individual to an acquittal under the American system of justice. This principle is not accepted easily, however, by some Marine colonels. There goal is discipline, not justice. Idiot Six had made his views known to the three members of the special Court Martial Tribunal, carefully selected from H&S and Weapons Companies for their daily contact with the Colonel and the obeisance he demanded of them.

Then occurred a quirk of fortune that may have saved White. Just before the court convened, orders came for the Battalion to saddle up and move back into the attack, this time against a rumored Chinese buildup north of the Hwachon Reservoir. The Weapons Company Commander who served as Chief Judge was particularly anxious to get back to his company. He advised both counsel that the presentation of evidence and arguments was to be of the briefest possible duration. We were happy to comply. The testimony took no more than twenty minutes, arguments five, and the judges' deliberation three.

A unanimous "not guilty" vote was hastily announced and the participants ran for their packs and weapons. It must be added that all three judges held a healthy respect for Jones and a matching distaste for the Colonel.

I was briefly a hero to the company, although I hadn't achieved much fondness for Sergeant White in the process. White had managed to convey a certain contempt for young replacement lieutenants without combat experience.

White was serving as the platoon guide of the 2nd platoon when, less than a week later, the long-rumored Chinese spring offensive burst upon us. Charlie Company was situated west of the Hwachon Reservoir, dug in after a day's advance of perhaps 2,000 yards up a north-south ridge line, when the Chinese hit the 6th Republic of Korea (ROK) Division off to our left flank.

For the first time in the nine weeks I had been in Korea, the Chinese used their carefully-husbanded artillery to bombard our positions. That night, Baker Company took heavy casualties in a sharp encounter on Hill 313 on the ridge line to our east, just above the town of Hwachon. We spent most of the night watching tracers arching through the night on our flanks. Baker Company held firm, but to our west, the tracers and flares steadily moved south.

By morning, the word came that the 6th ROK Division had completely broken, that the famous British "Gloucesters" had been overrun, allegedly while celebrating St. George's Day with a grog ration. The First Marine Regiment had been called up out of reserve and was heavily engaged in a desperate battle several miles to our rear, trying to prevent the Division from being surrounded and cut off.

We made a forced march back from Hwachon to a point in the Pukhan River Valley where we were picked up in "Dukws," big, rubber-tired amphibious vehicles, and ferried several miles further back down the valley of the Pukhan. We passed an unforgettable sight, the burned out hulks of the self-propelled 155 mm. guns and quad-50 halftracks of the "Triple Nickel" 555th Field Artillery, U.S. Army.

We had slogged past the same outfit a few days earlier in the advance north and had marveled at the firepower and mobility of the huge guns, tractors and halftracks of the army unit. Marines were not blessed with such magnificent weaponry.

The 555th's security had been lax, however. The Chinese had swarmed down on their lowland position from a nearby ridge, killing or capturing most of the artillerymen and burning their trucks and tents. The blackened ruins and dead bodies were a sobering sight, and a lot of us quietly said a word of thanks that Jones and our Executive Officer, Spike Schening had been forcing us to climb and dig in on mountain-tops each night.

Years later I read that the "Triple Nickel" unit had suffered a similar fate during the Naktong Perimeter fighting in August, 1950, with their lowland position overrun and several guns destroyed. Their leadership hadn't learned much from the first massacre.

The retreat south from Hwachon had other awesome moments. At one point, we plodded south past one of our own 105 batteries of the 11th Marines, with its howitzers pointing in three directions, north, west and south.

The psychology of the retreat, we learned, was far different from that of the attack. We *knew* the Chinese were behind us; with how many men and with what speed and determination they were coming wasn't yet clear, but the situation inspired fear rather than the confidence we had felt during the previous weeks of advancing while the Chinese withdrew.

Late in the afternoon we linked up on an east-west ridge line with George Company of the 1st Regiment, which had battled overwhelming numbers of Chinese, thereby giving us the chance to get back to join them and prevent encirclement.

I had the left flank platoon of our regiment, tying in with a platoon of George Company led by an old friend from the platoon leaders' class at Quantico, Fred Redmon.

Late that afternoon, feverishly digging in along the military crest, we saw—the only time we were to see it during the year—swarms of Chinese in the valley below, braving our air and artillery in broad daylight, massing for the attack on us that night. The attack came, around midnight, with the customary bugles, cymbals, whistles and shouts of "Marine, you die!" The first inkling we had was the triggering of a trip flare 10 yards in front of our forward foxholes, disclosing a surprised Chinese machine gun squad which had somehow managed to pull their heavy gun cart up a cliff in front of us which we had thought nearly unscalable. When the flare burst, and the bugle sounded, my veteran machine gun section leader, Sergeant Cliff Lansil, holder of a Silver Star from the Reservoir, yelled

"They're playing 'Open the Door, Richard'" a popular song of that day.

And indeed they were.

The attack failed, largely because of huge cargo planes which from midnight on flew above the valley below us, dropping flares every 3 minutes which illuminated the hillsides up which the Chinese had to come to dislodge us.

On several occasions, however, it was touch and go for George Company of 3/1 down the ridge line on our left. We could hear Chinese being spoken amongst George's foxholes and at one point near dawn, I pulled one of my machine guns out of our front line and turned it down the George Company ridge where it was apparent the Chinese had penetrated at least part of George's defense line.

Some weeks later, my wife sent me a headline from the San Francisco Chronicle:

"FIRST MARINE DIVISION SAVES UN LINE."

It was really two battalions of the First Regiment which had done the job.

Nearly 17 years later, on my first day as a Member of Congress, a rangy congressman from Indiana introduced himself to me as a former Marine, and I learned he had been in one of those George Company foxholes within a few yards of my platoon position that memorable night in April, 1951. It was Andy Jacobs, the same 17 year old who had turned down a West Point appointment for the chance to serve in combat as a Marine Pfc.

The next day, we pulled back again, and by evening were digging in on a wooded ridgeline some miles further back.

That night was to renew my acquaintance with Sergeant White, and under unique circumstances. Well after dark, we got the word to roll our gear and stand by to move out to the rear again. It wasn't clear just where, but the orders were to go south along an old railroad track which ran down the valley on our western flank.

It was a black night save for the tracers and flares in the distance to the west and southwest. There were also a lot of fires lighting the sky directly to the south toward Chun'chon. To the north, there was only an ominous quiet.

Around midnight, we moved off the hill in silence and started down the railroad track in a column, my platoon at the rear. The Chinese were clearly behind us, and on our right flank, but the fires directly ahead of us indicated possible danger there as well.

A rifle company on the march has an accordion effect. If a man at the front of the column falls back a step, then closes the gap, the 200 men behind him have to do likewise. If 20 men each drop back a step, then the 180 men behind them have to close up 20 steps.

At the tail end of the company, we had to almost run to keep contact with the platoon ahead. As my own platoon got further and further spread out, I finally decided it was better to keep us all together. I stopped and waited until the whole platoon had closed up. We then moved out down the railroad, much more slowly, determined to keep the platoon intact at all costs. After awhile, we came upon a small group of the 2nd Platoon in the darkness, clustered around Sergeant White, whose position as Platoon Guide on the march was at the rear to keep his platoon closed up.

He had also given up trying to maintain contact, and had the idea that the fires ahead meant enemy; that the rest of the company must have left the track and gone east, away from the firing to the southwest on our right. He was hell bent to go east and pled with me to go with him. He was clearly panicked, and although he was a seasoned veteran, and I had had no real combat experience up to that time, I ordered him to stay with us and had to threaten him to have the order obeyed.

Only two or three of his men and mine were close enough to hear our exchange, but he finally agreed, and we kept moving down the railroad track, finally at dawn linking up with the rest of the company and a lot of miscellaneous troops, tanks and the first full Colonel I had seen since arriving in Korea. It turned out that the fires we had seen were the destruction of our supply dumps west of Chun'chon, to keep them out of the hands of the still-advancing Chinese.

A few days later, in early May, the veteran platoon sergeant who had been my mentor in the first platoon, Sergeant Caret, was rotated home. Captain Jones asked me if I would like Sergeant White, obviously wanting me to have an N.C.O. of experience and competence to steady the platoon. I begged off for two reasons—White's thinly veiled disdain for me and reserve officers in general, and the panic I had seen that fearsome night of the great railroad track retreat. I didn't tell Jones or anyone else what I had seen of White's state of mind that night, but it stayed in my mind.

Delbert Klein, head of the Company's anti-tank rocket section was assigned as my platoon sergeant, and E. J. Clark, 130 pounds of vitality and good cheer, moved from squad leader up to platoon guide.

It was only a few weeks later that I had another unusual experience with White. This time it was a confrontation late on the afternoon of June 2, as the 1st Platoon was moving forward for the final attack on Hill 610.

It had been a very bad day, particularly for White and the 2nd Platoon, which since mid-morning had been under almost continuous 120 mm. mortar fire on the wooded ridge leading to 610. At least half of his platoon including both corpsmen had been hit, and White's situation was doubly difficult because we all knew that the next rotation draft was to leave a few days later when the monthly replacement draft caught up with us. White had landed at Inchon in September, and many of the Inchon people had been rotated home by early May. Having been with a rifle company for his full tour of duty, White had every right to believe he would be going home when the new replacements arrived. Also, by June 2, the wear and tear of too many tense nights in forward foxholes, coupled with increasing North Korean resistance, had led to more than one "psychological casualty." The day before we had had to take a grenade away from a member of one of my machine gun squads who had gone a little crazy under incoming mortar fire. He had pulled the pin of the grenade while lying in a rice paddy alongside our tanks, but 1,000 yards from the nearest enemy.

In any event, while leading the platoon up to the rear of the 2nd Platoon's position, down the ridge came Sergeant White, crying and calling for his mother. It was clear he had cracked up, and fearful that he would shake up my own people, I clubbed him with my carbine when he tried to go by me. Again, only the closest Marines behind me saw what happened.

The assault went forward and the incident slipped my mind. Three weeks later, when the Soviets and Chinese asked for truce talks, I was rotated to the rear, to become Assistant personnel officer (S-1) for the 5th Regiment, some 300 miles south at the Division Rear Echelon at Masan.

Several weeks passed in relative peace, both at the front and at Masan while the truce talks ground forward. There weren't any guerrillas in our area, but nearby Army units gave us ice cream and we saw our first young women in four months, Red Cross volunteers. These were momentous events.

The famous "Big Foot" Brown came down from the First Marines to command the scattered headquarters units which made up the rear echelon—personnel, supply, legal, graves registration, and the like—and put us all to work building an officers' mess. *There will be an officers' Mess wherever Marines are stationed,*" roared Big Foot at the first officers' meeting. This had been his experience since serving in China in the 1930's, and it was Big Foot's creed. We lieutenants obeyed with alacrity. One fortunate soul was given the periodic "booze run" to Japan, to bring back cases of V.O. and Canadian Club—the popular, or at least available, liquor of that age. He was later to become famous as the Reverend Pat Robertson of the "700 Club" and a candidate for President of the United States in 1988.

One fall day, the 5th Marines' small personnel office, occupied by me and three other lieutenants, one from each of the three battalions, Bill "The Pube" Heer, Ken Scheel and Tom Johnston, was visited by another Californian, T. J. O'Reilly, a lawyer in the Division Legal Office. O'Reilly told me that a Marine he had just unsuccessfully defended on a deliberate-disobedience-of-orders charge had asked if I would say a word for him before the seven-member General Court Martial Board passed sentence.

O'Reilly said: "He says he knows you. His name is White."

O'Reilly told me the story. It seemed that White had *not* gone home with the June rotation draft as he had anticipated and, indeed, was entitled to.

He had instead been assigned to a supposedly-safe billet at the battalion headquarters. The assignment was an unlucky one. As a result of being taken out of a line company, he missed the July and August rotation drafts, as the last remaining Inchon veterans in the rifle companies were selected first for rotation.

Finally, in late August, probably the last Inchon/Seoul/Chosin veteran left in the Battalion, White was told he would be going home in the September draft for sure. Then one dark night, with the Battalion in a forward position and the three companies spread out well to the front, a Chinese combat patrol infiltrated behind the lines and cut the wires leading back to the battalion CP.

A new Headquarters Company lieutenant, fresh from the states, looked around for a patrol to send out to restore communications and take on the Chinese infiltrators.

He found some cooks and bakers and finally White, whom he ordered to lead the patrol.

White said flatly, "No Sir."

"What do you mean 'No Sir'?" "I mean I'm going home next week, sir; get somebody else."

Had there been any veteran officers around, White's situation would have been understood and the matter forgotten, but nearly all the headquarters personnel were new arrivals. No one was still around who remembered White's heroism at the Reservoir. The new lieutenant put White in custody and he was promptly shipped to the Division Rear at Masan to stand trial. The penalty for deliberate disobedience of orders had been death by firing squad in World War I. Even a generation later it could mean years of imprisonment.

O'Reilly had argued the case well, but the Court had been unanimous in its decision. The offense was one for which the sentence could easily have been 10 years and a dishonorable discharge.

I went with O'Reilly over to the court martial building and spoke for perhaps 10 minutes, arguing for clemency on the basis of the two occasions I believed White had clearly shown he was suffering from combat fatigue; the railroad track incident in April and Hill 610 in June. I described in detail the respect Captain Jones had relayed on to me for White's earlier combat performance at the Reservoir. I mentioned the Company's other psychological casualties during May and June and my observation of the understandable magnification of men's fears when they have survived combat for a sustained period and are finally on the verge of relief. I was myself a case in point. The day that Jones was hit, the assault later that afternoon on the unnumbered ridgeline west of Hill 808 had left me in considerable doubt that I wanted to do or die for Idiot Six. After the terrible casualties taken by Able and Baker Companies and our aborted attacks on Hill 907 at the Punch Bowl on June 17 and 18 I had never been quite sure I was up to another headlong assault. It was unfair, and a pure accident, that Sergeant White was even *asked* to take that patrol. None of us who knew his record and the circumstances would have asked him to do it. Only the bad luck of having a new lieutenant fresh from the States had put White in his unfortunate position.

The Board retired and shortly returned to give White a sentence of the loss of one stripe—reduction to Corporal, and if I recall correctly, loss of two month's pay. The Chief Judge thanked me afterwards and told me that they might have acquitted White if they had heard my testimony before reaching their decision.

Another quirk of fate. I was probably the only person in the world who had seen White on those two occasions in April and June and also knew, through Captain Jones, of his outstanding record earlier. Jones, Schening, Daly and most of the Marines who had served with White were in Naval hospitals back home in the States. Had I not survived and been sent to that unique job in the rear, White might well have been imprisoned for years.

What a stroke of fortune that some of us who had less combat than Sergeant White were never asked to meet that final test which we too might have failed.

Instead we return to civil life, honored for our alleged good deeds, but ourselves knowing that it was only rare good fortune that the demands of combat leadership ended for us before we too were asked too much. Sergeant White was asked too much.

I hope he is well today.

Chapter 7

A Corpsman Saves Two Lives

One of the happier souls in Charlie Company was a young Navy hospital corpsman, Don Dickson. Dickson was 23, and like most of our corpsmen, had volunteered for combat duty with the FMF, joining the Company on Christmas Day, 1950 while the Division was resting and rehabilitating after the arduous fight around the Chosin Reservoir.

Dickson was assigned to the Second Platoon, first led by Chosin veteran Bill Kerrigan, but in April taken over by a new reserve second lieutenant, Chuck Straub. Straub was a superb officer, caught on quickly and was perhaps the best platoon leader in the Company when the heavy fighting began in late May.

The Company had had an easy time of it in the balmy weather of early May; the Chinese had been badly battered in their first spring counter-offensive in late April, and quite a distance, perhaps 10 miles, had opened up between the positions to which the 8th Army had withdrawn in the central front below the Hong'chon River and the steep wooded mountains to the north of the Soyang River where the Chinese were dug in.

After a month's quiet, marked mostly by long-range patrolling and one vicious fight involving the 7th Marines, the Chinese struck hard at their favorite target, the Second Army Division and its flanking ROK units, in the mountains to our east.

On May 23rd the Fifth Regiment was sent to bolster the badly-mauled Second Division. The 38th Infantry Regiment had been particularly hard hit, and for five days the Company advanced cautiously north in heavily-wooded mountains, scooping up demoralized stragglers from both the 38th and its Chinese attackers.

On the 27th, however, the Chinese General moved a North Korean Division into place on the ridge lines in front of the advancing Marines to screen the Chinese withdrawal. From advances of two or three miles a day, the 7th Marines on 1/5's left came hard up against a strongly-held mountaintop known only as "566." There they stalled, through the days of the 27th and 28th, unable to advance against the complex of bunkers, machine guns and perhaps 200 infantrymen dug into 566, a cliff on the left flank and a steep, wooded finger ridge on the right which provided mutually-supporting firing positions.

By the late afternoon of the 28th, the Second Battalion of the 7th Marines had been badly bloodied from a series of unsuccessful frontal attacks to take 566 from the north-south ridgeline on which 566 sat squarely astride.

With the Fifth Regiment unable to continue its own advance with an open left flank, Charlie Company was ordered up to assist the 7th Marines, followed by Baker Company to help if needed.

It was a hot, forced march uphill, and several Marines dropped out with heat exhaustion. Doc Dickson dropped behind to assist those from his platoon who had fallen out.

Charlie's C.O., Spike Schening, sizing up the situation when he arrived at the right flank of 2/7's position late in the afternoon, determined to attack.

From the Marines' ridgetop, some 100 yards long and slightly lower than 566 in elevation the Marines of Fox Company of 2/7 were lined up above Chairle Company's left, almost as if on a rifle range, exchanging occasional fire with plainly-visible machine gun bunkers and connecting trench lines a few yards down from the crest of 566.

566, also 100 yards in width, flat-topped and wooded, lay perhaps 600 yards away. Both Fox Company's hilltop and 566 had narrow finger ridges perpendicular to the main north-south ridge line, slanting down to the valley on the right. A cliff to the west made 566 invulnerable from that side. Fox Company had plainly run out of gas, with a large number of seriously-wounded on the reverse slope.

Standing on the shoulder on the reverse side of the finger ridge, and on the flank of Fox Company, Schening turned to Hank Straub whose platoon had been first in line as the Company came up the hill.

Spike's order was simple. "Hank, take your platoon back down the ridge until you're in defilade, cross over the ravine and attack up that ridge line. We'll give you cover fire from here."

Hank asked "What do I do if we can't make it?" Spike replied: "If it's too tough, pull on back and we'll take it in the morning."

It was late in the day. The sun was setting and darkness was not far off.

The Company had the advantage of Spike Schening's self-confidence and no real understanding of what had held up the 7th Marines so long; the rest of the Company got into position down the slope to give fire support from the side hill as Hank moved back down the ridge.

After awhile, the Second Platoon could be seen, well down the ridge leading to 566, moving up through the trees. When they reached a point perhaps 200 yards below the flank of the enemy position, there was a burst of fire from 566. Straub came up on the radio, "Charlie Six, this is Charlie Two. We've got a machine gun firing directly down the ridge at us and there are gooks down below us. This is apparently their MSR (main supply route)."

Spike snapped, "Well, what are you going to do about it?" Straub in deference to Spike's earlier comment that he could pull back if necessary, did not give the reply Spike wanted to hear.

It was unfortunate. Spike's blood was up. He looked around; to the first officer he saw he barked: "Get over there, take over the Second Platoon and assault." To Hank Straub: "Turn your platoon over to Sergeant Murphy and stay where you are."

The sun was down, as the lieutenant checked his gear. Doc Dickson, short, stocky and open-faced, one of the Second Platoon's two corpsmen, had not reached the hilltop when his platoon had taken off down the ridge and had been helping with Fox Company's badly-wounded. Dickson said: "Hey Lieutenant, that's my platoon. Can I go with go with you?" The lieutenant said "Sure, Doc," and off they went, running. They had to go perhaps 400 yards down the back of their finger ridge before they were out of sight of the enemy positions on 566. They then crossed the several hundred yards of rice paddies that ascended the ravine and started diagonally up the ridge to where they had last seen the Second Platoon in the trees.

After three and one-half months in Korea, the lieutenant was in reasonably good shape, and Dickson was just a little heavier and slower. The lieutenant finally got up on the narrow crest of the finger ridge, but no Marines were in sight, and looking back at Charlie Company's position, it looked as if he might still be below the Second Platoon's location. He started up a trail on the crest of the narrow ridge, with Dickson thrashing through the brush well behind and below him in more difficult terrain.

Moving up perhaps 100 yards, the lieutenant could find no sign of any Marines, and looking across the ravine it seemed he was getting far too high on the ridge. The dusk was deepening and there was an ominous quiet. He stopped near the edge of what looked to be a clearing in the tree line, blending into the brush. Across the little clearing, uphill perhaps 30 yards, there was a movement in the bushes. Then he saw a rifle, with a bayonet that looked to be two feet long, moving around to point in the direction of the panting Dickson who was now nearly parallel but perhaps still 10 yards down the side of the hill. What had looked like a bush now turned out to be the upper body of a Chinese or North Korean rifleman with padded jacket and helmet bedecked with tree branches and leaves like the underbrush in which he was kneeling. Dickson was not quite in his view, but the rifle was pointed at the point he would shortly appear.

The lieutenant was scared stiff.

It took what seemed like minutes to stop shaking and zero in his carbine at the rifleman and pull the trigger. Nothing happened; the carbine was on safe. He pushed the safe lever and after some effort to steady the weapon, finally squeezed off 2 or 3 rounds. Even shaking as he was, it would have been hard to miss at 30 yards. The lieutenant was ever after thankful, however, that he wasn't carrying a .45 pistol, a weapon that he had never learned to fire accurately in his brief days at Quantico and Camp Pendleton. Having fired, he took off running and was probably a foot off the ground when he passed Dickson, muttering, "Let's get the hell out of here."

Forty years later the lieutenant had a chance to call Dickson by phone. Dickson remembered the incident well. He said the lieutenant was white as a sheet when he roared past him saying that he had just shot someone for the first time. That was true enough, but the lieutenant had no memory of any conversation until the two were 400 yards down the ridge line where they ran into Baker Company, slanting up onto the finger ridge in single file, Lt. Jim Cronin at the head of the company with his troops strung out behind him. The last platoon leader in the column was Charlie Cooper. It was now quite dark.

Upon the lieutenant's inquiry, Cronin told him Baker Company had orders to get up on some ridge which was supposedly unoccupied.

The lieutenant told him what had happened to him, still not knowing where the Second Platoon had gone. Baker Company kept going, now in almost total darkness.

It wasn't until years later that Charlie Cooper related that Baker Company had walked diagonally past the enemy position on 566 in the blackness, had heard some clicking of rifle bolts, done a left face, and made a grenade assault only to find themselves amongst bunkers holding unknown numbers of enemy. Cooper had been wounded by grenade fragments, and Baker Company had retraced their steps back down to the battalion CP.[1] It wasn't much of an event, but it came back to the lieutenant

---

[1] In Cooper's words:

"In the late afternoon of 28 May, Idiot Six Sent B Company up a very steep hill to "occupy ground the enemy had supposedly left undefended." My 3rd Platoon was the tail end of a company column that followed a well used path. We had no means of flank security in the heavy brush. I was terribly concerned about our vulnerability; it was quite dark by the time we reached the summit. Using a low voice, I called Cronin on the radio, telling him we were in the middle of an enemy position, bunkers were all about, bolts were clicking, and I expected to be fired on any minute. I simply told him I was going to halt my platoon, face left, use verbal orders to assault up the hill on line ... to preempt what surely was going to be turkey shoot. He simply replied, "Do it!"

Yelling and screaming like a banshee, I shouted out the commands, told the troops to assault, firing from the hip, to form a perimeter on the high ground some 40 yards up the hill. We did just that, sounding like a Confederate cavalry troop. They opened up too, but we got on top. My corpsman got shot through the knee, but we were tying in together when I noticed I was sitting right under a bunker slit. As I reached for a grenade, one went off right by me.

many times in later years how lucky he had been that evening that Dickson had fallen behind on the way up that ridge line, diverting the camouflaged sentry's attention from what otherwise would have been the lieutenant's sure demise. The North Korean could scarcely have missed had it not been for Dickson's noisy progress.

The next morning, the 1st Platoon was sent up the same finger ridge, fortunately with some early morning fog for cover. The unlucky soldier was still there, the screening of twigs and branches still stuck in his padded uniform. His outpost position turned out to be no more than 100 yards below the main enemy position on the flank of 566.

The fog lifted a bit when the lead Marines had closed to within perhaps 60 yards of the North Korean's position. The Platoon was able to rush the first trench line and take the hill.

The day, like the one before, was a hard one for Hank Straub. Assigned the 60mm mortar section, he was with Spike Schening and the company command group on the crest of the newly-taken 566 when North Korean mortars dropped in three devastatingly-accurate 120mm rounds on the crest, seriously wounding both Hank and Spike.

Straub's wounds looked fatal and he asked Doc Dickson if he was going to make it. Doc said "Sure Lieutenant" but he didn't believe it. He helped put Hank on a stretcher and four chiggy-bears started to carry him down the ravine. More 120mm's came in, however, and the chiggy bears dropped Straub and started to run away.

Dickson grabbed a carbine, shot a round at their feet and yelled at them to pick up Straub, which they did.

Hank Straub survived to become a successful educator in the St. Louis area.

Doc got his own disabling wounds four days later when his platoon successfully assaulted the intermediate ridge of Hill 610, only to again fall under effective 120mm mortar fire from another group of highly accurate North Korean gunners.

Doc, following prolonged hospitalization, returned to civil life where he has taught elementary school and served as an assistant principal for many years in Las Vegas, Nevada. He will not be forgotten by the Second Platoon of Charlie Company nor the two lieutenants whose lives he saved in a span of less than 15 hours on Hill 566.

I went down the hill, ass over teakettle, thinking I had bought the farm. In what must have just been seconds, my platoon sergeant was shaking me to see if I was alive. It obviously was a concussion grenade; I couldn't hear much, but did get up, grab my weapon and report to Cronin that Baker 3 had the high ground, but we still were amongst the bad guys.

To make a long story short, it was my first wound, lots of small holes, one less ear-drum, but still functioning. We consolidated B Company and Jim Cronin walked us back down another route with my platoon providing rear security. I had to carry that 200 lb. corpsman on my back all the way down to the Battalion Aid Station. I had some fragments removed, bandaids over others, was given antibiotics and had to report to Idiot Six on what had happened. (Meeting him again that night was to haunt me later. Thereafter, he frequently specified that I was to lead the company or tasked me, by name, to conduct separate platoon combat patrols, usually under his direction.)

It was the same hill Charlie Company fought over so fiercely the next day, and Spike Schening got caught up in the 120mm concentration. I recall watching the third and final USMC assault when it became bedlam, hand to hand. The Platoon Leader became famous for a classic yell to the troops, "We've got 'em by the balls! Let's squeeze 'em."

The Second Platoon leadership, along the Honq'chon River, May 21, 1951; Lt. Hank Straub second from right.
Doc Dickson and Pfc. R.V. Lee in foreground.

2nd Lt. Hank Straub and family, St. Louis, 1988.

Platoon Leaders 1st and 2nd Platoons, Charlie Company, May 21, 1951, east of Honq'chon, just before the final attack north to the Punch Bowl. The grins stem from just having rolled some large rocks down on the Colonel's tent in the valley below, eliciting howls of rage from our esteemed leader.

Chapter 8

Second Lieutenant Robert Munday and Others. In Memoriam

O f the 355 members of the First Special Basic Class at Quantico which graduated on December 22, 1950, 40 were flown to Korea in January, and 39 other arrived by ship on February 16, 1951.

During the first six months of 1951, nearly all of the 79 lieutenants went to rifle companies, led rifle platoons and were wounded, some on several occasions. Eight were KIA.

Those that were killed were our best. The survivors have probably felt some guilt over the years, knowing that had we really done our jobs well, we too would have been killed in the process. There was no way to be a truly good platoon leader without leading, and there was no way to lead on the ridgelines of Korea without sooner or later getting hammered. It was just a question of time and luck.

The first member of our First Special Basic Class to be killed was Felix "Bill" Goudelock of South Carolina. Bill was everything that his State's Wade Hampton had been in the Confederate Army of 1861-65. He was kind and considerate to a fault. Above all else he was dedicated to learning to be a good Marine officer in the tradition of The Citadel and the South Carolina regiments of Lee's Army of Northern Virginia. He was killed by rifle fire shortly after his arrival in January, climbing a ridge at the head of his platoon in the guerrilla hunt around Pohang.

The second to be killed was Carey Cowart, a husband and father who had had World War II experience and was beloved by officers and men alike. Carey, with his friend Jim Ables, bunkmates aboard the troopship, both volunteered for the two vacancies in the famous Baker Company, 1/5, which had earned permanent fame at the Pusan Perimeter. Carey was seriously wounded while acting as a forward observer for Baker Company's 60mm mortars in the March advance to the Soyang River. He died of his wounds a few days later, to be joined within weeks by Jim Ables, killed during the late April withdrawal from Hwachon.

The First Special Basic Class' top graduate, Tom McVeigh, was everybody's choice to become a regular Marine officer. Son of a New York City police commissioner, Tom was tall, strong and straight. He had earned the distinction of being designated commander of the student battalion at our graduation parade in December and volunteered for the first group to be sent to Korea. He was killed in May while acting as a forward mortar observer for the 81mm mortars in the 3rd Battalion, 7th Marines.

Another member of our Special Basic School platoon (we had all the McC's—McConnell,

McCue, McVeigh, McWilliams, etc.) was Jim McGoey, a quiet member of my own squad bay. Jim was assigned to be a liaison officer with a Korean infantry unit, and was seriously wounded while trying to keep his unit organized in a night withdrawal under Chinese attack. We heard of his death only after the truce commenced in late June.

Another quiet good human being was Bob Buchmann, killed while leading his platoon of Fox Company of the 7th Marines on an almost suicidal ridgeline leading to Hill 566 on May 29. Bob had confided to his roommates aboard the Breckinridge that he didn't expect to survive.

Another member of our platoon at Quantico, joined belatedly to fill a vacancy in the L-O alphabetical group was Bob Baumgart. Bob was the best looking man in the platoon (he looked a little like Rock Hudson), and earned the reputation at Quantico of being top achiever in the number of week nights on which he jumped in a car for the 30 mile drive to Washington, D.C. for a night on the town with the hostesses of the Foreign Officers Club.

Since the only other young women within range of Quantico were the well-chaperoned students of Mary Washington College at Fredericksburg, the week night run to Washington was fairly popular. That a 20 to 23 year old 2nd Lieutenant could survive a twelve-hour, 6:30 a.m. to 6:30 p.m. classroom or field training day, take a quick shower, race to D.C. to return between 3:00 and 6:00 a.m. was a marvel of its time. Baumgart had no peer.

Assigned to 2/5, Bob survived some perilous situations only to be killed inadvertently in May by tripping a booby-trap set out by an adjoining platoon from 3/5. 2/5 didn't follow the practice of using grenades in ration cans as warning devices, and it was a tragic accident.

The loss that seemed most grievous, however, was that of Bob Munday.

Bob had played football at Villanova, and was big, rough and humorous.

A Catholic of the best kind, Bob routinely did thoughtful things that none of the rest of us even considered.

On more than a few weekends of our eleven weeks at Quantico in the fall of 1950, Bob, instead of driving up to Philadelphia to see his parents, would go to Washington and take a young orphan out of the local orphanage for a day, treating him to a movie or a picnic.

He could always be counted upon to puncture the balloon of any of our more blustering classmates, or to mutter some appropriate remark about our sometimes-austere regular platoon commander, Lt. "Digger" Odell, an Annapolis graduate with all the pomposity that being in the top 10% of his class could occasionally bring forth.

By the luck of the draw at graduation, Bob was assigned to a 90-day Motor Transport school.

It was May before he reached Korea and was assigned to command a 6 X 6 truck platoon in one of the Motor Transport battalions.

When the Chinese Second Spring Offensive hit, the Fifth Marines were ordered up from reserve to help the badly-hurt Second Army Division. Our battalion was in a double column plodding up the Hong'chon River road on May 22, 1951 when Munday's trucks came down the dirt road from the north, having ferried troops of one of the Regiment's other battalions up to the jumping-off point to stop the Chinese.

Bob was in a jeep at the head of his column, and seeing me, broke out in a big grin, jumped out, stopped his whole outfit and walked along with me for perhaps 200 yards, both of us catching up on the whereabouts and exploits of our other classmates at Quantico.

Finally Bob broke off and ran back to the head of his truck column. Its drivers no doubt wondered what had caused the delay.

As we kept moving, the boom of artillery and the uncertain state of the Chinese strength up ahead caused me to have the first of the only three philosophic musings I can remember from that year in Korea.

Thinking back on the purity and honesty of Bob and those wonderful qualities of service to others which made him so unique, I said a quiet thanks, walking along, that he was in Motor Transport and not a rifle platoon leader. It seemed important that his gentleness and kindness be preserved for the benefit of society. The rest of us, with our innate tendencies towards drink, women and foolishness were expendable. He wasn't. He was too valuable to the world to be lost running some ridgeline.

Coming out of the lines a month later, I learned that only a few days after our meeting along the Hong'chon Road, Bob's driver had pulled off the road to turn around and hit a buried mine of tremendous power, killing Bob instantly.

I tried to locate his parents years later, to tell them a little of how well Bob was loved by his friends, but they had both passed away. No other relatives were known, so on March 25, 1955, my youngest son was given the name John Munday McCloskey in the hope that he might somehow learn just a few of those human-caring qualities of his namesake. Fortunately he has. Bob would be proud of him.

Graduation Day, Dcember 22, 1950 ("L through O"), 1st Special Basic Class Quantico, Virginia. 1st Platoon, B Company, Captain "Digger" Odell, USNA Commanding. Lt. Bob Munday is in the second row behind Odell's left shoulder. Of the 20 who went to Korea, Munday, McGoey, McVeigh and Baumgart were KIA. McVeigh, the 355 member Battalion's honor man, is on Munday's right. Jim McGoey is directly behind Munday, two rows back. Bob Baumgart is in the back row third from the left.

Chapter 9

Harry Truman's Two Friends
Louis A. Johnson and Frank E. Lowe

Harry S. Truman was a salty, no-nonsense and surprisingly competent President of the United States.

He had reached the White House through the death of Franklin Delano Roosevelt just prior to the end of World War II, and to his lot fell some tough choices. First, to use or not to use the atomic bomb to force the surrender of the Japanese, and second, the demobilization of the vast military machine America had built to vanquish Germany and Japan.

The sudden invasion of South Korea by the North Koreans on June 25, 1950, five years after V-J Day, posed a third major decision, whether or not to send unprepared American troops into combat.

Truman had served as a captain of artillery in the American Expeditionary Force (AEF) in France during World War I. Indeed, his command of Battery D of the 119th Field Artillery, 35th Division, in France remained one of his most successful achievements prior to a series of unexpected successes after entering the White House.

Like most veterans of the AEF, Truman treasured old friends with whom he had served, and like many Army officers, he had built up a certain resentment over the years with respect to his perception that the Marines in our two great world wars had managed to achieve press coverage and public acclaim far beyond that of their Army counterparts. The Army had done at least an equal amount of hard fighting, and Truman thought the Marines had hogged the limelight with well-honed cultivation of the press corps.

Truman's was an understandable point of view.

The Brigade of Marines at Chateau Thierry, Belleau Wood and Soissons seems to have attained a great deal more publicity than the units fighting alongside them in the Army's Second Division.

A generation later, the hard fighting of the Army on New Guinea and Okinawa in the Pacific never quite reached the magnitude of public attention given the Marines at Guadalcanal, Pelelieu, Tarawa, Iwo Jima and finally Okinawa.

With the rapid demobilization and efforts towards armed services unification and economy after Japan's surrender, it was appropriate for Truman to choose an old A.E.F. buddy, Louis A. Johnson, as Secretary of Defense. As President he gave solid approval to Johnson's efforts to reduce the Marine Corps to little more than the Navy's police force they both believed it should be.

Sworn into office in March, 1949, Johnson ordered that the Marine Corps' 11 understrength battalions be reduced to 8 in 1950 and 6 in 1951. His plan was clear: the Marine Corps air-ground teams would be abandoned, with Marine air squadrons merged into the Air Force and Marine ground units reduced to a point where they could be transferred into the Army.

Luckily, one of the titans of the Congress, Michigan Congressman Carl Vinson, Chairman of the House Armed Services Committee stood in the way. Even so, by June, 1950, there were only some 28,000 men in the Fleet Marine Force (FMF), the fighting arm of the Corps, stationed primarily at Camp Pendleton in California and Camp LeJeune in North Carolina. The entire Corps was down to 70,000 men, scattered aboard ships and on posts and stations around the world, guarding embassies and doing ceremonial duties in Washington, D.C.

There were also some 33,000 civilian "active" reserves, however, attending weekly drills at 138 small reserve units around the country and a few thousand "inactive" reservists, mostly officers who had kept their commissions largely for sentimental reasons after World War II.

Finally, there were several hundred recent graduates of the Platoon Leaders' Class (PLC), an ingenious program conceived to attract young college students into obtaining a reserve commission solely through six-week summer sessions at Quantico, Virginia. If one had served a year as an enlisted man, he could qualify by attending a single summer camp; if he had no prior military experience, two successive summer camps were required. No further service was necessary; a Second Lieutenant's commission was awarded upon graduation from college.

In the laid-back days of the late 1940s, with no war in sight, the idea of becoming an officer in the fabled U.S. Marine Corps, with no college courses and no peacetime obligation, was simply too good a deal to pass up for a large number of the high school graduates of June, 1945, who had promptly enlisted only to see the war ended unexpectedly by events at Hiroshima and Nagasaki 6 weeks later. To active young men who hankered for a chance to visit the historic Civil War battlefields of Virginia, Maryland and Pennsylvania it was a great way to spend six weeks in the summer of 1948 or 1949.

This, then, was the Marine Corps of June, 1950, which Truman and his Secretary of Defense Johnson wanted to abolish. A few old Generals from World War I, some old Colonels from the 1920s in Nicaragua and other Caribbean trouble spots, a lot of seasoned officers and NCO's from World War II, perhaps 65,000 17 to 20 year olds serving time in the legendary Corps in order to be with the best and another 35,000 to 40,000 civilian reservists with no thought of possible assignment to combat. There was considerable fear of the demise of the Corps itself at the hands of the two old World War I Army cronies. The Corps had had an illustrious fighting record dating back to 1775, but in 1950 its future was highly dubious, if not bleak.

Luckily, one understrength regiment, the 5th Marines, with only two rifle companies in each of its three battalions, was in shape to fight. Its commanding officer, Victor "The Brute" Krulak, had made it so. In a long and illustrious career, putting the 5th Marines Regiment into the physical condition it was during the peacetime months of early 1950 was perhaps Krulak's finest achievement. The Fifth Regiment stood in stark contrast to the four Army divisions stationed in Japan, and its preparedness may have saved not only the Pusan Perimeter but the Marine Corps itself.

The Regiment's six rifle companies, Able and Baker of the First Battalion, Dog and Easy of the Second, and George and How of the Third, were in rare physical condition on June 25, 1950, having been marched, run and driven for months in the punishing hills and mountains of Camp Pendleton. The North Koreans' attack across the 38th Parallel on June 25th set in motion an unpredictable chain of events. In retrospect, several fortuitous circumstances and personalities combined to create a result no one could have foreseen.

That the United States would decide to resist the North Korean invasion was not at all a certainty.

With a President of other than Truman's background and personality, the matter might have been referred to the Congress for exercise of its constitutional prerogative of declaring war. In that great body there could easily have been a long and prolonged debate which might well have ended in no action at all. Nobody knew much about Korea and Koreans in 1950, and as late as January, 1950, our Secretary of State had proclaimed that it was outside our defense perimeter against communist aggression in the Pacific.

A land war on the Asian continent was not an option our military planners had considered.

South Korea was not even included in General MacArthur's Far East Command in early 1950. The four Army divisions on occupation duty in Japan were garrison troops, their heavy weapons and tanks unused and in some cases unusable. Their troops and officers were merely serving out their time in a peaceful world.

Duty was easy. There was lots of ice cream and the good life. Even the lowliest enlisted man could have his own Japanese home and attentive "wife" for $8 per month in the devastated Japanese economy of 1950. Outside Camp Otsu, near the shrine city of Kyoto, 18 year old Marines could rent a "bad" house and a beautiful girl, or a less-attractive girl but a fine house for the same $8 per month rate. There may be some justice in the recent dominance of the U.S. economy by Japanese auto makers; they had to pull themselves up by their bootstraps after their crushing defeat in 1945.

The four regular Army divisions, the 7th, 24th, 25th and 1st Cavalry, were understrength, untrained and unready for combat. Their leadership and discipline at the company level was judged mediocre at best, and worst of all, they were in no physical condition to maneuver rapidly against the hardy North Korean infantrymen in the grueling heat of a South Korean summer.

If one had asked, on June 24: "Should the United States fight an infantry war in Korea?", he could easily have received the response: "With whom and with what?"

Neither the Army nor the Marine Corps was ready to fight the 70,000 hardy North Koreans in the seven North Korean divisions which attacked across the 38th Parallel. An apathetic American postwar attitude and Harry Truman's friend, Louis Johnson, had seen to that.

Within 90 days, however, the situation had radically changed.

Within hours of the North Korean invasion it became obvious that the South Korean could not hold. They literally had no weapons capable of stopping the North Koreans' T-34 Russian tanks. They had little artillery and no air force. While they had nearly as many men under arms as the North Koreans, their rifles and machine guns were no match for Russian tanks and modern artillery.

But Truman was too feisty to ignore the challenge. The recently-enacted United Nations Charter was worth fighting for; its principle that no nation should ever again be allowed to take the territory of another by force had been achieved only after 4,000 years of warfare culminating in the 50 million deaths of World War II.

On June 27, Truman ordered American air and Naval units to support the retreating South Koreans.

The Russian U.N. Security Council delegate, Jacob Malik, had been boycotting the U.N. and was back in Moscow when the Council convened in emergency session on the same day. In his absence, with the Soviet veto power unable to be exercised, the Council voted unanimously to request each member of the United Nations to furnish "all necessary assistance" to South Korea in order to repel the North Korean invasion.

On June 30, Truman authorized General MacArthur to send U. S. ground troops to Korea. As the South Koreans continued to flee the rapidly-advancing North Koreans, elements of the 24th Division met the enemy for the first time on July 5 on the road below Suwon.

Meanwhile, the Marine Corps' two highest ranking officers, Commandant Clifton B. Cates and Lieutenant General Lemuel B. Shepherd, Jr., had asked the Joint Chiefs of Staff for permission to call up the Marine Corps Reserve. The Chiefs, still looking to the Corps' ultimate dissolution by their boss, Harry Truman, refused.

Nevertheless, alert orders went out from Headquarters Marine Corps to California to prepare to send the 5th Marines and supporting air and other units to the Far East. This force, to be called The First Provisional Marine Brigade, started forming up on July 7. On July 10, FMF Commander, Lieutenant General Shepherd and his operations officer, Colonel Krulak, flew to Japan to call on General MacArthur at his headquarters in Tokyo. The 5th Marines were now commanded by Lt. Col. Ray Murray.

By then, it had become apparent that the U. S. Army troops, fed piecemeal into the path of the onrushing North Koreans, were being slaughtered.

Shepherd and Krulak, mindful of MacArthur's successful use of the First Marine Division at Cape Gloucester in World War II, allowed to the Supreme Commander that if MacArthur could convince the President to override the Joint Chiefs and order a call-up of Marine reserves, they could give him a Marine brigade in two weeks and a division in six.

MacArthur jumped at the chance and agreed to call the President. He was already thinking of a counterstroke amphibious landing, to recapture Seoul and break the back of the advancing North Koreans.

Truman might not like the Marines, but when General MacArthur requested mobilization of its Reserve, Truman acted swiftly. The arrival of elements of three of the Army's four divisions in Japan had not materially slowed the North Koreans, and it seemed highly possible that the North Koreans would drive the U. S. and U. N. right off the Asian mainland in a matter of weeks.

On July 19, the President approved mobilization of the 138 Marine ground reserve units, and on the 22nd, the Corps' air reserve units as well. Within 15 days, all Marine ground reserve units and nine fighter squadrons had been ordered to active duty. Meanwhile, the 1st Provisional Brigade and supporting air units had boarded ships by July 14 and headed to the Far East. Their fighting edge consisted of the six rifle companies, averaging perhaps 200 men each. The Brigade landed in Pusan on August 2nd. By August 8th, Marines summoned from all over the world were commencing to load aboard ships to form the two additional rifle regiments, the 1st and 7th Marines, which would shortly make up the First Marine Division.

The Marine Brigade was thrown immediately into a fire- brigade role, being rushed to various break-through points on the shrinking Pusan Perimeter. On three separate occasions in four weeks, the six Marine rifle companies with supporting tanks and artillery battled the heat and the North Korean advance to a standstill, holding the line at critical terrain features and providing a rock-hard basis for defense by adjoining Army troops.

By August 15 the tide had begun to turn and there was hope that the North Korean advance could be stemmed. Back home, however, Truman's underlying hostility to the Marine Corps had not been dissipated by the Brigade's successes.

Stung by a letter from a conservative Republican Congressman, Carl McDonough of California, who pointed to the Corps' illustrious history and suggested that the Commandant of the Marine Corps be made a member of the Joint Chiefs of Staff, Truman fired off a typical salty letter. It read:

"My Dear Congressman McDonough: I read with a lot of interest your letter in regard to the Marine Corps. For your information the Marine Corps is the Navy's police force and as long as I am President that is what it will remain. They have a propaganda machine that is almost equal to Stalin's.

"Nobody desires to belittle the efforts of the Marine Corps but when the Marine Corps goes into the Army it works with and for the Army and that is the way it should be.

"I am more than happy to have your expression of interest in this naval military organization. The Chief of Naval Operations is the Chief of Staff of the Navy of which the Marines are a part.

"Sincerely yours,
"Harry S. Truman."

McDonough did not hesitate to make the letter public, and on August 29, as Pohang fell to the North Koreans, and fears rose that Pusan was next, a veritable fire storm of Marine Corps advocacy and anti-Truman oratory broke out across the nation.

Typical front page news stories from the Seattle Post-Intelligencer are shown at the end of this chapter.

But if his friend Louis Johnson had shared Truman's unflattering view of the Marine Corps, the President had another old friend from the A.E.F. who speedily learned otherwise. Distrusting MacArthur and the usual Army channels of communications, Truman saw fit to assign his second World War I pal, retired Major General Frank E. Lowe, to visit Korea and report back to him why the Army was doing so badly and the Marines so well.

Lowe first attached himself to Chesty Puller's First Marine Regiment when it landed at Inchon. Puller personally led his regiment on the rough road to retake Seoul. What Lowe saw he wrote about directly to Truman.

Later Puller's First Marines held the perimeter at Koto-ri, permitting the entire Division to battle its way back from the Chosin Reservoir.

Lowe's reports may have done a little to alter the President's historic understanding of the relative merits of the Army and the Marine Corps.

Extracted from the Truman Library in Missouri, they are published in full as follows:

"SUBJECT: 1st Marine Division in Korea

MEMO: To the President

1. On my itinerary, TAB, you will note that a great portion of my time in Korea has been spent with the 1st Marine Division, and I feel that this special memorandum regarding the activities of the 1st Marine Division in Korea is in order.

2. Having always desired to participate and observe an all Navy-Marine Corps amphibious operation, I decided to accompany the Marines on the Inchon invasion. Departing Pusan, Korea, on the twelfth of September we proceeded for Inchon Korea, arriving on the fifteenth of September. The actual invasion procedure and success you are already aware of, but I would like to re-emphasize that the co-ordination of the Navy and the Marines during the "off loading" and "ship to shore" assault was outstanding. The teamwork involved left little to be desired, or improved. Once the Marines were ashore, the operation proceeded rapidly and efficiently, each and every member of the Corps knowing what to do, and how to do it. It proved concisively to me that the U. S. Marine Corps training programs excels the Army Basic Training Programs.

3. The close cooperation and co-ordination existing between officers and enlisted men exemplified the true "Espirit De Corps" that is so easily recognizable in a Marine unit.

4. I stayed with the Marines until the conclusion of the Inchon-Seoul operation October 6, 1950, at which time I was with Colonel Homer Litzenberg, Jr., and his 7th Marine Regiment in Uijongbu. This operation was indeed the telling blow of our victory in the first war, which ended on 30 October 1950.

5. In late November and December 1950, I again visited the 1st Marine Division. At this time they were located in the treacherous Hagerru-ri Kotori, Pusan Reservoir Area. It was during this phase of the operation that the Chinese Intervention came into being. By infiltration techniques, and mass technique, the Marines were surrounded and in some instances cut off from their supporting elements. On 5 December 1950, Major General Oliver P. Smith, Commanding General, published his "attack in a new direction" operation order (see TAB). At no time did the Marines retreat or withdraw during this operation, they continually fought their way out of the trap, and effectively destroyed the combat effectiveness of (2) two Chinese armies. Their casualty toll was heavy, primarily due to frostbite. But they succeeded in carrying their wounded and dead with them, and did not lost any of their equipment. Indeed, a magnificent performance.

Conclusions

1. <u>The 1st Marine Division is without a doubt the best fighting unit in Korea today.</u>

2. The success of the Hungnam Evacuation in late December 1950 was primarily due to the ability of the 1st Marine Division to fight their way out of the Fusan Reservoir Area with the minimum number of casualties, and with complete co-operation and co-ordination with the Army divisions in the same sector.

3. The ability of the Marines to maintain a fighting force regardless of the number of replacements received definitely proves the value of their basic training, and our Army would do well to study their training ideas and techniques.

4. Future amphibious operations should be an all Navy function.

5. Tactical air support provided by the Marine air wings for the Marine ground units is precisely the answer to the controversial air support of advancing ground units, problems. The teamwork and co-ordination exhibited in Korea has certainly proven the value of this type training.

Recommendations

1. The U. S. Marine Corps strength be re-established and (3) three full war time strength divisions be activated and be assigned the mission of readiness for aggression against the United States.

2. Marine basic training ideas and techniques be studied by the Army, and similar procedures adopted in Army basic training programs.

3. A study of Marine "strength and fire power" within a Marine Division be made, and incorporated into our Army Divisions.

4. Future amphibious operations be a Navy affair complete, from the planning stage to the securing of the beachhead.

Frank E. Lowe
Maj. Gen., USAR"

The White House
Washington

"PERSONAL
EYES ONLY

April 30, 1951

Dear Mr. President:

The purpose of this letter is to confirm to you in writing certain statements I made to you verbally on Tuesday, April 24th, and to give you, condensed as much as possible, certain of my reactions.

(a) Throughout this tour of active duty I have obeyed your orders implicitly and have at no time exposed myself in a reckless manner.

(b) At all times while on duty with the ground and Naval forces, an officer wearing two stars or more has been ahead of me, with me, or immediately behind me. In the matter of air reconnaissance flights over enemy territory I took such flights only when I deemed it necessary in carrying out my mission. Furthermore, general officers of the Air Forces flew repeatedly on similar missions.

(c) I am in no way responsible for some of the wild tales about me that have come to your attention. I do not wish to appear suspicious nor cynical, but War Department attitude toward me in certain channels entitles me to the opinion that said channels will be both relieved and pleased at my relief from extended active duty—and well they may be. All through the summer, fall, and winter the going was tough and hard; it grew tougher and harder in the winter and the outcome was none too sure. Association and force of example are powerful factors, especially in the Army. It did no harm for a two-star General to be seen at the front, especially when said General was known to be "serving in executive capacity to the President." You know there can be no secrets from the soldier. I am not ashamed of the fact that I came to be known as the G. I.'s friend. Never did I coddle them nor support their gripes, rather the reverse, and I choose to believe that it had some good effect; at least I was told so repeatedly by Division Commanders and their subordinates. Also, all concerned did not miss the point that their Commander-in-Chief had sufficient interest in them to have a subordinate in the field. I carried a photostatic copy of your letter of instructions with my identification card and showed it as rarely as I did my original Truman Committee identification card and only when official procedure required it. Very, very few saw it. Whether those who saw it told about it, I do not know. At first my position was a bit difficult, but it did not take long for all concerned to learn that this executive had been thoroughly indoctrinated in the philosophy that an executive must be committed to anonymity and to keep eyes and ears open and his mouth shut.

I have seen many things on land, on sea, and in the air that have inspired me greatly; I have seen other things that have irked me no end; and I have seen things that disgusted me. Almost all of the last have been in the Army and <u>not</u> in combat.

When you sent me abroad in August I told you I had one mission of my own, to wit, to learn if we were still continuing to breed young Americans with guts and virility. The answer is an unqualified "yes." Our young soldiers are superb and our Marines are both superior and supreme. It's all a matter of training. Every Marine receives the same basic training, (I believe it is now 14 weeks). Consequently he is always a Marine. Furthermore, and regardless of whether they are on duty on land, on the sea, or in the air, they are required constantly to take refresher training to the end that they will know their weapons and will be able to fight on the ground. I could expand this theme with a dozen pertinent examples of the wisdom of such training. In the Army this was not true. In the occupational forces in Japan it is my opinion that just one Division, the First Cavalry Division, was kept at a high standard of field training and this because of the superior ability of the Division Commander, Maj. Gen. Hobart R. Gay. Sometime I hope for the opportunity to tell you more about this officer and his Division. Suffice it to say that he has had more actual battle days of experience than any officer now on duty in the Army and I challenge anyone to disprove this statement. Presently he is a temporary Major General and, in my opinion, he should have been wearing three stars long ago and hence be eligible for selection upward to the top. He is not a graduate of the U. S. M. A. In my judgment, the lack of a coordinated, axiomatic program of basic training for everyone entering the Armed Forces, especially the Army, is tragic. I have seen the wisdom of such program in the Marine Corps. I have seen how it permits the Marines to keep a Division at full war strength and to adopt a sane, sensible, and axiomatic program of relief and rotation, something the Army has not done and cannot do, in spite of their statements to the contrary, if we are to maintain a competent fighting force in the battle lines for the next few months. This is another point I would welcome opportunity of discussing with you.

You will recall my return to the States in August to stress to you the necessity for (a) replacements and (b) intensive training for all personnel committed to overseas assignment. The cold facts are that the Army has sent six Infantry Divisions into Korea. Not one of them went to Korea at TO and E strength; not one of them had attained TO and E strength up to the day I left Korea and I doubt if they reach this strength unless there is a great slacking of hostilities.

Our triangular Divisions call for a personnel strength of 18,834, if I remember my figures correctly. They are heavily mechanized, (over-mechanized, in my opinion). Hence you will note that the total TO and E strength of our Divisions was roughly 114,000. On or about February 1st of 1951, after we had been fighting for eight months, we were 40,000 short in replacements and very nearly, if not quite, 70% of the replacements we were receiving in Japan were MOS'd for service, not combat, assignment. This figure had to be reversed by additional training in Japan or else, as was frequently the case, send the soldiers to the front with inadequate schooling and physical training.

Another point that is important, when G-1 tells you that this or that Infantry Division is up to, say, 80% of its TO and E strength, he is saying automatically that the rifle companies, the men who do the fighting, are at 50% to 60% strength. Also, you will never convince me, based on my eight months' experience, that the number of officers and men behind the Divisions are not wholly disproportionate to the number of men on the firing line. Just read the record and compare the figures. Figures never lie, even though liars will figure, is an axiom that still holds true.

No, Mr. President, the old Army that trained you and trained me, the Army we respected and loved, is dead. Make no mistake about it, it is well nigh as extinct as the dodo. All that's left of it are a few old-timers, exemplified by most of the Division Commanders and Assistant Division Commanders in Korea, who were youngsters in our war, (World War I), plus some youngsters whom they have indoctrinated into a primary love of field command rather than staff assignment.

What is the reason for this situation? Well, in my opinion it is because we have allowed Staff to become the master rather than the servant of command. We are bogged down with Staff and Bureaus. There can be no higher accolade for an officer than his ability to care for, train and lead successfully in battle, his fellow citizens. TI and E, (Troop Information and Education); Career Management, (I call it "Career Manglement); and MOS, (Military Occupation Specialty) innovations are not calculated to the basic "how Jerry gets his oats" training that you and I received. For eight months I sought diligently, but never found, an MOS that specified the soldier as being an expert with a rifle and bayonet. Also, I take a very dim view of this Special Services activity as I saw it overseas and <u>especially</u> in the front lines where the need for it and the almost complete lack of it were all too evident; too much in the rear and not enough at the front.

Please understand that I found much to inspire and thrill me no end. The initiative, endurance, and sheer guts of our soldiers, sailors, marines, and air men—enlisted, non- commissioned, and commissioned—at the front beggars description. <u>The First Marine Division is the most efficient and courageous combat unit I have ever seen or heard of.</u> First it was Brigade, down on the South front in August, then it moved into Inchon as a Division and an expanded Division at that. It maintains its strength at 105% of TO and E and is an expanded force of over 25,000. It has its own transportation, engineer, medical and air units. As long as that Division is let alone, not emasculated or broken up, the enemy may annihilate it, (I doubt it), but they will never overrun it. Sometime I would like to tell you the particulars of this Division and what it did in Korea, also what happened to it and the part it played in saving the military situation time and again.

This Division is commanded by an officer, Maj. Gen. Oliver P. Smith, who is one of the very ablest Division Commanders I have ever known and he should, in my opinion, have been a Corps Commander long since. His subordinates, within their respective spheres, are equally superior. He has our concept of the basic fundamentals of leadership, namely, that there is as much obligation for loyalty downward as their is upward, and the higher you go the greater that obligation.

In the Far East Command our Quartermaster Corps, (Brig. Gen Hastings); our Signal Corps, (Brig. Gen Back); our Ordnance Department, (Brig. Gen. Niblo); and our Medical Department, (Maj. Gen. Hume) have been superb. Under present War Department policy these agencies do not, in my opinion, have authority commensurate with their responsibility and, lacking this authority, it is axiomatic that they cannot be held responsible. There is far too much interference and dictation in the conduct of their affairs by Logistical Command and G-4 authorities to suit me. The officers at the head of these Services are expert in their respective lines and all too frequently those over them are not so qualified. I would be very glad to amplify this statement to you if you wish. I have many examples to sustain my point.

U. S. NAVY. Our Navy in the Far East is superb and is under the command of one of the finest and ablest gentlemen I have ever met. Admiral Joy is a "team" officer who has the complete confidence, affection and respect of his officers. I shall never forget the kindness and courtesy extended to me by Admiral Joy and his subordinates. In all eight months I found just one sour note in the Navy and by keeping my eyes and ears open and my mouth shut I found that my estimate of this particular officer was not without foundation. Below the surface, on the surface, and in the air our Navy has been superb and superior. Also in the Navy I found the closest of harmony and cooperation between Washington and Tokyo. Incidentally, you may like to know that your subordinate has been made an honorary member of the crew of the USS VALLEY FORGE.

U. S. AIR FORCE. All that I said about Admiral Joy applies to General Stratemeyer. He is a tireless worker, kindly, considerate, and a natural leader. Above all, he is a team player. You may rest assured that perfect unification has been accomplished in the Far Eastern Command. General Stratemeyer has a superb staff—able, experienced airmen and every one of them a field soldier. In the field he had Lt. Gen. Earle Partridge, commanding his Fifth Air Force; Maj. Gen. Emmett J. O'Donnell, Jr., commanded his Bomber Group; and Maj. Gen. Tunner commanded his Air Transport. They were, and are, top superior officers. Had it not been for our Air Force, we would never have gotten into Korea in the first place, nor would we have been able to stay their five minutes.

The first time I ever met General Ridgeway was on the Harriman mission in August and I did not see him again until I met him in Seoul, soon after he assumed command of the Eighth Army. I shall never forget his unfailing courtesy and his many kindnesses to me. He has my unqualified admiration and respect. Just the same, and with utmost frankness and in spite of his present assignment, I cannot feel that he, Admiral Joy, and General Stratemeyer should be preferred, one over the other, in promotion to four-star rank. All are highly deserving and, again in my opinion, for the good of the Services and in the interests of unification, promotion should go to all three.

HELICOPTERS. I cannot close this memorandum without special mention of this craft. Recalling the days of our old Committee, you will be pleased to know that the helicopter has come into its own and ground, sea, and air forces now realize the merits and the value of this type of craft. The Marines pioneered in the use of the helicopter in Korea; the Navy now carries them as standard equipment on all aircraft carriers and other ships and ground installations as well; the Air Forces are using them extensively and so are the ground forces. Helicopters are used for transportation, communications, observation, reconnaissance, and especially for the evacuation of wounded. In this last item they have accomplished miracles in rescuing wounded who would have unquestionably died had it not been for helicopter evacuation. In future wars I believe they will very nearly displace the wheeled ambulance on the ground. I saw many instances of remarkable rescue work accomplished by means of these craft and several times I evacuated wounded in the helicopter which I was using. You will remember Commander Frank A. Erickson, USCG, who commanded the Helicopter School at Floyd Bennett Field and from which I graduated in the second class. The Air Forces were having some operational difficulties with helicopters last year. I told Maj. Gen. Crabbe, then Deputy Chief of Operations, USAF, that I was quite sure he could solve his operational difficulties if he could borrow Commander Erickson, then on duty with the Navy at Pawtuxet. Commander Erickson came to Japan and Korea and now the Air Force has as high a regard for him as you and I have.

FUTURE NATIONAL SECURITY PROGRAM. In conclusion, you may recall that I have been actively concerned, and interested in, a program calculated for adequate national security since the year 1912. During that period of time I have arrived at certain conclusions and convictions. My experience in the Far East have served to firm-up some of these convictions. If and when appropriate, I would welcome an opportunity of registering my thought with you on this subject. In the meantime, there is one point I wish to stress; I think we should be very, very careful in drawing any over-all conclusions affecting our national security program by reason of our experiences in Korea; too many factors were distorted and out of proportion over there to permit of drawing logical over-all conclusions.

Yours faithfully,

FRANK E. LOWE
Maj. Gen., USAR

Honorable Harry S. Truman, President
The United States of America
Washington, D.C."

It may have been happenstance that Harry Truman's old friend was able to watch two of the most famous Marine Corps combat leaders in history, Chesty Puller and O. P. Smith, fight their way to Seoul and then to the Chosin Reservoir and back, but there can be no doubt that the words of this old-time Army officer was as great a tribute as the Marine Corps may have ever received.

Not just a tribute, but a reminder to constant attention in peacetime to those principles that every man should be a rifleman, and every unit in good physical condition in peacetime. What the Brigade did at the Pusan Perimeter should stand for all time as an example for every Marine Corps officer, regular and reserve.

Truman Marine Slur Bitterly Protested

League Asks Apology

WASHINGTON, Sept. 5. — (AP) — President Truman today drew a storm of bitter protest from Marine veterans groups and senators by charging that the Marine Corps has a "propaganda machine that is almost equal to Stalin's."

The Marine Corps League called the statement an "insult" and demanded a public apology.

The Marine Corps Reserve Officers Association said it felt the statement must have been a "monumental misunderstanding" on the part of Mr. Truman.

Sentors hopped on Mr. Truman, too.

Typical comments:

Senator Thye (R, Minn.)— "Shocking."

Senator Aiken (R, Vt.)— "Indiscreet, incorrect and uncalled for."

THE LETTER—

One was from Representative McDonough (R, Calif.) He wrote asking the President to name a Marine to the joint chiefs of staff, along with the Army, Navy and Air Corps.

Mr. Truman's reply, dated August 29:

"My Dear Congressman McDonough: I read with a lot of interest your letter in regard to the Marine Corps. For your information the Marine Corps is the Navy's police force and as long as I am President that is what it will remain. They have a propaganda machine that is almost equal to Stalin's.

"Nobody desires to belittle the efforts of the Marine Corps but when the Marine Corps goes into the Army it works with and for the Army and that is the way it should be.

"I am more than happy to have your expression of interest in this naval military organization. The chief of naval operations is the chief of staff of the Navy of which the Marines are a part.

"Sincerely yours,
"Harry S. Truman."

'HE MADE BREAK'—

By coincidence, the Marine Corps League, which has 40,000 members, was gathering here for its annual convention starting tomorrow.

The league had invited Mr. Truman to attend a banquet. He first had accepted, but later had turned it down because of the press of military affairs.

Clay Nixon, Seattle lawyer and commandant of the league, told reporters:

"We feel he (Mr. Truman) should come to the American people and to the Marines, and

MARINE SLUR STIRS STORM

President Rebuked By Veterans, Senators

through our organization he should make an apology.

"We think it is up to him to come to our convention and not for us to go to him asking for any explanation. After all, we are not in the position of a supplaint. He's the one who has made the break."

Nixon pointed out that the league can't speak officially for the Marines. They kept quiet since, after all, Mr. Truman is their commander in chief.

'FEEL BITTER'—

But Nixon said he's sure that every Marine feels "bitter resentment that the blood of the Marines shed from 1775 to today in Korea should be characterized as propaganda."

He said it "is an insult to the Marine Corps which stepped into the breach at this critical time when that service alone was ready for emergency combat despite its inadequate numbers and appropriation."

Nixon told a news conference the Marines have the smallest publicity staff of any service.

He figured that Mr. Truman— an old Army man—still carries some resentment toward the Marines for the front page publicity they have received.

'ILL-TIMED'—

The Marine Corps Reserve Officers' Association was indignant, too.

It got out a three-page statement sprinkled liberally with such expressions as "profound sense of regret," "monumental misunderstandings," "most unfortunate."

"The fundamental tragedy of this ill-timed statement of the President," it said, "is that it is quite obvious that there is no one available in high places to advise the President as to the mission and functions of the Marine Corps.

"It is quite evident that the President's thinking is only a reflection of current Pentagon reactions to the Marine Corps."

The association advanced this conclusion:

"We submit that nothing has so dramatically pointed up the absolute necessity of representation of the Marine commandant on the joint chiefs of staff as this exchange of correspondence and the misunderstanding on which it is so obviously

McDonough Says: 'Unfortunate'

BISMARCK, N. D., Sept. 5.— (AP) — Rep. McDonough (R, Calif.) tonight termed "unfortunate" President Truman's statement the Marine Corps has "a propaganda machine that is almost equal to Stalin's."

The President made the statement in reply to a letter from McDonough suggesting that a Marine be placed on the Joint Chiefs of Staff which included representatives of the Army, Navy and Air Corps. The President also wrote that the Marine Corps is the police force of the Navy.

"This is no time to stir up dissension," McDonough said. "We need unity and that was my main reason for suggesting the Marines be included on the Joint Chiefs of Staff. It was merely a belief on my part that the Marines are entitled to equal recognition because of their fine battle records throughout the years."

McDonough stopped in Bismarck briefly en route to the Hungry Horse Dam project near Missoula, Mont. He is driving with his wife and they expect to arrive in Missoula tomorrow afternoon and inspect the dam.

Some of his constituents, McDonough said, "who might possibly have some indirect connection with the Marine Corps, have written me urging that the Marines be included on the Joint Chiefs of Staff, but no Marine Corps official has in any way inspired my letter."

The articles on these two pages are taken from photocopies of the Seattle Times, *Wednesday September 6, 1950, Vol CXXXIX, No. 6, using parts of the front page and other pages. The front page headline was* **POHANG LOST; REDS AT PUSAN ROAD** *and the articles refer to President Truman's statements concerning the Marine Corps which he made in a letter to Congressman McDonough (then R,-Calif.) dated August 29, 1950. The letter was sent in response to a request by Congressman McDonough that Mr. Truman name a Marine to the joint chiefs of staff. Mr. Truman stated that "the Marine Corps is the Navy's police force . . ." and that ". . . they have a propaganda machine that is almost equal to Stalin's" among other things. Great exception was taken to these comments, since they coincided with the 50% casualties the First Marine Provisional Brigade was taking while literally saving the UN Line at the Naktong Perimeter.*

An Insult To The Marines

PRESIDENT TRUMAN has lowered himself unbelieveably and immeasurably, and quite despicably, in the esteem of the American people by his gratuitous and insulting libel against the United States Marine Corps.

Coming so close upon the heels of his public condemnation of the patriotic acts of the American longshoremen who refused to build the armaments of Soviet Russia by unloading enemy cargoes, this disparagement of a great fighting force leaves the American people with an even deeper sense of shame and humiliation.

What possesses the President, that he speaks so loosely and so readily in this incomprehensible manner—first, of a demonstration of loyalty and devotion to our country that was an inspiration to the American people; and now, of a branch of the armed forces which is steeped in honored tradition and hallowed memory.

President Truman was not content with mere belittlement of the Marine Corps, speaking of it derisively as "the Navy's police force."

He was impelled by some mysterious quirk of mind to speak with utter venom and malice, calling the Marine Corps "a propaganda machine that is almost the equal of Stalin's."

THESE ARE THE MARINES who are since cherished jewels of a proud and grateful country.

These are the Marines who have bled and died on a thousand beaches, and in the bloody mire of battlefields and trenches on every continent.

These are the Marines who have been sent into the desperate Korean warfare within the last few weeks by the order of President Truman himself, and hundreds of them are already dead and many more are the maimed and tortured prisoners of our maniacal Communist enemies.

Many times in our history, the Marines have turned up the light in our dimming lamp of national hope by their dramatic and sacrificial example of patriotic integrity.

TODAY, AS SO MANY TIMES BEFORE, the Marines have been ready to defend America before most of the rest of us, and they are paying with their blood and their lives for the ultimate peace which is the aspiration of us all.

What is President Truman thinking of, that he has only words of contempt and disparagement for fighting men who are traditionally and rightfully honored by all Americans?

Who is he, that he holds in disdain that which America holds in highest pride and honor and affection?

What evil counsel is he listening to, that he offends and cheapens and defames that which America cherishes and loves?

President's Prior Stand On Curtailment Bared

By William P. Flythe
Post-Intelligencer Washington Bureau

WASHINGTON, Sept. 5.—How President Truman tried to curtail the Navy and demote the Marine Corps to a shore patrol in 1947 was revealed today by Former Rep. Walter C. Ploeser of Missouri.

Said Ploeser:

"The President is more intemperate today when he says the Marine Corps has 'a propaganda machine almost equal to Stalin's.'

"But he was impatient with the corps as far back as the fight for armed forces unification.

"His thinking now is the same as his thinking then.

"I am dumfounded."

FIGHTING FORCE—

"The world has never seen a greater fighting force. We should take advantage of that, not belittle it."

Ploeser, a member of the naval subcommittee of the House Appropriations Committee during the unification fight, learned President Truman desired to reduce the Marine Corps to a continental guard, detailed to patroling naval bases and acting as shore police.

He also wanted to take the anti-submarine patrol from the Navy and give it to the Air Force.

"I wrote the President," said Ploeser, "and pointed out that in the continental Army the Marine Corps was the expeditionary force.

"I said that if we went back to tradition we would expand the Marine Corps for our expeditionary force instead of the Army."

IMPATIENT—

The President replied expressing impatience with the corps, said the former congressman. He could not recall the precise content. The letter is in his files in St. Louis.

Ploeser's subcommittee fought President Truman's plan to transfer the Navy's anti-submarine patrol duties to the Air Force.

It put in an item in the appropriation bill for flying "turtles" to enable the Navy to increase its patrol effectiveness.

"I received a letter from James Forrestal, then head of the military establishment," Ploeser recalled. "I don't have the letter handy, but he closed with something like this, 'Thank God for this action. You saved the Navy.'"

Angry Senators Assail Remark On Marine Corps

(Compiled from dispatches of the Associated Press and United Press.)

WASHINGTON, Sept. 5 — A presidential remark that the Marine Corps has a propaganda machine "almost equal to Stalin's" evoked angry senatorial retorts today.

Senator Hickenlooper (R-Iowa) called it an "insult" to the Marines.

He said it was inconceivable to him how the Marines could be mentioned along with Russia's propaganda machine.

"The most corrupt, dishonest and dishonorable propaganda machine the world has ever known is that of Joe Stalin's," Hickenlooper told the senate.

He said it was one of the most "astoundingly insulting letters" ever written about such an organization as the Marines.

"I think every American should take just exception to

Sen. Joseph R. McCarthy (R-Wis.), a Marine Corps veteran of World War II, called the President's statement "a fantastically unpatriotic thing to say about the boys who are dying out there in Korea."

Sen. Edward Thye, (R-Minn.) said the President's letter was "shocking."

Most of the criticism in Congress came from Republicans.

But Senator Kefauver (D-Tenn.), a member of the Senate Armed Services Committee and a leading administration backer, told reporters he thinks it was a "very unthoughtful letter."

Senator Douglas (D-Ill.) told a reporter he had no comment on the matter. He is a World War II veteran of the First Marine Division.

"I am loyal to the President and I am also loyal to the Ma-

Chapter 10

The Wetback's Son
"He'll Do To Take Along"

At the turn of the century, cowboy Eugene Rhodes wrote that the highest accolade which could be said of a man in southwest New Mexico was: "He'll do to take along," whether riding fence, herding cattle or on a posse.

I have known a few such men. In our times of relative ease and comfort, it isn't often, however, that we see that combination of physical stress and challenge which gives us the chance to measure our friends against this standard of the old frontier.

In 60 years of observing friends do extraordinary things, an event which involved performances of quiet excellence by two men many years ago stands out. One acted with true heroism, the other with great common sense. The act of heroism, like most such, received neither public acclaim, nor indeed public knowledge.

In writing about my two friends at this late date, I owe them a double apology, first for not making sure they received proper commendation at the time, and second for embarassing them by comment now, when in old age they have achieved that total success in their professions and community which makes them no longer needful or desirous of public notice.

Somewhere a little over 30 years ago, after a week's work on the San Francisco Peninsula, three young fathers, one doctor, one lawyer and one banker, piled their three oldest sons (average age 6) fly rods and camping gear in the back of a family station wagon and headed north for a long weekend on one of the loveliest fishing streams in California , the Fall River. As on all spring-summer Friday nights, traffic out of the Bay Area towards Lake Tahoe and the High Sierras was heavy, and remained so on the broad freeway across the Sacramento Valley.

My banker friend, son of a Mexican wetback we knew only as "Alphonzo," was driving; the doctor was dozing in the center of the front seat, and the three boys had long since gone to sleep in the back. We were full of warmth and anticipation, the radio was playing softly; everything was well and in its place.

For one reason or another, we missed the Winters' cut-off to the north at the famous Nut Tree Inn. A mile or so later, in the broad grain fields of the valley, as our mistake became clear, we started looking for a road crossing to make a turn-around. It was a starry night, no lights on the highway, save for the headlights of heavy traffic, two full lanes in both directions. A grassy median strip, perhaps 50 feet wide, with a drainage ditch half that width and perhaps 20 feet deep in the middle, divided the east/west lanes.

A sudden cloud of dust swirling toward us on the opposite side of the freeway drew our attention. Suddenly an old car materialized out of the dust, spun off the highway into the median ditch and flipped over onto its back. My friend jammed to a stop on the right shoulder, and wholly on instinct, he and I jumped out and ran across to the median, down the slope to where the battered car was resting wheels up, in high weeds at the bottom of the ditch, with a small trickle of flame starting up from the engine.

My friend wrenched open the front door nearest us, reached down and lifted up an old man who seemed unconscious. We carried him up on to the dirt bank above the ditch, and looked back down at the wrecked car, where the flames were growing around the engine. The old man groaned, and seemed to be saying, "Anna . . . Anna."

My friend ran back down the slope with me following and got down to look inside the car. There was no one in the front seat, and there seemed to be nothing but jumbled cushions in the back seat. The flames were inching back toward the gas tank, and I, for one, was ready to retreat to safety, when my friend insisted on a last look. He pushed halfway into the car and finally located a foot we hadn't seen. He yanked at the foot which was attached to the thick stockinged ankle of an old lady, and we were able to pull her out of the car, although with scant attention to whatever additional injury we caused her in the process. She was unconscious, and remained so as we hauled her up the slope and laid her out beside her husband on the edge of the road where the doctor was now attending her husband. A few seconds later the gas tank, only a few feet away and below us, exploded, turning the car into an inferno.

Only then did we think about the three sleeping boys we had left at the edge of the highway with 60 mile an hour traffic rushing by just inches away. I have always thought that the doctor's coolness, in *not* rushing across the highway to help until he was assured that the boys would stay in the car, was of nearly as much value in the great order of things, and perhaps saved as many lives, as the quick thinking and courage of my friend who undoubtedly saved a woman's life under circumstances where others have received medals for bravery of the highest degree.

A few minutes later, we were back on the long quiet road north, and after a good weekend on the river, returned to our suburban lives and work.

Years later, I tried to find a highway patrolman in the area who could remember the incident, thinking to see my friend receive his proper honor, one of the life-saving medals the Red Cross awards for such action. By then, however, a new highway patrol headquarters served the area, no one could remember which hospital the old couple would have been taken to, and my banker friend had moved on to the highest levels of entrepreneurial capitalism and exclusive suburban living, admired for his leadership in country fox-hunting, business and charitable enterprises. No one would recognize in his current portly affluence a man who in his youth performed as courageous an act as I ever saw amongst the combat Marines of the famous Fifth Marine Regiment in Korea. The doctor likewise lives a quiet and respected existence in another typical American suburban town, his exceptional coolness under fire to await recognition until the next wholly-unexpected emergency or common disaster.

The name of the doctor: William W. Tevis, Atherton, California.

The wetback's son: Albert R. Schreck, Portola Valley, California.

Both will do to take along.

"I never shot at officers. I considered them somewhat harmless."
. . . a Civil War Rifleman

"Someone looked on as more a source of entertainment than an asset: a new second lieutenant."
. . . Charles R. Anderson, *The Grunts*

Chapter 11

Mistakes To Remember

This book of essays, being written primarily for fellow Marines, past and future, would not be complete without a list of the many mistakes I made as a platoon leader and some lessons I learned from those mistakes. Listing them here may conceivably help some second lieutenant in a future conflict, whether it be in Iraq, the Dominican Republic or Afghanistan, to keep a few Marines alive. After 40 years the mistakes are indelibly seared into my memory, far more so than the hazy details of some of the successes the Company enjoyed in the heat and turmoil of our relatively-few days in combat.

The two occasions when I had my weapon on "safe" when coming face to face with an enemy rifleman have already been enumerated. Those were minor, since they involved only my own safety. On other occasions my mistakes endangered others.

The 60mm Mortars

The first two mistakes occurred during my first two weeks in Korea, and were by far the most embarrassing.

The newest second lieutenant is invariably given the smallest unit in a rifle company, the 19-man 60 millimeter mortar section. There's not much for the mortar officer to do if he has a good sergeant, and luckily Charlie Company's mortar sergeant was one of the best, Emery Naboni, a grizzled Vermonter of long experience.

On our very first day in the attack north from Wonju, the rifle platoons were advancing in the low hills on either side of a narrow valley through which ran the road to Hoeng'song. The company headquarters, mortar section and various air and artillery observers moved up the dirt road, somewhat behind the rifle platoons. There was some snow on the ground, but it was being turned into slush by intermittent showers.

Ahead of us was a low hill. By some quirk of fate Captain Jones and I reached its crest before the rifle platoons on either flank. There were some unfamiliar hissing sounds which, because of Jones' reactions, I took to be hostile bullets. Beyond the hill, perhaps 800 yards away, was a small village. The village appeared deserted save for a few Chinese snipers whose firing continued. At that range they weren't very accurate. Jones calmly stepped back over the brow of the hill, turned to me and said, "Put a marking round into that village." As the lead company, we had a flight of four Marine Corsairs overhead, and the Air Observer was already setting up his "Angry 9" radio transmitter to call in the strike.

Too late, I realized that I had forgotten the details of the two-hour class back at Quantico on how to give the fire order for 60 mm mortars. Panicked, I looked helplessly at Naboni, who quietly said to one of the mortar squad leaders, his mortar already in place, base plate well set and the tube mounted, "Direction 20 degrees, Range 800, one round WP" (white phosphorous). The gunner made some adjustments at the tube, took a patch or two off the tail fins of a 60mm round handed to him by one of the ammo carriers, and dropped in the round. There was a thunk and the round soared off towards the village. It was short, but Naboni adjusted: "Up 200, one round WP."

This time the round landed n the middle of the village and the planes roared in, dropping first a 500 lb. bomb from under one wing, and then a napalm tank from the other. They then made several runs launching "Tiny Tim" rockets, and finally made four strafing runs with their machine guns.

On their last pass, the First Platoon under Lieutenant Gene Brown moved out across the flats from our right and secured the village without incident, the snipers leaving before the Marines arrived.

Neither Jones nor Naboni said anything, but I had the feeling they were being kind. That evening I asked Naboni for some careful instruction on fire orders.

There was another lesson learned that day. The terrible fire power of our planes had not bothered the Chinese riflemen left behind to slow us down, but the napalm, 500 lb. bombs, rockets and machine gun fire had wreaked terrible havoc with some 85 old people and little children who had hidden beneath the floorboards of their thatch-roofed huts. Our corpsmen spent the better part of the afternoon tending to the wounded civilians.

Two nights later I made another dumb and even more embarrassing mistake, in fact two of them.

After advancing north several miles, the Battalion was ordered to do a right flank and attack to the east, ostensibly to cut off a Chinese supply route.

Snow had fallen and the Company at evening was digging in on the forward slopes of a high and fairly-steep, north-south ridgeline. At dark, with the mortars safely set on firing platforms just behind the crest, laboriously hacked into the frozen ground, a runner came up with the word that I was wanted back at the company CP.

It took me what seemed like an hour to stumble down the hill in the dark through the trees and snow, to find a squad tent set up at the bottom. Pushing through the flap, I found the headquarters group were already in their down sleeping bags, an oil stove giving off some warmth. I timidly announced my presence and the Executive Officer, Spike Schening, lying on his back, his bag zipped up tight, with only his nose protruding, grumbled, unzipped the bag a few inches and produced a crumpled piece of paper and a flashlight. He grunted at me and read from the paper:

"Congratulations.

Daughter born February 16, 8-1/2 pounds. Mother fine.

Grandmother"

I don't remember saying anything more than "Thanks, Spike" and starting back up the hill. It must have taken an hour and a half to get back up the mountain in the deep snow to the mortar position. Everybody was in their bag, save one man on watch. I found my pack, but the idea of carving out a sleeping platform on the reverse side of that steep slope in the snow was not inviting. I went up to the top of the ridge, perhaps five yards above the mortars and rolled out my bag on the narrow crest. I can't remember feeling any great exultation over the privilege of having fathered my first child, Nancy, born eight days earlier, the same day we had landed in Korea. I was too tired and cold.

Climbing those steep slopes was not easy for newly-arrived replacements. We weren't in shape, and the combination of wearing three thicknesses of clothing, long johns, two pair of pants, sweatshirt, dungaree jacket, field jacket and a heavy knee-length parka, plus pack and carbine, were a real test those first few weeks. Lieutenants had it easy. The BAR men, machine gunners, mortar and machine gun ammo carriers were all carrying 10 to 15 pounds more.

Around midnight, I awakened to a new experience, the passing of tracer bullets a few inches over my head. I rolled off the back of the crest in a panic, clawed my way out of the bag and looked back over the hill.

Perhaps 500 yards away in the valley below were the winking flashes of a machine gun, sweeping our ridge back and forth.

This time I was ready. "Direction 270, range 500, one round HE" (high explosive). The round, however, lit at least 500 yards to the right of the still-firing machine gun.

Quickly I shouted "Left 500, one round HE." At least I *think* I said "Left 500." The gunner heard it as *Right* 500. The round landed off in the distance and a howl went up on the radio net: "This is Baker Company. Who the hell is shooting at us?"

Baker was on the forward slopes of the ridge on our right, and it sounded as if the round had hit right in front of their perimeter.

"Left 1000, nine rounds for effect," I ordered, trying to sound calm and with command presence.

The nine rounds, traversing in a box shape, were right on target, but it is probable that the Chinese machine gunners were long gone. No blood was found in the snow the next morning.

That was the last night in the lines that I didn't dig a foxhole. The very next night we learned another hard lesson. We had advanced east to yet another north-south ridgeline, this time overlooking the so-called Chinese supply road to the south.

There were some long-range exchanges of rifle fire, but no casualties. That night we dug into a tight company perimeter, two-man foxholes on the forward crest, with a sound-power telephone hooked up to every fifth or sixth foxhole.

We were standing a 25% watch, one man awake in every other foxhole and every 15 minutes, each of eight forward posts were supposed to check in. The company CP and mortars were perhaps fifty yards behind the forward positions, back on the reverse slope.

I had the CP telephone watch at midnight, and everyone checked in. "Post No. 1, OK," "Post No. 2, OK," and down the line.

There was a snow blizzard in progress.

At 12:15, one of the posts didn't report. "Post No. 5," then silence. Finally "Post No. 7, OK." Captain Jones organized a fire team, and we went forward, somewhat cautiously, to the silent Post No. 6.

We found a sad sight. In the swirling snow there were a lot of footprints, and 10 yards down the slope an empty sleeping bag. One Marine was sleeping at the bottom of the two-man hold; his buddy's boots were in the hole with him.

It was easy to visualize the cold and miserable Marine, his sleeping bag pulled up around his neck, the sound power phone at one ear, sitting on the edge of his foxhole, shivering in the snowstorm and waiting to be relieved at the end of his two-hour watch. A hardy Chinese patrol, watching where the forward holes had been dug the afternoon before, had patiently crept up, and probably were just below the foxhole when the sentry called in his 12 midnight report. They then moved up and snatched him, leaving his buddy sleeping at the bottom of the hole and with no notice to the sleeping men in the foxholes 10 or 12 yards on either side.

Without boots, no one expected the captured Marine to survive. His name was not among those returned when the war ended 2-1/2 years later.

From that point on, platoon leaders checked each foxhole at least twice every night, and whenever the enemy was nearby, the watch was set at 50%, one man awake in every foxhole.

Custer's Regiment, The Seventh Cavalry

Gene Brown was rotated home in early March and I moved up to the exalted position of platoon leader of the First Platoon, still fairly heavily made up of veterans of the Inchon-Seoul and Chosin Reservoir campaigns. Luckily, the platoon sergeant, Sergeant Caret, was a solid veteran who saw to it that I got through most of the rest of the month without endangering myself or others too seriously.

The Chinese were continuing to slowly withdraw northwards towards the Soyang River with the Marine regiments cautiously advancing, two regiments up, one back, two battalions up, one back, and each rifle company alternating between the forward advance and being back in reserve.

There was a lot of patrolling, and occasional fire fights with Chinese patrols as winter turned into spring, and at Easter the Battalion found itself dug in on a fairly-high east-west ridge line northeast of Hong'chon. Three days later on March 28, we got a taste of how lucky we were to be Marines. That day, Charlie Company was moved forward to occupy Hill 663, located on the extreme left flank of the Division boundary, there to tie in with the famous 7th Cavalry Regiment of the First Cavalry Division.

The 7th was Custer's regiment of Custer's Last Stand fame at the Battle of the Little Big Horn. They wore a yellow patch with a black diagonal stripe with a horse's head, and it seemed an historic event when I met their lieutenant at the top of 663 to work out our night defensive positions. I was no admirer of General Custer, but I had studied the battle as a youth. The names of Captain Benteen, Major Reno and Sitting Bull were household words, and the 7th Cavalry a title worthy of awe.

Hill 663 was the commanding terrain feature of the whole area. It was a triangular mountain, with three ridges at almost equal 120° angles, one running due north, one southeast and one southwest. The only dangerous avenue of approach was from a saddle in the ridge to the north.

Going by "the book" as taught at both Quantico and West Point, it was agreed between me and the 7th Cavalry lieutenant that the unit boundary would be to the left of 663 itself, with my platoon having a machine gun on either side of the nose and several foxholes on the forward slope of the southwestern ridgeline. The platoon line extended perhaps 200 yards down the southeastern ridge line, with the rest of the Company to the right.

We had plenty of time left in the day to dig in and camouflage each foxhole, and because of the unknown strength and proximity of the Chinese in the wooded ridges stretching north to the Soyang, we set a 50% watch. Because my platoon had by far the hardest position to defend, the Company machine gun officer put four of the Company's six machine guns in my position.

Captain Jones and Spike Schening came up to inspect the line and pronounced themselves satisfied with the placing and camouflage of each foxhole, the fresh dirt at the front parapet disguised with weeds or grass to avoid glinting in the moonlight, and some foliage behind so that an enemy creeping uphill would not be able to note the distinctive shape of a Marine helmet on the skyline. Our practice was four grenades and the occupants' two bayonets set out on the forward parapet of each foxhole. Given time, we could string empty ration cans with a few pebbles in them on communications wire 20 yards or so down the slope, sometimes with an illumination grenade as well. Barbed wire was not available in those days, and our battalion did not follow a practice of setting out live grenades in front of our lines. If was too easy to trip one by mistake.

In any event with darkness falling and warm with the satisfaction of having Jones' and Schening's rare praise for a well-prepared defense position, I set off to check how well my left flank foxholes were tied in with the Army's.

My last hole on the left was perfectly-positioned. It protected the machine gun's position at the left of the nose, and I started down the military crest of the Army's ridge. 10 yards, no foxhole. 20, 30 yards, still no sign of either foxholes or soldiers. I moved up on the crest of the ridge and finally, at least 100 yards from my position, found a squad of soldiers, eight already in their sleeping bags on top of the ridge, with one man on watch.

It was pitch black and I almost walked on him before he challenged me.

It brought to mind the last time we had seen an Army squad in their sleeping bags, nine men frozen beneath a bridge on the road to Hoeng'song, one shot while on watch and eight bayonetted while they slept. The whole company had walked by them in the snow in late February and said a quiet thanks for the 25% and 50% watches demanded by Jones and Schening.

The sentry woke his squad leader at my request, and I learned that no foxholes had been dug, and that the next squad was 100 yards further down the ridge, also standing a one in nine watch.

I asked where his officer was, and he said: "Down at the bottom of the hill. That's where he stays." It seems that everyone had had hot chow earlier at the base of the hill and that that company, at least, wasn't accustomed to digging foxholes.

I went back to our position and pulled our two machine guns on the right flank out of line, placing them on either side of the Army's ridge pointing *down* the ridge into the Army's position.

If the Chinese overran the Army, they at least wouldn't find it easy to roll up our flank. My own foxhole was just on the reverse slope of 663, now with four machine guns within fifty yards, covering both the Company's front and left flank.

The next morning, up the Army's ridge came a Major, a Captain and several lesser ranks. They took one look at the two machine guns covering them as they approached and the Major gave me a royal chewing-out. I sent for help and Captain Jones and Spike Schening came up, sizing up the situation at a glance. In his gentle way, Jones explained to the Major how the Marines did things and would he please forgive our quaint ways. As the Army officers departed, somewhat appeased but still in high dudgeon, Schening gave me a wink and said I had done just right.[1]

The Man in the Bearskin Hat

I was to make a serious mistake the next day, however, one that would draw a rare admonition from Captain Jones.

On the night of the 29th of March, my platoon was ordered to leave our machine guns and packs behind and move at night many miles north up the main north-south ridge line, almost to the Soyang River. Just short of the highest peak on the ridge, overlooking the Soyang, we were to turn right and move down a finger ridge to a point overlooking a small village known as Anhyon-ri. It was hoped we might garner a prisoner or two to learn what the Chinese were doing.

For the previous week, our patrols on the valley floor had been approaching Anhyon-ri from the south, sometimes getting in fire fights and sometimes not. Intelligence reports were received indicating that the Chinese remained south of the Soyang in small units and were busily engaged in ransacking the rice and other food stuffs from the remaining farmers and small villages in the valley, using Anhyon-ri as a base.

Our job was to get *behind* Anhyon-ri and try to catch the rice-gatherers in an ambush.

The Platoon departed shortly after midnight and found a fairly good trail along the ridge, reaching the turning point just before dawn and moving down the wooded finger-ridge to the designated blocking position, perhaps 300 yards west of the village and 50 meters higher in elevation. As dawn broke we were in a perfect ambush position, in low brush, each rifleman and BAR man prone, in an arc perhaps 150 yards from end to end. About half of the village was in our view, the other half shielded by the toe of the ridge.

To the north, another finger ridge like our own was 600 or 700 yards away, with rice paddies in

---

[1] The 7th Cavalry got away with their lax security, but in late May we were to see the tragic results of a similar failure of command in the 38th Infantry Regiment of the Army's Second Division. The regiment fortified the low ground, but only outposted the commanding peak in an area north of the Hong'chon River. The Chinese overran the outpost and swept down the ridge. Moving through the area on May 23, we found dozens of Army bodies. An Army major in pajamas lay dead in his tent in what must have been a battalion or regimental CP. That night a straggler from the 38th Infantry came into our perimeter. He had been hiding from the Chinese for four days. He said something we never forgot: "Thank God I'm with the Marines and we're on the high ground."

between. To the south there was a similar but lower ridge some 400 yards away, again with rice paddies in between.

Shortly after dawn, we were privileged to see a rare sight. Plodding out from the village at the base of our ridge, went a column of Chinese, a bag of rice on each man's back. They were headed diagonally up towards the finger ridge to the north, the nearest man 300 yards away.

We passed the word for "the book" solution; our left squad to take the furthest one-third of the line, the middle squad the middle third, and the right-hand squad the third closest to the village.

Waiting until there were at least fifty men in sight, at roughly five yard intervals, I gave the word to open up. For a few minutes it was a ball. I remember ruing the fact that we had not brought along the machine guns. It was fairly long-range shooting, but a few men were dropped, and quite a few dropped their bags and ran back into the village. Those furthest away kept plodding, however, and suddenly, into view on the opposite ridgeline, came an impressive, unusually-tall figure, 600 or 700 yards away. Fully silhouetted in the morning light, he stalked up and down the ridgeline, shouting and exhorting the rice-bearers. I took a look at him through the field glasses and saw that he was wearing what looked to be a Russian bearskin hat and carrying what looked like a Marine Corps swagger stick. We had all heard of the political commissars rumored to be attached to the Chinese units.

The Commissar, if that was what he was, certainly had no fear. I think every Marine on our line forgot our carefully-laid fire discipline to take a shot at this commanding Mongol leader. Even our attached S-2 scout, Whit Moreland, later to win the Congressional Medal of Honor posthumously, asked for my carbine to try his luck.

There was no luck. Our line was squeezing off aimed shots much as at the rifle range at Quantico or Camp Pendleton, but nothing fazed the man in the bearskin hat.

I raged and stormed at my squad leaders, but to no avail. Rice bearer after rice bearer plodded up, over and out of sight as our bullets kept kicking up dust at the feet of the pacing commissar. Finally, when his last man was over the hill, he waved at us and departed.

It was a shameful failure of leadership on my part. I had allowed the platoon to expend at least half of our ammunition, there were a few men down and a lot of rice bags out in the fields, but no prisoners. We now began to take some fairly heavy return fire from the village below as well as from above us on the finger ridge we had come down an hour or so before.

We had stirred up a hornet's nest. From the volume of fire, it appeared that there might be more Chinese in the village than there were of us. There was certainly a sizable force on the ridge above us to block our return route. There was a big mountain up there called Hu Bong which looked capable of hiding a Chinese division.

Jones asked over the radio if we had taken any prisoners, and I had to confess not only that we hadn't but that I thought it would be the better part of valor not to assault down into the village and try to get some.

We were at least five miles out in front of our lines; there was no help in sight. We couldn't go back up the ridge to our west; our only escape route was across the rice paddies to the south, but this was in full view of the village and its occupants below us. We weren't sure but that there were other Chinese units in that direction. With one or two machine guns the Chinese in the village could have been as lethal to us as we had been to the rice bearers earlier. Luckily we had been subject only to rifle and burp gun fire at that point, neither of which was as effective as our M-1s and BARs.

We moved into a tight platoon perimeter, exchanging occasional fire with the Chinese above and below us. The day wore on and the stalemate remained.

In the middle of the afternoon, we saw what could mean our undoing. A single platoon-sized column of 30 or 40 men came around the base of the ridge line to our right, led by a Korean in the familiar white clothing of a farmer. Through the field glasses, I couldn't tell whether they were Chinese or Americans. We held our fire as the column drew within range of the village below us. If the Chinese welcomed them into the village we had them dead to rights.

As the Korean farmer in the lead got to within 300 yards of the village, the problem was solved. There was a crackle of fire from the village and both the Korean and the lead soldier went down. We opened up on the village and the column hastily withdrew, dragging the dead soldier with them.

We learned later it was yet another misfortune for the ill- fated 7th Cavalry. They were continuing to live up to Custer's legacy.

Their misadventure hadn't helped us much. It had demonstrated, however, that there were no Chinese south of us, and that we had an escape route in that direction if we could get past the people in the village below.

It was getting late in the afternoon and it was a long way back to friends and home.

I finally made the decision to head back to our lines by crossing the rice paddies to the low ridge line to the south.

There were four hundred yards of open fields to cross, but the Chinese riflemen appeared to be running low on ammunition and they weren't all that accurate in any event. If they had machine guns, they hadn't been used, and it was a chance we had to take.

The plan was to have one squad make a run for it, well spread out, while two squads gave covering fire into the village and on the ridge above us. The first squad across would set up a fire base on the far ridge and the second squad cross, followed later by the third. Everything went fine for the first two squads. The M-1s and BARs kept the Chinese pinned down in both directions, return fire was light and no one was hit.

I stayed behind and was the last man at the end of the 3rd squad as we started our run across the open ground.

A few rounds whistled by, but things looked good until we reached and started to pass a single mud-walled, thatch roof hut in the middle of the field. From a small patch of brush at our right, a beautiful ring-necked Chinese pheasant suddenly whirred into the sky to an elevation of perhaps 20 feet, and commenced coasting past us down towards Anhyon-ri.

The Marine running ahead of me was a veteran trooper from Texas I remember only as "Smith," notable chiefly for a walrus mustache and a pearl-handled pistol he insisted on carrying. Smith could not resist his Texas heritage. In front of my horrified eyes, he dropped to one knee and slowly squeezed off a full eight-round clip from his M-1 rifle at the descending pheasant. I grabbed him and yelled, but without result. His last round was into the village itself as the pheasant landed at its edge.

Only then did he get up and resume the foot race to the far ridge, he and I now 200 yards behind the nearest Marine.

We made it over the top and into cover, and I was too exhausted to tell Smith what I thought of him.

Personal Comfort

It took us hours to make the return trip to 663, laboriously climbing several ridgelines en route, but finally just before sunset our position was in sight. There were several footsore and straggling Marines, and the Colonel had promulgated a rule a few days earlier that there would be no cooking fires after sunset, even on reverse slopes.

I looked at how low the sun was, and decided to send those in good shape on ahead to start cooking C-rations so everyone could have hot chow when the stragglers got in.

As the last group of stragglers, duly shepherded by me, made our painful way the last 1,000 yards up to 663, Captain Jones was at the summit watching us come in.

When I arrived, he took me aside, and told me I had committed a grievous error ... that the most vulnerable time for a patrol was on its return, that never, *never* should the platoon be allowed to spread out, that had the Chinese wanted to, the good results of the day could have been wiped out by my putting hot food ahead of safety.

I was chastened and humiliated. His advice turned out to be only too correct. Within days, a platoon patrol from 2/5, similarly strung-out on a similar return to base, had been rushed from a ridge-line by a Chinese unit, cutting the platoon in the middle and causing several casualties. The lesson was clear. Neither food nor comfort was worth endangering your troops.

Nevertheless, only a few weeks later, in June, faced with fording a four-foot deep river at dusk and having the whole platoon spend the night wet, cold and miserable, I made the decision to put them aboard tanks to stay dry. Had the enemy chosen to use its 76mm direct fire artillery as it did only an hour later, that decision too could have gotten a lot of my men needlessly hurt. If lives are at stake, personal comfort should be disregarded.

Respect for Command

In early March while I still had the mortar section, Captain Jones asked me to tour the Company's perimeter with him one morning. It was a quiet day, and the perimeter stretched from some rice paddies, up and around the military crest of a low hill.

Later I realized that Jones was giving me the first lesson in terrain appreciation. He would discuss likely avenues of approach, and then jump into a foxhole, ask me to join him, and point out how different the terrain looked from 6" above the ground in a firing position. Little folds of ground, that standing erect weren't noticeable, could mean life or death to a rifleman by blocking the view to the foxholes on his right and left, or by providing cover in front of him allowing an enemy to creep up into grenade range.

Jones pointed out how even in the most forbidding of ridge lines, there were indentations on the curve of the ridge which could allow an attacker to approach safely in defilade from fire on the crest. Selection of foxhole location, how far out on a nose one had to bend the line, was a crucial decision and one which could only be made by lying prone.

I have never been able to look at hills and valleys since, even on pleasure backpacks in the Sierra, without mentally estimating how I would attack or defend them with a rifle platoon.

But what most stands out in my mind about that morning nearly 41 years ago was the way Jones greeted each Marine, whether sitting in his foxhole, cooking a can of C-rations or cleaning his weapon. To every Pfc, Jones would say "Good morning, McDonald," calling them by name if he knew them, or "Good morning, Marine," if he didn't. He was recognizing them as equals, and they knew it. They were Marines; he was privileged, not ordained, to be their leader. They had their jobs, and if they had done them well, he was humble in their presence. If a rifle wasn't oiled and ready to fire, or the foxhole not clean and defensible, or gear not rolled properly, he would leave them with the impression that he was a little dismayed that their work wasn't quite up to Marine standards. It was clear that he wanted them to be nothing more than good Marines. It was equally clear that those men would do anything he asked, simply because he was a good Marine.

Doing each little thing right was the Marine Corps tradition. If rifles were clean and sighted properly, men were in good physical shape and their gear in order, the big things would take care of themselves. Marines would lead and disciplined Marines would follow orders. The job would get done, whether it was taking a hill, or defending one. It had been done at Guadalcanal and other places; nobody wanted to let the tradition down.

There was a sense of pride from the fire team, up through the squad, platoon and company, that each unit would be the best it could be, the very recruiting slogan the U.S. Army has now adopted in the 1990s.

To be a good rifle platoon leader was the greatest achievement a lieutenant could ever seek. To become a Captain and command a rifle company was the greatest of all ambitions, but somewhere in the indefinite future. Majors and higher officers were thought to be on the road downhill. Generals, other than O.P. Smith and Chesty Puller,[2] were to be distrusted, particularly Army generals. The world began and ended with your fellow Marines in the rifle company.

Sometime on that morning, our unloved battalion commander caught up to us with some instructions for Captain Jones.

Even in the few days I had been with the Company it had become apparent to me that the officers and troops were not happy about the Colonel.

Yet Captain Jones would not hear a word of criticism in his presence. He must have felt the same frustration as the others at some of the more stupid orders the Colonel handed down, but he never said a word and he immediately silenced any expression of resentment on our part.

That morning the Colonel had some project in mind which seemed questionable even to me, and involved some considerable discomfort to the troops which has long since escaped my memory.

Jones tried to politely change the Colonel's mind, but without success. Finally he drew himself up to his full height, saluted smartly, and said "Yes, sir; it will be done."

There was no sarcasm or irony in his words. An order had been given by another Marine and he would carry it out.

He looked me into silence and I thought, "What a great man this is."

A Courtmartial Offense

My worst day in Korea was on June 13th. I had been slightly wounded by 76mm shrapnel on the evening of the 11th, and had seen Chuck Daly and Charlie Bunnell, Charlie Company's other two platoon leaders, wounded and evacuated on the morning of the 12th.

The Colonel ordered me to report to the aid station that morning, and I fell asleep and slept until the following morning.

Around 7:00 a.m., Major Jones, now the S-3, came to wake me up in the native hut where the minor casualties were being treated, and asked me if I would go with him up to where Baker and Charlie Companies were now moving up the final ridges to the Punch Bowl. I scrambled to find a new pair of pants (the shrapnel had taken off the left pantleg) only to run into the Colonel who ordered me to stay at the CP until the doctor checked my leg. It looked bad but the wounds were not serious.

Jones took off with his radioman, and I followed an hour later.

The trip up the ridge was eventful only because I passed a liberated Chinese pony which the ever-resourceful Buzz Lubka of Able Company had impressed into service to carry his extra ammunition.

I finally reached the top of the ridgeline running northwest on which Charlie Company was supposed to be advancing, but it wasn't until around 10:00 a.m. that I caught up with the rear of the Company, slowly moving ahead. The 3rd Platoon was at the rear, led by a new lieutenant I'd never met, then the Company mortars and headquarters. I was moving right along, but didn't recognize anybody except John Goodrich, the XO, and our new CO as I passed alongside the column which was fre-

---

[2]Chuck Daly in April, had to report back to Division headquarters for his physical examination for promotion to First Lieutenant. There he met General Puller.

Daly's account:

"I went from there to a squad tent that was rigged up as a shower where we could drop our filthy uniforms at one end, drown ourselves with all the hot water in the world and then pick up clean dungarees at the other end. While I was taking a lengthy shower a little runt came in who had seen my gear and knew I had come from the front. He made a remark to the effect that everything was very quiet up there. I replied that it was so goddamn quiet that even you rear-echelon geniuses will be visiting us soon. He responded it wouldn't be quiet very much longer. Then a Colonel came in and addressed the runt as "General." I realized that I had been growling at Chesty Puller; therefore, I completed my shower in some haste. The next time I saw him was in May when he visited Charlie Company. He observed that I hadn't had any showers recently."

quently stopping, apparently because of the point's occasional stops. Ahead of the headquarters group, I recognized some Marines from the Second Platoon and realized with a shock that the new CO had put my platoon, the only one without an officer, at the point.

The First Platoon was being led by Corporal Eck and the three squads by Pfcs. They were all good men, but I felt the new CO had no business putting them where they were.

I quickened my pace and finally caught up with a Marine I recognized as one of my men.

At that very moment all hell broke loose.

There came a burst of automatic weapons fire through the trees up the ridge and I hit the deck, literally shaking with fear. Machine gun fire was raking the ridge, knocking bark off the trees, and the leaves off the branches. Luckily, if one lay flat, some sort of rise up ahead caused the rounds to be a foot or so off the ground.

The fire slowed and became sporadic, but I remained frozen to the ground, trying to dig a hole with my nose. I knew I should be moving up to take over the Platoon but I was absolutely terrified and afraid to raise my head. Minutes must have passed, and finally the fire slacked off. I turned my head a little and saw, a few feet to my right, the unmistakable shape of Gunnery Sergeant Kerman, known semi-respectfully as "Beer Belly Kerman, Always In the Rear With the Gear."

Kerman was obviously as scared as I was. I could see him shaking, but he hadn't yet seen me.

The fear that Kerman might see me shaking was even worse than the fear that the machine gun fire would resume. I got up, and crawling by fits and starts finally got to a little swale behind a grassy rise where most of the men of the platoon were fanned out. The ridgeline at that point widened to about twenty yards, and Corporal Eck, Phil Elson, the machine gun section chief and four or five Marines were lying around prone with one body and several wounded. There were others down the steep cliffs on either side.

Eck said, "Man, are we glad to see you, lieutenant," and told me about their situation.

It seemed that the point man, a replacement, had gone over the grassy rise, only to be riddled by fire from at least four automatic weapons emplaced in log bunkers some 200 yards ahead.[3] Beyond the rise, the ridgetop was said to widen out to perhaps 50 yards in width, but there were 200 yards of open grassy area to cross, and the cliffs on each side made any envelopment maneuver impossible.

To demonstrate his point Eck held up a ration can on a stick and it immediately drew a hail of fire over our heads. I wormed my way around to the side of the hill, looked cautiously through a bush and verified that what he said was only too true. Across the 200 yards, up a gentle slope, there were four apertures in four log bunkers, two of them covering the cliffs on the flanks making any movement across that 200 yards of open grass clearly suicidal.

Worse, there was no way to bring any supporting machine gun fire to bear. The gunners would have been cut down just getting into position.

Then came the final blow. Word came over the radio that Jack Jones had been wounded and evacuated. Now there was no one trustworthy left between us and Idiot Six. From his safe ravine a mile to the rear, the Colonel could coordinate supporting fires to his heart's content but there was no available supporting fire I could think of that would let the thirty or so remaining men of my platoon get across that 200 yards of open ground.

Nor did any of our peerless forward observers or the company commander seem to want to come up to appraise the situation.

What did come up, however, was the radioed order: "The Colonel wants you to take that hill

---

[3]The young Marine who was given the point had been chosen for that perilous position because three nights earlier, extra rations had come up, and he had purloined one box of C-rations rather than share it with his fellow Marines. Such deeds were customarily rewarded by assignment to the point when the Platoon was moving forward in uncertain circumstances.

by noon."

I radioed back that perhaps the CO might like to come up and see what we were facing. Or better yet, he might have Able Company come up the deep ravine on our left and try to get behind the bunkers. We had cliffs on both our right and left which were impassable. Baker Company was heavily engaged on a ridge line off in the distance to our right.

Time passed. I didn't see anything we could do. The loss of Jack Jones was heavy on my mind. It seemed like all my good friends were gone and the Company at the mercy of unknowns in the rear who didn't understand our problem. Every once in awhile the North Koreans would let off a few bursts of fire. They passed about 18" over our heads, and apparently everybody was safe back along the ridge so long as they kept flat.

About noon, an inquiry came over the radio as to how I was proceeding. I didn't give a Marine-type answer. I said we weren't going anywhere until somebody gave us an air strike or sent up an artillery FO. I may have indicated my troops were a hell of a lot more valuable than some imbecile in a command tent in the rear.

The next order was, "The Colonel has ordered you to attack at one o'clock; he's getting you some artillery support." None came. One o'clock came and went.

The next order from the CO was, "McCloskey, either get moving or you'll be courtmartialed. Regiment wants that hill taken by two o'clock." I raved a little over the radio telling the CO in effect to stuff Regiment. Only John Goodrich came forward to check out our position. No artillery came in, and whenever anyone twitched a little, the machine guns up the ridge mowed the grass again at the head of our swale.

Finally, the CO (still remaining well back down the ridge) got really upset. "You will attack at 3:00 p.m. Division insists that we keep moving." I flatly refused and told him something to the effect that he could get his own warm body and an artillery FO up to join us or he could courtmartial me at his pleasure.

Finally, after 3:00 p.m. an artillery FO and his radioman from the 11th Marines wriggled their way up to our pleasant little haven. The FO said that he'd been authorized to have something like thirty-six guns of the 11th Marines fire a simultaneous "Time-on- Target" (T.O.T.) barrage at 4:00 p.m.

I had heard of that terrifying use of firepower, but had never seen it happen. The FO had a few marking rounds fired and we were able to hear some satisfying explosions amongst the bunkers up ahead. We weren't looking over the rise to check the damage, however, as the machine guns kept firing a few rounds every once in awhile to keep us thinking.

We worked out a deal with the FO. He would fire thirty-six rounds of high explosion (H.E.) simultaneously 50 yards in front of the bunkers, followed by thirty-six rounds 25 yards further, followed by the final thirty-six rounds right on top of the North Korean bunkers. The T.O.T. was set for exactly four o'clock.

One round of 105 HE is a terrifying experience. We had had a little taste of that by mistake back on Hill 610. Thirty-six rounds at one time, in a 50 yard square area, was awesome, but I remained concerned, if not deeply skeptical, that our small band could make it to those bunkers.

In any event, there was no way *not* to go forward. I was mad enough at the long chain of command back to Division not to think rationally about the matter.

The squad leaders lined up our three rifle grenade launchers, each with two of the new white phosphorous rifle grenades we had stolen from an Army depot back at Inje. Phil Elson had his two machine guns rigged with wire handles for a one-man carry so they could be fired from the hip, the ammo belts flapping.

Our plan was to wait until the first artillery rounds came in, fire our six WP rifle grenades like mortars, and then take off running, every man of the platoon over the rise at the same time, me in the middle, with a machine gun on each side, firing as soon as we cleared the rise.

We fixed bayonets and waited for 4:00 o'clock.

The artillery FO was as good as his word.

On the dot of 4:00, we heard the distant boom of the guns and the whisper of the shells passing over our heads. The squad leaders each let go their two WP grenades and when the shells hit there was a tremendous crash and we took off. Crossing over the rise I expected to get it between the eyes, but nothing happened. There was only chaos in front of us, with flying branches, smoke and dust obscuring the bunkers. The second salvo came in, and we heard, but couldn't see, the result through the smoke and dust. We ran on and into the smoke and dust as the third salvo hit just ahead of us.

Then suddenly we were through the smoke, past the bunkers and in clear air on the reverse slope. There was a neat row of still burning cooking fires twenty yards past the crest, and down in the woods several hundred yards in front of us the backs of some fast- disappearing North Korean infantrymen. We had taken one casualty from the third 105 barrage.

We hit the deck in a hasty defense position and let the dust settle, blessing the 11th Marines that there hadn't been a single short round.

Two North Koreans came back up the hill with their hands up to surrender, but still carrying their burp guns. I went out to meet them, but ten yards away, one of them panicked and ran and both were cut down by every weapon in the line behind me.

I took from the body of one of them a family photograph. It was like an old Civil War daguerreotype, showing a family of at least twenty or more, old people, young people and little children, posing for a family portrait in front of a mud hut, with a wooded mountainside behind.

This led to the last of my three philosophic thoughts in Korea. What right did I, a big American from 10,000 miles away, have to be killing a poor kid who probably lived within 100 miles of where we were fighting? His family, standing so proud and happy in that picture, old grandparents to little kids, didn't deserve what was happening to their peasant sons.

It turned out later, from a prisoner we took, that the North Korean unit defending the hill had been ordered to hold us until exactly 4:00 o'clock and then retire back to the main enemy positions on the south rim of the Punch Bowl.

Luckily they had jumped the gun.

They had pulled out just before the artillery hit. Had one or two stayed behind to man just one of their four machine guns, even firing through the smoke and dust they would have had most, if not all of us as easy prey.

So much for luck and timing. I could, and probably should have been courtmartialed for the four-time repeated disobedience of orders to attack, first at noon, then at one p.m., two p.m. and finally, at three p.m. It wasn't fear that caused me to disobey orders, but simply pure rage at the idiocy of the orders from the rear.

Had Jones not been hit, I probably would have attacked rather than let Jones down, and the whole platoon might well have been wiped out. Then again, had Jones not been wounded, he undoubtedly would have come up and seen the situation, and either gotten that Time-on-Target a lot earlier, or figured out some other way to proceed. Some of us might have made it to the bunkers.

When we got back to Camp Pendleton some eight months later, Bill Heer, another second lieutenant who had participated in that drive to the Punch Bowl, and I wrote a letter to Headquarters Marine Corps recommending that there be developed a better rifle grenade launcher, and that a rifle platoon receive a reasonable supply of those WP rifle grenades. They were the perfect way to provide a smoke screen to allow an attack across two or three hundred yards of open ground, and WP is scarier than shrapnel.

I've always wondered whether our letter played a part in the development of the M-40 grenade launcher which worked so well in Viet Nam in the late 1960s.

Thus endeth the story of lessons, mistakes and unjustified good fortune.

THE ATTACK NORTH TO THE PUNCH BOWL
JUNE 8-18, 1951

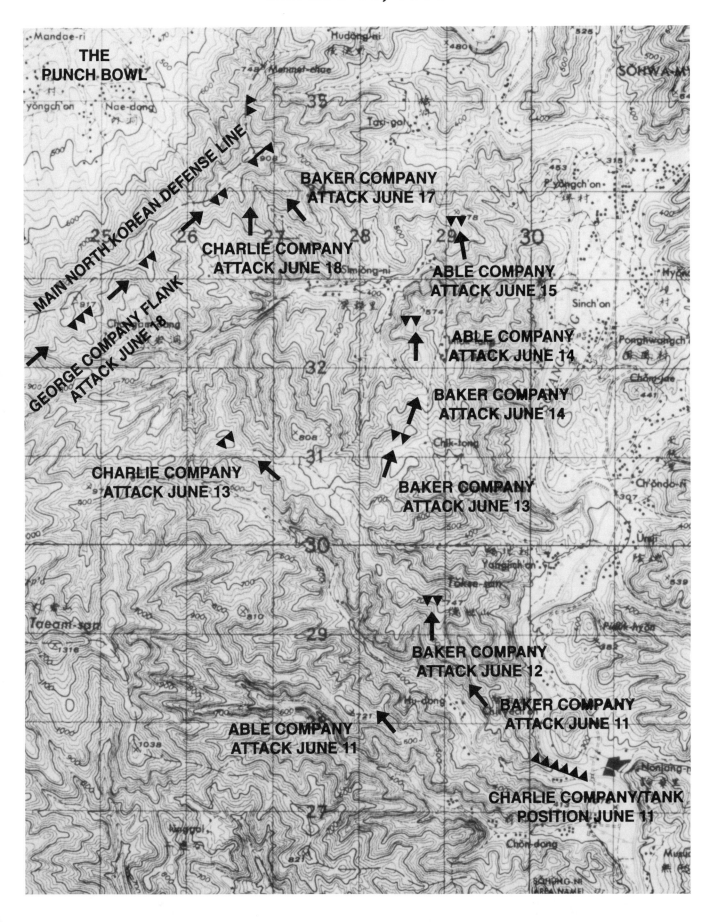

THE ANHYON RI AMBUSH
MARCH 30, 1951

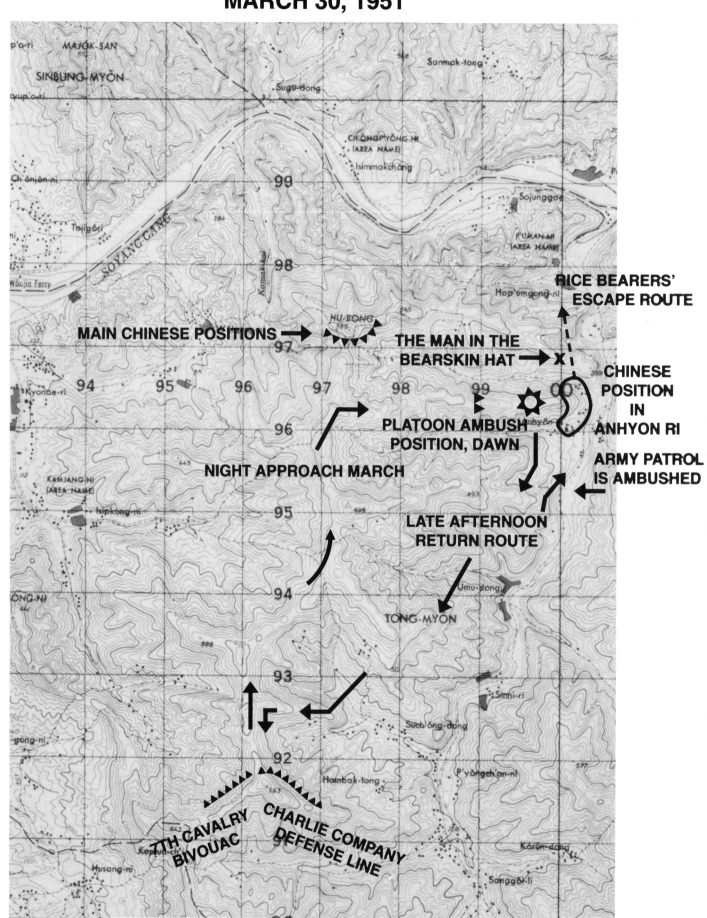

MAIN CHINESE POSITIONS ➡

THE MAN IN THE BEARSKIN HAT ➡ X

RICE BEARERS' ESCAPE ROUTE

CHINESE POSITION IN ANHYON RI

PLATOON AMBUSH POSITION, DAWN

ARMY PATROL IS AMBUSHED

NIGHT APPROACH MARCH

LATE AFTERNOON RETURN ROUTE

TONG-MYON

7TH CAVALRY BIVOUAC

CHARLIE COMPANY DEFENSE LINE

P U N C H B O W L

(1179)

This Army photograph shows the south rim of the Punch Bowl at the top of the photograph. The ridges at the far right are those attacked by the Fifth Marine Regiment, June 7-18, 1951. (Taken from Department of the Army booklet, Korea, 1951-53, page 187.)

The author and Ralph "Parson" Blaylock before Easter Services, 1951.

Chapter 12

The Liquor Officer

I had a proud Southern heritage—honor Grad from military prep school, Golden Gloves boxer, Phi Beta Kappa at Washington and Lee, *"Marine combat officer in Korea,"* etc.

from *Shout it From the Housetops*,
The autobiography of Reverend Pat Robertson

In the fall of 1986, a new type of politician and a new style of campaigning entered the American political arena.

A charismatic minister and former student at the Marine Corps officer training school at Quantico, Virginia, the Reverend Pat Robertson, claimed the unique talent to be able to receive occasional messages from God.

With supreme self-confidence in this rare blessing, Robertson had built up a highly successful television program, "The 700 Club," reaching a following of some fourteen million people, many of whom gave unstintingly of their financial means to Robertson's cause. Robertson proved time and again that he could raise as much as $500,000 in a single-hour of "spirit-filled" dialogue with his loyal followers across the nation, healing the ailments of born-again Christians in front of an audience of millions.

In late 1986, Robertson announced in a closed-circuit, nationally-televised press conference that he would run for the Republican nomination for President if three million people would each contribute $100 to his campaign ... a total of $300 million.

This was no small sum. George Bush and Bob Dole, the major Republican candidates, were preparing to campaign for the presidency with realistic hopes of no more than 1/10th of this amount.

In the two years preceding his announcement, Robertson had been organizing an effective army of his religious followers to restore God to American politics. He did this by plain old-fashioned grass-roots political organization. He had correctly perceived as early as 1985 that, in caucus states such as Iowa and Michigan, less than 10% of the American voters actually participated in the nominating process. 5% of the Republican voters in a majority of the voting precincts could be enough to win the delegates of an entire state.

Bush and Dole considered themselves lucky if they could obtain one out of five hundred Republicans to do volunteer work in their campaigns; three hundred volunteers in a congressional district of 500,000 people would be an enormous number ... usually enough to outstrip any opposing candidate.

Robertson *knew* he could get 1,000 dedicated evangelists in most of America's 435 congressional districts, and if he couldn't, they could be brought in by bus from bible-belt areas to dominate straw-vote conventions.

The television pulpit was a bully place from which to organize. There were enough examples of political corruption, increasing drug use and loose morals on the national scene to cause millions of people to yearn for a return to the good old fashioned religious values as defined by articulate television personalities such as Robertson, Jimmy Swaggart and Jimmy Bakker.

Robertson planned carefully and well. His announcement of his potential candidacy in September, 1986, brought forth a tremendous outpouring of cash contributions.

He seemed to have all the qualifications the nation yearned for. In his autobiography he had noted his superb academic achievements, Phi Beta Kappa at Washington and Lee, a law degree from Yale, and, having been "*a Marine combat officer in Korea.*"

A man who spoke with God and who had been a Marine combat officer was a rare combination indeed. Such a man might well be able to lead the nation on to glory, banishing sin, corruption and Godless communism forever.[1] At least a number of true believers wanted to think so.

One thing was sure. There was no better way to raise money than by waiving the flag at prayer meetings while the orchestra softly played "The Battle Hymn of the Republic" in the background.[2]

It conjured up marvelous images to those in attendance, or at their televisions sets, of God's terrible swift sword rising from the ashes of Armageddon in the hands of a great religious and Marine combat leader. With the music rising to a crescendo as the collection plates were passed, who would not be thrilled to contribute to such a glorious cause?

There was one small catch.

Marines who have been in combat do not commonly refer to themselves as "combat" veterans. The word is too respected, if not revered, in the Corps to permit its acceptable use by way of self-characterization.

A Marine or former Marine might modestly allow, upon inquiry, that he had been on Iwo, or Tarawa or at Guadalcanal. Any one of those words would earn instant respect. But "I was a combat Marine" had never before been honorably spoken or written, to the knowledge of most Marines. It just wasn't done.

Because of the incongruity of Robertson's claim, coupled with his announcement of his candidacy for the Presidency, an old and disquieting story was retold that Robertson's combat experience had been somewhat overstated. It was really a humorous, (not a sarcastic) tale, dating back to 1951.

---

[1]In all the Marine Corps' illustrious history, the Corps' connection with godliness has not received undue attention from historians. Alone among the services, the Marine Corps has no chaplains. They are furnished by the Navy when needed.

---

[2]"Mine eyes have seen the glory of the coming of the Lord.
  He is trampling out the vintage where the grapes of wrath are stored.

  He will loose the fearful lightning of his terrible swift sword.

  His truth goes marching on.

  Glory, glory, hallelujah ... glory, glory, hallelujah.
  Glory, glory, hallelujah, His truth goes marching on."

The theme of the story had four parts:

(1) Robertson, as a young Marine lieutenant en route to Korea in 1951, had asked the assistance of his father, Virginia Senator A. Willis Robertson, to keep him out of combat.

(2) His father had intervened and gotten his son and a friend taken off the troopship and kept in Japan. Four other young lieutenants had also been taken off the ship for cover so that no political influence would be inferred.

(3) Some months later one of the four had caught the ear of a General's aide at a cocktail party and volunteered all six for transfer to Korea, much to Robertson's anger and dismay.

(4) The six had gone to Korea, where several were forthwith wounded, but Robertson had been assigned as the "liquor officer" with frequent booze runs to Japan.

In a fiction novel published in 1979 by a former Marine who had served in Korea in 1951, there had been mention of the fictional son of a fictional southern Senator who had gotten his father to pull strings to keep him out of combat, taking him off a ship carrying the Fifth Replacement Draft to Korea in February, 1951.[3] Later, a friend's comment to a General at a cocktail party had gotten him transferred to Korea where he was given a cushy headquarters job, looked after by a bantam, but very tough, Chief of Staff. The fictitious lieutenant had been named Richards, but Marines who had been on the Fifth Replacement Draft would immediately remember that a young Second Lieutenant, Marion G. "Pat" Robertson, had told everyone in the ship's wardroom that his "Daddy," the Senator was going to keep him out of combat, and that Robertson had indeed been pulled out of the Draft when the ship, the *U.S.S. General J. C. Breckinridge*, reached Japan. The bantam but very tough Chief of Staff sounded very much like the famous Victor "The Brute" Krulak who was serving as Division Chief of Staff when Robertson finally arrived in Korea from Japan in late June, 1951. Krulak had also served as General Shepherd's Operations Officer (G-3) at FMFPAC during February, 1951, at the time Robertson was pulled off the troopship. He could be relied on to serve General Shepherd loyally and well.

The story was printed with some humor by two of America's leading political columnists, Evans & Novak and Jack Anderson. Most Marine veterans chuckled over the "liquor officer" publicity. The designation was an honorable one in the Corps, but it apparently resulted in some difficult questions from those of Robertson's devoted following who were teetotalers.

Robertson vehemently denied that he had sought to evade combat or that he had ever been a liquor officer. He was particularly incensed about the slur on his deceased father's reputation. That Senator Robertson would *ever* seek political favors for his relatives or friends was an outrageous lie, his son said.

Robertson consulted two noted conservative political advisers, Paul Weyrich and Marc Nuttle, who advised him that he should bring a libel suit against the source of the story to the press, Congressman Andrew Jacobs of Indiana, as well as the man who had related it to Jacobs, one of his shipmates aboard the Breckinridge. The lawsuit would at least keep the story from being circulated by the media during the campaign. No newspaper would want to take the chance of itself being sued for libel until the truth were established.

Jacobs had served in Korea while Robertson was in Japan, had been wounded and in the 1980s, while in Congress, had been characterized by Robertson as one of those who were "soft on communism."

Acting on Weyrich's and Nuttle's advice, Robertson on October 21, 1986 filed a $35 million libel suit against the two former Marines, who responded that a jury trial was not a bad place to ascertain the truth.

Then began a 16 month search through old records and for even-older Marines who could

---

[3]*The Vicar of Christ*, Walter Murphy, The MacMillan Company, 1979.

enhance the faded memories of over 35 years. By the summer of 1987, Robertson's political campaign was developing well, but enough records and former Marines had been found to suggest that he had indeed asked his "Daddy" to keep him out of combat, and that Senator Robertson had communicated on the subject with Robertson's Commanding General.[4]

Senator Robertson's correspondence files, unearthed from the archives of his alma mater, William and Mary College, were illuminating. Several letters written while his son was aboard ship headed to Korea were of particular interest. They thanked General Shepherd for his assurance that his son would "get further training before being sent to Korea," and advised his friend, the President of Washington and Lee that both their sons would be taken off the troopship when it reached Japan.

Robertson had sailed for Korea in January, 1951, as a new young Second Lieutenant fresh out of Quantico's 11 week basic platoon leader training course. With him was his friend and classmate from Washington and Lee, Ed Gaines. The First Marine Division had taken fearful casualties at the Chosin Reservoir in December when the Chinese had entered this war with a vengeance; new second lieutenants were needed badly and the rumored life expectancy of platoon leaders in combat was only six minutes. Robertson was one of 71 officers and 1900 enlisted men in the Fifth Replacement Draft aboard the U.S.S. General J. C. Breckinridge. The full draft was needed to bring the Divisions' three rifle regiments up to strength for General MacArthur's planned February counter-attack against the Chinese. On the last day before leaving for Korea, however, Robertson and Gaines had been pulled off the ship in Kobe, Japan, with four others whose names had the misfortune to be listed next to Gaines on the roster of lieutenants assigned to the 7th Regiment. The reason: ostensibly to train young Marines coming out of the hospitals after the Chosin Reservoir battle.

Both the First Marine Division personnel office and those officers aboard the Breckinridge who had had combat duty were offended. Captain Harry Steinmeyer, a decorated veteran of Guadalcanal wrote on February 14, 1951:

"Happy Valentines:

✳✳✳

Here's one I have to tell you. Lt. Gaines & a Lt. Robinson (Whose Father is Senator from Va) were taken off in Japan. In short there were 80 men and 8 2nd Lts pulled on the pretense of training men who came from Korea to go back there. Gaines slipped 2 days before we got to Japan and said he & the other one were going to be pulled off there. It's really rotten politics. I'd sure like to write Winchell on it. See what Walter & Daddy say about that. At least I can live with my conscience. Well so much for that"

First Lieutenant David Hartstein, the Draft's adjutant, wrote his wife the same day:

"Hi There Valentine:

✳✳✳

---

[4]As General Krulak later said: "Marine Corps Generals of that day and age were "expected" to stay in contact with and report to powerful Senators." The threat of abolition of the Marine Corps by President Truman and his Defense Secretary Louis Johnson was very real in 1950 and it was understandable that the leaders of the Corps would want to keep the respect of powerful Senators. In General Shepherd's words in 1989: "We needed to keep them buttered up." Every Marine would understand and agree that in 1950, this was a necessity if the Corps was to survive Truman's axe. To drop off two lieutenants in Japan for a few months was a small price to pay for the survival of the Corps. Both General Shepherd and Colonel Krulak played a major role in saving the Corps in 1950, General Shepherd by flying to Tokyo to convince General MacArthur to ask the President to allow the Marines to call up their reserves, Colonel Krulak by having kept the Fifth Regiment in top combat-readiness in peacetime. That combat-readiness was to impress the world at the Pusan Perimeter as the Marines performed incomparably better than all of the Army units save one, the 27th Infantry Regiment commanded by Lt. Col. John H. Michaelis.

Oh yes, there is one thing I wanted to tell you about. When we were in Kobe yesterday a Col. came aboard to choose several officers to retrain casualties that were getting ready to go back to Korea. He chose 6 second Lts. none of whom have ever had any combat. Its interesting to note that two of them had said they wouldn't have to go to Korea. One was the Robertson that General Sheppard wanted to see and I'm sure that his father being the Senator from Virginia had nothing to do with it and the other was a kid named Gaines whose father is president of Washington and Lee university. It is interesting though isn't it. See that's what you get when you choose the wrong parents. Incidentally they are both very nice guys but no more anxious to go than the rest of us."

What had caused this extraordinary salvation?

As the trial date of March 8, 1988 approached, Robertson found himself in an increasing dilemma. He had shocked the Republicans by strong second place finishes, in Iowa, South Dakota and Minnesota; he had nearly won Michigan, and expected to win South Carolina on Saturday, March 5. March 8, "Super Tuesday" with its 22 separate primaries, was expected to provide perhaps even a majority of delegates in the bible belt states where from whence came Robertson's strongest support. His lawsuit had suppressed any media comment on his alleged "liquor officer" background.

It appeared that the bright and shining religious leader could conceivably get enough delegates to the Republican convention in New Orleans to be the determining power broker between Bush and Dole, perhaps with as many as 20% of the total delegates. The Religious Right would be a factor no Republican could ever again ignore.

But Robertson's very success brought new problems. The press began to examine his credentials with more interest. Questionable claims about his date of marriage, his allegation that Soviet missiles were still in Cuba, an alleged knowledge of the location of hostages in Lebanon and that George Bush had leaked the sins of Robertson's fellow evangelist, Jimmy Swaggart, received national attention.

Also of concern, the press was beginning to talk to witnesses in his libel suit whose deposition testimony was now of public record.

A Marine bunkmate at Quantico was found who remembered Robertson's comment upon seeing his name posted on the list to go to Korea:

> "Pat also expressed that he wasn't very happy about the prospect of going to Korea and said that he was going to have to talk to his Daddy to see whether he could do something so that he didn't have to go to Korea."
> ". . . there was no question that he let you know that his father was a Senator in Congress and that his father was pretty influential, so it was no secret to anyone that he probably asked his father to do something and there probably was a good chance that his father could do something."[5]

The Steinmeyer and Hartstein letters proved unequivocally that Gaines and Robertson had *believed* they were going to be taken off the ship when it reached Japan. When Robertson's name appeared on a roster of lieutenants assigned to one of the rifle regiments, two other lieutenants remembered accompanying him to a dockside telephone facility at Kobe where he called his father.

> "My memory is that he said words to that effect, that, "I called my Daddy and I'm going to try to have him get me off," or "I will see if I can get stationed in Japan," or something of that sort."[6]

---

[5]Deposition of Herbert W. Marache, Jr.

---

[6]Depositions of Michael Sydney Rogers and John Gearhart.

Steinmeyer and another combat veteran, First Lieutenant Hugh Scott remembered Robertson asking the Draft Adjutant to send a cable to his father asking for help, and that when the orders came to take him and five others, including Gaines off the ship, a second one- word cable, "Thanks."[7]

Evidence began to accumulate that "Daddy" had intervened with his friend General Shepherd who, from his headquarters in Hawaii, commanded the Fleet Marine Force Pacific (FMFPAC) which included not only the First Marine Division in Korea, but also the First Casual Company in Japan and the Fifth Replacement Draft.

The Draft Commander, Major Paul Groth, had served with the General in World War II. A reserve, he had been recalled to duty when the Korean War broke out.

At Camp Pendleton, just before the Draft left for Korea, General Shepherd had come to inspect the troops. He called Major Groth to his quarters.

Major Groth testified at his deposition:

> "And so he sent for me, and I thought it was for—it was just to recall or reminisce about some of those times, you know, at that time, so I went over to see him at his quarters ... And he said, 'Paul it's good to see you,' in his Virginia drawl. And he said, 'Y'all have a fine young —' He said, 'You have a fine young man in the young gentlemen in that organization,' he said. 'His name is Robertson.' He said, 'Take good care of him.' And I said, 'Yes, sir,' . . . he said, 'His daddy is Chairman of the Senate Military Appropriations Committee.'"[8]

Another friend of General Shepherd's from World War II, Colonel Burns, had been assigned to command The First Casual Company at Camp Otsu, Japan, an organization used as a stop-over for casualties returning from hospitalization and other Marines en route to Korea. Colonel Burns had boarded the Breckinridge on its last day at Kobe. He had asked for the Draft roster, and was given the roster which showed Robertson as being assigned to the First Marines and Gaines to the Seventh Marines.

In Major Groth's words:

> "He took the roster, and then he was sitting right beside me on kind of a couch that we had there, and he went down the roster, and he went to Robertson, and he checked Robertson. And then he went on the roster and he checked some other officers' names. And I said, I said to him —I said, 'That was an interesting selection process. How did you do that?'
>
> And he said, 'Well, I don't know.' He said, 'These officers will be fine.' and that was that."[9]

A "smoking gun" was finally found, the testimony of the officer who had actually transmitted the orders from FMFPAC removing Robertson from the ship on the ground that "a Virginia Congressman wanted his son to get further training before going on to combat."[9]

By October, 1987 it was clear that Robertson no longer had a case on the evasion of combat issue. Gaines' letters had confirmed the Shepherd-Robertson-Gaines relationship. (See Appendix E)

The libel suit, however, was still viable if no one could be found who could verify that Robertson had been the liquor officer. A lot of Marines remembered the story but, by November, just weeks before the deposition cut-off date, no one had been found who could positively verify that Robertson

---

[7] Depositions of Harry Steinmeyer and Hugh Scott.

[8] Deposition of Major Paul H. Groth, Appelton, Wisconsin, October 21, 1987.

[9] Deposition of Goode Burleson.

had actually been "the liquor officer" at the Division rear echelon headquarters. Most combat Marines had never been near Division headquarters, save when arriving as replacements or upon their rotation home.

A fine young Washington lawyer for the defense, George Lehner, spent hours poring through the personnel records in the Corps' archives trying to track down individuals all over the United States who had once served in headquarters units.

Lehner finally hit paydirt in November, 1987.

Paul William Brosman, Jr., an ROTC reserve officer, had been called up and sent to the regular Basic Class at Quantico in September, 1950, graduating in April, 1951 and thereafter being sent to Korea as part of the ill-fated Ninth Replacement Draft, arriving in early June. Brosman had been assigned to Item Company in the First Marines, and as a platoon leader had survived the bloody battles around the Punch Bowl in June and September. He had been rotated to the Division Rear Headquarters at Masan in October, 1951.

Brosman had earned a Doctorate in Linguistics from the University of North Carolina and thereafter became a Professor of Linguistics at L.S.U. and then Tulane, retiring in 1979. His memory of the Korean War remained remarkably clear.

While in Item Company, Brosman had heard a funny story about three lieutenants, Pat Robertson, his buddy, Ed Gaines and one John Gearhart. Brosman had met Gearhart in reserve in August while the story was being told by another Item Company lieutenant named Dennis. Everybody had had a good laugh over it, and it stayed in his memory.

The story was that a Virginia Senator had had his son (Robertson) pulled out of the Fifth Replacement Draft with Gaines and four others so that it wouldn't look like political influence was a factor. Gearhart was one of the four. The six had been given fairly cushy jobs at Camp Otsu's Casual Company until General Shepherd came through in late May on an inspection tour.[10]

General Shepherd's old friend, the Casualty Company Commander, Colonel Burns, threw a cocktail party for the General, and at the party, John Gearhart had cornered the General's aide, complained that he wanted to see combat duty in Korea, and volunteered all six of the non-combat lieutenants for transfer to Korea.

The aide had walked him over to General Shepherd who had commended him for his initiative and agreed to send the six to Korea forthwith.

Robertson was furious. As the story went, on going back to the officers' quarters he had tried to knock Gearhart's door down to get at Gearhart and had to be restrained by a couple of other officers.[11]

Gaines and Gearhart were sent to Korea shortly thereafter, where both were wounded at the Punch Bowl. The fighting both in June and later in August and September was very fierce.

Robertson, however, had not been sent to Korea until after the Russians and Chinese asked for a truce. Gaines had written the following in a letter home on June 1:

> "General Shepherd came through the other day (if I've written you this, forgive the repetition) and had a long chat with Pat and me at the Colonel's cocktail party. He informed us we'd be leaving for Korea in about a month. Shortly thereafter I was notified I'd be leaving June 6 to

---

[10] Most VIP inspection tours were rumored to occur on the last day of one month and the first day of the next. The visitors thus qualified for "combat pay" for both months.

---

[11] In Brosman's words:

"And Pat Robertson became very upset about that . . . then it was that when he was drunk that he got violent. But at any rate he got violent, or attempted to, and went down and pounded on Gearhart's door . . . wanting to get at him and had to be restrained by a couple of guys." The full deposition of Paul Brosman is reproduced in Appendix E.

ply the couple hundred miles to Korea. Pat will stay here for awhile at least. But it was just the luck of the draw I'm sure."[12]

Arriving in Korea in late June, after the fighting had stopped temporarily, Robertson, unlike practically every other untried Second Lieutenant, upon arrival at the Division CP where Colonel Krulak was now Chief of Staff, was promptly sent to the Division Rear at Masan, 300 miles south. Krulak, a veteran of the infighting in Washington in the late 1940s when Harry Truman was trying to abolish the Marine Corps[13] certainly understood what General Shepherd had meant when he had said six months earlier: "Take good care of him; his Daddy is Chairman of the Senate Armed Forces Appropriations Committee."[14]

Brosman had remembered the humor of the story about Gaines and Gearhart and asked Gaines about it when he first met him at Masan.

Gaines confirmed both the truthfulness and the humor of the story. Gaines, Robertson and Brosman were billeted together in the same building at Masan, along with two other lieutenants. Brosman remembered that Robertson was referred to commonly as "the liquor officer," and that Robertson himself had referred to himself as the liquor officer, "jollily, of course." It was "somewhere between scuttlebutt and common knowledge" that Robertson's periodic trips to Japan were to purchase liquor for the officers' club.

Attorney Lehner asked Brosman:

Q: "Now at Masan, did you ever hear Mr. Robertson referred to as the 'Division Liquor Officer'?

A: Well, I heard him referred to as the 'Liquor Officer.' I don't know about the 'Division Liquor.' I thought he was the 'Masan Liquor Officer.'

Q: How did that reference come about or how did you hear that?

A: Because he frequently made trips to Japan, I would have said, to buy liquor, maybe. But I guess from the point of view of the guys at Masan, or the real purpose was to buy liquor. But I suppose some trumped-up excuse was devised so that he could — for an official trip.

And then he could go over and do something and then bring liquor back.

Q: Who referred to Pat Robertson as the 'Masan Liquor Officer'?

A: Well I guess just about everybody in our barracks, or whatever you want to call it.

That is, I'm not sure he didn't do it himself, as I think I said earlier . . .

It was just more or less general jocular reference by people there.

---

[12]Gaines' letters home are reproduced in Exhibit E.

---

[13]See Krulak's book, First to Fight, Chapter 8.

---

[14]Had I been in Colonel Krulak's shoes, I certainly would have made sure that nothing happened to the Senator's son. Preservation of the Marine Corps was very much in the Senator's hands and the latter had made his views known. Krulak's first duty was to the Marine Corps where in his lifetime he compiled a distinguished record of service. His leadership of the Fifth Regiment imediately prior to the Korean War paid rich dividends in that Regiment's performance at the Pusan Perimeter, and may have been the critical factor in both stopping the North Koreans and saving the Marine Corps itself.

Q: Did he ever buy you liquor?

A: Oh, no. He brought—I had to buy my own liquor at the Officers' Club. We had an Officers' Club at Masan.

It was that cushy a setup. And he brought the liquor back to the Officers' Club, this is my impression."

The foregoing was elicited from Brosman at deposition in New Orleans on November 17, 1987, and caused considerable joy to the defendant and his lawyers. The confirmation that Robertson was indeed believed to be the liquor officer at Masan in 1951 by a man obviously unconnected with the lawsuit, who did not know the defendants and had no axe to grind, effectively ended any chance of Robertson's winning the libel case.

Mr. Lehner ended his questioning with a sigh of relief.

But Robertson's lawyer was not content with Brosman's answers. He pressed on.

Q: "Do you recall any specific conversations you might have had with Pat Robertson?

A: Well, yeah. He was scared to death he had gonorrhea, and was very relieved when he found out it was what the corpsmen called 'non-specific drip.'

(This may have been the death knell for Robertson's presidential campaign; one can only imagine a Barbara Walters' interview . . . "Tell me Reverend, why do the Marines call you 'Non-Specific Drip Robertson?'")

Robertson's lawyer, perhaps unschooled in political matters, tried again:

Q: "Well, isn't it true that this 'Non-specific drip' is not the kind of disease transmitted by sexual intercourse or anything else, that it's an infection of the urinary tract?

A: Right. But he *thought* he had gonorrhea. And I don't think he got that from any other source."

If this wasn't enough, Robertson's attorney then made a fatal mistake. It is a general rule in the legal profession *never* to ask a possibly-hostile witness a question to which the attorney doesn't know what the answer will be.

Robertson's attorney opened the door wide.

Q: "How do you recall Pat Robertson being in those days?

A: Well, I—it's hard to say. I liked him a lot less than Ed Gaines. But it's hard to say why.

One thing was, he was—well, he was more inconsiderate, pretty inconsiderate for, I mean, things like the cleaning girl.

We had a cleaning girl who came in. It's like the story of the fraternity house and the nineteen (19) year-old housemother. We had a cleaning girl who was nineteen (19) who was our maid in our barracks. But she was a nice Korean girl.

And we had a lot of prostitutes around there, for example. And, well, Pat used to fool around with her all the time. That is, pinching her and carrying on.

And every once in awhile, he would chase her outside the house and then he would continue chasing her and pinching her outside the house.

That would terrify her because the Koreans would see.

And, of course, these prostitutes were dead meat when we left because they had ruined their lives to make money off of the Americans.

But once the Americans left, they were really finished.

And she didn't want the Korean men to see her fooling around like with an American. And she'd plead with him to stop and he wouldn't stop. *And none of the rest of us would have done that.*

Q: You never saw anyone else messing around with women?

A: Oh, not none of the—not with that maid.

Oh, a lot of guys messed around with the prostitutes that wanted to get messed around with, including Pat."

That about did it.

Messing around with prostitutes, molesting a nice young Korean maid in front of men who could make her life miserable . . . those were matters the American voting public could well understand. The youthful conduct could be forgiven, but the later hypocrisy and false claim that he had been "a Marine combat officer" did not sit well. The coup de gras came a few weeks later from an unexpected and previously-unknown source.

Watching Robertson earnestly repeat his claim of "combat" experience over national television, a former reserve Marine who had served with Robertson at the Division CP in 1951, ten miles behind the front lines, was moved to write his local paper.

On February 15, 1988, barely three weeks before the trial date and "Super Tuesday's" twenty-two Republican primaries, the *Marin County* (California) *Coastal Pilot* published the following letter on its front page:

COASTAL POST

MARIN COUNTY'S NEWS WEEKLY

Vol. 13, No. 7
Feb. 15-21, 1988

Pat Robertson "No Combat Marine"

This is a story I would like to see in your paper; it is timely and timeless. It is really an update on a 38-year old story. It may not make much sense but I think that's alright because it was going on. It changed a lot of people.

It really started on August 1, 1950. We got on buses in Kentfield that took us to Oakland where we boarded a special train that took us to Camp Pendleton. The Korean War had come to Marin County. Two hundred Marine reserves from Company C were called to duty. We laughed excitedly with bravado. We were getting into a war that would be over before it really got started.

Later that year, things were different for us.

I saw one of these former Marines last Wednesday at the Civic Center. He's a school teacher in Kentfield and was showing his students the workings of county government. We spoke.

There is a score of these special ex-Marines still in Marin. Another is a title insurance executive in Novato. Yet another that I see from time to time is a stock broker in San Francisco.

Although they look like us and talk like us they were "line" company Marines and although my company had the highest number of casualties of any company in the First Marine Division in the first year of the war, it came in short bursts of terror.

It was not a line company. The line companies went about this war business day-to-day, in the mud, in the rain, in the snow, with the smell of death, and a constant concern that there be another day for yourself and all of the members of your line company.

I saw truck-loads of frozen dead line-company Marines. I saw a line company which began with 238 fall to seven, led by a 20-year-old corporal. It was 30 below zero, in a howling wind off the Gobi Desert. This company from the Seventh Marines turned back the charge of a now-battered Chinese battalion. The charge began with the notes of "mess call" by the enemy bugler and ended in silence.

There is a person who calls himself a combat Marine. He is not. His name is Pat Robertson. I saw him often in the division headquarters where he was clean-shaven and clothed and showered.

He was in charge of making sure that the officers' booze ration was handed out and re-supplied. He was a lieutenant. He was in my battalion.

The line company marines I saw smelled badly, looked poorly. For months at a time they were cold, eating C-rations. Trying to stay warm and dry was a constant battle. These line-company men were the combat Marines of the First Marine Division.

Neither Pat Robertson nor I could carry their gear. He is trying to get elected by standing on those frozen bodies I saw, by putting himself in the company of those seven Marines who repulsed the enemy.

Imagine a person who aspires to be President being so loose with the truth, so lacking in grace and so dishonorable.

He says God talks to him. I'd like to hear what God says to him about this.

LEO T. CRONIN
Former Corporal U.S.M.C.

Editor's Note: Cronin was activated on August 1, 1950. Forty-five days later he was with the first wave of amphibious Marines that stormed and took the North Korean held Port of Inchon.

This Letter to the Editor was re-typeset and reformatted from the original layout.

This was the final blow. There were now *two* unimpeachable witnesses to Robertson's "liquor officer" status, a role he had denied under oath at his deposition, as well as over television to millions of Americans. Plainly and simply, Robertson had not told the truth.

On March 4, 1988, Federal Judge Joyce Hens Green gave Robertson the Hobson's Choice of either going to trial on March 8 and hearing the parade of former Marines testify against him, or dismissing his libel suit with prejudice. Robertson chose to dismiss. But the judge added a condition:

> "For the reasons set forth below, the Court concludes that defendant McCloskey is, for this determination, the prevailing party."

> "Dismissal of an action with prejudice is a complete adjudication of the issues presented by the pleadings."

> "Because a dismissal with prejudice is tantamount to a judgment on the merits, the defendant in this case . . . is clearly the prevailing party . . ."

> "If plaintiff [Robertson] does not accept the dismissal of this case on that condition, the case shall proceed to trial on March 8, 1988 at 10:00 a.m."

On March 3, four Korean combat veterans watching Robertson's tortured explanations of his dilemma on television at a bar in Columbia, South Carolina, had wired Robertson's trial opponent:

> "Maintain Contact. Expect Counter Attack. We're Depending on you."

South Carolina, home of The Citadel, is not just a strong bible belt state. It is the heart of the South's legacy of Civil War chivalry and military tradition dating back to Frances Marion "The Swamp Fox" and Wade Hampton.

Two days later, on March 5, the voters of South Carolina rendered their decision. Robertson plummeted from his expected victory to a distant third in the vote.

On March 6, a Robertson supporter told the Washington Post:

> "This business is hurting him, hurting him bad . . . people who should be for Pat are asking if he did it why didn't he just admit it? Or if he didn't why didn't he go to trial if he's got the evidence?"

At 9:00 a.m. on Monday morning, March 7, 1988, Robertson really had no choice. He agreed to accept the judge's condition, dismiss the lawsuit with prejudice and pay his opponent's court costs. He had chickened out in federal court as he had chickened out on the way to Korea thirty-seven years earlier.[15]

The next day, "Super Tuesday," the voters of Louisiana and eighteen other states rendered the verdict the jury could not. Robertson's political challenge was dead.

The bubble had burst. There would be no power brokering at the Republican Convention.

Litigation had not been able to suppress the truth. As Abraham Lincoln once remarked:

> "You can fool all of the people some of the time, and some of the people all of the time, but you can't fool all of the people all of the time."

---

[15] It's really rather a shame. Had Robertson survived a rifle platoon leader's experience in Korea, his manifest charm and leadership ability might have made him a great political leader as well, and possibly even allowed him to reach the White House. Many of our ablest political leaders, George Bush, John Glenn, John McCain, Bob Dole, Elliot Richardson, Chuck Robb, Warren Rudman, John Chafee, Bob Kerrey and John Kerry, to name a few, have either been former combat pilots or platoon leaders.

Ms. Martha Lofton of the Red Cross, Lt. Tom Johnston, G-3-5, and friends. The Division Liquor Officer is not shown. Masan, Korea, July, 1951, upon arrival of the 10th replacement Draft.

Chapter 13

The Long Arm of Congress

The Great Biscuit Fight

Shortly after joining Charlie Company in February, 1951, I was privileged to gain my first understanding that a far-off body, the Congress of the United States, had a certain importance to the Marine Corps, even in the front lines.

The triggering event was what could be called "The Great Biscuit Fight," one of the more humorous incidents of early March, 1951.

After the first week of the push north from Wonju, the First Battalion was pulled off the line and into a reserve area just off the Wonju-Hoeng'song road. The 7th Marines had taken over the attack and were having a tough time pushing the Chinese off the ridges north of Hoeng'song.

It was still winter, there was snow on the ground and there were a lot of breakdowns on the main supply route (MSR) as the engineers and truckers tried to cope with blown bridges, washed out roads and heavy mud.

The reserve bivouac in a little valley among low hills was better than the snowy ridgelines of the previous week, but not much. I speedily got dysentery again.

Mess tents and hot chow lines were set up, but weapons were carried in the mess line, following an incident during the Pohang guerrilla hunt a few weeks earlier when a few random shots from the hills had interrupted the evening meal. During the first few days in reserve, bad roads and general logistical problems delayed supplies from reaching our bivouac area.

There was a two-day stretch where the only noon meals were a canteen cup of soup and two biscuits per man.

Marine units have a unique custom. In mess lines in the field, the officers eat at the end of the line.

On the second day at noon Charlie Company had almost reached the end of its mess line, with perhaps twenty men and seven officers standing in the snow, waiting to be doled out their soup ration and two biscuits. Ahead of us, a mess cook managed to mishandle his delivery to a Marine's mess kit, and the biscuits fell in the snow, where they were immediately dived on and fought over by two ravenous Marines.

The fight in the snow for the biscuits caused a ripple of amusement along the line waiting to be served until a large guffaw was heard from the mess tent behind the mess cooks.

All eyes turned to see, standing in the doorway of the mess tent, his backside warmed by the stoves within, the lanky, handsome battalion commander, a biscuit in one hand, two in the other and a fourth stuffed in his chuckling mouth.

Grins in the mess line turned to growls, but the incident passed and was forgotten . . . for six days.

In that primitive time, it took five days for mail to reach the States.

Exactly six days later, the Battalion was back in the attack, now in the tangled brown ridges north of Hoeng'song. The weather was warmer now, with the snow melted and spring in sight. The biggest problem in the advance was not the withdrawing Chinese but the fires they kept setting in the wooded hills to slow us down.

The Battalion pushed ahead fairly cautiously, with only sporadic long-range fire fights, more to delay than to stop the advance. Suddenly a unique message was received all the way from Headquarters Marine Corps in Washington, D.C.:

"The First Battalion, Fifth Marines will retire to a reserve area for an official investigation of why the officers are getting more to eat than the enlisted men.
Commandant Marine Corps"

Obedience was immediate. The Battalion moved off the lines to the rear, and for a full day, struggled to respond to its first-ever direct order from the Commandant himself. Typewriters were extracted from field desks, paper was produced from somewhere and official statements were taken from all possible witnesses.

An erudite Pfc in line between the biscuit battlers and the Company's seven officers had written home, his letter reading somewhat like this:

"Dear Mom,

We are well and back in regimental reserve now. It's cold and we have outrun our supplies. The Company got only 2 biscuits and a bowl of soup again at noon today.

My buddies, Bill and Snuffy, fought over two biscuits that fell in the snow, and the Colonel laughed at them. It was funny, Mom, but the Colonel, whom everybody calls Idiot Six, had four biscuits.
Love,
Jimmy"

It was a pleasure to be pulled out of the attack for a day, but an even happier privilege to be able to confirm the Colonel's perfidy in writing.

The hero of the hour was the young Marine who had written home.

His mother must have been a campaign chairman for someone like a later powerful Chairman of the House Armed Services Committee, Mendel Rivers of South Carolina,[1] and she must have called him immediately.

---

[1]Mendel Rivers was one of a long line of powerful Southern committee chairman who were able to dominate their contemporaries. Shortly after he came to Washington to be President Nixon's chief of Staff for Domestic Affairs, my law-school classmate, John Erlichman, told me of a posh dinner he had attended at one of Washington's largest hotels, featuring the titans of the defense industry. The elevated head table ran the width of the room, faced by tables of eight seating over 1,000 representatives of the major defense contractors in America. The room quieted when the famous "Fishbait" Miller of Mississippi, Doorkeeper of the House of Representatives announced that the 30 dignitaries to be seated at the head table were due to arrive. The lights dimmed, the Marine Corps Band commenced a soft playing of the Battle Hymn of the Republic and a spotlight focused on a side doorway. "The Senator from Washington, the Honorable Scoop Jackson," intoned Fishbait. Thunderous applause. 30 seconds later, "Secretary of Defense Melvin Laird," Less thunderous applause. Another 30

The outraged phone call produced instant results. First, a stern demand for justice to the Commandant of the Marine Corps, and, within 24 hours, an order from the Commandant all the way to Korea to pull a front line infantry battalion out of the attack to obtain an answer to a Congressman who could vote yes or no on Harry Truman's plan to abolish the Marine Corps.

It was a powerful lesson to young Marines.

In just six days, the handscrawled letter of an 18 year old had brought at least a small demonstration of the enormous power of Congress with an organization whose leaders desperately looked to the Congress for salvation.[2]

There was great glee in the rifle companies that the Colonel had gotten his comeuppance, but once the statements were taken and so painfully typed, the Battalion returned to the lines and continued the advance north towards Hong'chon. There was no indication that the Colonel was ever reprimanded for his violation of one of the most long-standing customs of the Corps in combat. An enlisted man eats first, an officer last, and an officer never gets more to eat than an enlisted man.

The Robertson Letters

Upon his death, Senator A. Willis Robertson of Virginia left a number of his papers to his alma mater, William and Mary College at Williamsburg, Virginia, with instructions that they were to be available only to scholars until all persons mentioned therein had passed on.

In September, 1986, however, the Senator's son, Reverend Marion G. "Pat" Robertson announced his candidacy for the Presidency of the United States, shortly thereafter filing a lawsuit in the Federal District Court for the District of Columbia against two former Marines, the author and Congressman Andrew Jacobs Jr. (Democrat, Indiana). In his lawsuit, Robertson claimed that he had been libelled by the publication of an ancient story that (1) in February, 1951, he had sought to invoke his father's assistance in order to evade combat duty during the Korean War, and (2) that after his father had successfully kept him out of the combat zone until the truce talks commenced in June, 1951, Robertson had served as "liquor officer" at Division headquarters. The Reverend Robertson expressed particular outrage that his deceased and honorable parent had been accused of exercising "political influence" on anyone's behalf.

In the lawsuit, however, Senator Robertson's papers were ordered to be produced by the Court.

The papers confirmed a solid friendship amongst three distinguished Virginians from the little town of Lexington, Virginia, home of the famous Virginia Military Institute (V.M.I.) and its neighboring university, Washington and Lee. The three friends were Senator Robertson, Dr. Francis Gaines, President of Washington and Lee, and Lieutenant General Lemuel Shepherd, commander of all Marines in the Pacific Theatre. Robertson and Shepherd had served together as trustees of V.M.I. The Senator's son, Pat, and Dr. Gaines' son, Edward, had graduated from Washington and Lee in June, 1950. Both young men had attended the Marine Corps' Platoon Leader course at Quantico and were commissioned as second lieutenants that same month.

seconds. "The Chief Justice of the United States." Polite applause. "His Excellency, the Ambassador of Great Britain." Scattered applause. "The Chairman of the Federal Reserve Board, the Honorable Arthur Burns." Polite applause. "Chairman of the House Armed Services Committee, the Honorable Mendel Rivers of South Carolina." To a man, 1,000 well-fed tycoons roared to their feet shouting and twirling their napkins. Two full minutes elapsed before the revelers quieted and resumed their seats. A shocked Erlichman realized that Congress, or at least a few Congressmen, had more power than he had first thought.

---

[2]Dating back to the days of Smedley Butler, the Marine Corps has been preserved, on occasion, by powerfully-placed Members of Congress. Lt. Colonel Oliver North did the Marine Corps no favor when he deliberately concealed the truth from Congress about the Iran-Contra scandal and Israeli involvement. The faith of Congress and the American people in the truthfulness, as well as the fighting capacity of Marines is an asset of inestimable value.

The deposition testimony of Robertson's fellow Marines, taken with their letters home, and most particularly the letters of the Senator himself, confirmed that the allegedly-libelous story was accurate in excruciating detail.

More than that, the Senator's letters reflected a pattern of Senatorial intervention to obtain favorable military assignments for his friends and relatives dating back to 1946 and continuing until at least 1954.

Those letters, reprinted here for the edification of students of the American political system, reflect a depth of political favoritism which can only dismay the families of U.S. servicemen of that era.

They are arranged chronologically:

Section #1 In 1946, the Senator demanded of the Army that his nephew, Frank Robertson, be sent to the European Theatre instead of the Orient. His demand was successful.

Section #2 In 1947, a year later, the Senator requested that his nephew, Frank, receive an early return home from Europe. Again he was successful.

Section #3 In October, 1951, the Senator advised a military friend:

> "I shall see what I can do in behalf of a transfer. Colonel Cox of the Air Force who is our Liaison Officer is a close friend of mine and *always willing to interest himself in appropriate assignments for my friends without putting anything in the nature of political influence in their files.*"

Section #4 While his son Pat was aboard ship en route to Korea, on February 6, 1951, the Senator wrote General Shepherd, expressing regret that he had missed the General's visit to his office a few days earlier, and thanking the General for his assurance that Pat would "get some more training before engaging in combat duty in Korea."

The next day, February 7, the Senator wrote Francis Gaines:

> "February 7, 1951
>
>
> Dr. Francis P. Gaines,
> Washington and Lee University,
> Lexington, Virginia
>
> Dear Frank:
>
> Three years ago I was able to help Senator Knowland and Mayor Knox of San Diego on a ten million dollar water project there left unfinished by the Navy. When Pat went out to Camp Pendleton Knowland notified Knox that he was there. I enclose copy of the letter I received today from Knox.
>
> On Yesterday I received a letter from General Shepherd stating that Pat and Edwin were going to an interesting and historical part of Japan where they would be given some valuable training before proceeding to Korea.
>
> With kind personal regards, I am
>
> Sincerely yours,
>
>
> A. Willis Robertson"

Dr. Gaines sent a handwritten note back on February 9:

"Dear Willis

Shall always be grateful for everything you have done.

My best always.

2/9/51   Frank"

Six days later, on February 12, the Senator wrote to a friend or relative named "Josephine:"

"I think Pat and a few others in his category will be dropped off in Japan for further train-ing and naturally Gladys and I hope that before that is completed the issue in Korea will either have been settled or the United (Nations) line so stabilized that there will be no excessive casu-alties as in the Marine retreat from the Reservoir area."

The Senator didn't know that the word hadn't yet reached the First Marine Division. An officer from the Division met the troopship when it arrived in Yokesuka on February 10, and on February 11, Robertson's name appeared on the list of those assigned to the First Regiment. His friend Ed Gaines was on the list going to the Seventh Marines. On February 13th, however, the orders were finally con-veyed from FMFPAC (General Shepherd's headquarters) to the Breckinridge via the Marines' liaison office in Tokyo that "a Virginia Congressman wanted his son to have further training." An old friend of General Shepherd's, Colonel Burns, commanding the First Casual Company at Camp Otsu boarded the Breckinridge, sat down with the draft commander and the list of officers, and picked Robertson, Gaines and four other lieutenants appearing just above and below Gaines' name to be pulled off the ship, ostensibly to train returnees from the hospitals prior to their return to Korea.

All six officers were brand new second lieutenants without prior experience.

All but four of the thirty-nine remaining second lieutenants were killed or wounded in the next four months in Korea.

Twenty-six officers *with* prior combat service in World War II were not considered for the "training" assignment. Two of those officers were killed and one seriously wounded in Korea.

Section #5 The same day he thanked General Shepherd, the Senator wrote Secretary of Defense George Marshall enclosing a letter he had written in June, 1950, recommending General Shepherd to be the next Commandant of the Marine Corps.[3]

Section #6 In June, 1952, the Senator asked the Navy Judge Advocate General to honor his son Pat's desire to transfer to the Navy's legal department, noting that he didn't think General Shep-herd would object.

Section #7 Again, in June 1952, the Senator wrote a "Dear Lem" letter to General Shepherd, this time indicating a willingness to appoint a young nominee of the General's to West Point.

Section #8 In November, 1952, the Senator asked his friend General Shepherd to bring a friend's son, Pfc. Otto Halstead, home from Korea because his mother was upset.

Section #9 In December, 1952, the Senator wrote a friend, Garland Gray:

"I shall do what I can . . . to get Tommy . . .home next spring . . . without in any way hurting

---

[3]General Shepherd didn't need Senator Robertson's recommendation and was too much of a gentleman to have ever asked for it. When President Truman had named General Clifton Cates as Commandant in 1948, he had called Shepherd into his office and told him that he was making Cates Commandant only because he was older. The two had had identical distin-guished careers in World Wars I and II. Truman told Shepherd he would be made Commandant when Cates' four year tour of duty expired in 1952. This was related by General Shepherd to the author at the General's home in La Jolla in 1988.

Tommy's military future. In other words it is a matter I shall have to handle not only personally but with some one in the Army or Defense Department who is my friend . . . It may be next month before I can make the necessary contact with the right person."

Section #10 In October, 1954 the Senator wrote another "Dear Lem" letter to General Shepherd, indicating that his favorite fishing partner's son was now in Marine recruit boot training, but that the senator hoped "he will develop for you into a very fine platoon leader."

It is not known whether the young man who had failed to make the grades necessary to keep him in college was transferred into the Platoon Leaders Class which required a college diploma.

Section #11 For comparison, a letter from current Virginia Senator John Warner is inserted here. Hopefully Senator Warner is correct that the days of Senatorial influence on military assignments are long gone, but there were few sons of congresspersons who served in Viet Nam, and none are known to have died there. The letters follow.

LIBERTY TRUST BANK

ROANOKE, VIRGINIA

H. C. ROBERTSON
PRESIDENT

November 8, 1946

In re: Pvt. Frank Robertson, 13228525
         Co. "B" 11 Bn. E. T. C.
         Fort Belvoir, Virginia
- - - - -

Dear Willis,

As you already know, Frank enlisted in the Army on the last day of September. He gave as his preference the Army Engineers and is now in this branch of the service at Fort Belvoir. He has had about one month of basic training. As explained to you over the telephone, there is a great likelihood of his outfit being sent overseas within the next week or ten days. He would much prefer, if it is in order, to be detailed to one of the specialist schools.

He writes us that it appears very difficult to get into any of these schools. I wrote Frank yesterday to make application to his Commanding Officer for admission to one of the schools for which he has best qualifications. He is especially good in Math, Physics, Chemistry and Mechanical Drawing. We are anxious for him to be in some branch of the Engineers where he can learn something as well as be of service to the Army.

If it is in order, and you have any contact whereby you can be of assistance to him in this matter, it would mean a whole lot to Frank and be greatly appreciated by the folks at home.

We were all elated over the fine vote that you received. Sorry to hear that Pat hasn't been well. Hope you, Gladys and Pat can come to see us between now and Christmas.

Fondly yours,

Harold

COPY

November 12, 1946.

Harold G. Robertson, Esq.,
c/o Liberty Trust Company,
Roanoke, Virginia.

Dear Mr. Robertson:

I have just talked with Mr. Robertson with reference to your son's case. The Adjutant General of the Army advises me that he completed his training at Fort Belvoir, Va., last Saturday and is scheduled to go to Camp Stoneman, California, on the 19th for overseas shipment.

The Adjutant General said that he would like to be able to comply with the Senator's wishes in this matter, but that since your boy is in the Regular Army and it is necessary to replace draftees now overseas with men in the regular establishment, his hands are tied.

He explained that the overseas Commander had full and complete jurisdiction over the assignment of troops under his command, and that in view of your son's outstanding work in college in electronics, mathematics, chemistry and physics, he felt confident that he would be given an assignment commensurate with his training in those subjects.

Mr. Robertson asked me to tell you that he would be glad to communicate with Frank's commanding officer after he arrives overseas, if he will send him his name and address.

With kind regards, I am

Sincerely yours,

J. P. Stratton, (Secretary)

JOSEPH L. EGAN
PRESIDENT

The filing time shown in the date line on telegrams and day letters is STANDARD TIME at point of origin. Time of receipt is STANDARD TIME at point of destination

WA88 14 GOVT VIA BU MVD FROM HOB=LEXINGTON VIR 13 11:54A
J F STRATTON SECY=

WILLIS ROBERTSON SENATE OFFICE BLDG=

=ASK WAR DEPARTMENT TO ASSIGN FRANK ROBERTSON TO UNIT GOING

EUROPE INSTEAD OF ORIENT=

=A WILLIS ROBERTSON=

WESTERN UNION

1206

A. N. WILLIAMS
PRESIDENT

Send the following telegram, subject to the terms on back hereof, which are hereby agreed to   Washington, D. C.,
                                                                                                 November 14, 1946.

Mr. Harold G. Robertson,
c/o Liberty Trust Co.,
Roanoke, Virginia.

FRANK WILL BE SENT TO MEDITERRANEAN THEATER OF
OPERATIONS

                              A. Willis Robertson, USS

        AG says they are overstaffed in European Theatre,
        but they have arranged for his assignment as in-
        dicated above. He will probably be sent to Italy.

                              S

LIBERTY TRUST BANK

ROANOKE, VIRGINIA

H. C. ROBERTSON
PRESIDENT

November 23, 1946

Dear Willis,

Thanks for your letters regarding Frank's work. Glad to know that he did a good job. He is at home this week. He reports at Camp Kilmer, November 26th for overseas duty. He seems to be very well pleased about the whole situation and thinks it would be well for every young fellow to have at least twelve months of military training. He expects to learn something while he is in the Army.

Jack Burroughs asked me to tell you that his brother, Bill would like very much to be postmaster at New Market. Anything that you can do for him will be appreciated.

Hope to see you, Gladys and Pat, Thanksgiving.

Fondly yours,

WESTERN UNION

1206

A. N. WILLIAMS
PRESIDENT

CHECK

ACCOUNTING INFORMATION

TIME FILED

Send the following telegram, subject to the terms on back hereof, which are hereby agreed to

Washington, D. C.,
November 14, 1946.

Mr. Harold G. Robertson,
c/o Liberty Trust Co.,
Roanoke, Virginia.

FRANK WILL BE SENT TO MEDITERRANEAN THEATER OF
OPERATIONS

A. Willis Robertson, USS

EXXXXXXXXXXXX

December 9, 1947

Honorable Kenneth C. Royall,
Secretary of the Army,
Department of the Army,
Washington, D.C.

Dear Mr. Secretary:

My nephew, Corporal Frank P. Robertson, 13228525, is serving with the 427th Replacement Company, 149th Replacement Battalion in Italy. His outfit was scheduled to come home on December 3rd and all of them left at that time except about sixteen hundred, including Corporal Robertson. Those boys were told that it was not known when they could come home.

On the assumption that he would get home in December, my brother has enrolled his son, Corporal Frank P. Robertson, in a University to continue his technical training. Upon my advice this boy volunteered for service and did not wait to be drafted. If he had waited a few weeks longer and gone into the draft he would have been discharged from the service some months ago. I realize, of course, that you are having difficulty in obtaining your authorized strength and that it may be necessary for you to maintain some troops in the Trieste area after the 16th of this month when under the Italian Treaty our troops must be withdrawn from Italy. I feel, however, that it would be unfortunate if you have to use for that purpose boys who want to reenter college in February and who would have the privilege of doing so but for the fact that they were patriotic enough to volunteer.

If Corporal Robertson can't enter college in February he would lose one half a year in his college work in order to serve about thirty days longer in the Army. That, of course, would work a great hardship on him.

With best wishes, I am

Sincerely yours,

A. Willis Robertson

December 9, 1947

H. G. Robertson, Esquire,
President,
Colonial-American National Bank,
Roanoke, Virginia.

Dear Harold:

I took up with the Adjutant General of the Army what you said in your note to me of the 5th about holding troops in Europe and he has sent a radiogram to the Theater Commander for information.

He said it would probably be ten days or more before he can let me have a reply. The Adjutant General said he did not think that troops would be kept in Italy in violation of the Treaty Agreement but that some might be kept in the Trieste area. I shall do what I can to see that your boy is not among those so held.

Fondly yours,

December 11, 1947

In reply refer to:
CSLLD 200.3-1059

Honorable A. Willis Robertson

United States Senate

Dear Senator Robertson:

The Secretary of the Army has asked me to acknowl-edge receipt of your letter of December 9, 1947, in which you indicate your interest in Corporal Frank P. Robertson, ASN 13228525, 427th Replacement Company, 149th Replacement Battalion, Italy, and request informa-tion relative to his return to the United States.

Pursuant to a telephone conversation between Mr. Stratton of your office and Colonel Scott of this Divi-sion, a radiogram was dispatched to the appropriate overseas command on December 8th, requesting informa-tion on the return of Corporal Robertson to this country. As soon as a reply is received you may ex-pect to hear direct from Secretary Roynall.

Sincerely yours,

C. O. BLAKENEY
Colonel, OSC
Legislative & Liaison Division

7 DEC 1947

Honorable A. Willis Robertson

United States Senate

Dear Senator Robertson:

I have your letter of December 9, 1947 in which you discussed your nephew Corporal Frank P. Robertson, ASN 13228525, 427th Replacement Company, 149th Replacement Battalion, whose scheduled departure from Italy on December 3rd was cancelled. You also stated your brother had enrolled his son in a university to continue his technical training and that you are interested in his release from the Army in time to enter college in February.

Pursuant to your inquiry a radiogram was dispatched to the appropriate overseas command requesting the date of Corporal Robertson's return to this country. I have just received a reply to my message and have been informed that Corporal Robertson is being returned to the United States for discharge aboard the ADMIRAL SIMS which departed from Leghorn on December 14th. This vessel is scheduled to arrive in New York harbor on Christmas Day but the exact hour of arrival is not known at this time.

The usual procedure in processing personnel in Corporal Robertson's category is to ship them from New York to Camp Kilmer, New Jersey, where they will be separated from the service. The records of the Department of the Army indicate that he enlisted for 18 months on September 30, 1946, and that under present policy of the Army he is eligible for discharge upon his arrival at Camp Kilmer if there is no military reason to the contrary. Hence your nephew should be out of the Army in sufficient time to enter college in February.

I trust the above information answers your inquiry in behalf of Corporal Robertson.

Sincerely yours,

Kenneth C. Royall
Secretary of the Army

December 19, 1947

Honorable Kenneth C. Royall,
The Secretary of the Army,
War Department,
Washington, D.C.

Dear Mr. Secretary:

Your letter of the 17th advising me that my nephew is being returned to this country this month and upon arriving will be eligible for discharge is much appreciated.
With best wishes, I am

Sincerely yours,

A. Willis Robertson

Section #3   Noting that he would try to get a son's friend transferred to an ROTC unit without a record of "political influence."

October 20, 1951a.

Major Giles B. Cook, Jr.
P. O. Box 626
Barksdale AFB, Florida

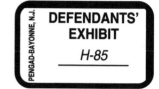

Dear Bim:

I have received and read with much interest the letter that I got from you today. The most interesting item in your letter was the fact that you are looking for Bim, Jr., in December. Frank and I some days ago commented on the fact that we had not heard from you for a long time, that if you were not expecting an addition to your family you were not properly discharging all of your public duties and, therefore, we sent you a copy of Infant Care which is generally considered the best publication on that subject.

When you find a school which has an ROTC Unit let me know and I shall see what I can do in behalf of a transfer. Colonel Cox of the Air Force who is our Liaison Officer is a close friend of mine and always willing to interest him-self in appropriate assignments for my friends without put-ting anything in the nature of political influence in their files.

This has been a really tough session of the Senate and I am glad that it will end today. Some weeks ago I and other members of the Appropriations Committee had planned to go to Europe for six weeks on the assumption that we would adjourn by October 13 but when we could not meet that deadline or find out definitely when we would adjourn we were forced to abandon the plan.

I have accepted an invitation for Mrs. Robertson and me to attend the reception at the British Embassy on November 1 for Her Royal Highness Elizabeth, a meeting of the Virginia Manufacturers Association at Hot Springs the next day and a speaking engagement at Miami, Florida on the 12th. However, Mrs. Robertson called me yesterday and said that she was feel-ing so badly that she doubted if she could keep any of these

engagements. She worried a great deal about Pat when he was
sent to Japan after only two months training but finally became reconciled to the situation. In June, Pat was sent to
Korea as a replacement for the First Marine Division which
has suffered very heavy losses. He and Edwin Gaines went
about the same time. Pat was assigned to the Adjutant's Office
at Division Headquarters and Edwin to a combat company. The
third day that Edwin was in action he got a shrapnel fragment
in the hip which put him out of commission about three weeks.
When he was returned to active duty Pat managed to have him
assigned to his Headquarters which, of course, will make it
pleasant for them both. Pat thinks that under the rotation
plan he can come back next March. He plans to enter the Yale
Law School next September.

Taddy who is now a Lieutenant (j.g.) in the Naval Reserves took a Summer training cruise but has not yet been
called to active duty. At the end of that cruise he made
the highest examination of the men in his class from twenty-
five States on the subject of radar information in which he
has specialized. Taddy has a fine job with Transcontinental
Gas and Oil of Houston, Texas. His present Headquarters is
in Atlanta where he is in charge of sales plus some work on
rate making which he studied for over a year in Washington.
Alfred Glassell, Jr., of Houston is a Director of that Company. His father lives in Shrevesport and is a wealth oil
man. A few years ago Secretary of War Patterson took me to
Louisiana for two days of duck hunting with him. Some time
when you can conveniently do so call on Mr. Glassell and tell
him that you are a friend of mine. He can put you and your
wife in touch with some nice people in Shrevesport.

With all good wishes for you and Mountie, I am

Sincerely your friend,

A. Willis Robertson

Section #4   Noting General Shepherd's assurance that Pat and his friend Ed Gaines would be taken off the replacement draft headed for Korea.

AIR MAIL

February 6, 1951a.

Dear General Shepherd:

Thank you so much for your nice letter of the 3rd and for your encouraging message concerning Pat. I think he is going to make you a good officer and naturally I am happy that he will get some more training before engaging in combat duty in Korea.

I was very disappointed to miss you when you came by my office week before last but I received the note that you left with my Secretary and that evening called Mrs. Robertson over the telephone and gave her your message.

The First Marine Division has added new glory to the record of a great Corps. And needless to say we in Virginia take great pride in the record that you and other VMI men have made in the Korean war. However, we would like to see that war brought to a definite conclusion as soon as possible. Partly because it is tying down in the Orient the best fighting forces we have which may be urgently needed before the year is out in Europe and secondly because of the vacillation of our allies with respect to Communist China, leaving everyone in this country in doubt as to what the real objective of the current fighting in Korea is.

In the last war, the Marines had six Divisions and without them we could not have defeated Japan. Last Fall in testifying before our Appropriations Committee General Cates said that while he was going along with the present decision of the Joint Chiefs of Staff for two fully equipped and trained Marine Divisions he personally would like to see an authorization for four such Divisions. Consequently, last month I united with Paul Douglas and several other Senate friends in the introduction of a bill to authorize four Marine Divisions and hope that we can get early action on it.

At the moment we are somewhat disturbed over the effect of pending draft proposals on military schools such as VMI. We hope to have incorporated in the law that is passed suitable provisions to utilize the facilities of our military colleges

COPY

to the fullest and best advantage. At the moment everything
is going well at VMI. I and two other old members retired
from the Board last June but our places were filled with some
fine young men. General George Marshall while retiring as
Chairman of the Board remained on the Board and Mike Sale was
named as Chairman to succeed him. Mike is a friend and admirer of the Superintendent and will work in harmony with him.

I am forwarding your letter to Mrs. Robertson who will
appreciate the good wishes sent by you and Mrs. Shepherd.

With kindest regards and all good wishes, I am

Sincerely your friend,

A. Willis Robertson

February 7, 1951e

Dr. Francis P. Gaines,
Washington and Lee University,
Lexington, Virginia

Dear Frank:

        Three years ago I was able to help
Senator Knowland and Mayor Knox of San Diego
on a ten million dollar water project there
left unfinished by the Navy. When Pat went
out to Camp Pendleton Knowland notified Knox
that he was there. I enclose copy of the
letter I received today from Knox.

        On yesterday I received a letter from
General Shepherd stating that Pat and Edwin
were going to an interesting and historical
part of Japan where they would be given some
valuable training before proceeding to Korea.

        With kind personal regards, I am

                Sincerely yours,

                A. Willis Robertson

Dear Willis —
Shall always be grateful
for *everything* you have done —
My best always —
Frank

2/9/51

Dear Willis—
    Shall always be grateful
for <u>everything</u> you have done—
My best always—
        Frank
2/9/51

February 12, 1951a.

Dear Josephine:

I am delighted to learn from your nice letter of the 9th that the ham finally arrived. My only regret is that I can't send you a whole steer because I really sympathize with you in these austere days. It is good to know, however, that before too long you and John will be returning to Lexington where opportunities for making money are possibly less than in some foreign city but the chances for gracious living a bit better.

I appreciate so much what you say about Pat. He finished two months of basic training at Quantico on December 22nd and reported for duty at Camp Pendleton, California the second week in January. After he had been there about ten days he sailed with Marine replacements some of whom were headed for Japan and some for Korea. I think Pat and a few others in his category will be dropped off in Japan for further training and naturally Gladys and I hope that before that is completed the issue in Korea will either have been settled or the united line so stabilized that there will be no excessive casualties as in the Marine retreat from the Reservoir area.

I regret that Gladys is worse instead of better and while she dreads to go through another operation, which means being in a plaster cast for four months, I am very much afraid that such an operation cannot be avoided. I know she will be delighted to learn that you and John will soon be her neighbors.

With best wishes for you both, I am

Sincerely your friend,

A. Willis Robertson

Mrs. John D. Rogers
3, Eldon Road
Kensington, W.8
London, England

Section #5 On the nomination of General Shepherd to be named Commandant of the Marine Corps.

February 6, 1951a.

Dear Mr. Secretary:

I am taking the liberty of enclosing to you a copy of the letter that I wrote on June 14, 1950 to your predecessor with regard to my friend, Lieutenant General Lemuel C. Shepherd, Jr.

Faithfully yours,

A. Willis Robertson

General George C. Marshall
Secretary of Defense
Washington, D. C.

THE SECRETARY OF DEFENSE
WASHINGTON

Feb. 12 1951

Dear Senator Robertson:

Thank you for your letter of February 6 with reference to Lieutenant General Lemuel C. Sheperd, Jr.

I am referring that letter and the copy of the letter you wrote to my predecessor to Secretary Matthews for his consideration when a decision with reference to the next Commandant of the Marine Corps is made.

I am sure that Secretary Matthews will give your letter every attention.

Faithfully yours,

G. C. MARSHALL

Honorable A. Willis Robertson

United States Senate

COPY

February 13, 1951a.

Dear Mr. Secretary:

Thank you very much for your kindness in referring my communication concerning General Shepherd to the Secretary
of the Navy.

Faithfully yours,

A. Willis Robertson

General George C. Marshall
Secretary of Defense
Washington, D. C.

*Author's Note: On the following day, February 14, 1951, orders were delivered to the troop ship U.S.S. General
J.C. Breckinridge, removing Senator Robertson's son Pat from the list of officers ordered to join the First Marine
Regiment in Korea, and reassigning him to Camp Otsu, Japan, where he remained until commencement of truce
talks in late June, 1951.*

THE SECRETARY OF THE NAVY

WASHINGTON

14 February 1951

My dear Senator Robertson:

    The Secretary of Defense has forwarded to me
a copy of his letter to you dated February 12th,
together with your letter to him dated February 6th,
referring to the matter of Lieutenant General Lemuel
C. Shepherd, Jr., U. S. Marine Corps.

    I wish to assure you that I personally share your
hgih tnthusiasm for the outstanding professional and
personal qualities of General Shepherd and will give
your letter every consideration at such time as the
matter you refer to is pertinent.

    With best wishes, I am

        Sincerely yours,

        Francis P. Matthews (signed)

Honorable A. WillisRobertson
United States Senate
Washington, D. C.

copy

February 16, 1951a.

Honorable Francis P. Matthews
The Secretary of the Navy
Washington, D. C.

Dear Mr. Secretary:

I am indeed happy to learn from your letter of the 14th that you share my high regard for Lieutenant General Shepherd and will give consideration to him when the time comes to select a new Commandant for the Marine Corps.

With best wishes, I am

Sincerely yours,

A. Willis Robertson

November 15, 1952e

General Lemuel C. Shepherd, Jr.
Commandant of the Marine Corps
Department of the Navy
Washington 25, D. C.

Dear General Shepherd:

Mr. Roland Halstead of Back Bay, Virginia, is one
of my very best friends. Several of his sons served
in World War II and his youngest boy for nearly two
years has been with the Marines presently stationed
in Korea. This boy is PFC Otto V. Halstead, 1185897,
Second Battalion, Fifth Marine Division. He was supposed to be rotated about October 18. On November
2d Dr. Ira L. Hancock, the family physician, wired me
that the report that her son would not be rotated on
October 18th was having a very serious effect on his
mother who was suffering from a bad heart condition.

On November 3d I presented the situation to Colonel
LaHue of your office who sent a dispatch to the boy's
commander to get information concerning the boy's
rotation. On November 10th your Liaison Officer called
my office and said that Halstead was well and his "return
from active duty is contemplated in the near future".

Last March this boy was wounded in Korea but soon
recovered and returned to active duty.   When his mother
learned of the terrific casualties being suffered by the
Marines last month and heard that her boy would not be
started home as she had hoped and expected on October 18th
it upset her so that both her doctor and her husband des-
paired of her life.

I have taken the liberty of informing Mr. Halstead that
the Marine Corps will rotate his boy just as soon as he
was entitled to rotation under existing rules and would
not hold him on the fighting front simply because there
was urgent need for replacements. I regret, of course,
having to bother you with a detail of this character but

2.

Halstead is such a good friend of mine and I feel so concerned over his wife's condition that I hope that you will forgive me for bringing this particular case to your personal attention.

As soon as you can give me some encouraging word to forward to Mr. Halstead I shall greatly appreciate it.

With kind personal regards, I am

Sincerely yours,

A. Willis Robertson

COPY

[handwritten] Halstad

November 19, 1952

General Lemuel C. Shepherd, Jr.
Commandant of the Marine Corps
Department of the Navy
Washington 25, D. C.

Dear General Shepherd:

Your letter of the 17th concerning
Private First Class Otto V. Halsted is
being forwarded to Senator Robertson at
Lexington.

Meanwhile, I can assure you that he
will appreciate your interest in this
matter and especially the action which a
member of your staff advised you were
taking in writing personally to Mrs.
Halsted.

Sincerely yours,

Warren A. McNeill,
Administrative Assistant
to Sen. A. Willis Robertson.

*[handwritten] cy to Lex
11-1---*

June 21, 1952a.

Dear Pat:

I mentioned today to Admiral Nunn, Judge Advocate General of the Navy, your desire to transfer to his Department. He said that he would like to have you provided the Marine Corps would agree to let you transfer.

Admiral Nunn will call you to his office one day next week for a personal interview and then he will take the matter up with General Shepherd. In the meantime, brush up on your Naval law because he may ask you some questions on that subject to see what you have learned since you have been in the legal section at Quantico. He suggested that you could get the Marine Corps to designate you to attend their Legal School but that is a three months course and I told him that would not fit into your present plans because you wanted a little vacation and then you would enter Yale in September.

Since you will soon go on an inactive status I don't believe General Shepherd would raise any objection to your transfer. It has to be accomplished before you return to a Civil Service status because after that time you would have to be passed by the Civil Service Commission before the Navy could commission you in its Legal Department as a civilian. If necessary, you could, of course, delay your retirement from active duty a few days while the transfer was being put through because undoubtedly now is the time to change over to the Legal Department of the Navy on a Reserve Officer status.

Fondly yours,

Lst. Lieutenant M. G. Robertson
Headquarters Battalion
Marine Corps Schools
Quantico, Virginia

June 24, 1952a.

General Lemuel C. Shepherd, Jr.
Commandant of the Marine Corps
Department of the Navy
Washington 25, D. C.

Dear Lem:

        Thank you for your letter of the 23rd in behalf
of Randolph Maury Browne, III, who is desirous of
securing an appointment to West Point for the session
commencing in June of next year. I have previously
received some high testimonials in his behalf, including one from our mutual friend, Colgate Darden, his
High School principal, Mr. Pruet and the Rector of
Christ Church in Alexandria. I note with interest from
your letter that the brother of this boy's mother is
from Norfolk and one of your VMI school-mates. I also
note that young Browne is taking a civil Service competitive examination this month either on Judge Smith's
list or Senator Byrd's or possibly both.

        For a number of years I have made my appointments
to the Service Schools on the basis of Civil Service
competitive examinations but found the plan to be very
unfair to Virginia high school graduates who could not
go to a preparatory school which specialized in coaching
boys to take the Civil Service examination. Incidentally,
in one year one of these preparatory schools secured an
advance copy of the Civil Service examination and naturally
all the boys from that School made top grades.

        This year, my appointments to the Service Schools
will be made on the basis of my personal appraisal of the
applicants. I expect to have one appointment to West Point
and three to the Naval Academy. If young Browne does not
win an appointment to West Point on the basis of the competitive
examination, I shall be glad to consider him when I make
my selections. In the meantime, you might ascertain whether
or not he would like to go to the Naval Academy and then

COPY

become a Marine if he fails to get an appointment to West Point.

With best wishes, I am

Sincerely yours,

A. Willis Robertson

December 5, 1952

Honorable Garland Gray
Waverly, Virginia

Dear Peck:

I know exactly how you feel about getting Tommy
and Flo home next Spring and shall do what I can in their
behalf without in any way hurting Tommy's military future.
In other words, it is a matter which I shall have to handle
not only personally but with some one in the Army or
Defense Department who is my friend. Since Tommy's three
year tour abroad will expire in August he no doubt has
accumulated a three months leave of absence. In the past
I think that it has been the policy of the Department of
the Army to include the leave of absence period with the
tour of foreign duty period and let the soldier come home
to take his leave where he will really enjoy it.

When I was in Europe last Fall I found that the
nations of Western Europe appear to be far less concerned
over the imminence of a Russian attack than we. Naturally,
I hope that they are right and considering the fact that
we now have an ample supply of atom bombs and a few hydrogen
bombs it would be difficult for me to assume that Russia
would intentionally and deliberately plunge the world into
another war. On the other hand, if by any chance the
Russians plan a shooting war, I don't see how they could
afford to postpone it longer than next summer.

It will give me pleasure to cooperate with you in
getting tommy and Flo home as soon as possible but it may
be next month before I can make the necessary contact with
the right person.

With kindest regards, I am

Sincerely yours,

A. Willis Robertson

Section #10 Just to let you know of my interest in a friend's son getting from Paris Island into Officer Training School.

<u>PERSONAL</u>   October 19, 1954a.

General Lemuel C. Shepherd, Jr.
Commandant of the Marine Corps
Department of the Navy
Washington 25, D. C.

Dear Lem:

    Just a note to let you know of my interest in
a Marine recruit named W. W. Wharton, Jr. This
boy's father, a prominent lawyer in Harrisonburg,
Virginia and a Commander in the Navy during the last
war, is my favorite fishing partner and in that way
I got to know his son Billie.

    When Billie finished high school he went, at my
suggestion, to VMI for one year. But unfortunately
he did not make grades high enough to get deferred
from the draft so this Fall he volunteered for service
with the Marines and is now taking his boot training
at Paris Island. Billie is about six feet tall, weighs about
one hundred and seventy pounds, is a good athlete
and has the type of courage and character that the
Marines esteem and I predict that he will develop for
you into a very fine platoon leader.

    With warmest personal regards, I am

        Sincerely yours,

      A. Willis Robertson

October 25, 1954a.

General Lemuel C. Shepherd, Jr.
Commandant of the Marine Corps
Department of the Navy

Dear Lem:

Your nice letter of the 21st concerning my
young friend, Wharton, is greatly appreciated.

I always shall be grateful for the fact that
my younger son, Pat, served with the Marines because, with all due deference to the Army in which
I served and the other two Services, I always have
said that in my opinion the Marine Corps was the
best.

With kindest personal regards, I am

Sincerely yours,

A. Willis Robertson

Section #11   Senator John Warner of Virginia, 1986: In 5 years of service as Secretary of the Navy during the Viet Nam years he never saw any evidence of congressional influence on duty assignments.

S.JP. 26 '86 10:44 777% CBN   804-< 4-7777--

89-26-86 FRI 10:29AM

JOHN W. WARNER
VIRGINIA

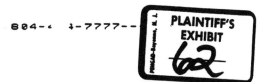

United States Senate
WASHINGTON, D.C. 20510

ARMED SERVICES COMMITTEE
  Chairman, Strategic and Theater Nuclear Forces
  Subcommittee

ENERGY AND NATURAL RESOURCES COMMITTEE
  Chairman, Energy and Mineral Resources
  Subcommittee

RULES AND ADMINISTRATION COMMITTEE

JOINT COMMITTEE ON THE LIBRARY OF CONGRESS

September 15, 1986

Dr. Pat Robertson
CHRISTIAN BROADCASTING NETWORK
CBN Center
Virginia Beach, Virginia 23463

Dear Pat:

I recently saw press accounts covering parts of your active duty Marine Corps Service during 1950-52.

As you will remember, I was on active duty about this same period, having volunteered for recall in August, 1950. Since graduating from W&L and receiving my commission, I had been affiliated with the U.S.M.C. reserve squadron at the old Anacostia, D.C., Navy-Marine Corps Air Station.

You and I were in basic school in Quantico in the fall of 1950, then were ordered our separate ways.

You went infantry, and I was trained as a communicator (having served in WWII in that field) and then ordered to aviation units in view of my duties with VMF 321, Anacostia.

We again saw each other in Korea — remember? Our old friend from Washington & Lee had been wounded while serving as an infantry platoon leader, had just been released from the hospital, and you and I welcomed him back to duty, following his recovery, in some location near the 1st Marine Division forward headquarters.

Earlier that day, I had been up on the lines working with battalion air controllers, assigned from the M.A.G. 33, where I was stationed.

I stopped on my return to see you and spent the night with our longtime friend in some old "dugout". We listened that evening to our friend recount his experiences and how he was now engaged in writing up citations. He finally put his W&L English major to work!

PR   136

09-26-86 FRI 10:30AM   P.03

I recall the night vividly for as we talked you could hear
the distant rumble of "H&I" artillery fire, and we were
expecting "bed check Charlie" to fly over and leave his
usual calling card. (He didn't as I remember).

Although I hold your father's seat in the Senate, I never
had the privilege of meeting or hearing from him. My loss,
for he had a most distinguished reputation. Had I known
him, especially during our Washington & Lee days together,
1946-49, perhaps I could today provide some observation
about his alleged participation in changes in your duty
assignments.

During my over five years in the Navy Department,
Undersecretary 1969-1972, and Secretary 1972-74, I recall no
incident where a Member of Congress personally approached me
in reference to a combat assignment of a constituent (or
relative) in Vietnam. While I have no means to comment on
practice during the Korean War, I do know that neither I,
nor another contemporary Secretary of Navy whom I consulted,
ever exercised our authority in a manner alleged to have
been done in your case.

Drop in to see me someday.

Sincerely,

John Warner

JWW/mmm

PR   137

Chapter 14

The Virginians, Regular and Reserve

In 1987, I read, for perhaps the tenth time, my favorite books, the three volumes of *Lee's Lieutenants*, written by Douglas Southall Freeman forty years earlier. Those books were the first I ever purchased, as a college student in 1947, and they played a major role in my decision to enlist in the Marine Corps Platoon Leaders Class the next year. The chance to spend six summer weeks at Quantico and visit the great battlegrounds of the Civil War, obtaining a Second Lieutenant's commission on graduation, presented an opportunity too good to miss.

Growing up in Southern California, my boyhood heroes had been Robert E. Lee, Stonewall Jackson and Jeb Stuart. *Lee's Lieutenants* added a whole new set of men to admire, a good number of whom were also Virginians. I read and re-read the stories of the Civil War from First Manassas to Appomatox.

The Army of Northern Virginia of 1862-65 has always seemed to me to have been the finest military organization ever formed on this continent. Their way of life was not a matter of glory and unexcelled heroism; the writings of Ambrose Bierce are perhaps more valuable than Freeman's in bringing home the awful carnage and suffering of the Civil War. The incredible casualty rates, the primitive nature of battlefield surgery with its lack of anesthesia, the long lines of battlefield dead, portrayed so graphically in Brady's photographs evoke images of misery, not glory. A visit to the scene of Pickett's charge at Gettysburg, the cornfield at Sharpsburg on Antietam Creek or the sunken road at Fredericksburg goes a long way to convince one of the truth of Sherman's famous comment, "War is Hell," and that the heroic statues of generals on horseback around Washington, D.C. should be viewed with caution, if not cynicism. From time to time during the tensest of times in Korea I remember reflecting on how lucky I was to be a platoon leader in 1951 rather than during the Civil War. The great leaders, to me at least, were the men who led regiments or brigades in the Civil War, often dying at the head of them, men like Dodson Ramseur, Thomas Rosser, Wade Hampton, Robert Rodes, John Pelham, William Pegram and John Bell Hood.

It was not lost on me that Hood had been a brilliant brigade and regimental leader, but later turned out to be a disappointment as a general officer at the Corps level. The Marine Corps has had its share of superb rifle company officers who later made only fair generals.

If there has been a modern parallel to the Army of North Virginia, it seems to me that the Marine units which held at Guadalcanal and assaulted at Pelelieu, Tarawa and Iwo Jima have come the closest to the Stonewall Brigade at First Manassas and Pickett's Division which charged the center of the Union line on Cemetery Ridge at Gettysburg.

I have mused for years over the connection between the Marine Corps and the Army of Northern Virginia. In many ways the Corps *is* the modern reincarnation of that Army.[1] Lemuel Shepherd, Chesty Puller, his son Lewis Puller III and Chuck Robb have carried on the same tradition in modern times as did Lee, Jackson, Stuart and Pickett between 1861-65. A large number of the Corps' most famous officers have graduated from the Virginia Military Institute (V.M.I.) at Lexington, Virginia, just as V.M.I. furnished not only Stonewall Jackson but over a third of the commanders of the 56 Virginia regiments formed in 1861. It was in Virginia's Shenandoah Valley that Jackson's "foot cavalry" outmarched, outmaneuvered and outfought Northern armies twice their size in the famous Shenandoah Valley Campaigns of 1862. With the end of the Confederacy in sight in 1864, the school boys of the V.M.I. Cadet Corps, led by the first General J. C. Breckinridge, had assisted in halting the federal army at New Market, Virginia.

A disproportionately large number of Marine Corps NCOs and officers have always been southerners.[2]

Of America's 138 Marine Corps Reserve units scattered around the United States in June 1950 when the Korean War began, the Virginia units in particular were up-to-strength, with young Virginians waiting in line for the first available vacancies.

The story of one such unit, Roanoke's 16th Engineer Company, chronicled in *One Bugle, No Drums* by William B. Hopkins, is a case in point.

Hopkins, a graduate of V.M.I.'s companion university, Washington & Lee, at Lexington, Virginia, had enlisted in the Marine Corps Platoon Leader Class in 1940 and had seen combat duty in World War II.

Hopkins, by 1950 a reserve captain and successful lawyer, was ordered to active duty with his unit on July 22, 1950, less than a month after the North Koreans had invaded South Korea. For every man who requested deferment from active duty for personal reasons, another Virginian stepped forward to volunteer. Within weeks most of the Roanoke Marines were assigned to the First Marine Regiment under Chesty Puller, winner of four Navy Crosses to that time,[3] and perhaps the most beloved Marine combat leader of the century. Puller was from Saluda, Virginia. By December 10, when the Division had extricated itself from the Chosin Reservoir, the Roanoke unit had suffered 8 killed and 34 wounded, a casualty rate comparable to that of Jackson's Stonewall Brigade in any similar two weeks of combat in the Civil War. Hopkins, later to become Speaker of the Virginia legislature, himself was wounded and evacuated in January, 1951, spending a year of convalescence at Portsmouth Naval Hospital, returning to his law practice in April, 1952.

Hopkins was typical of the sons of Virginia's Shenandoah Valley and its environs. Young men

---

[1] Robert E. Lee wrote to General John B. Hood on May 21, 1963, shortly before Gettysburg: "I agree with you that our Army would be invincible if it could be properly organized and officered. There never were such men in an Army before. They will go anywhere and do anything if properly led. But there is the difficulty—proper commanders—where can they be obtained?" That fairly well sums up the goal of every Commandant of the Marine Corps since World War I.

[2] Of all the men of courage honored by the Corps, perhaps none should rank higher than the black men who volunteered early in World War II for combat duty with the Marine Corps under NCOs most of whom had been inculcated with the doctrine of white supremacy since birth. These "Montford Point" Marines, so named after the segregated place where they trained, have the right to be the proudest of the proud. Even as late as the early Korean War, the U.S. Army maintained segregated units, black battalions commanded by white officers. It wasn't until I had been in C/1/5 over four months that the Company received its first Black Marine as a replacement. A black volunteer Marine was a special individual indeed in the 1940s and early 1950s.

[3] Puller's 5th Navy Cross was awarded for leading the First Marine's rear guard action and holding the vital passes and perimeter at Koto- ri as the Fifth and Seventh Regiments fought their way back from the Reservoir.

were proud of their state's history, proud of Virginia's distinguished military tradition and proud of the reputation of the Marine Corps as a worthy successor to the Army of Northern Virginia.[4]

Young Virginians knew what was expected of them . . . service to their nation in time of need, and if possible, service with the Marines. In June 1950, 20 year old Edwin Gaines of Lexington was commissioned as a Second Lieutenant in the Marine Corps Reserve; his great great grandfather had won the Congressional Medal of Honor at the Battle of Lake Erie in the War of 1812. The great Civil War battles of First and Second Manassas were fought within sight of Gainesville, Virginia. Ed Gaines was to be wounded at the Punch Bowl in Korea while leading a rifle platoon.

Members of the Gaines family and Virginians at every level had volunteered in every war since the War for Independence. Their commitment was essential, particularly in the Korean War.

When the North Koreans attacked across the 38th parallel on 25 June 1950, President Truman committed United States armed forces almost immediately, and within a few days, a supposedly combat- ready unit, the 24th Infantry Division, was pulled out of its comfortable billets in Japan and thrown into action against the advancing North Koreans. The result was disastrous. The 24th's men were not in good physical condition and their small-unit cohesion was woeful. Troops of the 24th were literally butchered in their early days in Korea and their commanding general was captured.

Three more U.S. Army divisions did little better. A hastily organized and understrength Marine regiment, the Fifth Marines, trained by Virginian Victor Krulak, was in action within weeks, and by early August United Nations forces, holding absolute control of the air and oceans, were finally able to stop a lesser number of lesser armed North Koreans, largely because of the extended supply lines of the invader through an unfriendly countryside.

On September 15, 1950, General MacArthur broke the back of the North Korean effort by landing the First Marine Division at Inchon and retaking Seoul. That landing had been made possible only by the emergency call-up of 138 Marine Reserve units from all over the United States just two months earlier. Virginian General Lemuel Shepherd, who had served under MacArthur at Cape Gloucester in World War II, had MacArthur's confidence and made that landing possible. MacArthur's brilliant landing at Inchon in September was largely negated by an intelligence and command failure of equally-monumental proportions a few weeks later when Chinese armies composed solely of foot soldiers, with neither artillery nor significant motor transport, were able to infiltrate undetected across the Yalu and nearly wipe out the American and ROK forces advancing towards the Korean-Chinese border.[5]

---

[4]A Virginian, later to become the First President of the United States, George Washington wrote in 1783:

"It may be laid down as a primary position, and the basis of our system, that every citizen who enjoys the protection of a free government, owes not only a proportion of his property, but even of his personal services to the defense of it, and consequently, that the citizens of America (with a few legal and official exceptions), from eighteen to fifty years of age should be borne on the militia rolls, provided with uniform arms, and so far accustomed to the use of them, that the total strength of the country might be called forth at a short notice on any emergency.

And that while the Men of this description shall be viewed as the Van and flower of the American Forces, ever ready for Action and zealous to be employed whenever it may become necessary in the service of their Country; they should meet with such exemptions, privileges or distinctions, as might tend to keep alive a true Military pride, a nice sense of honor, and a patriotic regard for the public. Such sentiments, indeed, ought to be instilled into our Youth, with their earliest years, to be cherished and inculcated as frequently and forcibly as possible."

---

[5]In retrospect one cannot help but feel enormous respect for the Chinese and North Korean Infantrymen, who, without air support, artillery, logistics or good radios, with rifles, grenades and automatic weapons generally inferior to those of their opponents, came close to driving the forces of 16 modern nations off the Korean Peninsula in August, 1950, and several hundred miles from the Chinese border in two short months in the winter of 1950-51. If we Americans thought it was a hard war, it was doubly so for the Chinese and North Koreans, facing napalm, bombing and massive artillery.

The extrication of the 2nd Army Division and 1st Marine Division from North Korea in late 1950 were perhaps military successes, but the experience at the Pusan Perimeter pointed squarely to a command failure with respect to combat-readiness. The greatest military power in the world led by two World War I combat veterans, Harry Truman and Douglas MacArthur, had sent thousands of men into combat without proper training and equipment. No amount of satisfaction over the eventual stabilization of the battle line north of the 38th parallel six months later could disguise that painful reality. Both the civilian and military leadership had failed to heed the admonition of General Light Horse Harry Lee, Washington's cavalry chief and also a Virginian:

"A government is the murderer of its citizens which sends them to the field uninformed and untaught, where they are to meet men of the same age and strengths, mechanized by education and discipline for battle."

The Korean War experience may provide the best guidance today's leaders can find for what U.S. armed forces of the 1990s will face: the need for an adequately-trained body of reserves to augment the initially-committed regular forces.

In the Virginia tradition, Shepherd, Krulak and Puller, the regulars, and Hopkins, Gaines and other reservists had led the way. Senator Chuck Robb of Virginia was one of the few relatives of national figures to volunteer for a Marine combat unit in Viet Nam. The Virginia tradition, from Washington to Robb, is worthy of careful note from military historians.

The system in 1950 worked perfectly.

Within 60 days, the Marine Corps administrative echelons completed the necessary paperwork to get hundreds of reservists into the three rifle regiments which made the Inchon landing on September 15. By Christmas 1950, the Marine Corps School at Quantico had given some 95 reserve second lieutenants enough training to replenish the First Division's ranks following the withdrawal from the Reservoir in December.

The 1st Battalion, 5th Marines, in February, 1951, was officered by 41 regulars and 2 reserve offices; by June 1951, four months later, with over 50% casualties in its rifle companies, the proportions were exactly reversed, to 41 reserves and 2 regular officers.

More importantly, the reserve officers had enjoyed the privilege of being absorbed into units of superbly-trained and experienced regulars who, both by example and advice, were able to impart their own experience and criteria of excellence to the reserves.

The success of the United Nations forces in the winter and spring of 1951, first stopping the Chinese attack at Wonju and then driving the invaders back north of the 38th parallel, can be traced almost directly to that mix of experienced regulars at the outset with a sufficient number of reserves who had been available for induction and training within the previous six months. The contribution of the Virginians was more than most.

A visit to the spot where Pickett's Division charged across a mile of open ground at Gettysburg on July 3, 1863, will cause any American to understand why Lt. Lemuel Shepherd did what he did at Belleau Woods in 1918 or how the Marines did what they did at Pelelieu, Tarawa, Iwo Jima and Hue City.

Pickett's Charge is the fundamental example of the ethic of the United States Marine Corps.

I suspect that this book will find little readership beyond the generation that fought in World II and Korea, but I hope these essays will help obtain some small support in Congress and the White House for continuance of three regular Marine Corps combat divisions and an adequate number of Army air borne and infantry divisions, in physical condition to fight on a day's notice, with Reserve units that can join them within 30 days. Whatever has to be paid to young Americans to cause them to be willing to train in the Arctic in winter and in the desert and jungles in summer must be paid. Instant combat-readiness is a national necessity. The words of Light Horse Harry Lee of Virginia set out a command responsibility for Presidents and Members of Congress to have constantly before them as military budgets are cut and forces reduced.

Colonel Victor Krulak had a Marine Regiment combat-ready in July, 1950. Commandant Al Gray had two divisions of Marines combat-ready for Operation Desert Storm in 1991. A country privileged to have peace and prosperity should preserve a record of gratitude for those performances, and whatever the cost, there should always be a few good men, with the will and ability to fight and the weapons, equipment and transport capacity to put them into action anywhere in the world within a few days.

Along with the life, liberty and pursuit of happiness mentioned by Thomas Jefferson, we owe a great deal to his fellow Virginians, George Washington, Robert E. Lee, Stonewall Jackson George Pickett, Lemuel Shepherd, Chesty Puller, Louis Puller Jr., Bill Hopkins and Chuck Robb.

A typical mobilization order issued for the transfer of Marines at various security detachments to Camp Pendleton to make up the 1st and 7th Regiments which landed at Inchon.

2445
MVH/jfn
Ser 55-50
25 July, 1950

MARINE DETACHMENT, HEADQUARTERS,
COMMANDER IN CHIEF, U. S. ATLANTIC FLEET,
U. S. NAVAL BASE, NORFOLK 11, VIRGINIA

From: Commanding Officer
To: Sergeant Leo R. TUCKER 857874/0336/5231 USMC

Subj: Orders

Ref: (a) CMC dispatch 24/1938Z

1. In accordance with the authority contained in reference (a), you will, on 27 July, 1950, take charge of the below named personnel and proceed to Camp Joseph H. Pendleton, Oceanside, California, and upon arrival, report to the Commanding General, First Marine Division thereat, for duty and futher assignment:

RANK	NAME	SERVICE NUMBER	MOS	COMPONET
PFC	ACKERMAN, Joseph E.	665032	0311	USMC
PFC	CAHILL, Thomas J., Jr.	664425	0300	USMC
PFC	ELLIS, Frederick P.	1101944	0300	USMC
PFC	EWING, William J.	1082809	0311	USMC
RFC	FEENEY, George	648018	0300	USMC
PFC	FULTON, Herman T.	1071717	0300	USMC
PFC	GAHM, Charles	1074088	0311	USMC
PFC	HALL, Kenneth A.	669934	0311	USMC
PFC	HIBBLER, Melvin A., Jr.	1082823	0311	USMC
PFC	HUMBLE, Ovid Jr.	664799	0311	USMC
PFC	IRWIN, John H.	659550	0300	USMC
PFC	KRIGBAUM, Floyd T.	669715	0300	USMC
PFC.	MCANDREW, Robert	668528	0311	USMC
PFC	MILANDER, Samuel H.	664051	0300	USMC
PFC	SMITH, Asa W.	1094460	0300	USMC
PFC	SMITH, Robert E.	660120	0311	USMC

2. The Supply Officer, Fifth Naval District, U. S. Naval Base, Norfolk, Virginia, is requested to furnish the necessary transportation and subsistance in the execution of these orders.

3. The staff returns for yourself and the personnel under your charge are entrusted to your care for safe delivery to the Commanding General, First Marine Division.

4. Proper decorum will be maintained at all times while in the execution of these orders.

5. The travel herein enjoined is necessary in the public service, and is chargeable to allotment number 10105, appropriation 1711105.18.

CERTIFIED TRUE COPY

M. V. HARLAN, JR.

Summer Camp 1953 TTU Coronado
Battalion Inspection by General
Lemuel C. SHEPHERD, Commandant of
the U. S. Marine Corps   June 1953

A Company, 7th Infantry Battalion, reserve unit of San Bruno, California, being inspected at summer camp, 1953, by the Commandant of the Marine Corps and the legendary Chesty Puller. Puller made a caustic comment about the varying trouser lengths of these 18 year old reservists. The Korean War would end a month later.

Chapter 15

"The Play"
Berkeley, California, 1982

Since the founding of Stanford University in 1891 (Herbert Hoover was in its first graduating class) there has been an historic rivalry called "The Big Game," between Stanford and the University of California at Berkeley across San Francisco Bay.

Both institutions are known more for their academic reputation than their football teams. Games between Stanford and California, like those between Harvard and Yale, have often been considered as little more than a joke by partisans of football powerhouses like Michigan, Penn State, Oklahoma and U.S.C.[1]

Occasionally, however, one of the two schools enjoys a rare day in the sun, with first class teams of scholars, who, rising to the occasion, can shock Notre Dame and even win the Rose Bowl.

Such a time occurred in the late 1940s when a lot of ex-Marines came back from the Pacific and chose to matriculate at Stanford or Cal. One famous Marine, Jim Cox, was wounded on Iwo Jima, but returned to the University of California for officer training where he captained the Cal football team, then, upon the end of the war in 1945, enrolled at Stanford and successfully captained the Stanford team team against Cal in 1946.

In 1990, a Stanford graduate was interviewed by a political science researcher from the Bancroft Library at the University of California on a matter of historical interest.

Before the discussion turned to more serious subjects, the following exchange ensued:

Interview with Stanford Graduate
October 18, 1990
regarding Point Reyes National Seashore

[Tape begins]

Stanford Graduate: from January '47 until 1950 when the Korean War broke out, we lost three straight Big Games to Cal, two of them on conversions. The turkey who kicked the points

---

[1]The redoubtable Charles U. Daly, masquerading as Vice President of Harvard University in the 1970s, once opined to a *Harvard Crimson* reporter something like this: "Me go to the Yale game? Are you crazy? If I wanted to see a football game I'd get a bottle of scotch, shack up in a local motel and watch the Bears play the Redskins on television."

tbeat us, 21 to 18 in 1947 and 7 to 6 in 1948, was a fellow named Jim Cullom, known as "Truck" Cullom. I grew to—I didn't hate Truck Cullom, but I didn't like him much. They had three teams that went to the Rose Bowl those years, 1947, 1948 and 1949. At Stanford we were hurting. My roomate at Stanford, an ex-Marine named Ken Peck, missed the tackle on Paul Keckley in the last few seconds of the 21-18 game in 1947. After an 0 and 9 season, we had battled them to a standstill for 59 minutes and a last minute pass from Jackie Jensen to Keckley beat us.

Interviewer: Those were the Pappy Waldorf years.

Stanford Graduate: Yeah. In any event, Cullom and a lot of other Stanford and Cal students ended up in the Marine Corps in Korea, partly out of respect for friends like Peck and Cox. I went to Korea as a second lieutenant on kind of a famous troop ship with Pat Robertson saying, "My Daddy's a Senator; he's getting me out of this."

Interviewer: Oh, you were on that ship?

Stanford Graduate: Yes. I came back home, and during my last six months on active duty, which was from January to June of 1952, I was at Camp Pendleton training other young lieutenants who were on their way to Korea on how to survive. One of those that came through was Truck Cullom, who had enlisted in the Marine Corps in his college days. I think he'd played pro ball a couple of years. But a marvelous guy, a big, genial tackle. So I rode him unmercifully. If we had to go on a ten-mile hike, I made him go fifteen or gave him the point or something. But I really ran his ass around the hills of Camp Pendleton.

Interviewer: Did he know why?

Stanford Graduate: Oh, he knew. Stanford and Cal, you know, it has been a long happy rivalry. But I later went into the D.A.'s office up in Oakland, where I was one of only two Stanford men, and there were about forty Cal men, so I got it the other way. Cullom and I finally became good friends.

But in any event, Cullom went over to Korea, and in his first couple of weeks went on a patrol. There's a famous story about that patrol. Cullom went along as an observer, and the squad leader was in front, and then Cullom, and then twelve Marines behind him. Cullom tells this story; he says they're walking along the trail and all of a sudden they hear a "ping!" The squad leader in front knew what he'd done, he'd tripped a trip wire with a hand grenade. He dove off to one side, shouting "Grenade!" and Cullom dove off to the other side. Cullom said, "Grenade!" and he heard the words going back along the line . . . "Grenade! Grenade! Grenade! Grenade!" until they got to the last guy. The last guy said "No shit!" And then there was an explosion and Cullom next woke up on a hospital ship.

Interviewer: He jumped the wrong way.

Stanford Graduate: Well, the grenade pretty much chewed up his leg and left him with a limp, and he couldn't play rugby like everybody else for a while. But in any event, he came back, and with a lot of Stanford and Cal folks played or coached a lot of rugby. Cullom became, as I recall, either the rugby coach or the junior varsity coach at Cal, and he insisted that their football team train with the lateral pass that you have to throw in rugby. So apparently for years the whole Cal football team under Cullom's urging would run up and down the field lateraling backwards to each other as they ran.

So when they had that famous play in the 1982 Big Game—I mean, Stanford had won the game with a last minute field goal. The game was over. There were four seconds left. All that was left was the kickoff, and all of a sudden these Cal guys start lateraling the ball. Five times, and the last guy runs through the Stanford Band and they had won the game. Everybody in the Stanford rooting section was sitting there in a state of shock. I jumped up and yelled "Hurray for Cullom!" [laughter] And everybody's looking at me like I'm nuts. But that's the story of Jim Cullom and "The Play."

Interviewer: So that's his legacy.

Stanford Graduate: It may not be totally true but that's my image of Truck Cullom. He may be the last of the "Big Blue" enthusiasts for Cal football. I think he wears blue and gold skivvies. That's the Cullom legacy.

Chapter 16

Kindness

This essay traces the evolution from Marine to peacemaker of Indiana Congressman Andrew Jacobs.

Strangely enough, the most peace-inclined men I have known all experienced combat service in their youth.

Senators Bob Dole, John Chafee, Warren Rudman, Chuck Robb, Al Gore and John Kerry were all combat platoon leaders; John Glenn and Bob Kerrey were combat pilots. None of these fine public servants have been warhawks during the challenging years of their tenure in Washington. Their judgment has not been affected by any need to prove their solid strengths.

Bob Reno, perhaps New Hampshire's most distinguished lawyer, left the Marine Corps after World War II and worked for years with Grenville Clark and Louis Sohn in efforts to achieve world peace under world law, and mechanisms to settle disputes other than by warfare. The best Marine battalion commander I ever saw, Paul Lafond, a tank platoon commander on Okinawa, has given his later years to peace keeping and peace making in his native New England. Lieutenant Colonel Bob Tunnell, recuperating in Oak Knoll Naval Hospital in 1965 after losing a leg in the early months of the Viet Nam War, was one of the first to state that the war couldn't be won and that peace should be earnestly sought.

General Matt Ridgeway told me in 1971 that he felt that his most valuable service to the nation had not been his distinguished combat leadership in World War II, nor his resuscitation of the defeated Eighth Army in Korea in early 1951. Ridgeway believed that his advice to President Eisenhower in 1954, counseling against sending U.S. forces to support the French at Dien Bien Phu, had been his greatest contribution to his country. That advice, strongly opposed by Vice President Nixon, remained good a decade later when President Lyndon Johnson obtained authority from Congress to "resist agression with agression" under the Gulf of Tonkin Resolution of 1964.

General David Shoup, who had won the Congressional Medal of Honor at Tarawa, was the first four-star General to suggest that the Viet Nam War was a misplaced commitment of American military resources.

Actor Paul Newman and Colorado Congressman Jim Johnson, both of whom worked assiduously to bring the Viet Nam War to an end were both subject to combat experience in their youth, Newman as a Navy Tail Gunner at the end of World War II, Johnson in the Marine Corps Air Wing during the Korean War.

It has always seemed to me that the Presidency is in safer hands when the occupant of the White House has heard a little hostile machine gun fire or the explosions of grenades and artillery shells in his formative years.

With all due respect to Dan Quayle, Bill Clinton and Pat Robertson, a President or Vice President with the combat experience of a Dole, Chafee, Glenn, Rudman, Robb or Gore may be a little less anxious to push the button for what may be mankind's next and final war than an individual who joined the National Guard to avoid combat service in his youth.

Our warhawk presidents, Lyndon Johnson, Richard Nixon and Ronald Reagan somehow missed the combat experience shared by the men of their age. Keeping America from becoming "a pitiful, helpless giant," "bringing the coonskin home," and assaulting Grenada and Lebanese villages perhaps seemed justifiable policies at the time, but they also served to prove the manhood of the "firm and strong" Commanders-in-Chief who ordered them.

Jack Kennedy, who had a PT boat shot out from under him at The Slot at Guadalcanal, felt no need to order the carpet bombing of Cuba, as recommended by the Joint Chiefs of Staff during the Cuban Missile Crisis of 1961. He chose instead to halt the Soviet cargo ships carrying missiles to Cuba and successfully faced down Nikita Kruschev with the potential nuclear holocaust of World War III hanging in the balance.

George Bush has been criticized for stopping the one-sided slaughter of fleeing Iraqi troops in Operation Desert Storm, but I am convinced that his memories of combat service in a war which culminated in Hiroshima and Nagasaki played at least a small role in his decision to stop the killing of helpless people in 1991.

It may be merely a personal preference, but Bush, Dole, Chafee and Rudman, Glenn, Robb, Gore, Kerrey and Kerry are people I would feel a bit more comfortable with at the triggering mechanism of wapons which can destroy the world during the balance of this century.

Kindness seems to have been a major characteristic in the later years of those privileged to have been shot at early in life.

There is much to say for a "kinder and gentler America."

But back to Congressman and former Marine Andrew Jacobs, Jr., a relic of Booth Tarkington's Indiana.

As a raw-boned Hoosier stripling of 18, son of a distinguished Indiana lawyer[1] and congressman, Jacobs was called to active duty in the summer of 1950 with his reserve unit, given several months of combat training and shipped overseas from Camp Pendleton, California in the 7th Replacement Draft. He arrived in mid-April, as the First Division was continuing an assault north against the Chinese which had started on February 21, 1951, at Wonju.

By April 22, elements of the 1st Division had recrossed the 38th parallel and were advancing on the various ridgelines running north in the rugged mountains west of the Hwachon reservoir.

The 1st Battalion of the Fifth Marine Regiment reached a point directly west of the town of Hwachon; Charlie company had moved during the day onto a commanding ridgetop position with Baker company on a similar ridgeline, perhaps a mile across a valley to the east. The battalion headquarters was located at the base of the ridgeline occupied by Baker Company, with our third rifle company somewhere on the right of Baker. We had tank support in the valley, and a battery of 105s from the 11th Marines.

My platoon had led the advance earlier in the day, and for the first time, had come across clear

---

[1]The senior Andrew Jacobs was one of Indiana's foremost trial lawyers. In his 80's he directed his son's defense of the Robertson libel case, and at one deposition, reduced opposing counsel to near-tears with a classic demonstration of cross-examination abilities in the tradition of Clarence Darrow.

evidence of the presence of the Chinese in our immediate front. During the morning we had found numerous propaganda leaflets suggesting that we surrender and turn ourselves over to the victorious Chinese Peoples Army. These leaflets bore no evidence of the customary morning dew and were attached to trees and rocks as we moved north along the crest of the ridgeline. Obviously the Chinese were only minutes in front of us. Late in the afternoon, our point fire team observed Chinese fleeing several hundred yards to our front, and as we dug in that night in our customary hilltop perimeter, for the first time since we had arrived in Korea two months earlier, we received several hundred rounds of artillery fire. The intelligence report was that a major Chinese counterattack was set for that night.

At approximately midnight, tremendous firing broke out on the ridges a mile to either side of us. It became apparent that Baker Company was engaged in a desperate fight, but was holding its own. Not so on the ridge to our west. The tracers and firing rapidly moved south, and it was apparent that the Chinese had broken through in a major counter-offensive.

At dawn, it became apparent that Baker Company too had been driven back several hundred yards to the reverse slope immediately above the battalion headquarters; our supporting tanks in the valley below were directing considerable fire at the top of the ridgeline where Baker company was trying to stem any further Chinese advance which would then bring the headquarters itself under fire.

Baker company had taken some casualties during the night's fighting, but the first round of our own tank fire nearly wiped out one of Baker's machine gun squads on the reverse slope of the ridge. Baker Company's Executive Officer happened to be down in the valley near the tanks when our battalion commander ordered the tank commander to fire on the troops on the reverse slope despite the tank commander's expressed reservation that they might be our own. We got the word that Baker's XO had come very close to shooting the Colonel personally when the first tank round burst among the Baker Company machine gunners.

During the day, the Battalion was ordered to retreat down the valley of the Pukhan River. As darkness fell, there was evidence of advancing Chinese in the hills immediately behind us. This was the first time we had made a withdrawal in the face of the enemy, and it was accompanied with a different sense of nervousness than we had ever felt during the previous two months of nearly daily attacks against the Chinese. We dug in well that night, prepared for the worst.

The night of the 23rd passed without incident, but the next day we were ordered to make a forced march westward towards a large east/west ridgeline, at the western end of which it appeared that a major firefight was developing.

We were not to learn until later that on the previous night, the First Regiment had been hurriedly ordered up from reserve to fill a gap created when the 6th ROK Division on our flank broke and ran. The famous British Gloucester Brigade, celebrating St. George's Day with a grog ration, had allegedly been overrun and almost destroyed by the advancing Chinese.

The 1st Battalion of the First Marines had been ordered to climb a 2700 foot peak during the night, and their leading squads had reached the top of the peak just in time to meet the advance elements of a Chinese Field Army which had broken through the ROKs and had advanced some 10 to 15 miles in a single night. The 1st Battalion fought desperately, and by morning, still held on to the mountain top, thus stopping, at least temporarily, the Chinese advance until daybreak, when our artillery and air support could be brought to bear.

In the afternoon, our company commander, Captain Jones, ordered me to make a speed march, to climb the east/west ridgeline on our left and to tie in with the 3rd Battalion of the 1st Marines, with whom we were expected to defend the ridgeline that night against an anticipated mass attack by the Chinese.

My platoon took off almost at a run up the ridge, as it appeared that the Chinese coming from ahead of us might reach the ridgeline before we did. Losing some people from exhaustion along the way, we got to the top of the ridge and moved down it to the west, finally meeting up with a friend,

Fred Redmon, who commanded a platoon in George Company of the 3rd Battalion, 1st Marines. The rest of his battalion was stretched out to the west along the military crest of the very steep ridgeline, and we dug in our forward foxholes perhaps 20 yards over the crest. My platoon had perhaps 400 yards of front with some 30 foxholes; the rest of our battalion came in behind us so that as night fell, the 3rd Battalion of the 1st Marines and the 1st Battalion, 5th Marines held a commanding position all along the ridgeline.

My platoon had a particularly difficult problem, inasmuch as a nose stretched out to our front which gave defilade protection, perhaps 100 yards in front of us to anyone coming up the nose. To cover this position, we stretched five separate trip wires with grenade booby traps every 20 yards or so out on the nose to where it dropped off steeply to the valley perhaps 1,000 feet below.

We were at the very top of the ridgeline which dropped off fairly gradually to the left.

Redmon and I had not seen each other since Quantico some four months earlier, but we didn't have any time to swap stories because it was a close question if we could get our foxholes dug in before nightfall. Spent rounds from a fire fight on a ridge in the distance occasionally fell on us. We could see the Chinese literally swarming over the lower hills and the valley below and it was clear that we would receive a major attack that night.

It was not until around midnight, after hours of eerie silence, that the attack hit us. Our first notice was when the Marines in our forward foxholes across the nose leading into our position heard the pop of the nearest booby trap. The explosion of an illuminating grenade surprised a group of 10 or 12 Chinese infantrymen pulling a two-wheeled machine gun cart they had somehow brought up the steep forward slope of the nose and gotten through our first four lines of booby traps without detection. We opened fire and immediately there were cymbals, bugles and a lot of shouting in Chinese and the battle was joined.

My platoon CP was about 20 yards back of the forward foxholes, just over the rear slope of the hill. I remember my machine gun section leader, Sergeant Lansil, yelling "they're playing Open the Door, Richard," a then-popular song which fairly well matched the notes of the Chinese bugler. The fire fight lasted until dawn, and while we held our own, at the left flank of our position it was apparent from the gunfire below us on the left, that the Chinese had broken through George Company in several places. At one point, with firing clearly on the reverse side of our ridgeline, I moved one of my two machine guns around to the reverse slope, pointing down into the George Company position, fearing that a break through there would move up and envelop us from the flank.

·The thing that saved us was a new innovation in aerial support. From somewhere, large transport planes appeared to fly up and down in front of us and behind the Chinese, dropping flares, each of which seemed to last up to three minutes, and which silhouetted the attacking Chinese. Had we not had those aerial flares during the before dawn hours, I am convinced that the Chinese with their massive numbers would have overrun us.

When morning broke, it appeared that George Company and the 3rd Battalion of the 1st Marines had restored their lines, and both battalions were able to retire during the day with little pressure from the pursuing Chinese. By that evening we were across the river to our south, dug into a strong hilltop defensive position.

It was not until over 16 years later, after being sworn in as a member of the House of Representatives on December 16, 1967, that I learned that now-Congressman Andrew Jacobs had been a Pfc in one of the forward foxholes of Redmon's platoon dug into next to us on that fearsome night of 24 April 1951. Some weeks later, I received a letter from my wife in California enclosing a headline from the *San Francisco Chronicle:* "1st Marine Division saves U.N. Line."

Significantly, this was the last headline to report any praiseworthy activities of the Marines in Korea. Some Army officer apparently put out the word that no further distinction would be drawn between the various branches of the services.

I would not have learned of Andy's involvement but for his modest comment one evening that he understood that I had once served in the Marine Corps in Korea. When we began to compare notes, we learned that we had been within 100 yards of each other on that night, although my position had been a good deal safer than his, being just over the reverse crest of the hill rather than in the forward foxholes which had been penetrated from time-to-time by the Chinese.

As it turned out, Andy's regiment, and particularly the 1st and 3rd Battalions, had indeed saved the U.N. line. The Chinese attack had hit them head on with only flank elements hitting portions of the Fifth Regiment.

The foregoing is not intended as a testimonial to any acts of heroism on Pfc Jacobs' part; I assume that he was as thoroughly scared as I was most of that long night when it seemed on several occasions that we would be overrun. I know both of us have long felt a certain gratitude for whichever Marine leader had had the foresight to have those transport planes ready with a six-hour supply of three- minute flares.

Andy later taught me and the rest of the Congress a little about the relationship between war-making and kindness.

After surviving the First Chinese Spring Offensive in April, Andy had gone through the May-June drive to the Punch Bowl without a scratch but was ultimately wounded in the heavy September battles, for which he was ultimately awarded a 10% disability pension. He has steadfastly refused to accept that pension, and has also turned down the recent congressional pay raise on the ground that until the budget is balanced, Congress doesn't deserve a pay raise. Andy is not your ordinary run-of-the-mill Congressman.

Considered a conservative on fiscal matters, he was tagged in the early 1980s as a dreaded liberal and "soft on communism" by the Reverend Pat Robertson by reason of Jacobs' opposition to the Viet Nam War, the mining of harbors in Nicaragua, and other American military actions. For a time the debate was heavy and at times ugly. Robertson was joined in his verbal attacks by a number of congressional and journalistic warhawks, nearly all of whom had taken student deferments or found some other way to avoid combat duty during the Viet Nam War. In response, Jacobs coined a tongue-in-cheek but salutary phrase, defining it in a brief speech on the floor of the House of Representatives on April 25, 1985:

"DEFINITION TIME

(Mr. JACOBS asked and was given permission to address the House for 1 minute.)

Mr. JACOBS. Mr. Speaker, it is definition time. The word is "War Wimp," noun, one who is all too willing to send others to war but never gets around to going to war himself.

The second term is "War Wimp Party," noun, singular, group of War Wimps."

The term "War Wimp" effectively quieted the debate, and subsequently led to a significant lessening of attacks on the patriotism of those who argued that American military restraint is sometimes preferable to headlong action.

An even greater contribution to American political debate in our time, however, was a wonderful essay on kindness that Jacobs wrote for the Indianapolis Star on August 4, 1979.

It pre-dated George Bush's call for a "kinder and gentler America" by some nine years.

Courtesy of the Star, that essay is reprinted here as a means of concluding this volume on the note that it began. Jack Jones, Spike Schening and Andy Jacobs were good Marines, but above all else they enjoyed an inordinate amount of that finest of human virtues, kindness.

Being Kind Doesn't Hurt

INDPLS.
STAR
8/4/79

By ANDREW JACOBS JR.

"Be very kind to each other," Gary Moore said at the end of his TV programs. "It's possible.

Take the late Asa Smith, a kaleidoscopic contradiction between agnosticism and reverence (well, at least for the Marine Corps Hymn); between right-wing politics (he hated the word "conservative" because he said it sounded "too liberal") and belief that states should be abolished in favor of one central authority in the Federal government. His booming voice wilted adversaries. But was he unkind?

Listen to this: When Colonel Smith came home from the Marines after World War II he became a judge for the U.S. Rent Control Board. And here was a case charging a boarding house landlady named "Grandma" with overcharging room rents by few cents a week. When the evidence was in and all the arguments made, Asa announced his decision and broke with convention for the millionth time.

"The United States government," he intoned, "has been invincible since its inception. In the revolution it toppled the King's English. In World War I it humbled the Kaiser's generals. In World War II it commanded the most awesome collection of admirals and generals in history. But this time," he declared, "the United States government loses to Grandma." Asa Smith, responsible for the 1925 conviction of Klansman D. C. Stephenson. Asa Smith, John Tinder Sr.'s chief deputy prosecutor of the Indiana highway scandals. Tough Colonel Smith, my father's friend. Heart of a lion. Mean as a kitten.

* * *

"Love thy enemy." Sounds good. Does it ever happen? I was a teen-aged Marine in the Korean War when my battalion was overrun by the Chinese one night. The next day about a third of my company managed to get back to our lines despite being mistaken for the enemy and strafed by our own Marine Corsair fighter planes.

Ironically, we had taken five Chinese prisoners with us. They were skin and bones from hunger. We, on the other hand, were sick with thirst, having spent two hot, grueling days in the mountains above the water line. We had C-rations. But when you're really thirsty it's hard to be hungry. So I gave my rations to the Chinese who smiled and gestured their joyous gratitude. Another Marine demanded an explanation and didn't I know

Political editor Edward Ziegner is on vacation. His guest columnist this week is Rep. Andrew Jacobs Jr., Indianapolis Democrat.

"these were the guys who were trying to kill us last night?" I asked my Marine buddy if he wanted the rations. "Of course not," he said, "my mouth's full of cotton." "Well then," I said, "it's either give the food to these starving guys or throw it away to get rid of the weight. The Chinese took a lot of Marine prisoners last night and are marching them north today. And I have a funny feeling that if we are humane to these guys, it might work the other way around, too." My friend looked down at his wounded leg for a moment, then looked back at me and said evenly, "I guess that's right."

Three weeks later, at the end of a battle near the North Korean "Iron Triangle," three other Marines and I saw our platoon leader blown away by burp-gun fire. But we were young and couldn't believe that our John Wayne-like lieutenant could in that split second be dashed from life to death. So we placed him on an improvised stretcher and set out in search of an aid station.

We went the wrong way. I mean really the wrong way, right into the sights of Chinese recoilless artillery (bazookas). Except for a final Our Father we didn't have a prayer. But we did have a miracle.

The Chinese held their fire and motioned for us to go ahead with the stretcher. And four American kids were given another chance to live and love and labor longer.

Was there somehow a connection between the kindness of Marines with their C-rations and the kindness of the Chinese with their *trigger* fingers? Is kindness contagious? The Lord works in strange ways.

There was a story from Japan just days after the beginning of U.S. postwar occupation. It was said that a young Japanese veteran, filled with hate, was on his way to an American headquarters with a concealed bomb when he saw an American soldier help an elderly Japanese lady onto a streetcar. That one random act of kindness changed the terrorist's mind.

"No act of kindness, no matter how small, is ever wasted." Aesop.

Appendix A

Charlie Company's Performance at the Chosin Reservoir
Excerpts from *The New Breed* and *Retreat Hell!*

&

Appendix A-1

Letter from Pfc. Fred Allen describing the defense at Hagaru-ri.

&

Appendix A-2

The Annex Able of the 5th Marines Special Action Report,
Chosin Reservoir Campaign, November 21-December 10, 1950.

The following narratives of Charlie Company, commanded by Captain Jack R. Jones, at the Chosin Reservoir in 1950 are taken from two books, *The New Breed*, Andrew Geer, Battery Press, (1989) and *Retreat Hell!*, Jim Wilson, Morrow Publishing Company, (1988).

(Pages 284-285 *The New Breed*)

Jones had arrived in Yudam-ni from the east shore of the reservoir after dark. There had been no opportunity for him to observe the terrain features of the area nor to make a reconnaissance of the rout of approach to the presently assigned objective. Displaying excellent judgment and great energy, Jones led his unit in the black of night over the treacherous terrain without a false turn or wasted moment.

Two hundred yards from the crest the unit came under heavy fire. Jones deployed his troops and pushed on into the CP area where he found remnants of Easy Company still clinging to the reverse slope. Snyder was the only officer left. Jones took command of all the Marines in the area and began to organize the attack to regain the crest.

✻ ✻ ✻

Day was breaking over the cold, white mountains of the reservoir when the order for the jump-off was given. With a fury that could not be denied the salient was retaken; the spirit of Jones' men reached fever pitch when they saw their leader in the forefront of the attack bayonetting and clubbing the enemy. Two platoons of Chinese were killed as they fought to hold the vital ridge. Corbet was wounded and First Lieutenant Robert Richter took command of the unit. By virtue of their speed Marine casualties were light.

(Page 338 *The New Breed*)

Fighting the rear guard, Jones' Charlie Company was attacked from the north by an enemy force estimated to be in battalion strength. The lone tank (Munsell) had been assigned to the rear guard. Under a concentration of rifle and machine-gun fire, Jones ran to the tank and directed it into a position where its fire could be brought to bear to support his troops. The enemy attack was finally repulsed at two o'clock.

(Pages 357-358 *The New Breed*)

Jones' Charlie Company received a heavy attack on the flank where it was tied in with Jaskilka. Eighty-one and 60 mm. mortar fire were utilized with maximum effectiveness on enemy troop concentrations. At one stage of the battle when the enemy had pressed to close range, Jones, under heavy fire, directed an Army Sherman tank into position where the weapons of the tank effectively supported the ground troops. The enemy attack withered and ended shortly before midnight.

✻ ✻ ✻

While the attack was underway against Heater, the enemy placed a second attack on Jones' front lines shortly after two in the morning. With skillful use of supporting arms and an Army tank on the left flank, Jones' unit quickly repulsed the enemy thrust. Throughout the remainder of the night small groups of the enemy attempted to infiltrate, but these were annihilated. At daylight Jones and his men counted two hundred sixty dead Chinese within two hundred yards of their company perimeter. Jones' casualties for the night were ten wounded in action.

November 28, 1950: Lt. Col. John Stevens, commanding officer of the 1st Battalion, 5th Regiment, sent a runner after Jones at about 1:00 a.m. The situation, Jones was told, was this: E Company of the 7th was on Hill 1282 and just about finished. Casualties were very heavy. Two relief platoons had already gone up, and they'd lost most of their men. But they were holding. D Company, 7th, was on Hill 1240 and in worse shape. It had been shoved off the hill shortly after 10:00 pm. but had gone back up.

"I was told to go up and hold Hill 1282," Jones said. "I had no orders to report to anyone. We didn't know if anyone would be alive when we got to the top."

"We could hear the firefight. The bugles. We could see the flashes," Jones said. "It was heavy. I mean really heavy . . . everything was busting loose up there."

He hurried back to his company and briefed his platoon leaders. He said he didn't know what to expect once they got to the top other than "We'll be involved in one terrific fight."

C Company—three rifle platoons, a machine-gun platoon, four 60mm mortars, headquarters personnel, an assault squad—was above strength, about 250 men. Jones had great confidence in his three platoon lieutenants, Merritt, Byron Magness, and Harold Dawe. He had a fine executive officer in Lt. Loren Smith. Of Sgt. Roger Wallingford of the company mortar section, Jones said: "He was outstanding. He could—and did—walk the 60s to within ten to fifteen yards of our lines."

Just before starting up Hill 1282 Jones was told to send Dawe's platoon up Hill 1240, where everyone could see and hear the fighting going on up there.

This didn't sit too well with Jones. He had counted on his full-strength platoon. But he also knew that a lot of wounded were coming down 1240.

It was tough going up 1282. "There were easier routes to the top," Jones said, "but we would have been silhouetted against the snow, so we took the harder ones."

"We just started working our way up the best we could," Merritt said, "There just wasn't much of a trail."

It took C Company more than two hours just to get within two hundred yards of the top. Along the way, Jones and Merritt talked to the wounded coming down. "We wanted to get a picture of what was going on up there before we walked into it," Jones said. The picture they got was this: The Chinese were up there, in force, and there weren't enough marines alive to do anything about it.

Those coming down were numb, stumbling, falling, sliding down a trail of red ice. Weapons were used as crutches. Medical supplies had run out on top. Ammunition was just about gone.

"I didn't know anything about the area," Jones said. "The maps we had weren't very good."

They worked their way toward the top in columns until they reached a point that from the sound of gunfire and explosions Jones felt was fairly close to the top.

"Then we formed a line with fixed bayonets and moved on up," he said. "It was very touchy. We didn't know what the situation was up there. If we saw people, would they be Chinese or marines? We didn't want to go up there firing into our own people."

About 150 yards from the top the company came under fire. Mortar rounds fell in front of Merritt's platoon. As they got closer to the top, rifle and machine-gun fire buzzed through the night air. About a hundred yards from the top, Jones found Sgt. Daniel Murphy of E Company's 3rd Platoon. "The Chinese are on top," Murphy said. "They've overrun the command post." He told Jones there were a few survivors on a spur out of sight along with what was left of Trapnell's relief platoon. What was left of Bey's platoon was there too, he said. The rest of the survivors of E Company and what was left of Snyder's relief platoon were on the reverse slope near where the command post had been.

"We were hit awful hard," Murphy told Wallingford. "He told me there were only twelve to fifteen men left in Bey's platoon."

As Jones's men were just about to the top they were hit with a grenade attack, but they were concussion, not fragmen-tation. "They didn't hurt you much," Merritt said. "They just knocked you silly for a while."

Jones and Smith led the men over the top as the marines shot, clubbed, and bayoneted the Chinese and drove the 3rd Company, 1st Battalion, 235th CCF Regiment, from their holes. Then they fought their way into the command post area and a sea of bodies. Close by were a few survivors. Snyder was the only officer. His platoon had been hurt badly.
"There wasn't much left up there," Wallingford said, "only bodies." Because of the heavy fighting, he hadn't had time to set up his mortars.

When PFC Winston Keating Scott, nineteen, got to the top, he was exhausted. He'd lugged four cans of .30 ammun-ition and extra water up the hill in addition to several clips for his car-bine. Gunfire dug up the ground at his feet, and he wondered why he wasn't hit. Bodies were everywhere. Chinese. Marines. Were the marines dead? There was no way to reach them with-out getting killed.

As it got light, Merritt could see marine bodies not too far away, but a captured .30 was spraying his men from about seventy-five yards to the left of where he was. "That damn thing just kept raking the top of the hill. Six of my men were hit," he said. To the right of Merritt's position the hill rose another fifty to seventy-five feet. A few of E Company survivors and what was left of Snyder's platoon were up there. "But we couldn't get to them," Merritt recalls. "All we could do was hold what we had on that ridge line."

Like Merritt's 1st Platoon, Magness's 2nd Platoon came under fire from that same captured machine gun as soon as his men reached the top and were pinned down.

Magness looked around, spotted Merritt, ran over, and dropped in the snow. "We gotta do somethin' about that damn gun," Merritt said. But first they had to locate it.

"I got to my knees to try and find out where it was," Merritt said. "I heard it, then I felt it. I got hit in the right shoulder and fell forward in the snow."

"I'll get a corpsman," Magness said, and crawled toward his platoon. "I didn't see him again until we were both back in the hospital," Merritt said.

"When we got to the top, we were ready to go," Scott said. "We wanted to take the Chinese on right then and there and settle this thing. We were so keyed up, the blood was really flowing."

He was tossing grenades and firing his carbine, when it would fire. The other men in his machine-gun section were firing their weapons, too, and hurling grenades. They hadn't had time to set up the machine gun. The Chinese were returning the fire, round for round, and giving a good account of themselves. A lot of marines were dropping.

Then, from one of the foxholes, the marines heard someone shout, "Hey, knock it off, knock it off? You'll get ten for every one you throw!"

"So we knocked it off," Scott said. Now they had time to set up their machine gun, set their fields of fire, distribute water and ammunition. Yet all around them the fighting raged.

"It was eerie," Scott recalled.

He and a few others then crawled forward to look into the nearest hole to see if any marines were alive. "First, we went through the bodies collecting ammo, rations, first-aid packets. We left the dead and started to drag some wounded back to our lines," he said. Then he heard someone shout from a foxhole about forty yards away, "Hey, anybody got any water? How about some ammo?"

Scott grabbed several bandoliers and a canteen and zigzagged to where he heard the shouting. He dropped to the ground, crawled forward, then peered over the edge as rifle fire dug up the earth around him.

"I saw two men reading a comic book," Scott said, "and I was really pissed. I risked my life to get to them and they didn't even cover me. I dropped the ammo and the canteen on their heads and ran back to the machine gun."

Fighting was so heavy and casualties so high that Jones's men couldn't do anything for the wounded. As it got light, his men were able to locate a few survivors. One over there. Two out there. A few in another foxhole. There weren't many.

Jones passed this word to them: Go down to the valley and help take the wounded. This was important. Get the injured to the aid tents before they froze.

Clements was on his feet, bloody, the right side of his helmet shattered. His head felt five times its normal size, as if someone had put it in a vise and spun the handle tight.

But he knew where he was, what was happening. "I saw this captain—I didn't know who he was—leading his men toward me. So I went out to meet him and turn over what was left of the company," Clements said.

"He took one look at me—my helmet, the blood—and told me to get down to the valley," he added. Clements showed Jones where his people were, the original company position, and pointed out some wounded. Then he started down.

✲ ✲ ✲

"Getting the wounded out of there was my prime concern," Jones said, "because I didn't know how long we'd be up there." So cooks, clerks, engineers, artillerymen, anyone who could climb to the top made their way up the hill to help bring down the dead and wounded.

There was no letup in the fighting. Magness's platoon was still heavily engaged. So was Merritt's. To the left of where Jones had set up a temporary command post about thirty Chinese were firing down at the wounded and the litter bearers. Smith shouted for Wallingford to grab six or seven men from his mortar section, fix bayonets, and together they drove the Chinese back. Once the dead and wounded were off the top, Jones set up a perimeter of about two hundred yards. Then he counterattacked to the left, to where the captured machine gun was still firing, and drove the Chinese from the top of Hill 1282.

The rest of Capt. James B. Heater's A Company, 5th Regiment, arrived to strengthen the defenses, and Jones knew that he was there to stay. But he also knew that the Chinese would be back. "There was some nice fortifications up there and we dug them a little deeper, improved them, then just waited," Jones said.

Jones spotted Merritt, blood running down his arm, ordered him to the valley, then gave his platoon to Lt. Robert H. Corbett of the mortar section.

Then the Chinese struck again, violently, furiously. They wanted that hilltop back in the worst way and were willing to pay any price. Jones heard the bugles first. Then the shouting. Then the Chinese attacked in waves. Grenades and small-arms fire cut them down. Others tried to attack C Company's rear, but this didn't work, either. Jones always had the backside covered, no matter what the situation.

Six times Jones ran forward to help bring back wounded. Grenade fragments hit him in a leg. A squad of Chinese charged into one of his machine-gun positions, and all were killed. Two other Chinese squads fell, side by side, before rifle fire and grenades. Still another squad tried to assault the summit and was cut to pieces. Marine air couldn't help. The Chinese and marines were much too close.

"We fought all day long," Scott recalled. "The machine guns never stopped. Some of them burned out."

Again, Hill 1282 lay under a blanket of dead and wounded.

✳ ✳ ✳

Then, late in the afternoon, Jones was ordered back down to the valley. He was replaced by Capt. Harold B. Williamson's H Company, 5th Regiment.

"Pack up and get ready to go down," the men were told.

The dead and wounded were removed first, then the men started to file down the trails, grimy, weary, but not beaten.

✳ ✳ ✳

The Chinese paid dearly for trying to take HIll 1282. In addition to the more than four hundred dead who covered its slopes, there were many hundreds of dead and wounded on top. Captured Chinese documents indicated that only six survived Jones's assault against the 3rd Company, 1st Battalion, 235th CCF Regiment. Of 116 officers and men in the 2nd Company, ninety-four were killed.

The price for holding the hill was high, too. E Company was reduced to less than thirty men, some wounded, most suffering from frostbite. The two relief platoons were badly hurt, suffering forty dead and wounded. Only six men could still fight in Snyder's platoon. Jones's C Company suffered fifteen dead and sixty-seven wounded.

After eighteen hours of fighting as savage as any in the history of small- unit warfare, Hill 1282 belonged to the marines.

Jones's C Company, 1st Battalion, 5th Regiment, was in the valley off Hill 1282, each man pleased that he was alive, sad that others were less fortunate. He learned that the two regiments were returning to Hagaru and that his company would have to go back up in the hills almost immediately and help keep the peaks clear of Chinese.

"Wear all the warm clothing you can comfortably wear, burn the rest, because we're moving out," he told his men. They moved high on the left, screening the convoy as it lumbered out of Yudam-ni. He had a good defensive position and felt certain the Chinese would not attack. To do so would be folly, he felt. Nevertheless, they did attack, and it was folly. They attacked head-on in great strength and quickly overran the front of his position.

"The guys called and told us they'd gotten through," Jones said. "We just told them to lay in their holes and we were going to shoot right back over their heads." We killed twenty-five or thirty on two different occasions.

But the fighting and the cold were taking a toll. "We took casualties consistently, Jones said. "The cold, frost-bite, were a drain on personnel, too."

C Company was absorbing engineers, cooks, bakers, company clerks to fill out its depleted ranks. Jones still had a good nucleus of veterans, and the newcomers followed their directions. Every man was dependable. No one ran.

"When we came down from the hills just before going into Hagaru, it was one of the blackest nights I've ever seen. You couldn't see your hand in front of your face," said Johnson, F Company, 2nd Battalion, 5th Regiment.

C Company, 1st Battalion, 5th Regiment, came down from the hills just short of the village, passed through the road-block at dawn, and moved into a deserted building. "It was the first time I'd been in a building since I got to Korea," said Jones, the company commander.

Jones's C Company and Jaskilka's E Company were side by side along the base of the hill to the north.

Although the marines had the hill for the first time since they got to Hagaru and were well dug in on top and in good position on the low ground, the Chinese weren't about to give up.

They attacked high and low throughout the night of December 6, first on the hill, then at its base.

Their losses were frightful. They came in great numbers, sometimes four abreast, marching, at times trotting, into the barrels of machine guns and Army tanks. They walked through fields of mortar fire.

When his company went into the perimeter at Hagaru, Jones was told, "Hold that ground in front of you." He did. So did Jaskilka.

"We were dug in pretty good. We were in some holes that were already there but we changed them the way we wanted them," Jones explained.

Wallingford had his 60s about fifty yards behind Jones's command post. When the Chinese struck again, at about midnight, he dropped the first few rounds out about two hundred yards, then carefully walked them in about twenty to twenty-five yards a round until they were exploding about twenty yards in front of company lines.

When it got really tight, he brought them in to about ten yards in front of the foxholes. This was a bit too close, but it worked. It stopped the Chinese.

"We felt good. We knew their tactics. We'd had waves of people coming at us, and we'd stopped them. We knew what to expect. Mass hordes. We had a couple of bad nights there. We didn't lose many people, but we sure took account of them," Jones said.

APPENDIX A-1

Pfc. Fred Allen of Mansfield, Louisiana described the defense at Hagaru-ri in a letter to another Chosin veteran of Charlie Company in 1991.

"To the best of my memory, we got into Hagaru about mid-morning, or about noon on the 6th of December. We were assigned our respective positions on the perimeter, and told to dig in and be prepared. Another man and I were the last position on the right flank, and we were the tie-in to Easy Company. About ten or fifteen feet to our right was one of Easy company's machine guns. I guess it might have been twenty-five yards to my left was a Charlie Company machine gun. D Company was on the east ridge directly in front of us. Someone had brought us some filled sandbags to use, and directly to our front there were three stacks of 105 and 90MM ammunition. There was a truck and about fifteen men out there loading it on the truck to get it out from in front of us. It took two truck loads to move it. Then someone came along and gave us some 03 ammunition—that's five rounds to a clip - and some clips for the M-1 rifle.

We sat down and unloaded the 03 clips into the M-1 clips. During this time, a new man came up. He was our BAR man—a reserve. He said he was from Texas, and his name was Luke. And it saddens me that I can't remember the other man's name. But I saw this man again in 1954 in the Panama Canal Zone. He was a Staff Sergeant. And he was wearing a Silver Star, and said that he was awarded it on 8 December.

Somehow, when they brought the ammo to us, they also brought a large can of pressed ham. We sat, filled clips, and ate ham. About dark, and when it gets dark there, it is as dark as hell, we saw three Chinese, about a hundred yards in front of us, sneaking along the railroad track. We didn't pay much attention to them, then.

From that time till about eleven o'clock we would take turns going back to the warm-up tent for about ten minutes. Then around midnight, there was firing to our left, and an illuminating flare was thrown up. As it was coming down, two more burst behind it, and as they were floating down it was hard to believe your eyes—it looked like half of China was coming down that valley. As the Korean said, there were "many, many, many". At this time those three Chinese that we saw earlier were looking down at us there in the foxhole. And I was down on my right knee, the BAR man was a little to my right in front of me. I couldn't get my weapon up in time. One of the Chinese said something to the others, then he fired two rounds at me. Those two rounds burnt the back of my parka. And I shouted, "Shoot, Luke!" He had his BAR in position, and he killed all three of them. Apparently, these three men were probing the line, because shortly thereafter, all hell broke loose. This was somewhere around 0100 on the 7th of December.

The machine gun in Easy Company began to shoot, and we were shooting for everything we were worth. And the gunner on the machine gun, instead of firing in bursts, was holding the trigger back. The barrel turned red, and he had to change barrels. The other man and I were alternating throwing grenades. The BAR man kept shooting, and behind us we could hear these tanks rumbling and clanking about. Then, the next thing we know, one pulled up within ten feet of us, about three feet from the dead Chinese. Then some turkey stumbled over my feet into the foxhole. He said, "Captain Jones sent this tank up," or something to that effect. This fellow said he had to get back - he was the Company runner. He gave us what ammunition he had, because we were running a little low. I learned, years later, this man was Gunther Dohse, and this was an Army M-24 tank with a 90MM gun. The tank commander was a Tech Sgt., and he was operating the 50 calibre machine gun on top of the tank. Just a few minutes later some man hollered, "The tank commander's been killed, and we can't get him out of the hole!" He yelled for help from us, but we couldn't get to the tank because of the intense fire.

Two men managed to get the tank commander out of the tank through the escape hatch in the bottom of the tank. Then a man began to fire the 90MM on the front of the tank. When he'd shoot, he'd yell, "We're going to fire!" so we could have time to close our eyes. He fired several rounds within the next thirty minutes.

The Chinese backed off a little, then they began to drop mortars in the direction of the tank. This was about 0200. The first round fell within sixty yards in front of the tank. The second round, about three minutes later, within thirty yards of the tank. One of the men yelled, "We've got to move this tank out of here!", and they began to move back. One man got out of the tank, and was leading it back to the rear. The tank had barely gone twenty feet, when the third mortar round fell about fifteen feet behind me, and that's when I got shrapnel in my left shoulder and back. Just think, what if there had been a fourth round! I remember hearing somewhere about the 'million dollar wound' and I thought to myself, "well, this is mine."

It took about twenty minutes for a Corpsman to get to me. He was from Easy Company. He helped me back to the First-Aid tent, stuck a cork in the wound, and put a bandage on me. The Corpsman wouldn't send me back to the line because of where the wound was—near my spine. At daylight the next morning, the top part of the tent looked like a sieve. I was transported from there to the airstrip, put aboard one of the C-47s and flown to Hungnam. I spent the night there in a hospital tent.

The next morning, December 8, those of us who could walk were looking for coffee. Some-one said the Red Cross tent had some right out front. As we were entering the tent, I saw a sign that said *Coffee and Doughnuts 5 cents*. A guy said, "You don't have to pay for the coffee, come on and go with me." We walked down a little way to another tent. It was a Salvation Army tent. We got a cup of coffee and two doughnuts and didn't have to pay a cent for it. This is one encounter with the American Red Cross that I will never forget.

That afternoon I was flown from Hungnam to Japan to the hospital. Chow was brought; we ate, and those of us who could, bathed. It was a great feeling because we knew we were safe and warm.

The credit goes to the leadership of Captain Jones knowing that we needed help, sent this tank over to us, and with the courage of Gunther Dohse who led the tank to our position. With the fighting spirit, leadership of our officers and NCO's, Charlie Company was second to none. I am proud to have been a Charlie Fiver."

Semper Fi

Freddie Allen

The battalion at 0830, 21 November departed via truck convoy to a new position at SINKUNG-HI on the east side of CHOSIN RESERVOIR. The convoy traveled up the one-way mountain pass which had to be cleared by 1200 to permit travel downward. The convoy arrived at the new area at 1300 and was guided into defense positions by members of the reconnaissance party of the previous day. One road block was established and approximately twenty (20) enemy were encountered at 0200 the next morning. Fire was exchanged with no known enemy casualties. During the period of 22 November to 27 November this battalion conducted local patrols each day to the north, northeast, and east, with light enemy contact generally of squad strength. Four outposts were established on the 22nd of November, one being a combat outpost of platoon strength. Thanksgiving Day, 23 November, was a definite boost to the morale of the officers and men of 1/5 as a hot meal of turkey with all the trimmings was served in the field. "C" Company (reinforced) with Captain J. R. Jones commanding, departed at 0700 the 25th on a reconnaissance patrol to a village about ten (10) miles to the northeast of the battalion area. This patrol encountered enemy of approximately squad strength and returned a 1600 with no other enemy contact. At 1700 contact was made with the 1st Battalion, 32nd Regiment, 7th Army Division which was to effect relief of the 5th Marines. A reconnaissance party departed at 1000 on 26 November for the new assembly area at YUDAM-NI and after reconnoitering the are returned to the battalion CP. At 1800 orders were received from the 5th Marine to be prepared to move on 27 November to YUDAM-NI. This battalion was to commence movement at 1300 and would provide one (1) company as a covering force for the 3rd Battalion's movement from their position to the following morning to YUDAM-NI.

"A" Company departed the battalion area at 0630, 27 November for the 3rd Battalion's positions to provide a covering force for their movement that commenced at 0800. An advance party consisting of the S-3, S-1 and an officer from each company departed at 0800 for YUDAM-NI and arrived there at 1200. The battalion, less forward elements, commenced movement to YUDAM-NI at 1210 and arrived there after dark, Personnel from the advance party guided the battalion into a Regimental reserve assembly area and local security was established. This assembly area was located in the flat ground to the right of the road in the village of YUDAM-NI; the 3rd Battalion, 5th Marines was on the high ground to the west and northwest; "D" and "E" Companies, 7th Marines were on the high ground to the north and northwest. "D" and "E" Companies, 2nd Battalion, 7th Marines were under operational control of 1st Battalion, 7th Marines at this time. "E" Company, 7th Marines occupied defense positions on the ridge leading from hill 1282 west and on the ridge leading south-southeast from hill 1282. These two (2) ridges were almost at right angles to each other with hill 1282 their origin. "D" Company, 7th Marines occupied defense positions on the southern sector of hill 1240. The top of this hill actually had two (2) high points of ground with a slight saddle of about two hundred (200) yards between the north sector and south sector.

For graphic picture of initial assembly area and action until 1400 on 25 November 1950 see sketch #3.

The defense sectors of the 3rd Battalion, 5th Marines and "D" and "E" Companies. 7th Marines were subjected to a heavy enemy attack at approximately 2300 and 1/5 was alerted for possible enemy infiltration. At 0030, "C" Company was ordered to the rear of 3/5's position to be prepared to counter a possible enemy breakthrough from the direction of 3/5's CP area.

At 0100. 28 November, the 1st platoon of "A" Company was ordered to reinforce "E" Company, 7th Marines and shortly thereafter the 3rd platoon of "A" Company was given the same mission. The 1st platoon with Lt. Trapnell tied in with "E" Company, 7th Marines' right flank while 3rd platoon with Lt. Snyder was integrated with elements of "E" Company, 7th Marines. The 1st platoon went into position under heavy enemy fire, and after close-in fighting, with grenades being used extensively, the enemy managed to penetrate the line between "E" Company, 7th Marines and the 1st platoon. About the same time an enemy envelopment of the 1st platoon's right flank began, forcing them to withdraw to higher ground to their immediate rear. There again the platoon tied in with "E" Company, and held the line against continuous enemy pressure that eased only after daylight. The 3rd platoon, integrated with elements of "E" Company, 7th Marines, was engaged in heavy grenade fighting and repeated attacks by the enemy which resulted in many casualties. Lt. Snyder, the surviving officer in that sector, assisted in the control of personnel of "E" Company. The enemy increased their efforts and the combined Marine force was driven from its positions on the high ground where the two ridges met. Lt. Snyder rallied the forces at his command and held the west ridge of the hill although not in possession of the high ground on his right flank. They remained in these positions until daylight.

The 3rd platoon of "C" Company was placed at 0400 under operational control of the 7th Marines and ordered to reinforce "D" Company, 7th Marines on hill 1240. Upon the platoon's arrival on the hill they found a confused and disorganized situation. The platoon commander, Lt. Dawe, could not make contact with "D" Company, 7th Marines, at this time. Lt. Dawe advanced his platoon to a northerly forward position on hill 1240 which was approximately one hundred and fifty (150) yards forward of "D" Company's positions and was immediately brought under heavy enemy fire forcing him to withdraw to the south sector of the hill where he assumed a defense position. During the remainder of the day a continuous fire fight ensued as "D" Company, 7th Marines and 3rd platoon, "C" Company, 1/5 attempted to defend and reorganize the south sector of hill 1240. The 3rd platoon commander estimated that there were two (2) battalions to a regiment of enemy attacking on hill 1240. The 3rd platoon casualties were four (4) KIA, one (1) MIA and seventeen (17) WIA.

At 0400, 28 November, "C" Company, (less one platoon), was ordered under operational control of the 7th Marines with the mission to reinforce "E" Company, 7th Marines and elements of "A" Company. The Commanding Officer of 1/5 realizing the seriousness if the situation on the ridge immediately above and to his right, also ordered the remainder of "A" Company to follow in trace of "C" Company, to assist in the accomplishment of the mission. "C" Company, having been previously alerted, immediately moved up the draw directly towards hill 1282. "C" Company upon reaching a point about one hundred (100) yards from the enemy on hill 1282 was subjected to intense enemy small arms, mortar, rocket,

and rifle grenade fire. Capt. Jones, "C" Company Commander, immediately
deployed his two platoons and assaulted the high ground. This assault regained
the high ground and defense positions were taken up. No officers of "E" Company,
7th Marines were to be found on the hill and Capt. Jones assumed control of all
units in that sector. Evacuation of approximately two hundred (200) casualties
was commenced with the aid of almost one hundred (100) men of H&S Company,
1/5. The men evacuated were dead and wounded of "C" and "A" Companies, 1/5
and "E" Company, 7th Marines. Reorganization of the ground was completed
between 0730-0830 after hill 1282 was secured. "C" Company, 1/5 occupied a
frontage of about one hundred fifty (150) yards on the high ground of hill 1282.
"E" Company was on the left flank of "C" Company and occupied a frontage of
about seventy-five (75) yards. A squad from "C" Company was used to outpost
and secure the left flank of the ridge leading west off of hill 1282. "A" Company
was tied in on the right flank of "C" Company with a frontage of one hundred fifty
(150) yards which extended down the ridge southeast of hill 1282. Lt. Lichten-
berger of "A" Company, 1/5 was ordered by Capt. Jones to command the remnants of "E" Company, 7th Marines. Lt. Dye of the 7th Marines arrived on hill
1282 about 1200 and assumed command of "E" Company. Throughout the day the
entire line was engaged in a continuous fire fight with the enemy to hold the positions on hill 1282. Capt. Jones could make no radio contact with the 7th Marines
therefore the reports of the situation were made to 1/5. The units of 1/5 that
were assigned to the 7th Marines for operational control never were committed as
such but remained under 1/5 control. At 1600, "A" Company, "C" Company, (less
1 platoon), and "E" Company, 7th Marines were relieved by "I" Company, 3/5.
"A" and "C" Companies returned to the battalion assembly area. Casualties for the
period: "A" Company, five (5) KIA and thirty-seven (37) WIA; "C" Company, (less
one platoon), ten (10) KIA and thirty (30) WIA. It is estimated that the enemy
encountered numbered about two (2) regiments. Capt. Jones estimated the enemy
dead to the immediate front of his sector to be between two hundred fifty (250)
and five hundred (500).

    For the following action see sketch #4.

    At 1400, 28 November, "B" Company began relief of "D" Company, 7th
Marines and the 3rd platoon of "C" Company, 1/5 in their positions on hill 1240.
"B" Company made a reconnaissance of the positions of "D" Company and the 3rd
platoon of "C" Company. "B" Company, with a machine gun platoon from Weapons
Company attached, began to effect the relief. The 1st platoon moving into position
was unable to contact any friendly troops on its left and was drawing enemy small
arms fire from its front and left flank. The platoon leader was ordered to continue
to attempt to occupy his assigned sector. The 2nd platoon was in position and the
3rd platoon attacked to seize its sector, the high ground around hill 1240. At this
time several casualties were inflicted by a mortar barrage on "B" Company CP
area. It soon became evident that the 1st and 3rd platoons could no occupy their
assigned sector by dark because of continuous strong enemy resistance. "B" Company requested an air strike on the area directly to the front of their 3rd platoon.
The air strike was delivered successfully just at twilight but failed to dislodge the
enemy and the 3rd platoon then withdrew to positions along the top of the south-

CONFIDENTIAL

Annex ABLE to the 5th Marines Special Action Report (Cont'd)
----

ern sector of hill 1240. 81mm mortar fire was also placed with effect on the enemy positions. "B" Company partially covered the saddle to their left flank by fire and physically occupied positions on the left slope of the hill. This position extended along the top of the hill and down the right shoulder and attempted to tie in by fire with the reported elements of the 7th Marines on the high ground to the right flank. The 81mm mortar platoon of Weapons company in support of "B" Company was in position at the base of hill 1240 occupied by "B" Company. "B" Company's artillery FO could not register artillery to their front because the position occupied by "B" Company masked the fire.

By 1600 the Commanding Officer of 1/5 had prepared and received approval of counterattack plans. The Commanding Officer of "A" Company were briefed on the plans. At 1900 the 3rd platoon of "C" Company rejoined "C" Company after release by CO, 7th Marines and relief by "B" Company.

At 0110, 29 November a warning order was received from 5th Marines for one (1) company to be detached and report to 1/7 CP for operational control. "A" Company was detached at 0915 for this mission and upon reporting to 1/7 CP was attached to the Provisional Battalion, 7th Marines. This Provisional Battalion immediately moved out to effect a relief of "F" Company, 7th Marines. The mission was cancelled soon after and "A" Company moved into a blocking position above the airstrip which was being constructed in the valley south of YUDAM-NI.

"C" Company upon being relieved on hill 1282 by "I" Company, 3/5, had returned to the battalion assembly area and occupied a sector in 1/5 defense perimeter. Two (2) provisional platoons of one (1) officer and twenty-four (24) men from the 11th Marines and one (1) officer and twenty-two (22) men from H&S Company, 5th Marines were attached to "C" Company. At 0900 one (1) platoon (Reinf) of "C" Company was ordered to take up defense positions on hill 1240. The 1st platoon occupied positions on the ridge of "I" Company's right flank and tied in by fire with "I" Company on the left and "B" Company, 1/5 on hill 1240 to its right flank.

At 0900 the 3rd platoon of "B" Company was ordered to take the north sector of hill 1240 and recover the one (1) dead of the previous day. This action was successful in the recovery of the one (1) dead but the platoon was driven back by heavy frontal and flanking small arms fire and grenades. The 3rd platoon was ordered to withdraw to its former position. The north sector of hill 1240 was then subjected to 81mm mortar fire and several air strikes were run. Early in the afternoon of 29 November a provisional platoon of one (1) officer and eighteen (18) men from the AT Company, 5th Marines was placed under control of "B" Company and positioned to cover the draw to "B" Company's left flank and 1st platoon, "C" Company's right flank. At 1300, "B" Company called for 81mm mortar fire on thirty (30) to forty (40) enemy to their front causing them to disperse. At 1500 enemy troops were reported coming down a slope in the direction of "B" Company's left flank. "B" Company requested and received 4.2" mortar support and at 1530 an air strike was requested which succeeded in breaking up the attack. A direct napalm hit on the enemy OP coupled with excellent strafing runs forced the attacking enemy to disperse.

At 1530 the 1st platoon, "B" Company with Lt. A. C. Jensen commanding was ordered by "B" Company commander to move two (2) squads into position to assault the northern portion of hill 1240. The assault was to be carried out while being covered by small arms and machine gun fire from the 3rd platoon's position. The 12st platoon moved to within ten (10) to fifteen (15) yards of the high ground on the northern portion of hill 1240 without receiving any enemy fire. At this point intense machine gun and small arms fire was received from its front and left flank. Many grenades were thrown down upon the attacking platoon by the enemy from their positions on the high ground which arose abruptly to a height of seventy-five (75) feet a short distance in front of the attacking platoon. "B" Company Commander, upon viewing the situation, ordered the 1st platoon to withdraw to its former position. The 1st platoon suffered ten (10) casualties, six (6) WIA who were evacuated and four (4) KIA including the platoon commander.

Very little enemy fire was received the night of 29 November. In the early dawn, night fighters dumped their ordnance very effectively on the reverse slope of hill 1240 while "B" Company used illuminating hand grenades to mark the Company's lines.

At 0700, 30 November, "B" Company observed enemy grouping to their front; mortar fire was called down and the enemy dispersed. At 0825 one (1) 75mm recoilless section from the AT Company, 5th Marines was attached to "B" Company and at 1000 reported scoring hits on three (3) enemy bunkers at TA 4182—I-2 on the northern sector of hill 1240. An AT Assault section of Weapons Company, 1/5 also scored hits with 3.5" rockets on the bunkers from the 3rd platoon's sector. Lt. Hancock, "B" Company Commander, estimated the enemy dead at eight hundred (800) on hill 1240 for the period 28 November to 30 November.

The night of 29-30 November, "C" Company, (less one platoon), occupied a sector in 1/5 defense perimeter. At 1100, 30 November it was ordered to relive elements of the 11th Marines on hill 1167 to the right of "D" Company's position. This relief was effected by 1330 and "C" Company was in position with its right flank anchored on the CHOSIN Reservoir and its left flank tied in by fire with "D" Company on hill 1240. No enemy contact was made during the night.

This battalion began preparation at 1200, on 30 November for movement of the CP to the southeast where the battalion was to withdraw the next day to its sector of a smaller and bi-regimental perimeter. A reconnaissance of the new area was made and at 1530 movement was started to the new CP location at TA 4179-S. Equipment and supplies were moved by trucks and jeeps with trailers. The greater part of H&S Company moved in route column to to the new CP location. A combat CP was opened directly behind "B" Company's position on hill 1240 to command the rearguard composed of "B" and "C" Companies while other units of the regiment withdrew to the new bi-regimental perimeter. Weapons Company Headquarters, AT platoon and the 1st and 2nd sections of the mortar platoon supporting "B" Company moved to the new area and occupied a position on the lower left slope of the high ground to the southeast of CHOSIN Reservoir (see sketch #5). The new Battalion CP was opened at 1630.

For the following action see sketch #5.

On 1 December at 0920, "B" Company ran an air strike in front of their positions and at this time "C" Company started their withdrawal to pre-determined

CONFIDENTIAL

Annex ABLE to the 5th Marines Special Action Report (Cont'd)
----

positions on the high ground to the southeast of CHOSIN Reservoir. "C" Company with one (1) provisional platoon attached, occupied a defense sector of 1000 yards extending along the high ground generally running east. From these positions "C" Company supported by fire "B" Company's withdrawal from hill 1240. The 1st platoon, "C" Company after withdrawal from hill 1282 rejoined "C" Company in its defense sector.

"B" Company began withdrawal from hill 1240 as soon as "C" Company was in position and at 1050 had effected withdrawal to the base of hill 1240. An artillery concentration shift to "B" Company's old positions on hill 1240 was requested to fall at 1050. The artillery forward observers radio was not operating and due to his distance from "B" Company Commander an air strike could not be called in lieu of the artillery concentration. The rapid displacement of machine gun sections in leap-frog fashion provided "B" Company with covering fire to its withdrawal across the flat ground between hill 1240 and its new defense position between the road and CHOSIN Reservoir. "B" Company, in its withdrawal, was subjected to heavy fire from its previous positions on hill 1240 now occupied by the enemy. Booby traps were placed by "B" Company prior to withdrawal and were successful in infliction; several casualties in the enemy closely following the company's withdrawal. As the last elements of "B" Company crossed the first bridge on the road from YUDAM-NI to HAGARU-RI that bridge was destroyed by Weapons Company, 1/5.

"B" Company occupied a defense position which extended from the road across the level ground and tied in with the left flank of "C" Company. At 1700, "B" Company was relieved by "D" Company, 2nd Battalion, 5th Marines and then moved into an assembly area on the west slope of the high ground to the rear of "C" Company's position.

Following the withdrawal of "B" Company a dispatch was received ordering the battalion to be prepared to move to HAGARU-RI on order. All equipment and supplies that could not be carried would be destroyed. The battalion less the motor convoy was to attack overland and move in the direction of HAGARU-RI. All organic vehicles were loaded and where possible trailer and truck loads were leveled off for carrying stretcher casualties and all other spaces were utilized for other casualties. All loaded vehicles were placed in an assembly area ready to move out on order.

"A" Company still in a defense position on the high ground to the right of the road and south of "C" Company's position was released by the 7th Marines and reverted to battalion control remaining in its defense position.

Between 2300, 1 December and 0300, 2 December many attempts at infiltration were made on the left front of "C" Company's position. Enemy troops in the approximate strength of one (1) squad infiltrated the perimeter but were annihilated. The enemy infiltration attempts then shifted to the center of "C" Company's position on the high ground and immediately thereafter the enemy attacked the position in force. A platoon from "B" Company was sent to reinforce "C" Company on the high ground. The attack was repulsed with heavy losses to the enemy. Shortly thereafter seventy-five (75) to one hundred twenty-five (125) enemy were observed crossing the ice on the reservoir to the right of "C" Company. Mortar and artillery fire were placed on the enemy troops resulting in many casualties and causing the remainder to move back. Attempts at infiltration continued until daylight, It is estimated that an enemy force of one (1) regiment was attacking "C" Company's perimeter. The following morning a force of approximately 375 enemy were observed to the right flank of the battalion sector evidently having crossed during the night. Estimated enemy killed was two hundred, (200). Fifty-one (51) enemy dead were counted in front of one machine gun. "C" Company had four (4) KIA and six (6) WIA, attached Weapons Company units had one (1) KIA and 2nd platoon of "B" Company one (1) WIA.

The morning of 2 December a verbal order was received to cancel and burn the order for the battalion to move overland to HAGARU-RI. The battalion was to proceed on order to HAGARU-RI along the road with two (2) companies acting as a flank covering force. All supplies and equipment that could not be carried were prepared for burning and destruction. At 1110 this destruction was ordered and the battalion began withdrawing to HAGARU-RI. "A" Company was detached to operational control of 2nd Battalion, 5th Marines, the rear guard unit. Order of march was H&S Company, Supply Train and Weapons Company. "B" and "C" Companies were deployed on high ground to the left of the road as a flank covering force. At 1600, "B" and "C" Companies were ordered to take up positions on Hill 1520 at TA 4274-Q and support 3/5 in breaking a road block holding up the column. As "B" and "C" Companies approached Hill 1520 with "C" Company as the point, enemy small arms fire from the hill forced "C" Company to deploy. At this time the road block had been broken and the Commanding Officer of 1/5 ordered "B" and "C" Companies to return to the road. Before "C" Company could disengage from the enemy and move down hill 1520 it had received one (1) KIA and one (1) WIA. "C" and "B" Companies returned to the road at 2400 and rejoined the battalion column at 0400. The rest of the battalion remained on the road until daylight under adverse weather conditions with the column moving only slightly. During the morning of 3 December, the battalion continued along the road in it position with other regimental elements. The column was halted several times by defended road blocks which were cleared. The battalion continued to move until 1530 at which time "B" and "C" Companies were set in positions at TA4475 to cover the withdrawal of division elements. H&S Company, Supply train, and Weapons Company proceeded on to HAGARU-RI arriving there at 2100 and going into an assembly area at TA 5171-T-4 .

At 0230, 4 December, "B" and "C" Companies moved from their defense positions to the road and had the mission of rear guard. Later the two companies were released as a rear guard and ordered to move forward in the column ahead of 3/7.

At 1240, "B" Company arrived at the assembly area and "C" Company arrived at 1300. At 1335, "A" Company rejoined the battalion from operational control of 2/5. At 1530 all of 1.5 attached units returned to parent organizations. While at HAGARU-RI the battalion was provided some tentage and warm-up facilities by the 1st Service Battalion, 1st Ordnance Battalion, Headquarters Battalion, and 1st Motor Transport Battalion. The 1st Service Battalion also assisted in providing hot food for the battalion, as all galley equipment had been destroyed.

Clothing and equipment were also issued to men of the battalion.

The battalion rested in this assembly area until 0900, 5 December at which time it was assigned a sector of the defense perimeter of HAGARU-RI. By 1600 the battalion had completely occupied its portion of the defense perimeter with a combat CP established to the rear of "A" Company's position. (See sketch #6). For the remainder of the day and night no enemy contact was made.

During the day of 6 December the Battalion remained in defense positions, strengthening them and being resupplied with equipment that was destroyed at YUDAM-NI. The battalion was alerted for movement the following day to KOTO-RI.

For the following action see sketch #6.

At 2100 the enemy launched a heavy attack on "C" Company's right flank where it tied in with "E" Company, 2/5. The attack was repulsed and it then moved to the right in the direction of "B" Company while small groups of the enemy continued exerting pressure on "C" Company's left front. 81mm and 60mm mortar fire and "C" Company's rockets were used with maximum effectiveness on enemy troop concentrations. One (1) USA M024 tank was used effectively during the late phases of the attack, The attack, except for several attempts at infiltration by small groups along "C" Company's left front ended about 2330.

At 2330, 6 December light enemy activity occurred along the entire battalion front. Activity increased before "A" Company's position and at approximately 0100 the enemy struck heavily on "A" Company's right front. The attack was stopped. Immediately the enemy's main effort shifted to the left front and the position was penetrated slightly but the enemy was immediately counterattacked by the 2nd platoon forcing the enemy to fall back.

The enemy continued to press the attack more vigorously. The main enemy pressure began to develop quickly against "A" Company's right flank forcing it back off the low ground to the high ground to its rear. Company 60mm mortars were used to their maximum.

At 0215, 7 December "B" Company in battalion reserve was ordered to reinforce "A" Company. The 3rd platoon, "B" Company was placed in position to effectively block by fire any envelopment across the river flat. The 1st platoon, "B" Company, integrated with "A" Company on the right sector if the hill. The 2nd platoon "B" Company was sent to reinforce "A" Company's left flank. "B" Company's 60mm mortars were placed in position near "A" Company's mortars to the left rear of the high ground. "B" Company mortars received missions from "A" Company. A bitter grenade and small arms fire fight went on for the remainder of the night.

At dawn the enemy attack decreased in intensity. Supporting arms with better visibility became very effective, aircraft made several close air support runs and the enemy attack stopped completely. The enemy became demoralized and fled. Several hundred enemy dead were found before "A" Company's positions. "A" Company casualties were twenty-six (26) WIA and seven (7) KIA. "B" Company casualties were seven (7) WIA and three (3) KIA.

While the heavy attack was underway against "A" Company, another attack at 0200 struck "C" Company's front lines. With the aid of effective supporting arms the attack was quickly repulsed. A USA, M-24 Tank gave support on the left flank. Infiltration by small groups of enemy was attempted throughout the remainder of the night. Two hundred sixty (260) dead were counted within two hundred (200) yards in front of the company perimeter the next morning. "C" Company casualties for the night's action were ten (10) WIA.

The battalion remained in defense position until 1100 at which time it withdrew from the perimeter and departed HAGARU-RI for KOTO-RI. "B" Company was employed as a left flank guard. The order of march was: "A" Company, H&S Company, Supply Train, Weapons Company and "C" Company. The battalion made the march during the day with negative enemy action. During the early hours of darkness great difficulty was encountered by the moving column. Where bridges had been destroyed, the by-passes were difficult to cross because of water and icy streambed and banks.

The battalion arrived in KOTO-RI at 2000 and went into assembly area at TA 5639-B. The men slept in the open in the snow for the most part. The battalion remained in this assembly area during the night of 7 December.

At 1100, 8 December, 1/5 departed from KOTO-RI. All equipment and supplies were carried in organic transportation. Troops moved on foot along the road. Division elements moving southward along the road were held up by enemy road blocks. Approximately 2,500 yards south of KOTO-RI at TA 5457-S the battalion less "A" and "C" Companies, set up defense perimeter, astraddle the road where it remained during the night of 8 December, No enemy contact was made on the perimeter.

Appendix B

History of the First Battalion, Fifth Marine Regiment, World War I, June 1917-August 1919.

HISTORY

of the

FIRST BATTALION

5th Regiment, U.S.Marines

—————

Published and Distributed from
Profits of Battalion Exchange.

—————

APPROVED :

MAJOR LeROY P. HUNT, U.S.M.C.
commanding

The Brass-Hat

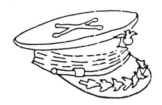

"History of the First Battalion, 5th Regiment, U.S. Marines" was sold to members of the Battalion on or after the date that Major LeRoy P. Hunt, Battalion Commander issued his statement of August 13, 1919. At the time the Battalion was in the process of disbanding, sending many of its members back to civilan life, and anxious to make the book available to as many as possible.

In order for the book to be available by that date it may have been printed in Germany and completed just about the time the Battalion was preparing to return to the United States. Otherwise, for it to be ready for distribution on or after the August 13, 1919 date would indicate a very rapid printing job in or near Quantico between the Battalion arrival time in New York in early August and the probable time the book was issued to members when the Battalion was disbanded, officially, August 13, 1919.

This unit history had few errors inherent and seemed to have had a better editor than "History of Second Battalion", (reprint 4 of this series) had when originally prepared. This book was re-printed at Quantico in 1935 on mimeograph paper with a total of 14 pages. Typewriters of that period did not perform as well as though it was set in type, therefore that edition has not stood the test of time.

It is hoped that this re-print will entice readers to get beyond the World War 2 syndrome and recognize that wherever or whenever U.S. Marines have served, they always did a hell of a job, giving the American public their money's worth, several times over. This is reprint number 3

George B. Clark

Additional copies available:

The Brass Hat, RR 2, Box 1B, Foster, RI. 02825

Organization

Battalion Headquarters
17th Company
49th Company
66th Company
67th Company
Medical Unit

Commanding Officers

From	To	Name
May 1917	Sept.23,1917	Major Julius S. Turrill
Sept.24,1917	Oct.24,1917	Lt.Col. Logan Feland
Oct.25,1917	Jan. 18,1918	Capt. George W. Hamilton
Jan.19,1918	Mar 12,1918	Major Edward A. Greene
Mar.13,1918	Aug 19,1918	Major Julius S. Turrill
Aug.20,1918	Aug.28,1918	Capt. Raymond F. Dirksen
Aug.29,1918	Sept.19,1918	Lt.Col. James O'Leary
Sept.20,1918	Dec.14,1918	Major George W. Hamilton
Dec.15,1918	Jan.15,1919	Capt. LeRoy P. Hunt
Jan.16,1919	Mar.20,1919	Major George W. Hamilton
Mar.21,1919	Aug.13,1919	Major leRoy P. Hunt

Composition

Every state in the Union is represented in the 1st Battalion. New York leads with 117, Pennsylvania 103, Ohio 103, Illinois 80, Missouri 55, Texas 33, Michigan 31, New Jersey 31, Tennessee 28, Massachusetts 27, California 21. Among miscellaneous addresses are 3 from England, 1 from Scotland, and 2 from Canada.

HISTORY of THE FIRST BATTALION

FIFTH MARINES

1917 – 1919

The assembling of the units of the First Battalion, Fifth U.S.Marines, under the command of Major Julius S. Turill, at QAUNTICO, Virginia, during the last fortnight of May, 1917, marked the beginning of a transformation by which that slumbering little village became a vast center of Marine activity.

The 66th and 67th companies were formed from prospective battleship's guards at the NORFOLK Barracks, and were joined in QUANTICO a few days later by the 49th Company whose ranks had been augmented by the U.S.S. New Hampshire's guard, commanded by Lieutenant George W. Hamilton.

The battalion was made complete by the arrival of the 15th company from PENSACOLA, Florida.

Following a brief period of drill on the banks of the Potomac, the battalion entrained for PHILADELPHIA on June 9, 1917. From the first the unit was blessed with an unquenchable spirit of acheivement, a factor that later carried the battalion through seemingly impossible situations when all other resources were at the lowest ebb. On the occasion of this first movement as an organized unit, divers inscriptions chalked upon the coaches in no modest type informed the yet unawakened citizens along the route that it was to be "Berlin or Bust" as far as the First Battalion was concerned.

After tenting for three days in the busy LEAGUE ISLAND Navy Yard, the battalion quietly embarked, 20 officers and 790 men strong, aboard the U.S.S.DeKalb, formerly the enemy ship Prinz Eitel Friedrich, which had engaged in high piracy before her internment in American waters. The embarkation was conducted after the fashion of the Corps, with no demonstration and with the greatest unconcern on the part of the troops. The DeKalb remained in home waters for two days, and on June 14, 1917, weighed anchor off STAPLETON, New York, and set out upon her zig-zag course eastward in convoy.

Conditions aboard the transport were somewhat cramped, but calm weather prevailed, and the voyage was accomplished with little hardship.

The only notable incident of the voyage occurred at 10:30 on the night of June 22, 1917, when two enemy submarines were sighted from the lookout. A light sea was running, phosphorescent glow of the whitecaps furnished the means by which the enemy craft were sighted. Two torpedos flashed their way toward the DeKalb, but missed their target by a narrow margin. Meanwhile, the guns of the transport fired a salvo at the submarines, and at full speed the ship plunged away from the scene of the near disaster, and encountered no other U-boats during the remainder of the trip. Part of the DeKalb's guns were manned by members of the battalion, who demonstrated their prowress in target practice from day to day during the voyage.

Around the old piano in the forward quarters of the ship, the members of the battalion improved acquaintances, and by the time the convoy glided into the welcome harbor of ST. NAZAIRE, France, on June 26, 1917, the unity of the four companies had become marked.

On June 27, 1917, the battalion disembarked, was greeted enthusiastically by the citizens of ST. NAZAIRE, and went into camp on the western outskirts of the city. The Fifth Regiment had been assigned to the First Division of the Army, units of which had crossed in the DeKalb's convoy.

The battalion remained in this seaport camp for over two weeks, entraining on July 15, 1917, for NAIX-AUX-FORGES, in the Department of Meuse. The trip was made in the little French box cars, but pleasant weather was again an alleviating factor. Throughout the two-day journey the men were warmly greeted by the French, and upon reaching NAIX on July 17, 1917, found the villagers in gala attire, standing along the little main street, over which a banner of welcome had been suspended.

NAIX furnished the First Battalion comfortable billets for the summer, and it was here that the long, hard period of intensive training was begun.

Practice entrenchments were dug among the peaceful hills of the region, and the organization to a man entered with a zest into the task of studying modern warfare. A battalion of Alpine Chausseurs, the 30th, was stationed nearby for the purpose of cooperating in instructing the Americans, and the high character of the organization, both as soldiers and men, had a lasting influence upon the First Battalion. The two units found that they had much in common, and through the remainder of the war the Alpine Chausseurs and the U.S. Marines were devoted brothers-in-arms. Social relations with the natives were here, as in succeeding localities, developed to a cordial extent, the French women from the first assuming a maternal benevolence toward the young men from over the seas.

While at NAIX the battalion was twice inspected by General John J. Pershing, who was accompanied upon one of the tours by General Petain, of the French Army.

"The finest body of men under our command" was the consensus of opinion of the General Staff after the inspection of the Fifth Regiment.

The strenuous course of training was highly effective upon the health of the men, and September, 1917 found the battalion in superb physical condition.

In the middle of the month General Silbert, commanding the First Division, bade farewell to the 5th Marines upon the occasion of their being detached from that army unit, and on September 23, 1917, the First Battalion, minus the 15th and 67th companies, entrained for BREUVANNES, Haute-Marne.

The 15th company was detached from the battalion at this time, and its place in the organization was not filled until January 1918, when the 17th company joined. The 67th company departed for England, where it remained on detached duty at the American Rest Camps in SOUTH HAMPTON, WINCHESTER, and ROMSEY, until March 7, 1918 when it rejoined the battalion in BREAUVANNES. Major Turrill accompanied the 67th company to England, and during his absence the battalion was commanded by Lieutenant Colonel Logan Feland (Sept.24 to Oct.24,1917), Captain George W. Hamilton (Oct.25, 1917 to Jan.18, 1918), and Major Edward A. Greene (Jan. 19 to March 12, 1918).

Upon its arrival in the BREAUVANNES area the 5th Regiment was attached to the 2nd Division, whose other regiments later became the 6th Marines, the 9th and 23rd Infantry, the 12th, the 15th, and the 17th Field Artillery, and the 2nd Engineers.

The winter of 1917-1918 proved a rigorous season in the BREAUVANNES area, and the light wooden barracks occupied by the battalion were of slight protection from the cold. But the hardness of the men obtained and increased during the period. A spirit of unrest, a longing for action became marked, especially so when it was learned that the First Division had proceeded to the front early in the winter and was engaging the enemy.

Thanksgiving, Christmas and New Year's Days were celebrated in little BREAUVANNES with as much of the home observance as it was possible to reproduce under the circumstances. Keen interest was aroused in football, and the battalion was creditably represented by teams from its companies in contests arranged with other units of the Regiment.

In January, 1918, the battalion was reinforced by the 12th and 26th companies, by means of which the strength of the respective companies was increased to the combat size of 250 men.

Travel orders finally arrived, and on March 17, 1918, the First Battalion entrained at daybreak. A day's journey brought the unit to LEMMES, a short distance from VERDUN. Disentraining under cover of darkness, the battalion set out upon a trying night march, made under great difficulties, which brought the organization at an early hour on the morning of the 18th to Camps DOUZAINE and NIVOLETTE, reserve positions in the old French sector southeast of VERDUN.

A week later, after a single day had been spent in the trenches opposite the two camps, the battalion hiked toward VERDUN, and on the first day of April, 1918, took over the lines before MOULANVILLE and AIX, in the sector known as MEUSE HEIGHTS, relieving the French troops.

The lines in this sector had remained stable since the early days of the war, in spite of the fact that the costly struggles for the possession of the VERDUN strongholds had been staged a few kilometers to the left. The tranquility of MEUSE HEIGHTS was chiefly due to the fact that the terrain rendered any extensive operation scarcely worth the price.

During the six weeks that followed the battalion gained invaluable experience in trench warfare at the cost of minimum casualties. The only contact with the German forces that occurred was gained by patrols and by a raid that was launched successfully by a French-Marine force out of AIX. The entrenchments in the sector were for the most part in low ground, and the accommadations consequently damp and crowded. But the long period of training had placed the health of the battalion beyond the effects of any of the unsanitary factors that existed from this period on.

On May 14, 1918, the Regiment was relieved, and the First Battalion entrained at ANCEMONT for a daylight trip to VITRY-LE-FRANCOIS, from which VITRY-EN-PERTHOIS was reached that evening on foot. In that pleasant village the battalion was billeted for a week, after which it entrained for BOURY, northwest of PARIS, to await further orders.

The brief period out of the lines was perhaps the happiest in the history of the battalion. Losses had been practically nil in the MEUSE HEIGHTS, and the confidence gained during that period brought the spirits of the men to the zenith. Then too, there was a goodly percentage of the men in the ranks of each company who had served in the Marine Corps for years, and who represented the traditions of the Corps. Subsequent battles caused this group of the older Marines to dwindle to the merest handful, but they left behind them, in the minds of the younger sea-soldiers, the traditions of which they were so proud. The columns whistled and sang while on the march, during this period, and racy songs were adopted in number. Chief among these was "Parlez-Vous", whose catchy melody appeared suddenly from an unknown source, but whose verses were added to daily from the ranks of the songsters.

Decoration Day, 1918, was passed peacefully in BOURY, but on the following morning, May 31, 1918, the battalion boarded camions and whirled east over white highways on the famed hurry call toward CHATEAU-THIERRY (BOIS-DE-BELLEAU).

The meeting near MEAUX, with a long plodding procession of refugees, for the most part women and children, trudging westward under heavy burdens, acted upon the men that afternoon like a powerful stimulant, bringing the situation home to every member of the battalion, and instilled a tense demand for vengence.

The organization slept in the open on the night of May 31st, a short distance from MEAUX, and continued to live in bivouac during the entire drive.

On June 1, 1918, a long march brought the battalion close to the lines, and on the following day the unit moved into position supporting the French, only to move off, during the night, in camions, toward a more vital point in the sector.

It was impossible for the men to realize what a tremendous crisis hovered in the vicinity. The French forces were in the depths of despair, and the rapid withdrawal that they had been forced to make had taken from them the pride and determination that alone could stem the tide. As for the men of the battalion, the situation in prospect held no terrors. The crack units of the German Army were coming on, and the "Leathernecks" had been given the honor post in the allied project of stemming the enemy's sweeping advance.

The daylight hours of June 4 and 5, 1918, were spent under the cover of woods near MARIGNY. On the latter day a number of enemy shells directed with fatal accuracy caused the battalion's first extensive casualties, and the incident served to fill the brim the cup of the avengers.

Daybreak on June 6, 1918, found the First Battalion deployed for combat a short distance before MARIGNY. Food had been impossible to bring up because of the speed with which successive moves had been made, and the galley forces had foraged practically all that was prepared for the men during the preceeding days.

The orders for the attack had not reached Major Turrill until midnight on the night of June 5-6, and the orders designated that the companies be in position three hours later. But the appointed hour found the stage completely set for the deadly drama that was to follow.

There was very little artillery available in the emergency, but all such handicaps were forgotten when the H hour, 3:45 a.m., arrived, and the battalion was deployed, pieces loaded and bayonets fixed. The 49th and 67th companies had been assigned to assault, and the 17th and 66th companies the support.

The hour had come, and the assaulting waves moved out across the first wheatfield, barely visable in the early morning mist, into its first combat with the Hun.

During this day's battle every man in the organization was called upon to give the best that was in him, and to a man, the unit responded.

Out ahead lay Hill 142, an elongated height extending approximately north and south. The course of the 49th company lay along the crest and on the right flank of the hill, bearing due north, while the 67th company's course led to the lower slopes east of Hill 142. Alternate woods and grainfields covered the region, and it was nearly surrounded from the enemy direction by commanding heights.

The two assaulting companies had advanced but a short distance into the first open when the Boche opened a machine gun barrage, and from that moment there was little cessation of fire until the noon hour.

The enemy forces opposing the Marines included two of the most highly trained units in the Imperial Army, the 28th, better known as "The Kaiser's Own", and the 362nd.

The 17th and 66th companies had been placed at the disposal of the 2nd Battalion during the two preceeding days, and it was not until later on the morning of the 6th that they took their places in the rear of the assaulting companies. The 17th company moved forward to the assault line when the objective was reached, reinforcing the 49th company's position.

The morning's objective lay along the northern extremity of Hill 142, a position which commanded the terrain on all sides. The attack orders had not been issued long enough before the battle began to permit of fully acquainting the subordinates with the plan of assault, and when the 49th company reached the objective with aproximately 90 per cent. of its officers and non-commissioned officers already on the casualty lists, the men pressed on down the north-eastern slope of the hill, holding tenaciously to their additional gain until recalled to the designated line.

Brave deeds and cool leadership went hand in hand on that day. The enemy's pride was shaken but not broken by the first attack, and he stood his ground more firmly than he did in any subsequent encounters with the Marines. Hand to hand engagements offered the only means of satisfying and avenging spirit long pent up.

The objective was reached before the sun was high, and by mid-morning the first of a series of enemy counter-attacks had been successfully stemmed. The teams who had become experts in handling the Chauchat automatic rifles were decimated early in the battle, but the trusty Springfield in the hands of men who had an inborn confidence in the weapon saved the day and completely confounded the enemy.

Individual deeds of heroism were legion. For a year the battalion had trained faithfully and awaited its chance, and the long-postponed day of action was welcomed. It was its own reward.

The tension lessened after the first day, and from June 7 to 19, 1918, the battalion clung to the ground gained, repelling counter-attacks and strengthening its position. Allied artillery had been rushed to the scene at the outbreak of the battle, and the positions of the enemy were shelled heavily during this period and until the great enemy retreat was taken up.

On June 19 the unit was relieved and moved back to SAACY-SUR-MARNE, a reserve position, only to be called back to the old sector on June 25 for two full weeks more of strenuous duty in and about what had become known as "Hell Wood".

On July 4, 1918, fifty members of the First Battalion took part in an inspiring parade in PARIS, during which the Marines were heavily "shelled" with boquets and hailed as saviours of the gay city.

From July 9 to 15, the battalion was billeted in CROUETTES, worn out, but well satisfied with the task it had completed. On the evening of the 16th the unit boarded camions and again whirled toward MEAUX, this time under cover of darkness, towards SOISSONS. On the following night a forced march was made through the FOREST OF RETZ in order that the battalion might be at its appointed post before dawn. The roads were fearfully congested by blockaded traffic of all kinds, and it was necessary to move the battalion in single file through the blackness of the night, worming between interminable columns of vehicles or plunging into the brush when the road became completely jammed. Remarkable leadership on the part of its commanders brought the organization to its designated post, and at daybreak on July 18, 1918, the battalion participated in the attack which drove the German forces completely out of the FOREST OF RETZ and forced them into an ignominious retreat.

From the moment of bitter combat with the enemy at CHATEAU-THIERRY (BOIS-DE-BELLEAU) the battalion gained a moral confidence, and ascendancy over the Hun that remained unshaken through the last day of hostilities.

A unit which had been on the road for upward of twenty-four hours and whose subsistence depended upon a small ration of hardtack cannot be considered liable to acquit itself in its standard degree. Yet the First Battalion, having reached its jumping-off point in the FOREST OF RETZ a few minutes before H hour on the morning of July 18, deployed into combat formation with its customary abandon.

At 3:45 the attack was launched. The battalion occupied the extreme left of the 2nd Division's line, with the 17th company and the 66th company in the assaulting waves, the 67th in support, and the 49th company in combat liaison with the forces on the left. The latter consisted of the 1st Division of French Colonials, a famous unit of Moroccans, whose cold-blooded manner of fighting had from the early days of the war struck terror in the hearts of the Germans.

In spite of the fatigue caused by the forced march, the battalion's prospects at SOISSONS were vastly more promising than they had been on the morning of June 6, for on all sides was evidenced the extensive preparation in all branches that later in the day forced the enemy into a retreat that more closely resembled a complete rout.

More tanks, great and small, than had been assembled for any previous American operation, were on hand, prepared to worm their way through the forest roads and pursue the enemy into the distant open. Likewise troop after troop of French cavalry, units with brilliant records, assembled close behind, awaiting their part in the drama, to harass the enemy's rear as soon as his expected retreat had been taken up.

At the given hour, the First Battalion disappeared from sight into the dark depths of the great forest. The enemy outposts were alert, and, within a few moments of the opening shot, the forest became the scene of a spirited combat. In the early morning light, good markmanship proved a difficult proposition. Snipers, perched high in the great trees of the forest, rendered our advance precarious, and machine gun nests could not be discerned until approached to a dangerous proximity.

The battalion's advance was, however, unimpeded, and at sun-up the unit had reached the edge of the forest, while the enemy scurried over the skyline, leaving in his wake only machine gun nests which held out in considerable number to the last.

Enemy aeroplanes rendered the advance from this point on, a considerable problem. Sweeping low over our lines, the Hun aviators operated their machine guns upon the infantry with considerable effect.

The 17th Company, finding its left flank exposed, boldly swerved to the left, under the direction of Captain LeRoy P. Hunt, and against organized resistance captured the village of CHAUDUN. This minimized danger from the exposed flank, and regaining its course, the 17th again closed on the 66th company, and the advance toward VIERZY continued.

At sunset on July 18, 1918, the battalion headquarters group, headed by Major Turrill and his staff, and accompanied by a platoon of the 49th company, entered VIERZY, and the battalion formed a line extending north from the village. Here the organization remained until the following night, when it was relieved, and dropped back into the depths of the great forest. A march brought the battalion to SILLY-LE-LONGUE, where it remained until July 25.

Casualties at SOISSONS were naturally much lighter than those at CHATEAU-THIERRY. In the latter battle, the battalion had reported 142 deaths and 405 lesser casualties, including the wounded, gassed, and sick, while the organization's losses at SOISSONS totalled 18 deaths and 216 lesser casualties. The Marines had gone into the June battle as "Leathernecks" and had come out as "Devil-Dogs". SOISSONS served only to increase their conscious superiority over the enemy, whose resistance grew rapidly weaker from this period on.

On July 25, 1918, the First Battalion was relieved from the SOISSONS sector, and by a series of marches and brief encampments, and transportation by rail from NANTIEUL to NANCY, reached the PONT-A-MOUSSON sector on August 6, 1918.

In this sector the battalion occupied a reserve position well back of the lines, and the fortnight spent here afforded comparative relaxation to the men who for two long months had performed assault and line duty with practically no respite.

On August 17, 1918, the battalion was sent out upon a two-day hike to GOVILLERS. At this point Julius S. Turrill, now a Lieutenant-Colonel, left the battalion, which was successively commanded by Captain Raymond F. Dirksen (August 20 to 28, 1918), and Lieutenant-Colonel James O'Leary (August 29 to September 19, 1918).

After five days of practice upon a rifle range in the area, the battalion was billetted in SELAINCOURT, where it remained from August 19 to September 1, 1918. This period, brief though it was, afforded an opportunity of giving valuable practice to the replacement men, who now filled the ranks in large numbers.

On September 1, the long march to ST. MIHIEL sector began. The distance was covered in easy stages, chiefly by night, and on September 12, 1918, the First Battalion took up the divisional attack in support of a battalion of the 9th infantry. The hasty retreat of the enemy forces in that day's battle was encouraged by the perfect work on the part of the 2nd Division's artillery. On the following day the battalion took over the front line on the northern outskirts of JAULNY, and remained in position during the three remaining days in the sector.

The casulaties sustained by the battalion during this drive, 4 deaths and 202 lesser casualties, were considered remarkably light for the amount of fire to which the unit was subjected.

Hiking out of the ST. MIHIEL sector on September 16, 1918, the battalion traversed TOUL and on the 21st was billetted in MONT-LE-VIGNOBLE. Four days later the organization entrained for CHALONS-SUR-MARNE. After two days in COURTISOLE, near CHALONS, the unit was transported by camions into the heart of the CHAMPAGNE sector, where going into the lines beyond SOMME-PY on October 2, 1918, and jumping off on the following morning, the 5th Regiment added another laurel to its wreath.

Looming up ahead was BLANC MONT, a commanding eminence for whose control the French had made many costly attempts. The secret of the enemy's success in stemming these attacks lay in the fact that the sole portion of the Hindenburg line remaining in German hands traversed this sector. An intricate double system of trenches known as the ESSEN and ELBE trenches rendered the position formidable.

The situation was rendered the more complex by the fact that our forces had gained a foothold in a part of these trenches, and that at points contact with the enemy was a matter of mere yards, a most precarious situation for the side unfamiliar with the intricacies of the entrechments.

All four companies, the 17th, 49th, 66th, and 67th, participated in the assault, and it fell to the lot of the 17th company to attack a hook-like salient of the enemy position which menaced our own security. This the 17th accomplished with great success.

Through the densest barrage of shell and machine gun fire that it had ever faced the battalion performed its advance as cooly as ever, and digging into the chalky surface of BLANC MONT formed its line and prepared to hold.

Liaison between the various French and American units was maintained with the greatest difficulty during this engagement, and gaps occurred in our lines that seriously threatened the success of the battle. It was thus when the 17th company, crashing through the enemy's center of resistance advanced into the town of ST. ETIENNE only to be oorced to fall back because the French forces operating on our left were not equally successful and failed to bring up the flank.

Another gap was discovered by the enemy in the course of the day's battle, and he proceeded to organize in the open for an attack upon the unprotected flank. Gunnery-Sergeant Arthur S. Lyng, 49th company, observed this preparation while scouting, and with the assistance of First Lieutenant Francis J. Kelly, 66th company, and Sergeant Robert Slover, 49th company, as well as other non-commissioned officers, Lyng organized a force of thirty men, all that were available in the emergency, and the small band burst from cover with their Springfields, opening fire on the run and howling in Comanche fashion. The Germans, whose number was estimated at between 250 and 300, were completely routed, and they left many dead and wounded upon the field, while prisoners and guns were taken by the little force, who became known in the organization as "Lyng's Comanches".

On the following day George W. Hamilton, now a Major, who had taken command of the First Battalion on September 20, 1918, received the following letter from Logan Feland, now a Colonel, and in command of the 5th Regiment:

"October 5, 1918.

"I am very happy to tell you that General Lejeune called me up this morning to ask me about our conditions and to assure you of his appreciation of your good work yesterday and last night.

He says that General Gouraud had called to assure him that it was the pushing out of this salient and especially our work of holding on last night that has made the Boche take up the big retreat now going on in all this RHEIMS sector. General Gouraud told General Lejeune that if we had given an inch the Boche would have forced us on, that he was giving us all he had to force us back and so prevent the necessity of his general retreat.

"General Lejeune is proud of you and sincerely sympathizes with us in our losses. I was so happy when I learned that the good work and devotion of you and your men are properly appreciated that I broke down. Let as many as possible of the officers and men know that the higher-ups know the great results gained by their holding last night, and give them full credit for it.

Yours,

(Signed) Feland."

Casualty reports consolidated at the close of the engagement in this sector showed 53 deaths on the field and 402 lesser casualties in the battalion.

On October 9, 1918, the organization was relieved from the lines and fell back to DAMPIERRE-AU-TEMPLE, where it was billeted until October 20. On the latter date a two day's march toward the lines was begun, but upon its completion the orders were countermanded, when the unit was encamped three kilometers southwest of SEMIDE. After a counter-march to CAMP MONTPELIER, the battalion boarded camions and reached LES ISLETTES, near ST. MENEHOULDE, on October 25, 1918.

The 31st of the month found the First battalion under cover of woods before EXERMONT, and during that night it moved up to the lines and awaited the hour of attack, which had been set for 5 a.m., November 1, 1918.

The First Battalion was designated to carry the assault to the first objective, two-and-one-half milometers into the enemy's lines. A violent artillery barrage by our guns from

3 to 5 a.m. was highly effective, and when at the latter hour the First Battalion passed through the lines of a battalion of the 42nd Division, the only stubborn resistance offered by the Boche was on the part of isolated machine gun nests which, however, inflicted many casualties before being destroyed.

The attack was entirely successful, and the companies, the 49th and 66th in assault, and the 17th and 67th in support, reached the first objective of the day at 8 o'clock, as per schedule.

The other battalions of the regiment then carried the attack to the second and third objectives, the First Battalion becoming the reserve of the regimental forces.

On November 3, 1918, the advance was resumed, and practically no resistance was met from the enemy, who was hastily withdrawing to the east bank of the Meuse.

From November 5 to 9, the battalion bivouacked in woods south of SARTELLE FARM, and on the night of November 10, 1918, it was designated to substitute in an attack across the MEUSE for a battalion of the 89th Division which had failed to reach the vicinity.

Under heavy shell fire from the enemy batteries on the opposite heights, the battalion crossed the MEUSE on frail foot bridges which had been thrown across the stream by the 2nd Engineers. Major Hamilton directed the combat of both the First and Second Battalions during the operation, while Captain LeRoy P. Hunt commanded the First Battalion.

The crossing was accomplished at 10 p.m., and the darkness of the night together with a heavy fog gathered just at that hour aided greatly in the success of the project. Before dawn on November 11, 1918, the battalion was dug in far beyond the east bank of the river, and had the situation well in hand.

Shortly before noon on the 11th, while the battalion was standing by for a further advance, the following order was received from regimental headquarters:

"Nov. 11,1918.-9:10 a.m.

"To Major Hamilton:
" All firing will cease at 11 a.m. today. Hold every inch of ground that you have gained, including that gained by patrols. Send in as soon as possible a sketch showing positions of all until 11 a.m.

"(Signed) Feland."

Three days later the battalion was relieved by a unit of the 77th Division, and hiking into POUILLY, a nearby village, was billeted there until November 17, 1918.

Casualty returns for the operation showed 46 deaths and 448 lesser casualties in the First Battalion from November 1, until the cessation of hostilities.

On November 17, 1918, as a unit in the American Army of Occupation, the battalion marched northeast through MOIRY toward the Belgian border, which was crossed two days later. Alternately marching and resting in billets, the organization took the following route to the Rhine: ETTALE, Belgium; ARLON, Belgium; RIECHLANGE, Luxemburg; COLMAR-BERG, MOESTROF, and GILSDORF, Luxemburg; HOLSEKEN, Germany; MERTSCHEID, OLZHEIM, STADTKYLL, ESCHE, ANTWEILER, AHRWEILER, OBERZISSEN, HONNIGEN, and NEIDERBREITBACH, Germany.

The Rhine was crossed at REMAGEN on December 13, 1918, and the battalion reached its destination, NEIDERBREITBACH, on Decemeber 15, and was billeted in and about the village for the remainder of the year, under the command of Captain Hunt, who relieved Major Hamilton when the latter the organization December 15 on sick leave.

The 66th Company was billeted at WOLFENUCKER, and later the 17th company moved from NIEDERBREITBACH to KURTSCHEID.

Athletics, entertainments, and various amusements helped relieve the monotony of the "Watch on the Rhine", keeping all in excellant physical condition, morale and spirit high. A rifle range was built at NIEDERBREITBACH. Frequent maneuvers and parades were held, demonstrating the battalion's fitness for its duty as a part of the American Army of Occupation.

Previous to the final presentation of the Peace Terms at PARIS, the battalion, under full combat equipment, moved to STEINEN at the perimeter of the COBLENZ bridgehead, prepared to move forward further into Germany if ordered. The troops remained in bivouac until Germany's delegates accepted the terms, whereupon the battalion returned to the NIEDERBREITBACH area, to await entraining orders for the return to the United States.

Leaving NIEDERBREITBACH July 17th and entraining at NIEDERBIEBER the same day, the battalion in high spirits left Germany for BREST by way of COLOGNE, LIEGE, ARRAS, VALENCINNES and other points in the areas where the Belgians and English had battled the Hun. July 24th, the First Battalion as a unit of the 5th Regiment boarded the U.S.S. George Washington, bound for NEW YORK. A battalion of the 6th Regiment was also aboard, together with Major General John L. Lejeune and Brigadier General Wendell C. Neville. The returning Marines were given a joyous and noisy welcome in New York harbor, the troops disembarking at HOBOKEN and proceeding to CAMP MILLS on Long Island.

As a unit of the 2nd Division, the First Battalion participated in the parade of the 2nd Division in NEW YORK CITY August 8th, entraining thereafter for QUANTICO, Virginia, at which point the Marine units of the 2nd Division again came under the jurisdiction of the Navy.

A considerable portion of the men of the battalion were "duration of the war" men, and preparations were made immediately to discharge these men as promptly as possible. In the meantime the First Battalion as a unit of the Marine Brigade, paraded in WASHINGTON, D.C., August 12th, being reviewed by President Wilson, various Cabinet members, Major-General George Barnett, Commandant of the Marine Corps, and Major-General John L. Lejeune, who had commanded the 2nd Division.

Carlyle believed that true history is nothing more or less than a narrative of individuals and their achievements as such. From this standpoint the above record of the First Battalion, 5th Regiment, U.S. Marines, falls lamentably short. From the first its ranks were filled with heroic men, men whose names should appear on these pages by merit of their deeds, but whose number is prohibitive.

Headquarters 1st Battalion
5th Regiment, U.S.Marine Corps
Quantico, Virginia
August 13, 1919.

To the Officers and Men of the 1st Battalion, 5th
Regiment, U. S. Marine Corps:

The time for demobilization has come and in another day
the 1st Battalion, 5th Regiment, will be but a memory.
We will soon be scattered to the four corners of the
land, never again to be together.

It is useless to go over the part played by us in the
war, for we all know it too well, and it speaks for
itself. Every one has done his bit well and faithfully
and deserves every possible bit of credit.

I wish to thank you for your hearty co-operation and
faithfulness and believe me, when I say that I consider
it the greatest honor of my life to have commanded such a
wonderful body of officers and men as the 1st Battalion,
5th Regiment, Marines.

The best o'luck and success to every one of you.

Sincerely,

(Signed) LeRoy P. Hunt,

Major U. S. M. C.

Appendix C

Special Action Report, First Battalion, Fifth Marines,
First Provision Brigade at the Pusan Perimeter,
7 July-6 September, 1950.

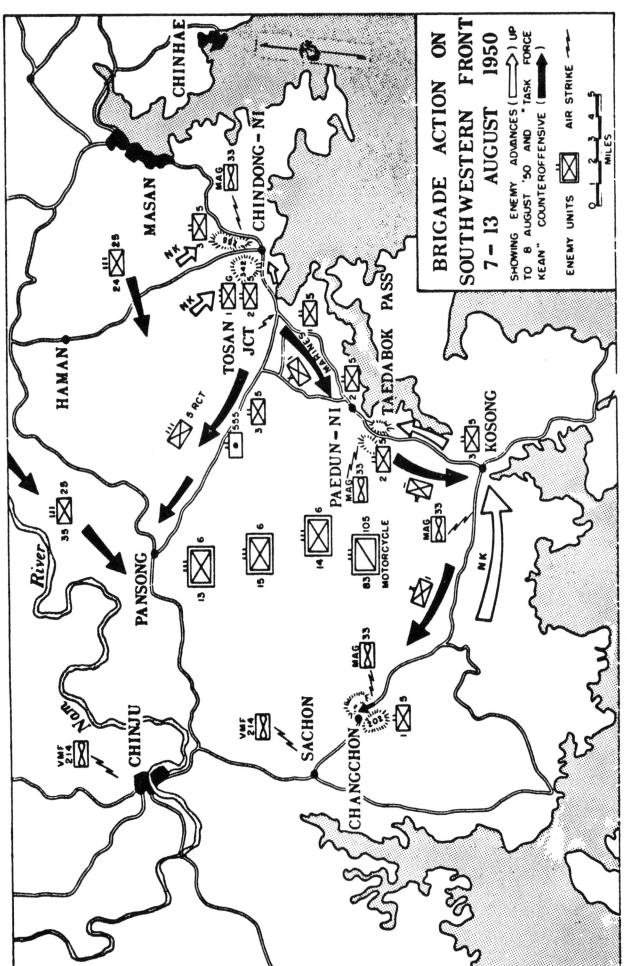

Taken from The Pusan Perimeter, by Edwin P. Hoyt. (pg 147)

1st Battalion, 5th Marines
1st Provisional Marine Brigade,
In the Field, Korea

9 September,1950

SPECIAL ACTION REPORT

Maps: Masan, ChinDong-ni, Kosang, Sach'on, Miryang, Yongsan
and Namji-ri sheets, 1:50,000, Korea.

Appendices: 1 through 6, sketches of special battle areas.

1. INTRODUCTION:

This report is submitted in accordance with a directive
received from the Commanding General, 1st Provisional Marine
Brigade and paragraph 11401.2, Marine Corps Manual. The purpose of this report is to provide a concise, complete record
of the actions in which this unit participated during the period of 7 July to 6 September, 1950. Missions assigned this
battalion were as issued by the next higher echelon, the
5th Marines.

2. TASK ORGANIZATION:

BLT 1/5   33 Officers 673 Enlisted   LtCol G.R. Newton

    H&S Company   Capt W.J. Godenius

        TACP   1stLt J.W. Smith

        NGF Liaison   Lt C.O. Grewe, USN

        Artillery Liaison   1stLt J.J. Snyder

    "A" Company   Capt J.R. Stevens

    " Company   Capt J.L. Tobin

    Weapons Company   Maj J.W. Russell

At various times, as noted in paragraph 7, elements of
the following units were attached, depending on whether the
battalion was in assault or reserve.

75mm Recoilless Gun Company, 5th Marines

One Platoon 4.2" Mortar Company, 5th Marines

1st Platoon, Company "A", 1st Tank Battalion, 1st Provisional Marine Brigade

Detachment of Reconnaissance Company, 1st Provisional
Marine Brigade

Detachment of Engineer Company, 1st Provisional Marine
Brigade

1

3. PRELIMINARY PLANNING:

The schedule, as set forth by higher headquarters, required this battalion to be ready in all respects to embark aboard ship at San Diego on 13 July 1950. All organizational equipment was prepared and packed for an amphibious operation. A preferred plan was formulated for an amphibious landing. An alternate plan was drawn up in the eventuality the battalion would be airlifted to its destination. The enemy situation in Korea was confused and very little concrete information was available at battalion level. No military maps of Korea were available prior to reaching our destination. The battalion carried sufficient water, rations and ammunition in its supply train to last for one days operations.

4. TRAINING AND REHEARSAL:

Prior to embarking aboard ship on 13 July, the battalion conducted three days dry net training and amphibious lectures at the debarkation mock-ups at Camp Joseph H. Pendleton. Approximately one half of the battalion had participated in Demon III on 12 May 1950 at Aliso Beach, near Camp Pendleton. Lectures were held on troop life and training aboard ship. On 17 and 18 July, while the APA-45 was at NSD Oakland for repairs, units held instructions in weapons, first aid and tactics and participated in calisthenics ashore. During the period 19 July to 2 August, shipboard training was conducted continuously to include weapons instruction, tactics lectures, calisthenics, amphibious doctrine and debarkation drill. While in bivouac near Changwan, night patrolling was practiced.

5. LOADING AND EMBARKATION:

Upon receipt of the order to be embarked by 13 July, all equipment and supplies of BLT 1/5 were packed for an amphibious operation. Transportation of supplies to San Diego and ship loading continued on a 24 hour schedule until completed. On 13 July, BLT 1/5 entrucked at Camp Joseph H. Pendleton and proceeded to San Diego. Embarkation was completed by 1600, 13 July.

6. MOVEMENT TO AND ARRIVAL AT OBJECTIVE AREA

The APA 45 sailed from San Diego at 0800, 13 July. On the afternoon of 13 July, in the vicinity of San Clemente Island, the ship developed turbine trouble and turned toward San Francisco, arriving at NSD Oakland on the afternoon of 16 July. Repairs were completed by the afternoon of the 18th. The ship rejoined the convoy on the morning of 2 August and arrived at Pusan, Korea at 1800 on 2 August. Personnel debarked at 0500, 3 August, entrucked at 0600 and proceeded to Ch'angwan, where the battalion covered the advance of the Brigade and remained in bivouac for three days.

7. DETAILED COMBAT NARRATIVE:

BLT 1/5 became a part of the 1st Provisional Marine Brigade on 7 July 1950. From 7 July 1950 to 13 July 1950 this unit was packing, training and preparing to board ship.

On 13 July 1950 at approximately 0800, BLT 1/5 commenced entrucking at Camp Joseph H. Pendleton, Oceanside, California and proceeded to the U.S. Naval Station, San Diego, California, going directly aboard the USS Henrico, APA 45. BLT 1/5 was completely loaded at 1600 on 13 July 1950.

On 14 July 1950 at approximately 0900, the APA 45 put to sea and proceeded to the vicinity of San Clemente Island when engine trouble, which developed at approximately 1430, caused the APA 45 to leave the convoy and proceed independently to Oakland, California.

The APA 45 put in at Oakland, California at approximately 1900 on Sunday, July 16, 1950. On 17 and 18 July, small unit training was conducted ashore at NSD Oakland while the APA 45 was undergoing repairs.

The ship departed Oakland, California at approximately 1800, 18 July, and while underway, the battalion conducted indoctrination, intelligence lectures on Korea and general and specialized infantry training.

APA 45 joined up with the convoy of the 1st Provisional Marine Brigade, in the early morning of August 2, 1950, and proceeded to Pusan, Korea, arriving at Pusan, Korea at 1800, August 2, 1950.

BLT 1/5 disembarked at Pusan, Korea at approximately 0500 on 3 August, 1950, entrucked at 0600 and proceeded to Ch'angwon, Korea. The battalion disembarked at approximately 1400 on 3 August and took up defense positions approximately one mile west of Ch'angwon astride the Masan-Pusan road with the mission of protecting the movement of the Brigade into the Ch'angwon area. Later, BLT 3/5 arrived, tied in on the left flank and relieved elements of 1/5 on left of road, and took up defense positions on left front, while this battalion extended their defense to the right front. Two casualties were suffered in "A" Company, BLT 1/5, one by accidental discharge, and the other during challenging procedure.

4 August 1950

The battalion remained in position at Ch'angwon. Continuous patrols were sent out by "A", "B", and H&S Companies to the front and right flank. No enemy were encountered and patrols continued on 24 hour basis.

3

5 August 1950

The battalion remained in position and continued patrol action. At approximately 2130, "B" Company reported enemy activity to their front and at 2145, "B" Company's patrol was fired upon and withdrew to friendly front lines. A short fire fight followed without any casualties suffered by "B" Company and enemy withdrew at approximately 2200.

6 August 1950

Continuous patrol action by BLT 1/5. No enemy encountered.

7 August 1950

BLT 1/5 entrucked at approximately 1000 and proceeded to the vicinity of ChinDong-ni, arriving at approximately 1230 on the same day. This battalion relieved "G" Company, BLT 3/5 at TA 1148-1347.9 (Sheet #6819 II), at 1500. New battalion CP was established at 1530 at 1148.2-1347.5 (Sheet #6819 II). The relief of "G" Company on front lines was completed at approximately 1700. Enemy activity was observed to the battalion front. One casualty suffered in "A" Company due to friendly short artillery round. Friendly supporting fires were placed on enemy to the battalion front. No enemy action was encountered during the night.

8 August 1950

BLT 1/5 departed from ChinDong-ni at approximately 0600 and moved in route column southwest along road towards Chinju, Sachon-Paeden-ni with the mission of following in rear of elements of the 5th RCT, (U.S. Army), to crossroads at Chinju and Sachon junction and to take the left fork in the road, proceed to high ground to the immediate front and relieve the 1st battalion, 5th RCT (U.S. Army) on position. Upon arrival at the crossroads, this battalion found that the 5th RCT (U. S. Army) had not cleared that point and acting upon Regimental Orders moved back approximately one mile and went into defensive positions with orders to move out again at 2300. The rear CP was established at approximately 1700 at 46.2-47.2 (Sheet #6819 II). At 2300, BLT 1/5 departed to relieve the 1st battalion, 5th RCT (U.S. Army) on position. The night march included the crossing of approximately 1 mile of rice paddies and a climb to positions on the high ground at TA 44.2-44.2 (Sheet #6819 II) where the battalion set up defense positions at approximately 0400, 9 August. No opposition was encountered. At 0430 this battalion received an order to attack and seize the high ground to the immediate front known as Regimental Objective #1.

At 0600, BLT 1/5 moved out to seize Regimental Objective #1 and advance to the west along ridge line and set up defense

4

positions on Regimental front lines at approximately 0900;
no resistance was encountered. At 1200, orders were received
to move to road and continue advance towards Paedun-ni. No
opposition was encountered and defense positions for the night
were set up at approximately 1800 with the battalion CP located
at 42.3-43.4 (Sheet # 6819 II).

10 August 1950

At 0100 the last of the column of BLT 2/5 passed through
1/5, becoming the Brigade Advance Guard. At 0630 the battalion
moved out behind the 2nd Battalion with orders to seize the
high ground east of Paedun-ni. This battalion was in position
at 0900. At 1500, the battalion was ordered to continue the
advance toward Paedun-ni, Korea behind the 2nd Battalion. At
1700 our column arrived at Paedun-ni, entrucked and proceeded
to TA 35-36 (Sheet # 6819 II). At 2000, the battalion passed
through BLT 2/5 and went into defense positions at 34.6-36 to
35.5-56 (Sheet # 6819 II).

11 August 1950

At 0800, the advance was continued westward toward Kosong,
Korea with this battalion following BLT 3/5, with orders to
patrol the high ground to the southwest of Kosong. At approximately 1200, BLT 1/5 arrived in Kosong, Korea, patrolled the
area assigned with negative results. The column was reformed
and departed from Kosong at approximately 1500, advancing westward behind BLT 3/5 at TA 29.3-30.2 to 29.3-30.7 (Sheet # 3819 I).

12 August 1950

At 0630, BLT 1/5 passed through BLT 3/5 and moved northwest
in advance guard formation along the road to Sach'on, Korea,
with a detachment of fifteen men commanded by Captain Kenneth
J. Houghton of the 1st Provisional Marine Brigade Reconnaissance
Company as the point and "B" Company, BLT 1/5, commanded by
Captain John L. Tobin, as the advance party. At approximately
1100 the point and the advance party had reached TA 14.6-37.8
(Sheet # 6819 III). No resistance had been encountered up to
this time. 50 enemy abandoned motorcycles with side cars,
twenty Russian built Ford jeeps, and numerous quantities of
small arms were passed, burned or camouflaged beside the road,
all having been abandoned by the enemy as a result of air strikes
and rapid movement of the Brigade.

The 1st Battalion was assigned the mission of seizing the
town of Sach'on, passing through, and seizing the high ground
to the north and west of Sach'on. Units attached to the 1st
Battalion at that time were a detachment of the 1st Provisional
Marine Brigade Reconnaissance Company, 1st Platoon of "A"
Company, 1st Tank Battalion and detachment of "A" Company, 1st
Engineer Battalion. The point and 1st platoon of "B" Company
was supported by two M-26 tanks, with three tanks of the same
type following "B" Company. At approximately 1300 the point

5

and "B" Company were in a valley in the vicinity of the small village of Changch'an, with high ground to the front, to the left flank, and to the right flank. The point had just entered the village when it observed two enemy taking cover; (shown as enemy position "E" on sketch #1) they were fired upon by the point, whose fire was resultant in precipitating the premature disclosure of enemy positions. The enemy obviously had planned a rear guard action of an ambush type to such an extent that the entire column would be allowed to come within their fields of fire before they commenced firing. The point was immediately fired upon by an enemy machine gun on the high ground to the right flank. (shown as enemy position "B" on sketch #1). "B" Company immediately came under intense automatic weapons fire from the high ground to the front and both flanks. (shown as enemy positions "B", "C" and "A" on sketch #1).

The point requested the 1st platoon, commanded by 2ndLt Hugh C. Schryver Jr. to move forward and assist them in the fire fight. The company commander, "B" company, immediately dispatched the 1st platoon to their aid by fire and manuever, engaging the enemy from positions in the ditch beside the road. The 1st platoon suffered 3 casualties while moving forward to this position.

While the 1st platoon was moving forward to the aid of the point, the company commander "B" company ordered the 2d platoon, commanded by 1stLt David S. Taylor, to move forward on the three tanks from the rear of the Company's column.

This platoon moved forward to the rear of the 1st platoon, deployed on both sides of the road and engaged the enemy from positions in the road ditches with small arms fire.

By this time company headquarters and the 3rd platoon were receiving intense fire from enemy machine guns and other automatic weapons from the high ground to the right flank. (shown as enemy positions "B" and "C" on sketch #1). The battalion commander directed the forward air controller, 1stLt James W. Smith, to call down an air strike on enemy personnel observed on the right flank. (shown as strike #1 on sketch # 2). The company commander, "B" company ordered the 3rd platoon, commanded by 2dLt David R. Cowling, to cross the rice paddies and seize the high ground to the right flank, as soon as the air strike lifted. (shown as enemy position "B" on sketch # 1). The battalion commander experienced difficulty in getting immediate supporting fires due to the fact that the units were in the column and had to get into firing positions. The Regimental Commander had been previously notified by the Battalion Commander, 1st Battalion, 5th Marines, that artillery fire was not available.

While the 3rd platoon was crossing the rice paddies, one rifle platoon and one machine gun section from "A" Company, 1st Battalion, 5th Marines, reported to the Company Commander,

6

"B" Company, for orders. This unit had moved forward upon order of the Battalion Commander. The Battalion Commander was at that time informed by the forward air controller of two planes with five minutes remaining on station prior to returning to the base. The Battalion Commander directed they search for targets forward of friendly troops. This flights immediately located enemy vehicles and personnel in strike area #2 (shown as strike area #2 on sketch # 2). They used their remaining ordnance and returned to base.

The Company Commander, "B" Company, ordered the two squads and the machine gun section from "A" Company to take up positions on the high ground to the right flank and to the rear of the enemy positions from which "B" company was receiving automatic fire, (shown as enemy position "C" on sketch #1), and the one remaining squad to move to the high ground to the left flank and place flanking fire on the enemy occupying positions on the high ground on the left flank (shown as enemy position "A" on sketch #1). The two squads and the machine gun section from "A" company succeeded in knocking out the enemy position. (shown as enemy position "C" on sketch #1).

While the 3rd platoon was moving forward to carry out their assignment, intense machine guns and automatic fire was being delivered on the company from the high ground to the left flank. (shown as enemy position "A" on sketch #1). The tanks and personnel on the left side of the road took these positions under fire, the tanks utilizing machine gun and 90mm fire.

When the 3rd platoon of "B" company was near the crest of the high ground, it received exceptionally heavy fires from machine guns positioned to deliver interlocking bands of fire from such well concealed positions that the 3rd platoon was forced to fall back a short distance down the slope of the high ground. Enemy strength in that area was estimated at approximately 60 in number. In this action one man was killed and 4 were wounded, one of the wounded being Lieutenant Cowling, the platoon leader. The battalion commander directed the company commander of "A" Company, Captain John R. Stevens to seize the high ground to the battalions right flank, thereby protecting the brigade's flank. The battalion commander, also at that time, ordered the Weapons Company, 1st Battalion, commanded by Major John W. Russell to place 81mm mortar fire on the high ground to the left flank. (shown as enemy position "A" on sketch #1).

The 3rd platoon, "B" company was ordered to fall back to the high ground where the two squads and the machine gun section from "A" company were in position, and "B" company mortars were ordered to fire on the enemy automatic weapons which the 3rd platoon had been assaulting. (shown as enemy position "B" on sketch #1). A total of 113 rounds, 60mm HE, was delivered on these positions.

The battalion commander, 1st Battalion, ordered an air strike on the automatic weapons positions on the high ground to the right flank immediately following "B" company's mortar fire. (shown as strike # 3 on sketch # 2). The air strike destroyed those positions. While the air strike on the right flank was being delivered, the Battalion Commander, 1st Battalion, ordered artillery, one battery of which had gone into position, to fire on the enemy positions on the high ground to the left flank. (shown as enemy position "A" on sketch # 1). At about 1700 all of the enemy positions had been silenced with the exception of the machine gun positions on the left flank from which "B" company had been receiving fire. An air strike was called which silenced this position. (shown as strike #4 on sketch # 2).

At about 1730, "B" company was ordered to take up positions on the high ground to the left flank and dig in for the night. "A" company was ordered to occupy the high ground to the right flank and dig in for the night. While "B" company was preparing to move out the battalion commander ordered an air strike (shown as strike # 5 on sketch # 2) on enemy position "B" where the enemy had once again placed an automatic weapon which was firing on "B" company. "B" company moved out with the 1st platoon in the lead, followed by the 2d platoon, then the remainder of the company. Progress was very slow due to the crossing of rice paddies and sporadic small arms fire.

When "B" company reached the far side of the rice paddies they located approximately fifty empty well prepared and well concealed infantry positions. (shown as enemy position "D" on sketch #1).

The battalion commander received a report from friendly aircraft, of an enemy concentration in the area shown as strike # 1 on sketch # 2. He ordered an air strike on the concentration (shown as strike # 6 on sketch # 2).

Upon reaching the crest of the high ground, the 2d platoon engaged the enemy of approximately one company strength, and in about 10 minutes had secured the high ground in their sector. During the engagement the platoon leader, 1stLt David S. Taylor observed some of the enemy withdrawing down a ravine on the reverse slope of the high ground. He ordered one squad to proceed down another ravine in an attempt to cut off the enemy's retreat. This squad succeeded in doing so and in the ensuing action a total of 38 enemy was killed and one wounded enemy officer captured, without any casualties to the squad. Despite all effort to get the enemy officer to Regimental Headquarters for interogation, he died upon arrival.

"B" company completed its movement onto the high ground and set up a perimeter of defense. The company had to complete its perimenter of defense under cover of darkness.

The 3rd platoon less one squad and with one machine gun section attached were place on hill 202; 1st platoon with one machine gun section attached, extending down from hill 202 to within 75 yards of the second platoon, which, plus 1 squad from the 3rd platoon and one machine gun section, were placed on the ridge on the company's right flank. (see sketch # 2).

Total casualties for the day were 13 wounded in action, 3 killed in action, and 2 missing in action.

The battalion commander received orders at approximately 2400 from the regimental commander to form the battalion on the road at 0630 and prepare to entruck for movement of the regiment to another sector to reinforce U.S. Army units. All companies were notified.

At approximately 0400 the following morning, all company commanders alerted their companies and every man was awakened. (As previously directed by the battalion commander). At 0450 "B" Company started receiving intense automatic weapons and small arms fire from the right front. "B" Company's 60mm mortars fired six (6) illuminating shells to the immediate front. The enemy was observed near the right front and was engaged with fire at approximately 0500; enemy strength in that sector was estimated at 60 in number.

At that time 3 flares (2 green and 1 red) went up to "B" Company's front and the company was immediately attacked on the left flank. The enemy attacking the left flank all appeared to be armed with automatic weapons and attacked from close, well-concealed positions, to which they had moved during the hours of darkness.

They succeeded in over-running the left flank, killing all but one man in the machine gun section and inflicting heavy casualties in the 3rd platoon.

Due to lack of communications and darkness, (the 1st and 3rd platoon 536 radios had become inoperative due to mud and water from crossing rice paddies,(and the telephone wires were believed to have been cut), it was practically impossible to determine the condition of the 3rd platoon's position. Two runners were dispatched from the company CP to the 3rd platoon to obtain information, but both were killed before they could get to the platoon. The enemy, upon over-running the machine gun section attached to the 3rd platoon, turned the captured machine guns on the remainder of "B" Company.

The company commander ordered messengers to instruct the remainder of the 3rd platoon, 1st platoon and company headquarters to fall back to the 2d platoon's position with the 1st platoon covering the movement by fire.

9

The company commander requested the battalion commander to place all available 81mm mortar, artillery, and 4.2" mortar fire on hill 202 to cover the movement to the 2d platoon's position.

The fire support was excellent. The 81mm mortar fire from the 1st Battalion, 5th Marines delivered immediate support, with 4.2" mortar and artillery fire getting on shortly after the 81mm fire.

It was daylight when the movement to the 2d platoon's positions was completed and at that time the captured machine gun positions were observed. "B" Company commander ordered the 3.5" rocket section to fire on them; both guns and enemy crews were destroyed.

By this time the entire company had the enemy under fire and with the assistance of supporting fires were driving the enemy back over hill 202. During the attack the enemy placed intense and effective mortar fire on "B" company's right flank and right rear.

It was practically impossible to move "B" Company off the high ground by 0630 since the counterattack was still very strong at that time so at approximately 0700 the battalion commander ordered "B" Company to leave the high ground and proceed to the road, ready for prior ordered movement. The company commander "B" Company requested all available supporting fires be placed on the enemy prior to and during the movement. All wounded personnel were collected and the company moved in an orderly manner, carrying the wounded off the high ground under covering fire set up by the 1st and 3rd platoons and supporting arms.

The company executive officer, Capt Francis I. Fenton, Jr. directed the column and movement of wounded across the rice paddies while the company commander directed the covering fire for the movement from the rear. When all troops were clear, an air strike was called on hill 202 by the regimental air controller.

Total casulties for both days actions were, 15 killed in action, 33 wounded in action, and 8 missing in action. There was an estimated 250 enemy killed in both days actions.

For reference to night defensive positions and action the following morning, see sketch #3.

It is the concensus of opinion of persons involved in the action that the enemy in the area was of battalion strength. It is also apparent that the enemy in this area was the rear guard for the main body.

The map reference for this engagement is TA 1113.9-1339.1
Sach'on sheet #6819 III.

13 August 1950

At 0900, "B" Company completed its withdrawal from its
position and all casualties were evacuated. At 1000, BLT 1/5
entrucked at TA 14.5-38 (Sheet #6819 III) to proceed to Miryang,
Korea in accordance with regimental movement plan. At 1330 BLT
1/5 arrived at TA 43.3-45.3 (Sheet #6819 II) and disembarked
from trucks and went into a tactical assembly area. At 2400
BLT 1/5 began a march to TA 48.2-45.8 (Sheet #6819 II), to board
on LST for further transfer to Masan.

14 August 1950

At 0230, BLT 1/5 embarked aboard LST #24 to proceed to Masan,
Korea. At 0600, LST #24 got under way for Masan. At 0930, LST
#24 arrived at Masan and troops disembarked and went into an
assembly area while awaiting rail transportation to Miryang,
Korea. At 1400, BLT 1/5 entrained at Masan and commenced movement by rail to Miryang. At 1730, BLT 1/5 arrived at Miryang
and entrucked at 1930 to proceed to bivouac area located at TA
76.4-96.3 (Sheet #6920 II). The battalion arrived at bivouac
area at 2000.

15 August 1950

Remaing in bivouac all day, personnel drew clothing, washed
clothes and unit was resupplied on all equipment shortages.

16 August 1950

At 1400, the order was received to move to the Naktong River
area, west of Yongsan. The 24th Division (U.S. Army) plus the
1st and 2nd Battalions, 9th RCT, 2nd Division (U.S. Army) were
occupying defensive positions in this area. The Naktong River
at this point made a large semi-circular bend, at which point
elements of the North Korean Army had penetrated to the east
side of the river. In order to maintain the Naktong River defense line, it was necessary to drive the enemy from this peninsula on the east side of the river.

Due to the scarcity of transportation, the 5th Marines were
shuttled to the front by battalions, the 1st Battalion being
the last to leave the Miryang area. The 1st Battalion entrucked
at 0515 on 17 August, making the 24 mile trip in shortly over 2
hours and detrucked west of Yongsan at 0730. It then proceeded
west in route march with "A" Company as the point followed by
"B" Company, command group, Weapons Company, H&S Company, and
the supply train.

At 0700, the 2nd Battalion, 5th Marines, had jumped off in the attack to take Brigade Objective #1 which consisted of Obong-ni Ridge and the low ground to the west. The attack had been preceeded by an air strike and a heavy artillery concentration.

By 1100, the 1st Battalion was being held in reserve, 1000-1200 yards in rear of Objective #2, with the battalion CP at TA 1144.1-1388. At 1330, the order was received to pass through and relieve the 2nd Battalion and to continue the attack to secure Objective #1. The Regimental Commander attached the 75mm Recoilless Gun Company and the 1st platoon of "A" Company, 1st Tank Battalion to the 1st Battalion. At this time the 2nd Battalion was in contact with the enemy at the bottom of the slope of Obong-ni Ridge, with "D" Company on the right and "E" Company on the left, extending approximately 1000 yards south of the road. LtCol. Newton was in the OP with the 2nd Battalion Commander. The 1st Battalion staff moved into the 2nd Battalion CP to operate in conjunction with them until the relief was effected. "B" Company, 1st Battalion, proceeded forward along the road to the right of the CP to relieve "D" Company, 2nd Battalion and "A" Company, 1st Battalion went forward over OP hill to relieve "E" Company, 2nd Battalion on the left. Weapons Company set up 81mm mortar positions as shown on the sketch. The relief was completed by 1600 and the attack was continued to secure Obong-ni Ridge before nightfall.

"B" Company went into the attack with the 1st and 2nd platoons in assault, the 2nd on the left, 3rd platoon in support and the machine gun platoon under company control delivering supporting fire from positions on the forward slope of OP hill and from the forward slope of the hill on the right of the road. "A" Company had the 1st and 2nd platoons in assault with the 2nd on the left, the 3rd platoon in support and set up on the forward and south slopes of OP hill to provide supporting fire. The machine gun platoon was attached to the rifle platoons by sections.

The 1st platoon of "B" Company proceeded across the low ground forward of OP hill and attacked up the draw leading to hill 102. When it was within 100 yards of the top, it was pinned down by fire from hill 109 and then manuevered to the right to take hill 102 along the spur leading up from the road. This manuever was successful and hill 102 was secured by the 1st platoon at approximately 1710, although they were then receiving fire from the village on their right rear. Shortly thereafter, the village on their right rear. Shortly thereafter, the 1st platoon of "A" Company gained the high ground (hill 117) on the right of the company's zone of action by manuevering up the draw between hill 117 and 109. However, upon reaching hill 117, they were pinned down by fire from the vicinity of hill 143. The 2nd platoon of "A" Company had proceeded up the draw between hill 117 and hill 143 to secure hill 143, but could not overrrun the position due to heavy casualties, including the platoon leader, 2ndLt. Thomas E. Johnston. The fire directed

12

on the platoon had come from machine guns set up on hill 143 and in the saddle between hill 143 and hill 117.

By 1725, the 2nd platoon of "B" Company was on hill 109 and the nose running forward of it. They had attained their position by working up the draw between hill 109 and hill 117 and had assaulted hill 109 from the left (south) side. Their advance had been supported by the machine gun platoon firing over their head from the forward slope of OP hill. In the final assault of the high ground, Captain John L. Tobin, "B" Company Commander, was seriously wounded and Captain Francis I. Fenton, Jr. took command of the company. An all-around defense position was set up with the 1st platoon on the right, 2nd platoon bending around hill 109 on the left, the 3rd platoon in the rear, and the Company CP and 60mm mortars in rear of hill 109. The machine gun platoon was called forward and attached to the platoons for the defense.

At approximately 1700, Capt John R. Stevens, "A" Company Commander, passed his 3rd platoon through his 2nd to continue the attack on hill 143. The 3rd platoon advanced up the draw between hills 117 and 143, but could not emerge into the saddle due to machine gun fire from flanking hill crests and slopes. The 1st platoon had been forced to withdraw to the forward (east) slope of hill 117 due to heavy casualties and concentrated enemy fire. During the entire afternoon, supporting fire had been called down on hills 117 and 143 and the whole of Obong-ni Ridge and could immediately replace their casualties when our supporting fires lifted. "A" Company continued the attack, but as darkness fell, was not on the high ground in force. The defensive positions set up on the ridge on the night of the 17th consisted of "B" Company extending from the nose on the right of hill 102 to the saddle on the left of hill 109 with "A" Company tying in there and extending along the east slope of hill 117 and on down the spur behind hill 117 to the low ground forward of OP hill, (See sketch #5).

At 2000, while the battalion was digging in for the night, "B" Company sighted four North Korean tanks approaching along the road leading into the battalion position. The rocket section of the anti-tank assault platoon was called up from positions near the CP and went into position on the right of the road by the curve just forward of the CP. The 75mm Recoilless Gun Company was already in position on the spur leading down to the road from OP hill, where they had been supporting the advance of the battalion with direct fire on Obong-ni Ridge. Three M-26 tanks were also called to take positions at the curve in the road just forward of the CP. As the first tank approached point X, (See sketch #4), it was fired on by a 3.5" rocket from the AT assault platoon and was hit in the right track assembly but continued forward. As it reached point Y, it was hit by fire from the 75mm Recoilless Rifle Company, where it was stopped, but continued to fire its guns at the OP. The 2nd tank was hit in the gas tank by a 3.5" rocket from the AT

13

assault platoon as it approached point Y, and ran off the road. The tank commander then opened the turret to fire the top machine gun when a 2.36" white phosphorus rocket from the AT assault platoon richocheted off of the turret cover and fell into the interior of the tank. As the 3rd tank approached point Y, it was hit by fire from the M-26 tanks and knocked out of action immediately. The M-26 tanks fired on all three enemy tanks until they were completely destroyed. The destruction of the 3 tanks from the time the first shot was fired, took ten minutes, only because the third tank was ten minutes behind the second tank. The fourth tank and accompanying troops never reached the position, being destroyed and dispersed by friendly aircraft well forward of "B"Company's positions. No enemy personnel escaped from the 3 tanks knocked out at point Y.

The plan of night defensive fires set up for the night of the 17th consisted of the 60mm mortars of "B" Company firing into the logical routes of approach forward of the Company. "A" Company's 60mm mortar section was ineffective due to a direct hit on the section by three white phosphorus shells. The 81mm mortars were firing into the draws leading into the battalion positions on the west slope of Obong-ni Ridge. 4.2" mortars were registered in the valley forward of Obong-ni Ridge. Artillery was registered in on the west slopes of Obong-ni Ridge, with the bulk of the registrations southwest of hills 143 and 147.

The enemy counterattacked the 1st Battalion positions at approximately 0230 on the morning of the 18th of August, comming down Obong-ni Ridge from the south, moving on both sides of hill 117, isolating the 3rd platoon of "A" Company on the spur running down behind hill 117, and penetrated through the 1st and 2nd platoons of "A" Company and on into "B" company's position around both sides of hill 109. (see sketch no. 5). Part of the 1st platoon of "A" company pulled back along the left flank of "B" company, leaving a gap between hill 109 and 117. "B" company restored its lines after the initial penetration and was able to drive out or kill all the enemy in their position within 45 minutes, however they continued to receive heavy automatic weapons fire from hill 117 throughout the night. "A" company was in such a position that the enemy was on the high ground immediately above them and was able to throw and roll grenades down into their positions. The enemy method of attack was to have one squad rise up and throw grenades and then advance a short distance, firing to their front and flanks with automatic weapons. They would then hit the deck and another squad would repeat the same movements. These actions were observed in the light made by 81mm illumination shells. They would not halt their actions when illuminated. The enemy was armed with automatic weapons and had set up at least one 30 caliber US light machine gun. The 2nd machine gun section of "A" company, in firing on the attack, was subjected to heavy grenades and automatic weapons fire in return. One trick of the enemy was to work in close to our machine gun positions, drawing their fire. When our machine gun position was

disclosed, it would be fired on by an automatic weapon set up
at a greater range. "A" company mortar section, as previously
mentioned, was down to 5 men and could not support the company
due to lack of accurate information on troop positions. At
0330, one red and one green flare were fired by the enemy, the
meaning of which was unknown. The intensity of the attack
diminished toward daylight, leaving the enemy in posession of
hill 117. "A" company reorganized and at 0700 resumed the attack
to secure hill 117. Heavy supporting fire was laid down on hill
117 and 143 and the saddle in between. One squad of "A" company
which had remained with "B" company throughout the night, attacked down the ridge from hill 109 and the 3rd platoon and the
remainder of the 1st and 2nd platoons proceeded up the draw
between hill 109 and 117. "B" company furnished supporting fire
from their positions on hill 109. The enemy was entrenched in
strength on hill 117 and only after a direct hit by a 500 lb
bomb on the east slope of hill 117, which knocked out 4 enemy
machine guns, was the 3rd platoon of "A" company able to reach
the top of hill 117. The 3rd platoon then advanced south across
the saddle toward hill 143 and was pinned down by fire from the
crest. An air strike was called on hill 143 followed by 81mm
and 4.2" mortar concentrations. The enemy then withdrew to the
west and 0830, "A" company had secured hills 117 and 143.
Supporting fires were continued on hills 147 and 153, ending
with an air strike.

Upon securing objective # 1, it was appearent that the MLR
had been penetrated and the enemy was in full retreat, without
arms in numerous cases. They could be seen fleeing beyond
brigade objective #2 in large numbers. LtCol Newton requested
permission to continue the attack immediately, in order to retain
the initiative and keep the enemy on the run.

At 1000, the battalion reveived the order to move south along
Obong-ni ridge and occupy hills 147 and 153. By 1230 this had
been accomplished and the lines extended on the forward slope of
Obong-ni ridge from hill 109 to hill 153 and down the spur behind hill 153 to the low ground. The 81mm mortar platoon displaced to positions at the foot of the draw between hills 109
and 117.

By this time, the 3rd Battalion, 5th Marines, had been passed
around the right flank of the 1st Battalion and had secured
Brigade Objective No 2, and was assaulting Brigade Objective No
3. The 2nd Battalion, 5th Marines, had been passed around the
right flank of the 1st Battalion and had taken up positions in
the valley forward of Obong-ni Ridge. Weapons Company, 1st
Battalion sent out patrols down the trail toward the village of
Obong-ni and on south of hill 153. No enemy was encountered.

When Objective No 1 was secured, "B" Company had 2 officers
and 110 men effective and "A" Company had 4 officers and 100 men
effective. In going over the enemy position, the battalion, in
a very brief inspection counted 18 heavy machine guns, both
American and Russian types; 25 light machine guns, 63 rifles and

15

sub-machine guns, both American and Russian types, one 3.5" rocket launcher with 9 rounds, 8 AT rifles and large amounts of ammunition and hand-grenades. 150 enemy dead were found in the area. "A" Company found that the enemy buried many of their dead in the fox holes where they were killed. During the entire operation, all the personnel of H&S Company acted as litter bearers, doing an outstanding job of evacuating the wounded of both front line companies to the battalion aid station minutes after they were hit and carrying water, ammunition and defense materials forward.

"B" Company, in overrunning the enemy positions, found one SCR 300 Radio and one SCR 536 radio, evidently captured previously by the enemy. The SCR 300 was in perfect working condition and was set on the frequency of the 1st Battalion, indicating that the enemy had been listening in on all conversations of the battalion throughout the attack on Objective #1.

An all around defensive position was set up for the night of the 18th of August with "A" and "B" Companies in position as previously mentioned; Weapons Company extending across the low ground on the left flank of "A" Company and the AT assault platoon on the nose of OP hill leading down toward Obong-ni . H&S Company continued around OP hill, tying in with Regimental H&S Company. The 1st Battalion CP was moved to the draw on the forward slope of OP hill. Protective wire was put out to the front of the rifle companies and trip flares and anti-personnel mines were installed down the valley to the left flank of "A" Company by engineer personnel, who had been sent up to remain with the 1st Battalion for that night. When the flares and anti-personnel mines were retrieved the next morning, 3 mines were found detonated, with pools of blood beside them. No bodies were found.

At daybreak on the 19th of August, "F" Company, 2nd Battalion 9th RGT. (U. S. Army) occupied hill 908 to the south of the 1st Battalion's position and had sent out patrols to tie in with "A" Company's left flank by 1000 of that day.

At 1400 on the 19th, the order was received to entruck and proceed to Yongsan and to go into bivouac. The battalion arrived at Yongsan at 1700.

During the engagement, 4 enemy were captured; 3 by "A" Company and 1 by "B" Company. Questioning disclosed that the 1st Battalion had been opposed by elements of the 19th Regiment of the 4th North Korean Division.

It is believed that Obong-ni Ridge was the enemy main line of resistance.

The map reference for this engagement is the Namji-ri sheet 6820-II; 1:50,000.

19 August 1950

At 1700, moved into bivouac area southeast of Yongsan, Korea and the CP was set up at TA 51.2-87 (sheet # 6820 II). The battalion established a local defense perimeter for the night.

20 August 1950

At 1120, BLT 1/5 entrucked from bivouac area to proceed to Miryang. At 1530 arrived at TA 76.4-96.3 (Sheet # 6820 II), north of Miryang and went into bivouac.

21 August 1950

At 0845, BLT 1/5 entrucked and proceeded to the train station at Miryang and embarked on train at 0930 for rail transportation to Changwan, Arriving at the debarkation point, 3 miles south west of Changwan at 1400. Troops disembarked at 1430 and went into bivouac in an area located at TA 1157-1360.6 (sheet #6819 IV).

22 August 1950

Remained in bivouac area all day, troops resting.

23 August 1950

Remained in bivouac, troops resting and taking showers.

24 August 1950

Remained in bivouac, troops resting, going swimming and taking showers.

25 August 1950

From 0800 to 1130 BLT 1/5 conducted infantry tactics and weapons training from bivouac area. From 1300 to 1600, weapons instruction and inspection was conducted by all units of BLT 1/5.

26 August 1950

BLT 1/5 remained in bivouac area conducting rifle platoon tactics, 81mm mortar instruction, anti-tank assault instruction from 0800 to 1130 on adjacent terrain. From 1300 to 1600 all units conducted care and cleaning of weapons.

27 August 1950

BLT 1/5 observed holiday routine.

28 August 1950

From 0800 to 1130, BLT 1/5 conducted company problems, 81mm mortar instructions, and anti-tank assault instructions. From

1300 to 1600 conducted weapons inspection, maintenance of equipment and shower details.

29 August 1950

At 0754 a combat patrol consisting of one reinforced rifle platoon from "A" Company, BLT 1/5, was sent out approximately 5000 yards to the right front. The patrol returned at 1235; no enemy encountered. Remainder of BLT conducted platoon problems, with Weapons Company conducting anti-tank assault training and 81mm mortar night firing exercises. From 1400 to 1600, all units of BLT 1/5 conducted practice marches.

30 August 1950

Infantry training was conducted in an area adjacent to the bivouac area. A patrol of a reinforced platoon size, patrolled the area around TA 1154.9-1363.5 (sheet # 6919 IV). No enemy were encountered nor was there any evidence of enemy having been in the area. The patrol returned to the bivouac area at 1120. Maintenance of equipment and weapons inspection was conducted during the afternoon.

31 August 1950

"B" and "C" Companies conducted training in squad and fire team tactics. Weapons Company trained 3.5" rocket teams in tracking targets and setting up road blocks. The 81mm mortar platoon rehearsed delivering night defensive fire and conducted training for forward observers. H&S Company, other than those attached to "A", "C", and Weapons Companies, conducted on the job training.

1 September 1950

The 1st Battalion, 5th Marines received a warning order at 1000 to standby for immediate movement, on order, to the Haman sector or to the Naktong River sector to reinforce U.S. Army forces. At 1100 orders were received, directing the battalion, to send out combat patrols to the southwest due to enemy penetration of friendly front lines. Before patrols could be dispatched an order was received, directing the 1st Battalion, to prepare for movement to Miryang to be used as 8th Army reserve for the Naktong River area. At 1630, all units of this command boarded a train in the vicinity of the bivouac area for transportation and proceeded to Miryang. The 1st Battalion arrived in Miryang at 1710 and disembarked immediately. Sufficient transportation was not available to transport the 1st Battalion to the assigned assembly area, consequently, the shuttle system was used and all troops were in the bivouac area by 2400.

18

2 September 1950

At 0230 a warning order was received which directed the 1st Battalion to prepare to move out, by truck, at 0800 and proceed to a forward assembly area and to be prepared for further movement on order.

By 0810 the 1st Battalion was entrucked and started the movement to the forward assembly area at 0820.

The 1st Battalion arrived at the forward assembly area at 0940, disembarked and moved into assigned areas. The battalion CP was established at TA 54.6-84.8 (Sheet #6920 III). At 1750, while in the assembly area, the 1st Battalion received a warning order, directing the battalion to standby for movement, prior to daylight, to the Yongsan area.

3 September 1950

At 0050 the 1st Battalion received the order to commence movement to the Yongsan area by truck prior to daylight and to be prepared to commence the attack southwest of Yongsan at 0800.

At 0400 the 1st Battalion started the approach march following BLT 2/5 toward U.S. Army front line positions southwest of Yongsan where BLT 1/5 and 2/5 were to pass through the Army's defense positions and take up positions at the line of departure with BLT 2/5 on the right, in preparation to attack to the southwest at 0800.

While enroute to the line of departure BLT 2/5 was held up by enemy mortar and small arms fire, thereby, causing a delay of approximately 50 minutes in starting the attack.

At 0850 the 1st Battalion was on line with BLT 2/5 on the right and commenced the attack at 0855 with the mission of seizing the high ground at TA 50.8-85.8 to 50.4-87.9 (Sheet #6920 III).

The supporting weapons that were attached to the 1st Battalion at that time was the 2nd platoon of the 75mm Recoilless Gun Company which was in position at TA 53.4-87 (Sheet #6920 III).

Immediately after the attack started "A" and "B" Companies moved out across the rice paddies, with "A" Company on the left, and immediately came under long range small arms fire from the high ground to their direct front, however, the enemy fire was not of sufficient intensity to halt the advance. The Battalion Commander, 1st Battalion directing 81mm mortar, 4.2" mortar and artillery fires be placed on the battalion objective while the companies were moving across the rice paddies.

19

At 0925, while crossing the rice paddies, "B" Company started receiving intense automatic weapons fire which pinned them down and halted the advance. The Battalion Commander directed the forward air controller to call down an air strike on Battalion Objective #1. Air support was immediate and succeeded in destroying the enemy positions from which "B" Company had been receiving fire.

The advance continued with "A" Company moving more slowly due to the mounting intensity of small arms fire coming from the high ground to their left front. The Battalion Commander directed an air strike, using Napalm, be placed on the area from which "A" Company was receiving fire. As the air strike lifted the Battalion Commander directed "B" Company to shift its lines to the right to maintain contact with BLT 2/5, for "A" Company to move abreast of "B" Company and for the advance to continue as rapidly as possible.

At 0950 "A" and "B" Companies were tied in, contact had been made with BLT 2/5 and the attack continued. Progress was very slow due to the crossing of 800 yards of rice paddies and constant enemy small arms fire from, the 1st Battalion Objective.

At 1015 the 2nd platoon of "A" Company started receiving heavy automatic weapons fire from the enemy positions to the left front where the air strike using Napalm had been conducted. The Battalion Commander directed the 81mm mortar forward observer to place mortar fire on those positions and directed the platoon leader of the 75mm Recoilless Rifle platoon to place white phosphorus fire and a small village to the direct front of "B" Company from which enemy small arms fire was being delivered on "B" Company's left flank.

At 1050 enemy heavy machine guns started firing on "A" and "B" Companies from positions on the forward slope of the 1st Battalion Objective. The Battalion Commander directed the 4.2" mortar and the artillery liasion officers to place 4.2" mortar and artillery fire on these positions. At 1055 as the 4.2" mortar and artillery fires lifted, the company commander of "B" Company reported his company was in position to start the assault on the forward slope of the 1st Battalion Objective #1.

At 1105, "A" Company was in position to start the assault and both "A" and "B" Companies commenced the assault on objective #1.

At 1110, "A" Company's left flank was pinned down by enemy automatic weapons fire from the military crest of objective #1 in "A" Company's zone of action. 81mm mortar fire was placed on the enemy positions and the assault continued.

At 1115, "B" Company had succeeded in seizing the portion of objective #1 within their zone of action and were receiving enemy machine gun fire from the reverse slope of objective #1. The Battalion Commander directed 81mm mortar be placed on the reverse slope of the objective in "B" Company's zone of action and that flame throwers be sent to the company commander of "B" company to be used on suitable enemy positions.

At 1205 "A" Company had completed seizing the portion of objective #1 within their zone of action.

At 1202 both "A" and "B" Companies were receiving small arms and automatic weapons fire from the next high ground to the 1st Battalion's direct front. The Battalion Commander directed the forward air controller to run an air strike on that high ground from which "A" and "B" Companies were receiving fire.

While the air strike was being conducted the company commander of "B" Company reported the enemy was leaving the reverse slope of objective #1 and running down the road to the next ridge line. The Battalion Commander directed artillery fire be placed on the enemy and excellent results were acheived.

At 1220 both "A" and "B" Companies requested a resupply of machine gun ammunition, grenades, 60mm mortar ammunition, water and additional stretchers to remove wounded.

Groups of enemy continued to break and run from positions on the reverse slope of objective #1 and artillery fire was continually brought to bear upon them.

At approximately 1350 both "A" and "B" Companies had received all necessary supplies and were about ready to move out in the attack of 1st Battalion Objective #2 located at TA 49.8-28.8 to 47.8-87.8 (Sheet #6920 III).

At 1415 the 1st Marine Brigade Reconnaissance Company was moving up on the extreme left flank of the 1st Battalion with orders to keep in visual contact with "A" Company's left flank and to block any enemy movement from the left flank.

At 1445 the Battalion Commander 1st Battalion, directed the forward air controller to call a five minute air strike on the 1st Battalion's Objective #2 and the artillery liasion officer to deliver a 5 minute artillery preparation immediately following the air strike.

At 1510, "A" and "B" Companies moved out in the attack of objective #2. There was light and scattered enemy resistence as the advance continued until 1545 when "A" Company started receiving enemy mortar fire on their front lines. An artillery observation plane spotted the enemy mortar position and directed artillery fire which destroyed the position.

At 1605 the company commander of "B" Company reported a large group of enemy running from his zone of action toward the low ground in front of BLT 2/5. The Battalion Commander, 1st Battalion notified BLT 2/5 of the presence of the enemy in their zone of action.

By 1630 both "A" and "B" Companies had seized Battalion Objective #2 and were directed by the Battalion Commander to consolidate their positions and dig in for night defense.

The Battalion CP displaced forward and set up at TA 50.9-88.7 (Sheet #6920 III).

There was no enemy activity during the night and the 1st Battalion was prepared to continue the attack the following morning at 0800.

4 September 1950

At 0800, "A" and "B" Companies moved out in the attack with the mission of seizing the portion of 5th Marines Objective #1 in the 1st Battalion's zone of action which was located at TA 46.7-88.6 to 46.4-87.5 (Sheet #6820 II). BLT 3/5 moved through and relieved BLT 2/5 on the right flank of BLT 1/5.

At 0820 the Company Commander of "B" Company reported the capturing of two Russian type T-34 tanks on his company's right flank, the tanks were unmaned and in excellent condition.

The advance continued very rapidly meeting no enemy resistance and many small groups of enemy were observed running in a disorganized manner away from advance elements. In all cases artillery fire was called down which killed and wounded many of them, and a total of 12 prisoners were captured by 1240.

By 1505, "A" and "B" Companies had completed the seizure of 5th Marines Objective #1. The Battalion Commander, 1st Battalion, received orders from the Regimental Commander to halt the advance and to remain on Regimental Objective #1 until further orders were received.

At 1515 the 1st Battalion was ordered to continue the attack and to seize the high ground at TA 44.9-87.9 (Sheet #6820 II). At 1600 the advance elements of the battalion CP moved forward and set up in position at TA 46.9-88.7 (Sheet #6820 II). At 1620 enemy activity was sighted on the high ground to "B" Company's left front. The Battalion Commander directed 81mm mortar fire be placed on the area in which the enemy were observed. At 1630 the 1st Battalion continued the attack. As "B" Company was starting across the rice paddies they were fired upon by enemy automatic weapons from positions on the high ground to their right front. "B" Company moved back out of the rice paddies to take cover from the automatic weapons fire, and the Battalion Commander directed an air strike be called on the enemy positions.

At 1710 the Battalion Commander, 1st Battalion, requested BLT 3/5 to place supporting fires on the high ground to their direct front, from which "B" Company was receiving enemy machine gun fire.

At 1725 the advance continued and both "A" and "B" Companies completed the seizure of the high ground, without further enemy resistance, by 1800.

There was no enemy activity to the front during the night.

At 2400 heavy caliber enemy mortar fire started falling on the 1st Battalion CP. Results of the mortar fire were one killed and two wounded.

5. September 1950

At 0750 friendly P-51 type aircraft on a noncontrolled mission strafed "B" Company's front lines causing one casualty.

At 0820, "A" and "B" Companies continued the attack with the mission of seizing the portion of 5th Marines Objective "A" within the 1st Battalions zone of action, the 1st Battalion's portion of the objective was located at TA 42.9-88 to 43.3-88.4(Sheet #6820 II).

BLT 3/5 was directed to move across the rear of BLT 1/5 and to tie in on "A" Company's left flank. BLT 1/5 was directed to maintain contact on the right with elements of the 9th Infantry Regiment, (U.S. Army).

The advance continued very rapidly and unopposed until approximately 0935 when enemy mortar and artillery fire commenced falling on the 1st Battalions front lines from enemy positions on Obong-ni Ridge. The Battalion Commander, 1st Battalion, directed artillery and 81mm mortar fire be placed on the enemy positions.

At 1025 the company commander of "B" Company reported the presence of one enemy artillery piece in the vicinity of Obong-ni Ridge and many enemy sighted on the ridge. The Battalion Commander directed 81mm mortar and artillery fire be placed on Obong-ni Ridge.

At 1105, "B" Company had reached the high ground located at TA 42.9-88.1 to 43.4-87.7 (Sheet #6820 II), and "A" Company the high ground located at TA 43.6-87.1 to 44.1-86.9 (Sheet #6820 II),when orders were received to halt the advance

23

and remain in present position until U.S. Army units could tie in on the right flank and BLT 3/5 could tie in on the left flank. At 1130 both "A" and "B" Companies were receiving enemy small arms and automatic weapons fire from Obang-ni Ridge at frequent intervals during the halt.

At 1420 the enemy launched a counter-attack against "B" Company with approximately 300 troops. The counter-attack was launched very rapidly from flanks and well concealed positions. The enemy used large quantities of small arms fire, automatic weapons fire, mortar fire, hand and rifle grenades (For direction of counter-attack and position of "B" Company see sketch #6). At the same time the counter-attack started the Company commander of "B" Company reported three enemy tanks moving down the road toward "A" and "B" Company positions. The Battalion Commander directed 81mm mortar fire be placed to the immediate front of "B" Company's positions and that the anti-tank assault platoon go forward and take up suitable positions for anti-tank defense. The anti-tank assault platoon took up positions as shown on sketch #6. One 3.5" rocket team from "B" Company had expended all their ammunition prior to the arrival of the anti-tank assault platoon, scoring hits and stopping the 1st tank. Prior to the arrival of the anti-tank assault platoon, two M-26 tanks moving up the road were knocked out by the enemy tanks immediately in rear of a U.S. Army tank which had previously been knocked out. (For position of tanks, see sketch #6). Four other M-26 tanks withdrew to positions from which they could fire in the event the enemy tanks continued to move down the road. (Position of tanks after withdrawal areas shown on sketch #6).

The anti-tank assault platoon fired on the three enemy tanks exploding the 2nd and 3rd tanks and making the final kill on the 1st tank. The anti-tank assault platoon withdrew and tied in on "B" Company's left flank.

While the tank action was going on "B" Company, with the aid of 81mm mortar fire had succeeded in stopping the counter-attack. "B" Company's casualties during the counter-attack were: 2 killed and 23 wounded.

By 1500, BLT 3/5 had relieved "A" Company and tied in with "B" Company's left flank. "A" Company, less the 1st and 2nd platoons, one machine gun section and one mortar squad, moved into reserve positions approximately 400 yards to the rear. The remainder of "A" Company was placed on line to reinforce "B" Company.

At 1530, U.S. Army units made contact and tied in with "B" Company's right flank.

At 1600, the Battalion Commander directed the Battalion Executive to resume control while he attended a Battalion Commanders conference at the regimental CP.

24

At 1725 orders were received to prepare to be relieved in position, under cover of darkness, by elements of the 23rd Infantry Regiment, U. S. Army, and for a route march to the vicinity of Yongsan where the 1st Battalion, in regimental order, would be entrucked for Pusan, Korea.

Enemy activity was light throughout the evening until 1855 when "B" Company received machine gun fire from the vicinity of Obong-ni Ridge. 81mm mortar fire was directed on the enemy machine gun positions and immediately large caliber enemy counter mortar fire was being delivered on the 81mm mortar positions. Artillery fire was directed on the enemy mortar positions.

6 September 1950

At 0030 elements of "K" Company, 23rd Infantry Regiment, affected relief of the 1st Battalion on position. The 1st Battalion moved out in route march following BLT 3/5 to TA 46.9-89.8 (sheet # 6820 II) where the battalion CP displaced and joined the column at 0230.

The route march continued toward Yongsan, arriving in the vicinity of Yongsan at 0430.

The 1st Battalion halted on the road west of Yongsan to await transportation to Pusan.

At 0750 all companies moved into adjacent assembly area and the battalion CP was established at TA 50.1-88.8 (sheet # 6920 III).

At 1430 the 1st serial of trucks departed and proceeded to Pusan, arriving and going into assembly area at the Port of Pusan at 1810.

At 1330 the 2nd serial departed and proceeded to Pusan, arriving and joining the remainder of the 1st Battalion in the assembly area at the Port of Pusan at 2130.

6. ENEMY TACTICS, ORGANIZATION, STRENGTH, DEPLOYMENT, PROBABLE ORDER OF BATTLE, AND EQUIPMENT

a. Enemy tactics

The tactics used by the North Koreans in the action of 3, 4 and 5 September resembled that of a retreating enemy fighting a delaying action. Small units, such as companies, platoons and squads were well camouflaged and concealed themselves in strategic positions on commanding terrain.

In the defense the enemy dug in on ridge lines some 10 to 15 yards down the reverse slopes. Their foxholes and positions were well prepared, being 15 to 20 feet apart.

25

In order to have concealment from air observation the enemy used scrub pines camouflage. The enemy constructed parpetts around the mounds of the graves on the ridges and by placing 4 or 5 men in this revetment with automatic weapons, established fortified positons or strong points.

In the attack the enemy consitently tried to attain igh commanding terrain. In frontal attacks the enemy tried to approach our lines as close as possible and employ hand grenades.

None of the enemy tactics either in attack or defense tended to be fanatical, such as the Japanese. When enemy attacks were repelled and the enemy driven from his defense position, he would give ground, surrender, or retreat in a very disorganized manner.

b. Organization

The enemy was organized in groups of 50 to 150 men. These units would be grouped together in a small area at strategic points, and not tied in with adjacent units. In this group there would be 1 or 2 50 caliber guns, sniper and automatic weapons. From POW reports it was learned that each group was leaded by a professional soldier and contained several other professionals, but that the buld was coscriptees and draitees who were not well trained and wanted to surrender but that their seniors threatened them with death. Moral was very low and the POW's stated that they were not properly fed. These POW's stat d that the enemy was well supplied in arms and ammuntion.

c. Strength.

Estimated total enemy strength opposing the 1st Bn. during this action was 1800 to 3000. Estimated enemy died in 1st bn zone of action were from 500 to 600. POW's taken by 1st bn.: 28.

d. Deployment.

The enemy was deployed on strategic ridge lines. They would occupy the forward slopes and positions on the flanks and in huts or small villages, if present, but when heavy fire was brought down on them they would withdraw either to their well prepared positions on the reverse slopes or on the military crest. When driven from their reverse slope positions the enemy would withdraw in disorganized manner using low ground to move to the rear of another ridge. The retreating enemy would not take position on the next ridge line or strong point. Their position would be occupied by fresh troops and the withdrawing enemy would proceed further to the rear. It was noted in their withdrawal that some enemy troops would take cover in rice paddies and houses and revert to sniping activity.

8. e. Enemy order of battle

(1) The enemy encountered on 12 August in a rear guard action at 1113.9-1339.1 (Sach'on sheet #6819 III), were elements of the 83rd Motorized Regiment of the North Korean 6th Infantry Division. The strength of the enemy encountered by BLT 1/5 was estimated to be one battalion of 300 to 400 men. The enemy was deployed on the high ground overlooking the road and town of Changch'on. The enemy used machine guns, small arms, small mortars and grenades.

(2) On 17 August the enemy encountered defending Obong-ni Ridge, located on the Namji-ri sheet, #6820 II, 1:50,000, was the 18th Regiment, commanded by Changi Ky Dok, of the North Korean 4th Infantry Division. The estimated strength of the 18th Regiment was 1000 men. The enemy was deployed with three battalions on line. All three battalions were placed to repel the attack on Obong-ni Ridge. The enemy was well equipped with automatic weapons, plus rifles and anti-tank guns. They also delivered sporadic artillery and mortar fire.

(3) Prisoners were captured from units of the 4th Infantry Division, 9th Infantry Division and the 16th Mechanized Brigade. The actual units which opposed the 1st Battalion, 5th Marines were the 2nd Battalion of the Independent Regiment of the 16th Mechanized Brigade, the 4th Battalion of the 16th Regiment of the 4th Division and the 1st Battalion of the 17th Regiment of the 9th Division.

f. Equipment

The individual enemy soldier was equiped with automatic weapons, sniper rifles, or a 57 caliber (clip of 5 gas operated or a single shot bolt action) anti-tank rifles and hand grenades. The 1st Battalion captured 2-122mm Howitzers, 4-120mm mortars, 4-82mm mortars, 5-76mm Howitzers, and 5-47mm anti-tank gun. One T34/85 tank was captured intact by the 1st Battalion. Three T34/85 tanks were destroyed by 1st Battalion.

Estimated Results of the Operation:

a. Sach'on Area against enemy 83rd Motorized Regiment.

(1) This battalion was in contact with the enemy on 13 August 1950 when ordered to return to Chin Dong-ni. On the 12th the enemy had fought a rear guard action with a force of an estimated battalion strength, and had counter-attacked at dawn of the 13th without gaining their objective, which was to force the withdrawal of "B" Company from the high ground on the brigade left flank. The enemy was attempting to delay the advance of the Brigade while their main body moved towards the Sach'on-Chinju Area. The enemy suffered severe casualties in

27

this action and it is estimated that over one half of the rear guard was killed. The Brigade could have moved towards Sach'on without too much opposition, especially in view of the breaking off of the attack by the enemy at dawn.

(2) It is believed that the operation resulted in the destruction of the mobility of the 83rd Motorized Regiment. The enemy was so badly cut up that it is believed that complete reorganization with replacements was necessary to make the 83rd Motorized Regiment an effective fighting unit.

b. Naktong River-Yongsan Sector.

(1) This battalion was in contact with the enemy on Obongi-ni Ridge on the 17th and 18th of August 1950. The 18th Regiment of the 4th Division was defeated and retired towards the Naktong River in confusion, leaving behind the majority of his small arms, supporting arms, and motor transport. The capture of Obong-ni Ridge resulted in the penetration of the main line of resistance and the eventual collapse of the enemy bridgehead on the Naktong River.

10. Comments and Recommendations of the Commander:

a. The enemy and his tactics.

(1) The enemy has defended hills with concentrations up to regimental strength. The enemy has defended roads with anti-tank guns, but not with personnel in any great strength. Villages have been defended by a few automatic weapons, but no great numbers of personnel. Enemy mortar and artillery fire has been accurate, but of small intensity when compared to ours. Enemy mortars and artillery have been previously registered in on objectives both to the front and rear of their positions. On entering these areas, our forces find themselves in comparatively heavy and accurate mortar and artillery fire of relatively short duration. The enemy fights for a hill, but so far, nothing else. He attacks at night rather than in daylight.

(2) The enemy makes excellent use of camouflage. He uses cover to a maximum at times, and then again, takes no advantage of it.

(3) The enemy has attacked at night rather than in daylight, breaking off his attack as soon as daylight comes, and makes maximum use of hand grenades and his short range automatic weapons. He is neither as tenacious nor fanatical as the Japanese, but does press home his advantages until separated from leaders. Attacks start suddenly and finish just as suddenly. He either does not like daylight close combat, or realizes the shortcomings of his poor marksmanship at ranges above 200 yards and his inadequate supporting arms. He obviously does not relish close support aircraft as used by the Marine Corps.

12. Unit Station List, 7 July- 6 September, 1950.

NAME	RANK	SERVICE NO	MOS	DUTIES
NEWTON, George R.	LtCol	05786	0302	Bn Comdr
OLSON, Merlin R.	Maj	08163	0302	Bn ExecO

S-1

FRITZ, Martin F.	2dLt	028390	0130	Bn Adj & S-1
RABE, Leroy D.	2dLt	032059	0105	Bn Pers Class-ification & Assign-mentO; RO;Custodian Registered Pubs; 4Aug-5Sep OinC Bn Rear Echelon

S-2

HANSEN, Dean B.	2dLt	049626	0302	Bn S-2

S-3

SMITH, Loren R.	1stLt	040624	0302	7Jul-8Aug&13Aug-5 Sep,Bn S-3;9-12Aug Sk
YOUNG, James R	2dLt	049647	0302 0306	13Jul-8Aug&14Aug-5Sep Ass't S-3; 9-12 Aug, S-3 5Sep, WIA, Evac.

S-4

MORROW, Clark D.	Capt	018480	0302	7Jul-3Sep,Bn S-4; 3Sep, WIA Evac
DAVIS, Warren A.	WO	042207	3010	Bn SupplyO

H&S Co

GODENIUS, Walter E.G.	Capt	027175	4960	CO
PETER, William J.,Jr.	1stLt	033632	2502	Bn CommO
NELSON, Bentley G.	Lt(jg)	523633		Bn Surgeon
SMITH, James W.	1stLt	037073	7302	FAC
GREWE, Carl O.	Lt(USN)	202105		NGLO
ALLEN, Merle W.	2dLt	049723	0301	NG Spotter;3-5 Sep,Bn S-4

A Co

STEVENS, John R.	Capt	014231	0302	CO
EUBANKS, Fred F. Jr.	1stLt	036407	0302	ExecO
SEDILIAN, Robert C.	1stLt	049292	0302	7Jul-17Aug,PlLdr 1st R Plt,17Aug WIA,Evac;17-20Aug Hospitalzed;20Aug Det

30

JOHNSTON, Thomas H.	2dLt	049718	0302	7Jul-18Aug PlLdr 2nd RPlt,18Aug,KIA
FOX, George C.	1stLt	047459	0302	7Jul-3Sep PlLdr 3rd R Plt;3Sep,WIA,Evac
MUETZEL, Francis W.	2dLt	049792	0302	MGun PlLdr
BLANK, Howard G.	2dLt	043444	0302	30Aug-6Sep,60mmMort Sec Ldr

B Co

TOBIN, John L.	Capt	011730	0302	7Jul-17Aug,CO,17Aug WIA Evac;17-24 Aug, Hospitalized;24Aug Det
FENTON, Francis I.,Jr.	Capt	015170	0302	7Jul-17Aug,ExecO; 17Aug-6Sep,CO
SCHRYVER, Hugh C.,Jr.	2dLt	049849	0302	Plt Ldr,1st R Plt
TAYLOR, David S.	1stLt	048493	0302	7Jul-17Aug,PlLdr, 2nd RPlt;17Aug WIA Evac.
COWLING, David R.	2dLt	049804	0302	7Jul-12Aug,PlLdr 3rd RPlt;12 Aug WIA Evac;12-15Aug Hospitalized;15Aug Det
HALL, Edward C.,Jr.	2dLt	049867	0302	7Jul-12Aug,MGPltLdr 12Aug,WIA,Evac;12-15Aug-Hospitalized; 15Aug Det
CLEMENT, Robert "A"	WO	048589	0310	7Jul-14Aug,60mmMort SecLdr;14Aug Sk,Evac;14-15Aug,Hospitalized;15Aug, Det
MORRIS, Edward C.	2dLt	050033	0302	20Aug-6Sep,PlLdr 3d RPlt
CHRISTOLOS, Nick	2dLt	049920	0302	20Aug-6Sep,60mmMo. SecLdr

Wpns Co

RUSSELL, John W.	Maj	07098	0302	CO
SOLLOM, Almond H.	Capt	024462	0302	ExecO
ALDERMAN, Harry L.	2dLt	049788	0302	81mmMortPltComdr
TULEY, Ralph J.	2dLt	049907	0302	Asst81mmMortPlt. Comdr
BROWN, Dale L.	2dLt	050020	0302	AT Asslt PltComdr

Appendix D

Excerpts from 1/5's Special Action report for the Inchon-Seoul Operation 15 September-7 October 1950.

&

Appendix D-1

A brief narrative of Able Company's actions at Inchon and the drive on Seoul, written by John Stevens, who commanded the company both at the Pusan Perimeter and at Inchon. Able Company had 1 platoon leader wounded and 2 killed in August, and 2 platoon leaders killed and 2 wounded in the Inchon-Seoul operation during the last 2 weeks in September.

A comparison of the fight as seen by a rifle company commander with the view of the battalion commander reveals some differences.

1st Battalion, 5th Marines
1st Marine Division, FMF,
In the Field, Korea

7 October, 1950

SPECIAL ACTION REPORT

Maps: Map of Korea, 1:50,000, AMS L571.

Sketches: 1. Inchon Landing
2. Battalion Operations South of Han River
3. Attack of Hill 105
4. Battalion Operations North of Han River

1. INTRODUCTION

This report is submitted in accordance with a directive received from the Commanding Officer, 5th Marines and paragraph 11401.2a, Marine Corps Manual. The purpose of this report is to provide a concise, complete record of the actions in which this unit participated during the period 30 August to 7 October, 1950. Missions assigned this battalion were issued by the next higher echelon, the 5th Marines.

1. TASK ORGANIZATION

BLT 1/5	37 Officers	1026 Enlisted	LtCol G. R. NEWTON
H&S Company			Capt W.E. GODENIUS
TACP 1st			Lt J. W. SMITH
FGF Liaison			Lt C. O. GREWE,USN
Arty Liaison			1st Lt J. J. SNYDER
"A" Company			Capt J. R. STEVENS
"B" Company			Capt F. P. FENTON,JR.
"C" Company			1st Lt. P. F. PEDERSEN
Weapons Company			Maj J. W. RUSSELL
Korean National Police Platoon			SSgt J. L. WILLIS

At various times, as noted in paragraph 7, elements of the following units were attached, depending on whether the Battalion was in assault or reserve:

75mm Recoiless Gun Company, 5th Marines

One Platoon 4.2" Mortar Company, 5th Marines

3rd Platoon, Company "A", 1st Tank Battalion, 1st Marine Division

Detachment of "B" Company, 1st Engineer Battalion, 1st Marine Division.

Detachment of Reconnaissance Company, 1st Marine Division

3. PRELIMINARY PLANNING

The schedule, as set forth by higher headquarters, required this Battalion to be ready in all respects to embark aboard ship at Pusan, Korea on 11 September, 1950. All organizational equipment was prepared and vehicles loaded for an amphibious landing. The preliminary planning of the Battalion consisted of reorganization and resupply. The reorganization consisted of joining a rifle company and additional sections for the Weapons Company. These units were newly arrived from the United States. The rifle com- pany was designated as "C" Company, 1st Battalion, 5th Marines.

Military maps of the landing area were received by this Battalion on the afternoon of 10 September, 1950. These maps were not used for preliminary planning prior to this Battalion's embarkation aboard ship at 1400, 11 September, 1950, inasmuch as an operation order had not as yet been received. The Battalion supply train carried sufficient water, rations and ammunition to last for a period of one day.

4. TRAINING AND REHEARSAL

Training aboard ship consisted of physical drill, instruction on amphibious techniques, briefings of the landing operation to take place at Inchon, estimate of the enemy situation, review of technique of combat in built up areas, debarkation drill and the use of scaling ladders and cargo nets as it was planned that the first five boat waves were to land shortly after the tide began to rise and the scaling ladders and cargo nets would be needed as an aid in reaching the top of the sea wall from the LCVP's hold "bow on" to the sea wall.

5. LOADING AND EMBARKATION

Upon arrival at Pusan, Korea on 6 September, 1950, BLT 1/5 commenced combat loading of the USS HENRICO, (APA 45) continuing on a 24 hour schedule, until loading was completed on the morning of 11 September, 1950. The first element of the Battalion to go aboard ship was the Battalion cooks who embarked on 6 September, 1950, followed by the messmen on 7 September, 1950. The main body of the Battalion commenced embarkation at 1400, 11 September, 1950. Embarkation was completed at 1600, 11 September, 1950.

6. MOVEMENT TO AND ARRIVAL AT OBJECTIVE AREA

The USS HENRICO (APA 45) sailed from Pusan, at 1450, 12 September, 1950, and was underway for a period of three days, arriving at the transport area off the port of Inchon at approx- imately 1300, 15 September, 1950. Troops began disembarking at 1530, with the first assault wave hitting Red Beach I at 1733.

7. DETAILED COMBAT NARRATIVE

On 30 August, 1950, while in 8th Army Reserve, 3 miles west of Changwon, Korea the Battalion Commander was summoned to the Regimental Command Post and Given information as to the general scheme of maneuver for the proposed landing at Inchon. After a short briefing, orders were received to return at 0800 the next morning for further planning and conferences. At 0800 on 31 August, the Battalion Commander returned to the 5th Marines Command Post, only to receive orders that the 1st Battalion would be prepared to move by 1200 to Miryang for operations against the enemy in the Youngsan sector. The single map of Inchon was turned in and no further planning was possible until the Battalion was returned to Pusan, Korea on 6 September after three days of continuous fighting in the Naktong River Bulge in the vicinity of Youngsan. The Battalion casualties during the period amounted to 11 KIA, 84 WIA.

The lead elements of BLT 1/5 arrived at Pusan, Korea at 1810, 6 September, 1950 with the last element arriving at the assembly area at 2130. Upon arrival at Pusan, a directive was received stating that at 0001, 13 September, 1950 the 1st Provisional Marine Brigade would be deactivated and would be absorbed by the 1st Marine Division, FMF under the command of Major General Oliver P. Smith, USMC.

During the period 7 September through 11 September, 1950, while waiting to board its assigned ship, the USS HENRICO (APA 45), the Battalion was reorganized and resupplied. Although billeted in a warehouse on the dock at Pusan, the men of the Battalion were fed aboard the USS HENRICO. The Commanding Officer of the USS HENRICO (APA 45), Captain Fradd, also allowed the Battalion the use of the ship's showering facilities. A limited amount of training, consisting of small arms firing for the Battalion and a conditioning hike for the newly arrived "C" Company was accomp- lished. The Battalion also furnished a detail of 25 instructors to train the Republic of Korea Marines in the firing of rockets and mortars. The USS HENRICO was being combat loaded and readied for embarkation of BLT 1/5 at this time.

On the night of 10 September, 1950 all companies were alerted to make preparations to board ship on order because of an approaching typhoon. Actual embarkation of the Battalion commenced at 1400, 11 September, 1950. After embarkation was completed at 1600 that date, the ship remained tied to the dock at Pusan until 1450, 12 September, 1950 when it got underway with BL T 1/5 and H&S Company, 5th Marines as the major units embarked. Also aboard were a group of war correspondents from loading American and British newspapers.

On 13 September, 1950 all units were informed of the overall mission of the 1st Marine Division and the specific mission of BLT 1/5. A series of briefings on the plan of operation of BLT 1/5 and on the estimate of the enemy situation were conducted regularly while enroute to the Objective area.

On 14 September, 1950 the Battalion supply sections issued ammunition and rations to the companies for further distribution to the troops. Upon debarkation, each man was to carry a basic load of ammunition, one days C-4 ration, and two canteens of water. During the afternoon of the 14th, a debarkation drill was held for all embarked troops and all boat teams of the first five waves were briefed in the use of the scaling ladders and cargo sets to be employed in clearing the sea wall at the landing beach.

On the morning of 15 September, 1950, all units completed last minute preparations and the Battalion stood by to disembark on order. For graphic picture of the Inchon landing see sketch No. 1.As the ship neared the transport area, all troops were ordered to their compartments. At 1530, the assault wave began disembarking from the USS HENRICO into the landing craft and proceeded to the rendezvous area. At this time, word was received that H-hour had been postponed for 30 minutes. During the approach of the landing craft to the beach, an intense naval and air bombardment of the landing area took place. Immediately prior to the arrival of the assault wave at the beach, LSM(R)'s fired a 2,000 round rocket concentration on the landing area. An air strike was called on Observatory Hill by the 1st Battalion FAC, 1st lt J. W. Smith, as he was enroute to the beach, using portable equipment in the landing craft. At 1733 the first wave arrived at the sea wall on Red Beach I and disembarked the troops through the use of scaling ladders. Three of the initial landing craft utilized holes blasted in the sea wall to unload their troops. The first three waves, consisting of 14 boats, carried "A" Company, commanded by Captain J. R. Stevens. "A" Company, with the mission of taking battalion objective No. 1 and their portion of the O-A line, landed amid heavy small arms fire and intermittent mortar fire coming from trenches and bunkers on the beach, from the exposed left flank, and from battalion objective 1 (Cemetery Hill). The left flank of Red Beach I was strongly defended, in contrast to a fairly week defense on the right flank. "A" Company assaulted objective I. Captain Stevens, at 1755, fired an amber star cluster signifying the seizure of objective I. "A" Company and attachments during this period amounted to 1 Officer and 7 enlisted KIA, 28 enlisted WIA.

The 4th and 5th waves, composed of "C" Company, commanded by First LIeutenant P. F. Pedersen, landed at H - 20 with a 5 minute interval between waves. Due to motor failure of an LCVP in the Company Commander's boat wave at the rendezvous area, the entire wave was delayed by order of the boat wave commander, and Lt Pedersen did not land with his boat team until the 6th wave had landed. The organization of "C" Company on the beach was delayed inasmuch as units of BLT 2/5 were over-lapping into the 1st Battalion's zone of action. It should be noted at this time that there was a great deal of confusion on Red Beach from H-hour to H - 180 due to the inability of coxwains to land in their assigned areas; units were intermingled and commanders had difficulty in organizing their commands. Added confusion was caused when a beached LST fired its 40 and 20mm cannon's over the heads of the troops on the beach,and on objective I and ABLE while they were being occupied by our forces. The second platoon, under the command of Section Lieutenant B. L. Magness, with the 60mm mortar section commanded by Second Lieutenant M. A. Merritt att- ained Regimental Objective ABLE at 1845, but due to the lack of communication facilities or the proper signal flare equipment, they were unable to notify the Battalion Commander that the objective had been taken. This lack of communication with the Battalion Commander resulted in friendly fire being delivered on Objective ABLE while it was being occupied by elements of "C" Company. Due to the difficulty "C" Company was experiencing in reorganizing, and inasmuch as the the units of "C" Company on objective ABLE were unable to inform the Battalion Commander or the Company Commander of their presence on the objective, the Battalion Commander deemed it necessary to order "B"Company, which had landed in support of the Battalion and was intact, to seize and occupy Regimental Objective ABLE. The rapid approach of darkness also influenced the Battalion Commander's decision to have "B" Company seize and defend objective ABLE. During this time Lt Pedersen reported to the Battalion Commander that he was reorganizing his copany on the beach. The Battalion Commander ordered "C" Company upon completion of reorganization to assume the mission of Battalion Reserve.

"B" Company upon attaining objective ABLE discovered that the 2nd platoon of "C" Company was occupying the right flank of the objective and had visual contact with "F" Company, 2nd Battalion, 5th Marines. "B" Company Commander, Captain Francis I. Fenton, Jr., contacted the Battalion Commander and notified him of the presence of the 2nd platoon of "C" Company. The Battalion Commander, ordered "B" Company Commander to leave this platoon in position and to occupy and defend the left portion of objective ABLE and to die in with the right flank of "A" Company. This was accomplished at approximately 2330. The remainder of "C" Company reorganized, and as ordered took up positions to the rear of objective ABLE, and assumed the mission of Battalion Reserve for the night. At 2240 on 15 September, the Battalion Commander reported to RCT-5 that objective ABLE was secured and by 2345 all units had made contact with adjacent units and had organized for the night. Casualties suffered by "B" Company during this period were 6 WIA, "C" Company suffered 5 WIA.

Weapons Company, which had landed after "B" Company, was placed with "C" Company in support of the Battalion to the rear of objective ABLE. The Command Post established ashore at 1755 and initially located at TA 8950-2-2 displaced at 0230, 16 September, 1950 to TA 8949-E-1.

As scaling ladders were used for the first time by Marine Units in the landing, inquiries were made as to their practicability. Captain J. R. Stevens, "A" Company Commander had the following comment to make:

"Boat 1-4 used aluminum ladders equipped with large books which were used to hook over the sea wall. These ladders proved extremely effective. The wall was estimated to have been at least 10 feet high and all reports are that unloading would have been very difficult if not impossible without the use of these ladders. In debarking it was estimated that each boat was unloaded in less than two minutes with a minimum of casualties.

The hooks on the wooden ladders proved ineffective. However, the ladders were placed vertically against the sea wall and the troops were able to disembark rapidly."

For graphic picture of BLT 1/5's operations south of the Han River see sketch No. 2.

At 0400, 16 September, 1950, a verbal order was received by the Battalion to move to an assembly area and to assume the mission of Regimental Reserve. At 0630, an operation order was received from RCT-5 confirming the warning order received earlier. At 0910 BLT 1/5 began movement to the designated assembly area. While on the move, additional orders were received directing the unit to proceed to a more forward assembly area. Orders were once again received to move to a third assembly area still further advanced. At 1930, the Battalion moved into an assembly area at TA 9750 X 2.

The Battalion Commander at 1900 attended a Regimental Conference at which time plans for the following days operation were issued. At 2300, an operation order was received directing this Battaion to move out behind BLT 2/5 at 0700, 17 September, 1950.

BLT 1/5, was unable to get underway until 1125, 17 September, 1950 because BLT 2/5 had been held up. At 1125, this Battalion moved out in trace of the 2nd Battalion. Movement continued very rapidly throughout the afternoon. No enemy resistance was encountered. During the late afternoon BLT 2/5 swung to the left to capture KimpoAirfield. BLT 1/5 continued forward and at 1900, objective EASy was seized and occupied by "A" Company, which was later strengthened by the addition of "B" Company. After seizure of objective EASy, the Battalion set up in defense positions for the night. The Battalion Command Post was located at TA 0655-W-4.

At dawn on 18 September, 1950, "B" Company Commander reported to the Battalion Commander that there were enemy troops in his left flank advancing in direction of Kimpo Airfield, attacking 2nd Battalion, the Battalion Commander immediately called for artillery and mortar fire to be added to the fire "B" Company was already bringing down on the flank and rear of the enemy. At the same time he ordered "C" Company to attack in order to cut off their retreat.

The coordinated fire of the 1st and 2nd Battalion, plus the attack to the rear and flank by "C" Company caused confusion in the enemy ranks, which forced him to make a hasty and disorganiz- ed withdrawal, suffering heavy casualties. Enemy resistance was light as they fled to objective FOX. The retreating enemy were again brought under artillery fire called for by units of BLT 1/5 and BLT 2/5. "C" Company, who had halted for the second artillery barrage were ordered to continue the attack and seize objective FOX, which was accomplished against light opppossition at 0930. During this time the remaining elements of the Battalion remained in position. The remainder of the day was spent with all units conducting patrols, capturing of 31 enemy, and various types of equipment, which included a large quantity of medical supplies found in an abandon enemy aid station to the rear of objective FOX. At 1600, BLT 1/5 displaced the Command Post to TA 0656-S-4. At 2110, the Battalion was ordered to send out a patrol of one platoon to locate an enemy radio team, believed to be located at TA 0959-B-2. "C" Company Commander was ordered to dispatch the patrol immediately. The patrol, let by Lt Magness, departed at 2130, encountered no enemy opposition enroute to the designated area. The patrol was engaged in a minor fire fight with an undetermined number of enemy on the return trip, but suffered no casualties. The patrol had no success in locating the enemy radio team, and returned to the Battalion Area at approximately 0200, 19 September, 1950.

At 2200, 18 September, 1950, BLT 1/5 was ordered to prepare to move out in the attack to seize Hills 80 and 85 and 0700, 19 September, 1950. At 0615, "C" Company began to receive heavy small arms fire and sporadic mortar fire from Hill 118. The Battalion Commander immediately called for artillery, mortar fire and an air strike on this position.

At dawn, groups of enemy, ten to fifteen per group, were observed advancing along the road toward the air field on the left of "C" Company. Other groups were moving across the rice paddies to the front of "C" Company's position. The advance of those groups was covered by heavy small arms and mortar fire. The enemy was taken under fire by 81mm and 60mm mortars located on the reverse slope of objective FOX. The "C" Company machine guns on the left flank played a major part in stopping and containing the attack. As the enemy were being held by "C" Company, "B" Company was ordered to attack and envelope Hill 118, which was directly in front of objective FOX. Preceeding the attack a heavy artillery barrage on an air strike were delivered. "B" Company quickly moving in under this preparation succeeded in taking its objective which resulted in the surronding and destroying of 100 enemy troops with no casualties to "B" Company. This move also enabled "C" Company to move forward and take the ridge to the left front with light casualties. Hill 118 was secured at 1055.

Approximately 500 enemy were involved in the attack on "C" Company's position. It was estimated that the enemy suffered 80 % casualties, with 56 enemy prisoners being taken. The casualties suffered by our forces were as follows: "B" Company, 1 WIA; "C" Company; 2 KIA, 6 WIA. "B" Company's casualty occ- urred in defense of Hill 118. At 1310, the Battalion Command Post displaced forward and at 1325 was located at TA 0957-M-1. "B" Company and "C" Company consolidated their positions on Hill 118 while waiting the arrival of tanks to assist in the attack on Hills 80 and 85. A large number of enemy troops were observed on Hill 80 by "B" Company. Due to the Battalion FAC not being able to observe from the Battalion CP, Captain Fenton called for and directed an air strike on that position causing many casualties and succeeded in routing the enemy from Hill 80. At 1430, the 3rd Platoon of "C" Company, commanded by Lt Dawe moved southwest along the highway, covered by company machine guns and mortar fire directed at Hills 80 and 85. This platoon seized and occupied Hill 80 at 1545. The 1st Platoon, commanded by Lt Corbet, supported by a platoon of tanks moved in column behind the 3rd platoon at an interval of approximately 500 yards, seized and occupied Hill 85 at 1650. The platoon of tanks remained to the rear of Hill 85 as a covering force. The 2nd platoon leading the company supply train moved to the rear of Hills 80 and 85. The 2nd platoon reinforced by Korean National Police was assigned the task of clearing the villages to the rear of Hills 80 and 85.

Upon occupation of Hills 80 and 85, "C" Company was subjected to artillery, mortar, and small arms fire. This enemy fire continued until night fall. A perimeter defense was set in on the reverse slope of Hills 80 and 85, with the company making all preparations to defend the position for the night. "B" Company was set up in their position on Hill 118. The Battalion Command Post was located at TA 0957-M-1 with H&S Company. Weapons Company occupied positions behind "B" Company on the reverse slope of Hill 118.

At approximately 1600, 19 September, 1950, the Battalion Commander was summonded to the Regimental Command Post. At this time, the Battalion Commander was informed that BLT 1/5 would withdraw to an assembly area at Kimpo Airfield when relieved by BLT 1/1. at 2030, BLT 1/1 began relief of BLT 1/5. Upon relief, units of BLT 1/5 proceeded independently, by foot, to the airfield. At 0130, 20 September, the last elements of this battalion arrived at the assembly area. The

Battalion Command Post was located at TA 0557-I-2.

For graphic sketch of BLT 1/5's operations North of the Han River See sketch No 4,

At 0145, 20 September, the Battalion Commander received an operation order from RCT-5 directing BLT 1/5 to cross the Han River on order, and after crossing to assume the mission of Regimental Reserve. The Battalion remained in its assembly area at Kimpo Airfield throughout the morning. At 1330, units of this battalion began embarkation aboard the LVT's in which they would cross the Han River. At 1355, the first LVT's left the assembly area and arrived at the Han at 1455. Cross-ing of the river was begun immediately. No enemy encountered. When the river cross- ing has been completed the Battalion disembarked and began a route march to the tactical assembly area located at TA 1063-F-4, arriving there at 1700.

At 1830, orders were received from RCT-5 to dispatch one company to objective ABLE (Hill 125) for flank security of the river crossing area and to clear out snipers which were harrassing personnel in the vicinity of the Han River crossing. "C" Company was assigned this mission and completed occupation of objective ABLE at 2130.

At 0730, 21 September, 1950, the battalion started in route march to objective DOG, "C" Company brought up the rear of the column after leaving its position on objective ABLE.

The Battalion proceeded in route march along the railroad tracks toward the city of Seoul. At 1050, the battalion established the Command Post at TA 1361-J-3. At this time "A" and "I" Companies were ordered to attack and seize Hill 96. "A" Com-pany jumped off in the assault of the hill located just to the right of Hill 96, this position to be used as the intermediate objective in the assault of Hill 96. At 1200, an air strike was put on the objective. The air stroke was immed- iately followed by an artillery barrage. As the artillery barrage lifted, "A" Company jumped off in the attach supported by fire from tanks located along the railroad tracks, and at 1315 they had seized and occupied Hill 96. "C" Company, follow- ing in trace of "A" Company, swept through the rice paddies and then moved around to the left flank of "A" Company to take over the assault for the seizure of Hill 68. "B" Company mov-ing on the Battalion left flank, continued the attack and at 1355 seized and occupied its objective, Hill 40. Throughout the attack, the assault companies were under mod-erate small arms fire the rear elements of the Battalion were being harrassed by sniper fire. All enemy fire was coming from the direction of Hills 96 and 68. With the support of machine guns and mortars of "B" and "C" Companies, "C" Com-pany swept the ridge and occupied Hill 68. Occupation of Hill 68 was completed at 1730. After Hills 40 and 68 were occupied by "B" and "C" Companies, "A" Company occupied the ridge between Hills 40 and 68. During the days operation, the follow-ing casualties were incurred: "A" Company, 5 WIA including 1stLt Eubanks, Com-pany Executive Officer, "B" Company, 1 KIA, 1 WIA; "C" Company, 1 KIA, 1 WIA. At 1600 the Battalion Command Post displaced and set up at TA 1559-$-1. At 1730, all companies had attained their obj- ective, consolidated their positions and were dug in for the night. Throughout the night, the Battalion positions was sub- jected to inter-mittant artillery and mortar fire.

For graphic sketch of action of Hill 105 see sketch No. 3

At 0730, 22 September, 1950, the Battalion Commander ordered an attack on Hill 105. The scheme of maneuver was that "B' Com- pany attack along the railroad tracks supported by a platoon of tanks and fire from"C" Company. This attack was to be coord- inated with an attack launched by the ROK Marines on the high ground to the front of Hill 104 in their zone of action. The railroad tracks was to be the boundary line between the 1st Battalion and ROK Marines. The tanks which were to support "B" Company were committed to the aid of the ROK Marines who were having difficulty in launching their attack. The initial plan call for an attack with companies in column.

At 0745, this plan was changed in that "A" Company, would pass through "C" Company and advance to the base of Hill 105, at which time "C" Company would envelope the objective from the right. "B" Company was to remain in position and deliver fire support from these positions on Hill 40. At 1030, "A" Company moved out with the 1st Platoon, in command of TSgt McMullon leading, and secured the high ground around the radio station. Capt Stevens passed the 2nd and 3rd Platoons through the 1st platoon to set up a base of fire from which he could support the attack on Hill 105. As the platoons were moving into position they received heavy enemy automatic and small arms fire from the front and left front of Hill 105. This fire pinned "A" Company down. During this fire Lt Mann, Platoon Leader of the 2nd Platoon was killed and Lt Schimmenti, Platoon Leader, 3rd Platoon was severely wounded.

During "A" Company's move, "C" Company had moved to the extreme right of the Battalion zone of action sweeping the rice paddies as it moved, and arrived at the low ground to the right flank of Hill 105.

"B" Company who had remained in their original positions were ordered by the Battalion Commander to send a two platoon patrol back to the vicinity of Hill 68, to investigate a reported 400 enemy soldiers in that area. This patrol was lead by 1stLt J. Hancock, Executive Officer of "B" Company. This patrol departed at 1235. The remaining platoon commanded by Lt Schryver returned to the Battalion Command Post as a security force. "B" Company's patrol returned to the Battalion Command Post at 1500, with a negative report.

At 1500, "C" Company with the 1st and 3rd platoons supported by a section of machine guns attacked Hill 105. The 1st Platoon commanded by Lt Corbet, was immediately pinned down by heavy enemy machine guns and small arms fire, from his front and right flank. At this time the 2nd Platoon commanded by Lt Magness swung to the right rear of the company's zone of action and both the 2nd and 3rd Platoons awaited the coordinated attack which was ordered with "B" Company.

At 1545, the Battalion Commander ordered "B" Company to pass throught "A" Company and attack the west portion of Hill 105, in their zone of action. At 1720, after an intense mortar, artillery and air preparation, "B" and "C" Companies assaulted Hill 105, supported by fire from "A" Company. "B" Company attack with the 2nd and 3rd Platoons, seized the west portion of Hill 105, with the 1st Platoon taking the low ridge to the rear of Hill 105. "C" Company enveloping from thr right with the 2nd and 3rd Plat- oons seized the east portion of Hill 105. The objective was secured at 1735.

During the attack on Hill 105, "A" Company, machine guns and "C" Company mortars delivered supporting fires. Excellent sup- porting fire was delivered by the 81mm Mortar Platoon of Weapons Company. This platoon was commanded by Lt Alderman, and had their fire directed by Lt Tuloy the Battalion F.O.

After Reaching the crest of Hill 105, "B" and "C" Companies consolidated their positions dispite heavy small arms fire and sporadic artillery and mortar fire. Due to the fact that "B" Company occupied the larger portion of the objective and that their 1st Platoon was occupying low ground to the north of Hil 1 105, which was under heavy fire, the 3rd platoon of "C" Company was attached to "B" Company for filling the line. As soon as was practical, the 1st Platoon of "B" Company was withdrawn from the low ground and placed on Hill 105 for support. At 1800, Hill 105 was secured and a perimeter defense established for the night. The casualties suffered by the attacking companies in the taking of the hill were; "B" Company, 1 KIA, 6 WIA; "C" Company, 9 KIA, 17 WIA; "A" Company, 2 KIA, 8 WIA.

During the attack of Hill 105 supplies were being rushed t o the assault companies by jeep. Many mines were encountered on the roads. One jeep struck a land mine, injuring the driver, killing the rider and destroying the jeep. At 1030, 22 September, mortar and artillery fire fell in the Weapons Company area causeing 1 dead and 15 wounded. At 1705, that afternoon a concentration of artillery shells fell in the Battalion Command Post and supply area, killing 5 and wounding 18.

At 0200, on 23 September, 1950, a counter-attack of approx- imately 50 enemy came up the east side of Hill 105 penetrating the 3rd platoon of "C" Company, over-running a machine gun, killing the gunner and the assistant gunner. The penetration was sealed off and enemy repulsed.

Throughout the following day "B" and "C" Companies remained on Hill 105 and were subjected to intense small arms fire, spora- dic mortar and constant fire from several high velocity flat trajectory weapons on the forward slope and either side of the hill. Movement was impossible during daylight hours. Water, rations and ammunition was supplied thes positions only after darkness, at which time the small arms fire subsided. The Battalion's position remained unchanged on the night of the 23rd.

At 0450, 24 September, 1950, the enemy, approximately 50 in strength, again counter-attacked in the same area as they had the night before. The counter-attack was repulsed with heavy losses to the enemy.

At 0700, 24 September, 1950, "C" Company was ordered to send one platoon to the right rear of Hill 105 on the Han River to secure a portion of the river bank for the landing of elements of the 1st Marines and to guide these elements into positions on the right flank of Hill 105.

At 0900, the patrol returned to its position on Hill 105 after accomplishing the mission.

At 1010, orders were received for the Battalion to move to Hills 216 and 296 and effect relief of BLT 3/5 and assume that battalion's mission of protecting the left flank of RCT-5.

At 1230, "A" Company began movement to the rear followed by "C" Company less the 3rd Platoon, which remained with "B" Company on Hill 105. At 1400, elements of the 1st Marines moved around the right flank of 105 and moved towards the high ground to the front, thereby allowing "B" Company with the 3rd platoon of "C" Company to withdraw at 1630 when ordered by Battalion Commanding Officer. The number of casualties suffered by the Battalion while seizing and occupying Hill 105 were: 27 KIA, 72 WIA.

At 2000 all units of BLT 1/5 had effected relief of BLT 3/5, "B" Company was placed in Battalion support. The Command Post was located at TA 1760-V-2.

At 0100, 25 September, 1950, "A" Company in its positions on Hill 296 repulsed a minor counter-attack. At 0300 an operation order was received directing the Battalion to move out, on order, in trace of the 3rd Battalion, with BLT 1/5 in reserve. The Battalion's positions would be occupied by elements of the 1st Reconnaissance Company.

At 1830, the Battalion was relieved in position by the 1st Reconnaissance Compnay and this Battalion moved out in route column to a new assembly area in the vicinity of TA 1850-V-2, arriving there at approximately 1900. At 2300, orders were received from the Commanding Officer of RCT-5 to move out immed- iately in trace of BLT 3/5. This Battalion moved out and cont- acted BLT 3/5 at 0100, 26 September, 1950, but inasmuch as BLT 3/5 did not continue the attack this Battalion remained in position at TA 1959, in the vicinity of "Chosen University". The Battalion set up a perimeter defense in this area and remained there until 1100, 27 September, 1950.

At 0200, 27 September, 1950, BLT 1/5 received orders directing the Battalion to move out on order following BLT 3/5 in trace to Middle School. Upon reaching Middle School, the Battalion made a left wheeling movements and seized Hill 338. At approximately 1045, orders were received to move out, and at 1100 the Battalion moved out in route column with "A" Company loading, followed by "B" , "C", and Weapons Companies. At 1300, "A" Company had reached Middle school, turned to the left and taken up positions on Observatory Hill in preparation for the assault of Hill 338. They were supported from this position by a section of 75mm Recoilless Rifle Platoon, one platoon of machine guns and the 81mm mortar platoon from Weapons Company. "C" Company moved on through the city to the Government Buildings and there, with the support of a platoon of tanks, they moved up that portion of the city that lies between Hill 338 and the Palace Grounds, moving in the direction of Hill 342. "B" Company, with Weapons Company, took up reserve and support positions around Observatory Hill with the Command Post being located at TA 2059-S-3. At 1300, following an air strike and heavy artillery and mortar preparation fires, "A" Company launched the attack against Hill 338. Just prior to the attack, a squad of Korean National Police was sent to clear the section of city between Observatory Hill and Hill 338.

As soon as the Korean National Police had accomplished their mission of clearing the section of the city in the path of "A" Company, the 1st platoon, commanded by Lt Trapnell, was assigned the mission of seizing the high ground to the front. This was accomplished against moderate resistance. The 2nd platoon, commanded by Lt Collins, was then committed to the left of the ancient wall that runs along the slope of Hill 338, and abreast of the 1st Platoon, their mission being to seize the portion of Hill 171 in their zone of action. As the attack continued, the 1st and 2nd platoons came under heavy mortar and small arms fire. While being held up, an air strike was called on the right portion of Hill 171. After the air strike lifted the 2nd platoon was still subjected to severe small arms fire and could not advance. The 1st Platoon, supported by fires from 81mm mortars and 60mm mortars, "A" Company and Weapons Company machine guns, attacked and over-ran the enemy on Hill 171. This action enabled the 2nd Platoon to move forward and secure their objective. The 3rd Platoon, commanded by TSgt Bolkow was passed through the 1st Platoon with orders to attack Hill 225 in line with the 2nd Platoon. Hill 225 was taken with light resistance, the 3rd Platoon, upon taking its portion of Hill 225, was ordered to attack to Hill 338, which was accomplished with light resistance. Hill 338 was secured at 1850. "A" Company set in defense positions on Hills 225 and 338.

During "A" Company's attack, "C" Company had progressed through their zone of action and proceeded up the slope between Hills 342 and 338, swinging to the left along the ancient wall moved up Hill 338 to tie in with "A" Company. Casualties for the day were: "A" Company 4 KIA, 7 WIA. BLT 1/5 remained in position for the night with no enemy activity. The Command Post was located in Middle School, at TA 6059-S-3.

At 0700, 28 September, 1950, BLT 1/5 was directed to give fire support to the 7th Marines on Hill 342, but was unable to do so, as information as to their front lines was not available. At this time "A", "B", and "C" Companies were assigned to sectors of the Battalion zone of Action in which to patrol. The mission was to seek and destroy all remaining enemy and to confiscate all enemy material. At 0800 all patrols had departed from company positions.

No enemy resistance was encountered, although there were many prisoners taken and large quanties of all types of enemy material was found and reported. At 1800, orders were issued for all units to proceed independently to the Battalion Assembly Area at Middle School, leaving one platoon of "A" Company on Hill 338. At

1600, all units of the Battalion were in the Assembly Area. "B" and "C" Companies were ordered to dispatch one platoon each to assigned areas in the Battalion zone as outposts. The Battalion established local security and remained in the Assembly Area during the night.

On 29 September, 1950, the Battalion utilized the building of Middle School for offices and barracks. At 1200, all out-posts were recalled to the Assembly area and an interior and security guard was established on a 24 hour basis. At 1700, the Battalion received 57 new replacements which were distributed to the com- panies. The period spent at Middle School was utilized for re- organization and administrative details.

At 1115, 30 September, 1950, the Commanding Officer of BLT 1/5 ordered "C" Company to be prepared to ontruck at 1300 and report to the Commanding Officer of BLT 2/5 at TA 0865-A-3 for further orders. At 1300, "C" Company departed Battalion Assembly Area and at 1700 reported to the Commanding Officer of BLT 2/5 for further orders. At 1350, the Korean National Police, attached to BLT 1/5 were ordered to send out three patrols of one squad each to investigate reports that North Korean Soldiers were located in the northern sector of the Battalion Zone. At 1600, these patrols departed from the Battalion Assembly Area, and remained over night, returning the following morning at 0700, 1 October, 1950, with 21 prisoners, both civilian and military.

At 1930, 30 September, 1950, BLT 1/5 received a one hour stand-by order to move out. BLT 1/5 remained in this status until 1430, 1 October, 1950, at which time word was received to begin movement to an assembly area at TA 1764. At 1530, BLT 1/5, less "C" Company, began route march, arriving at designated assembly area at 1730, with the Command Post being established at TA 1764-M-3. The Battalion dug in and established local security. At 1945, orders were received from RCT-5 that the Battalion, on the following morning would send out two patrols to assigned sectors and also to provide a security detail for BLT 3/5's supply train. At 2040, "C" Company rejoined the Battalion. There was no enemy activity during the night. At 0830, 2 October, 1950, BLT 1/5 Patrols 1 and 2, which were supplied by "A" Company, departed from the Battalion Assembly Area. The patrols covered their assigned routes meeting negative enemy resistance. Mine fields were located by both patrols. Information gathered from civilian sources indicated that small groups of enemy were raiding the villages. At 1900, the patrol returned to the Battalion Assembly Area. At 1940, the security guard for BLT 3/5 supply train departed BLT 1/5 Assembly Area. While enroute a truck overturned on a soft shoulder in the road slightly injuring three men of the security guard. The S-4 of BLT 3/5 supplied two jeeps and trailers to reload the supplies from the damaged truck and to deliver them to BLT 3/5. The security guard returned to the Battalion Assembly Area at 0800, 3 October, 1950.

At 0745, 3 October, 1950, Patrol 1 and 2 formed from "C" Com- pany departed the Battalion Assembly Area. Patrol 1 returned at 1500 and reported engaging in a slight fire fight with an undetermined number of enemy. One member of the patrol was wounded in the hand. At 1640, Patrol 2 returned to Battalion Assembly Area. Patrol reports indicated that the groups of enemy reported by the previous patrols had been withdrawing to the northwest.

It has been said many times that the Inchon Landing was unusual
in the annals of amphibious warfair. From a lead Assault
Rifle Company commander's point of view, the most unusual aspect
was the limited amount of time available to: 1. Absorb a large
number of replacements and additional elements that had had no
recent combat experience; and, 2. Absorb the landing plan and
complete the company level planning necessary to conduct a
"different" kind of landing (ladders on a sea wall, densely
populated area, dusk vs. dawn) without any practice or rehearsal.

Able Company, First Battalion, Fifth Marines had been operating
throughout the Pusan Perimeter with a skeleton staff of officers
and NCO's. Not very many, but good, dependable and experienced
men.

When replacements were received at Pusan, prior to the Inchon
Landing, one of the officers joining Able Company was Lt.
Baldomero Lopez. Lt. Lopez had been Able Company Executive
Officer while in Camp Pendleton in 1949 and early 1950. He
had received orders to go to school shortly before the First
Marine Brigade was formed in June, 1950 at camp Pendleton.
After Lt. Lopez had already started classes, he requested duty
in Korea with Able Company, First Battalion 5th Marines, when
war broke out.

When Lopez joined A-1-5- at Pusan he was assigned as Platoon
Leader 3rd Platoon.

Our experience, up to then, had indicated that if an officer
or staff non-commissioned officer could make it through an
initial fire fight, his chances for continuing were good.
Lt. Muetzel, Platoon Leader 2nd Platoon and Gy Sgt. McMullan,
Platoon Leader, 1st Platoon were excellent examples of this.
The Assault Plan at Red Beach called for Able Company to be
deployed with 2 platoons up and one platoon in reserve. The
1st platoon under Gy Sgt. McMullan and the 2nd platoon under
Lt. Muetzel were selected as the two assault platoons.
Lt. Lopez, with his 3rd platoon, was to be the reserve. It
was my thought that Lt. Lopez would have the least amount
of exposure by being with the reserve platoon.

Unfortunately, it didn't work that way. The 1st Platoon leader
and half of the platoon were delayed off shore by a boat
breakdown. The remainder of the 1st Platoon scaled the sea
wall from boat 2, but ran into heavy fire from the north flank
and from submachine guns in a bunker directly ahead. The others
were unable to advance more than just a few yards inland.
Boat No. 3, to the right of the 1st Platoon with Lt. Muetzel
and part of his platoon landed with no casualties.

Muetzel continued the attack towards his objectives, meeting
with very little opposition. Back in the 1st Platoon area, no
progress was being made against flanking fire and the bunker
to the front. At this time the 3rd Platoon under Lt. Lopez
landed. At the same time McMullan landed with the other half
of the 1st Platoon putting both units into a very crowded
and restricted area. Casualties mounted. As Lopez climbed
ashore he was hit. He moved against the bunker with a grenade.
He had pulled the pin on the grenade but was unable to throw
it because of his wound. He was killed when he smothered the
explosion with his body to protect the people around him.

I landed about that time in the 2nd Platoon zone (at H+5 min).
When I heard of Lt. Lopez's death, I asked 1st Lt. Eubanks,
the Company Executive Officer to take over on the left and get
them organized and moving. At the same time I radiod Muetzel
who had already reached the brewery without suffering any
casualties, and asked him to bring the 2nd Platoon back to
the beach to help out. On his way back he noted that the
southern slope of Cemetery Hill was a better route of approach
to the top. We had talked about the 2nd Platoon being asked
to sieze this high ground, if the job proved too tough for the
1st Platoon. With his usual display of excellent judgement
and initiative Muetzel launched his assault on Cemetery Hill
from the South. This assault moved rapidly, flushing out
about a dozen red soldiers who surrendered. When they got
to the top, the entire crest suddenly became alive with rifle
and mortar crewmen. They also threw down their weapons, filed
out from the trenches, and marched to the base of the hill
where they were kept under guard.

On the left side of the beach Eubanks had cleaned out the
bunker in a grenade duel, followed by a flame thrower attack.
He then took the 1st and 3rd Platoon out of its pocket and
drove inland to the edge of the city where he made contact
with the 2nd Platoon. At 17:55 I fired an Amberstar cluster
indicating that Cemetery Hill was secured. The thirty minute
fight in the area of the 1st and 3rd Platoons had cost us
8 killed and 28 wounded.

Accompanying me in my boat going into the beach were several
Time Life photographer/correspondence type's. The last time
I remember seeing those people, was head down on the top of
the sea wall digging for all they were worth.

JOHN STEVENS
2200 SACRAMENTO STREET
SAN FRANCISCO CA 94115

Appendix E

The letters of Edwin Gaines Jr. to his parents in 1951 (Appendix E-1), together with the deposition of Professor Paul Brosman Jr., taken November 17, 1987, effectively forced dismissal of Pat Robertson's libel suit in early 1988. The deposition of Brosman is reprinted here in its entirety because Brosman's words, taken down 36 years later, give perhaps the most accurate picture of the world of a rifle platoon leader in the front and rear Division headquarters of 1951.

&

Appendix E-1

The letters home of Second Lieutenant Edward Gaines of Lexington, Virginia, wounded in the mountains northeast of the Punch Bowl. They were prepared in the form shown as trial exhibits in the case of Robertson vs. McCloskey, dismissed March 7, 1988. Gaines, whose great, great-grandfather had earned the Congressional Medal of Honor at the Battle of Lake Erie in the War of 1812, came from one of Virginia's oldest and most distinguished families. His father was President of Washington and Lee University.

OF PROCEEDINGS

UNITED STATES DISTRICT COURT

FOR THE DISTRICT OF COLUMBIA

```
- - - - - - - - - - - - - - - - - - - - -x
                                          :
MARION GORDON ROBERTSON,                  :
                                          :
              Plaintiff,                  :
                                          :        Civil Action Number
       v.                                 :
                                          :        86-2878
PAUL N. McCLOSKEY, JR.,                   :
                                          :
              Defendant.                  :
                                          :
- - - - - - - - - - - - - - - - - - - - -x
```

DEPOSITION OF PAUL WILLIAM BROSMAN, JR.

New Orleans, Louisiana

Tuesday, November 17, 1987

ACE-FEDERAL REPORTERS, INC.
Stenotype Reporters
444 North Capitol Street
Washington, D.C. 20001
(202) 347-3700
Nationwide Coverage
800-336-6646

IN THE UNITED STATES DISTRICT COURT

THE DISTRICT OF COLUMBIA

MARION GORDON ROBERTSON,
        Plaintiff

        v.   Civil Action No.
                                    86-2878

PAUL N. McCLOSKEY, JR.,
        Defendant

        Testimony of PAUL WILLIAM BROSMAN,

JR., taken by the Defendant pursuant to notice and

within the stipulations at 7834 Willow Street, New

Orleans, Louisiana, beginning at 12:00 noon on

Tuesday, November 17, 1987.

B E F O R E: Goldie F. Kinchen,
              Certified Shorthand Reporter,
              Registered Professional Reporter -

APPEARANCES:

        For the Plaintiff:

                KAPLAN, RUSSIN & VECCHI
                1215 Seventeenth Street, N. W.
                Washington, D. C. 20036

                BY: JOEL E. LEISING, Esquire

        For the Defendant:

                SLOAN, LEHNER & RUIZ
                1920 N Street N. W., Suite 420
                Washington, D. C. 20036

                BY: GEORGE A. LEHNER, Esquire

S T I P U L A T I O N

It is stipulated and agreed by and between the parties that the testimony of the witness, PAUL WILLIAM BROSMAN, JR., is hereby being taken pursuant to Notice under the Rules of Civil Procedure for all purposes permitted under the law.

All formalities, including those of sealing, certification, signing and filing are hereby waived.

All objections, except those as to the form of the question and the responsiveness of the answer, are reserved until the time of the trial of this cause.

* * * * * *

Goldie F. Kinchen, Certified Shorthand Reporter, State of Louisiana, officiated in administering the oath to the herein witness.

PAUL WILLIAM BROSMAN, JR., 7834 Willow Street, New Orleans, Louisiana, who, after having been first duly sworn to tell the truth, the whole truth and nothing but the truth, was examined and testified as follows:

EXAMINATION BY MR. LEHNER:

Q.   Mr. Brosman, would you please state

your full name for the record?

    A.   Paul William Brosman, Jr.

    Q.   And your address?

    A.   Seventy-eight thirty-four (7834) Willow Street, New Orleans, Louisiana.

    Q.   Now, Mr. Brosman, turning your attention to the year 1951, were you at that time serving in the United States Marine Corps?

    A.   Yes, I was.

    Q.   In what capacity were you serving at that time?

    A.   I was a second lieutenant, if that's what you mean. I graduated from basic school and stayed around Quantico briefly after that and then went on leave.

    I'm taking it from the beginning of the year 1951.

    Q.   Okay.

    A.   Then went to Camp Pendelton and was-- spent about a month in the ninth placement draft in Camp Pendelton.

    And then went to Korea and served in the First Marine Division.

    Q.   Now you arrived in Korea approximately when?

A.   The first week of June.

Q.   And at that time, you were assigned to the First Marine Division?

A.   Right. Well, I guess I was assigned to the First Marine Division when I got on the ship going over there. But, yes, I was assigned to the First Marine Division.

And then do you want to know what I did in the Division?

Q.   Yes.

A.   Then I was assigned to Item Company, First Marines. And I was in Item Company, First Marines, from about the first week of -- First Marines is First Marine Regiment as opposed to Division.

And I was in Item Company from about the first week of June until early-to-mid October.

Q.   And then in early-to-mid October, what assignment were you given?

A.   I was assigned to the Division Board of Awards. Actually, it takes about a week. It took about a week for them to assign me. And I was assigned to the Division Board of Awards.

At that time, the Board of Awards, like many of the sections of the Division CP, was divided into a Main Board of Awards office and a Board of Awards, Rear.

And all of these Rear sections were assembled together at Masan, the town of Masan, Korea, which is a short distance from Pusan, at what was called Rear CP or the First Division, Rear.

So we had two (2) CPs. A main CP which was, well, some distance behind the Regimental CPs where Division CPs normally are and the Rear CP at Masan.

And I was assigned first to the Rear CP at Masan. Should I go on?

Q. Well, I just want to back up a little bit. For the record "CP" is what?

A. Command Post.

Q. That stands for Command Post?

A. Or headquarters.

Q. When you were serving with the First Marine Regiment, was that out at what was called "On the front" or "On the line"?

A. Well, we were on the line from the beginning of June until late July.

And then the entire Marine Division went into Corps Reserve. That is, we were the

Division of the Corps that was in Reserve.

And the entire Division was in Corps Reserve from sometime in late July until early September.

And then we got recommitted, piece-meal, in early September. And there was the September offensive. It was supposed to force the Communists back to the truce table, and did, apparently.

And then we were on the line the rest of the time I was in the company. Of course, toward the end of September, things sort of stopped.

Q. So when you were mustered out of the First Marine Regiment, you were on the line at that point, correct?

A. Right, I was.

Q. In October.

A. Right.

Q. Then you traveled back to the Regimental Headquarters?

A. Yes. I was sitting on the line in Item Company. And then just walked out of the evacuation area with some guys that were going back to Battalion for some reason. And they go back.

And I went back to Battalion CP and all because I was being rotated off the line, is what it amounts to. Because normally when a junior officer with no experience except basic school goes over to Korea, he is assigned to a line company.

And he spends four (4) or five (5) months in a line company commanding some small unit appropriate to his ranks.

And then he is rotated. His first rotation, he spends four (4) or five (5) months in some staff job in the Rear. In other words, the Marine Corps is taking advantage of this to make it a big training program.

And so this was my rotation. And what happens when you rotate, is you just go down to Battalion. If they've got a job for you, they just pick you off and put you in it. If they are full, they have no vacancies, then they'll send you back to Regiment to see if they can do something with you and they'll assign you a job at Regiment.

And so Battalion was full so they just put me in a Jeep with some guy who was going back to Regiment and sent me right back to Regiment.

I got to Regiment. They said they had nothing for me either, but they were going to keep me for a couple days because they expected two (2) or three (3) fellows from one of the other Battalions to come through, who were in the same circumstances I was. And they were going to hold me until they got there so they could send us all back to Division together and we could be assigned at once by Division.

But two (2) or three (3) days elapsed and they hadn't appeared. So then they said they would send me back by myself anyway. And so they sent me back.

They put me in a truck with a bunch of guys who were going back there and they sent me back to Division, that is, to the Division CP.

Q. Now do you recall approximately how far it was from the line where you were when you were rotated off the line, to the Division CP at that point approximately or how long it took you to get from the line to the Division CP?

A. Gee, I don't have a very good recollection. I would guess it's about twenty (20) miles. But it's pretty far. I mean it's a fair walk to Battalion. And I would guess that it's about twenty (20) miles, but not so much based on my impressions of traveling to Battalion, to

Regiment, to Division.

I got curious about it myself later on and tried to check into it, figure it out. But I think that's what I recall, twenty (20) miles.

But I'm not too reliable on that. No, my impression on that isn't too reliable because I was leaving the line. I wasn't, you know, measuring distance or anything. I was just glad to get off the line.

Q. So you arrived at the Division CP. Were you assigned a job at the Division CP at that time?

A. No, I was sent to see a guy. As soon as I got there, I was sent to see a guy. I'm pretty sure him name was Mike Young. He was a personnel officer of some sort.

And he sort of interviewed me and then he told me to go a Casual tent or something they had for itinerant officers and I could stay in that. I could live in that tent and just wander around the CP, check in with him every day.

And when he figured out something to do with me, he'd tell me. And so I spent about three (3) or four (4) days at the Division CP, just checking in with him every day.

And then finally one day, I checked in with him -- the fellows never did appear, by the way, these guys from the other Battalion. And then one day, I checked in with him and he said that they were going to sent me down to Masan to the Board of Awards, Rear.

And so the next day, I was to be out there somewhere and got on a truck that was going to take me back to an airstrip and they'd fly me down to Masan because Masan is, I don't know, two hundred (200) miles back -- south.

Q. Now is it correct then that you arrived at Masan sometime towards the middle of October?

A. That's right.

Q. Now when you arrived at Masan, did you have an occasion to meet another second lieutenant named Edwin Ganes (Phonetically spelled)?

A. Yes, I did.

Q. And when did you meet him approximately?

A. Well, the first day -- the day I was there or the day I got there. He was also assigned to the Board of Awards, Rear.

He had been in Fox Company, Item

Company, had been hit.

Q.   Also First Marine Regiment?

A.   Right.   And evacuated, eventually to the hospital ship at Pusan, I understand.

And I was coming down from the Division and he was coming up from the hospital ship at Pusan.   And we both were assigned to Masan.

And it's my impression that he arrived in Masan one (1) day or two (2) before I did.   And he was assigned to the Board of Awards at some point.   I found him -- when I went to the Board of Awards, there he was.

Q.   And then did you have an occasion to ask Mr. Ganes about his prior service in the Marine Corps when you met him?

A.   Yes, I did.   That's kind of normal procedure for the Corps.

Q.   Yes.   What kind of questions did you ask him?

A.   Well, I asked him what -- I knew he had been hit and come up from the hospital ship at Pusan.

I asked him what Regiment he had been in and he said First Marines.   And I said "Well, I was Item Company.   What were you?"   And he said "I was Fox."

And we exchanged a couple of questions and answers about what had gone on during the summer because Item Company -- I mean because my battalion, the Third Battalion which Item Company belonged to, had relieved the Second Battalion that Fox Company belonged to a couple of time and they had relieved us at least once. So we had crossed paths and "Were you among those guys?" and that sort of stuff. And I think partly he was. And partly he recalled and partly he didn't.

And then I asked him what draft he came over in because that's something one always asks because that's something one is always very conscious of when you are in Korea.

Q.   Why is that?

A.   Well, it's when you got there. They sent over a replacement draft every month after the landing at Inch'on.

And so what draft you were, just first draft, second draft, third draft, October, November, December and so on. So what draft you came over in, first, it means when you are going home. It's how long you've been there and when you are going home. And, of course, the companies, it also means whether you're a veteran or not.

Q. How much seniority you have, essentially?

A. Well, right. And, well, of course, you feel kind of meek when you first get there and they ask you what draft you came over in.

Of course, they don't have to ask you because you are clean. But if they ask you what draft you were on and it was last month, you're kind of apologetic.

And then very quickly -- things happen fast. Later on, you're senior and if you came over on old draft, then you feel real rough.

Q. So you had occasion to ask Ed Ganes what draft he come over on?

A. Right.

Q. And what did he tell you?

A. He told me -- well, he told me the correct number, but the fifth or sixth draft.

Q. And so that indicated to you that he had come in February or March, is that correct, sir?

A. Right. Several months earlier than I had.

Q. And then did you ask him what he had

done once he had arrived with the fifth or sixth replacement draft?

A.   Well, as I recall, no.   I didn't have to.   As I recall, I asked him what draft he came in and he said the fifth or sixth but that he hadn't come straight to Korea, that he had stayed in Japan.

He had been assigned to duty in Japan at first and had spent several months in Japan and then hadn't been reassigned from Japan until June so that although he came -- although he was in a draft several months earlier than mine, he actually arrived in Korea, or in the First Marines, a few weeks after I did.

I was interested in that.   I said "Well, how did that all come about?"   And he started telling me.

And at some point early on, I remembered a story from a Lieutenant Dennis (Phonetically spelled).

Q.   Who is Lieutenant Dennis?

A.   Lieutenant Dennis served with me briefly, for a few weeks in August, in Item Company while we were in Corps Reserve.

He had been a member of Item Company

many months before, long before I got there.

Q.   Uh-huh.

A.   And he had been hit and apparently hit pretty badly because he had been evacuated to Japan and apparently it took him quite awhile, he recuperated for quite awhile there in Japan.

And then, after recovering, instead of being sent back to Korea immediately, he was assigned to this Casual Company, or whatever it was, that Pat Robertson and Ed Ganes were assigned to in Japan.

Q.   So you met this Mr. Dennis in August or July?

A.   Right.   Then ultimately -- I'm pretty sure he was there from then until -- because his assignment there had nothing to do with their assignment there.

But he was there the rest of the time they were there, and I think for some time afterwards.   Well, I'm sure he must have been for some times afterwards.

And then eventually, he was sent back to Korea and sent back to his original company, Item Company.   And arrived, I would guess in August.   I'll guess in early August because he was there for a few weeks.

And then before we went back up in early September, he was transferred out. I don't know. He was about due to be entitled to go home but he was transferred out.

Q. Now you referred to a story that Mr. Dennis had told you. What story had Mr. Dennis told you then, when you met him in August?

A. Well, he told me that -- I'm confident that I have met Gerhart (Phonetically spelled). He told me, when he walked by John Gerhart to meet two (2) or three (3) of us in Item Company, he introduced us. And then he said "Let me tell you a story about this fellow, Gerhart."

Q. So John Gerhart was with Mr. Dennis when you had this conversation with Mr. Dennis?

A. Yes, standing there. Right. And there were two (2) or three (3) other people there, though I can't name then. But they would have been officers in Item Company, First Marines, at that time.

And his story was that Gerhart had come over in an early draft, the fifth or sixth draft. And that in the draft with him there had been the son of a United States senator. And the senator had used his pull to get the son taken out of the draft and assigned to this Casual Company or whatever in Japan so as to avoid having to go to Korea and probably be in combat.

And presumably to keep it from looking so obviously like special treatment, they pulled out about three (3) or four (4) other guys, too, along with the son.

Q.   This is what Dennis related to you?

A.   Right. And Gerhart was one of those three (3) or four (4) guys pulled out with the senator's son. And then they spent several months in Japan.

Then General Shepherd who was in charge of the Fleet Marine Corps, Pacific, came through on some kind of a tour and he went by this place where they were.

And there, he asked them how they were doing or something, and Gerhart told him that he was doing all right, but that he'd like to go to Korea. And he told the General that he had been in replacement draft headed for Korea but that he had been taken out of it when they got to Japan and assigned here.

Q.   All this, again, is what Dennis is

relating to you during this time?

A. Right. All this is Dennis' story quoting Gerhart because Gerhart was standing there.

But that he wanted to go to Korea and go to combat and couldn't the General -- of course, in telling him this, he told him that he and these other fellows, whoever, three (3) or four (4) of them -- and so he was disappointed that he was there at Otsu, was the name of the place. I guess that's a town in Japan.

And so General Shepherd said that he was glad to hear him talking like that and that he was surprised to learn this or something and that he would see to it that he would get sent to Korea. And he indicated that he would see that these other fellows who had been pulled out of the draft with Gerhart would be sent, also.

And Pat Robertson became very upset about that and incensed and, as I think I've told each of you, I believe that the reason that he got so violent was that he was drunk. But I don't want to swear that he got that drunk that night.

Q. This is your recollection of Dennis' story to you?

A. Because that's my vague, vague idea.

Dennis and Ed Ganes. But I think he started drinking because he was going to Korea, he thought.

Then it was while he was drunk that he got violent. But at any rate, he got violent or attempted to, and went down and pounded on Gerhart's door.

Apparently these guys had separate rooms or apparently they lived in separate rooms. I don't know. Anyway, Gerhart had a door.

And Gerhart had retired for the evening and closed the door and, perhaps, locked it. I don't know.

And Pat Robertson had gone down there and started pounding on Gerhart's door, wanting to get at him, and had to be restrained by a couple guys.

And then they all had been transferred to Korea. And that's where the story ended with Dennis.

Q. Now during this conversation when John Gerhart was standing there, do you recall whether Gerhart disputed anything that Mr. Dennis was relating to you?

A. Oh, no, he didn't. Now Dennis didn't identify Pat Robertson or Ed Ganes by name or any of the other fellows, anybody but Gerhart, I guess because he knew those names wouldn't mean anything to us.

And I don't know if he told us that it was -- if he identified the senator by name or not. I don't know if he said he was the senator from Virginia -- I mean the other senator from Virginia or Senator Robertson or what.

Q.   Now this conversation that you've just related took place some time in either August or September of '51 while you were with the First Marine Regiment somewhere near the front in Korea?

A.   Right. Conceivably the first week of September but I'm confident in August, some time in August of 1951.

At that time, I think Gerhart and Dennis both -- I don't know whether they knew that Pat Robertson hadn't had to go to a line company like Gerhart and Ed Ganes and all the others or not.

Q.   So picking up the story then, you began to say that you were having a conversation with Ed Ganes now.   The time frame being mid October of 1951, you've arrived at Masan.

A.   Right. This would be the first day or

two (2), as I've mentioned.

Q.   Right. And you were exchanging war stories, as it were, with Ed Ganes?

A.   Right.

Q.   And he began to tell you that he had been taken off of one of the replacement drafts and sent to Japan.

What was the next part of the conversation you had with Ed Ganes at that point?

A.   Oh, well, I said that that reminded me of the story that Dennis had told me. And I indicated to him that I heard a story about that from a guy back in Item Company about this and a fellow named Gerhart arranged for these guys to get sent to Korea.

And I said "Do you know about that?" or "Are you one of them?" or something. I don't know if I asked him he was one of them or not.

But he indicated -- I told him part of the story, and he indicated, yes, that he was one of those guys that Gerhart and Dennis had been talking about.

And so I said "Oh, so you were there with them."

And at some point, of course, he told

me that Pat Robertson was the senator's son because by this time, I knew who Pat Robertson was. He was living in the same BOQ as we were.

Q. At Masan?

A. At Masan.

Q. So you had already met Pat Robertson?

A. Yes, I met him the first day.

Q. The first day?

A. The first day or that night that I was there.

And so then I don't know to what extent I told Dennis the story and he verified it or to what extent he, who knew it firsthand, picked it up. And eventually he took it over, of course, because he did know it.

And so then Ed told me the story. And essentially, he told me the same story as far as Dennis carried it. But he added the names.

Q. He told you that he and Pat Robertson had been on the fifth or sixth draft?

A. Right. That's right. He added that. I don't believe that Dennis knew that Ed -- if he did, he didn't tell me -- that Ed was more than window dressing.

But he said that Senator Robertson--

Ed Ganes said that Senator Robertson had arranged for Pat Robertson and Ed Ganes to be pulled off, pulled out of the draft, and assigned to Japan to avoid having to go to Korea. And that three (3) or four (4) other guys, including John Gerhart, had been pulled off with them, presumably again, just to make it look more plausible.

Q.   Ganes offered that as an explanation for why these other people were pulled off the draft as well?

A.   Well, either he offered it or I offered it and he accepted it. I don't know.

Q.   He didn't dispute that if you were the one who made that suggestion?

A.   No. And then they were there for several months. And then General Shepherd came through. And Gerhart spoke to General Shepherd and the General responded to Gerhart as Dennis had said.

And the General said that Gerhart and the other guys who had been pulled out of the draft would all be sent to Korea.

And then, I'm pretty sure -- I think I said "Yes, and I understand Pat threw a tantrum that night" or something to that effect.

And he said yes, he remembered that Pat had tried to get at Gerhart, he was so upset.

Q. About the fact that they were now being assigned to Korea?

A. Right. Then Ed added what Dennis had not. That then, of course, Senator Robertson stepped in again and saw to it that although he couldn't avoid having Pat Robertson sent to Korea, he could see that he was in just about a cushy a place as in Japan and anyway keep him out of combat.

And so he had him sent to Masan.

Q. Ed Ganes told you that when the reassignment to Korea came through, that Ed was under the impression or told you that he knew that Senator Robertson had stepped in again?

A. Right. Stepped in again, and this time, he took care of Pat alone because it was getting kind of difficult I guess to -- I've never been a senator -- but getting kind of difficult to keep doing this.

Plus this was kind of a sudden emergency that came up. So they decided that Ed Ganes would have to fend for himself. And the Senator took care of Pat but he couldn't take care of anybody else.

Q.   Now did Ed Ganes tell you that he and Pat Robertson had been friends before they joined the Marine Corps?

A.   Yes, they were.   They went to Washington & Lee together, I guess were class mates all the way up through it.

And I suppose they knew each other earlier than that.   Wasn't the Senator from Lexington?

But anyway, Ed Ganes and Pat Robertson were close friends.   And they may have both been on a tennis team.   Ed was on the tennis team.   But anyway, they were close.   Ed Ganes and Pat Robertson were very close friends from Washington & Lee, if not from Lexington.

And then, my impression is that Ed's father, who was the president of Washington & Lee, was a friend of Senator Robertson.

Q.   This is something that you learned through conversations with Ganes in 1951?

A.   Ed Ganes.   That's right.   So the Senator took care of Ed out of friendship for Ed's father, I guess, primarily rather though.   But also Ed was a friend of Pat's.

Q.   Now when you were at Masan in October, '51, were you sharing quarters with Ed Ganes?

A.   Right.

Q.   Were you in the same tent?

A.   Well, but in Masan, we were in wooden barracks-like buildings. It was the kind of thing though that they were old things, the kind of things that are, you know, temporary, armed-forces buildings.

Q.   Yes.

A.   And we had a complex of about three (3) rooms in this old barracks building. And there were five (5) us, I believe, altogether, five (5) young lieutenants.

Q.   Now was Pat Robertson in that same quarters with you at that time?

A.   Right.   I was one.   Ed Ganes was the second. Pat Robertson was the third.   A fellow named Lester Tooley (Phonetically spelled) was the fourth. And a guy whose name I think was Dick, was the fifth.   And I'm pretty confident there were just the five (5) of us.

I can't recall what Lester Tooley did. And this fellow, Dick, he worked on the payroll. He was in the Division payroll office, if his name was Dick. I think it was Dick but I don't know his last name.

Q. Did you, when you were at Masan, have an opportunity to meet Pat Robertson and observe his work?

A. Well, I met him because we were there living in the same barracks. So I would see him every evening at least and at night.

I didn't observe his work.

Q. Do you know what area he was assigned to at Masan?

A. My impression was that he was assigned to the S & C Files. The S & C Files Section of the Division had an S & C Files, Rear, and that he was supposedly the S & C Files, Rear, Officer.

Apparently, he would have been the only S & C Files Officer there because after-- have I ever said in this deposition that we were consolidated, the CPs were consolidated?

Q. No, we haven't come to that part yet.

A. After, well, ultimately, the two (2) CPs were consolidated.

And once they were consolidated, he was definitely assigned to the S & C Files. And he was one of only two (2) officers there. The

Captain in Charge was one and he was the other, so I assumed.

Q.   When he was at Masan?

A.   He was along at Masan.

Q.   Now at Masan, did you ever hear Mr. Robertson referred to as the "Division Liquor Officer"?

A.   Well, I heard him referred to as the "Liquor Officer." I don't know about the "Division Liquor Officer." I thought he was the "Masan Liquor Officer."

Q.   How did that reference come about or how did you hear that?

A.   Because he frequently made trips to Japan, I would have said, to buy liquor, maybe.

But I guess from the point of view of the guys at Masan, or the real purpose was to buy liquor. But I suppose some trumped-up excuse was devised so that he could -- for an official trip.

And then he could go over and do something and then bring liquor back.

Q.   So you were aware that he was getting an assignment which would take him to Japan, is that correct?

A.   He went to Japan on at least a few

occasions.

Q. While he was your tentmate, essentially, did he go?

A. Well, that I can't swear to. I'm pretty sure he made one trip while we were there, while I was there, because I was there for only three (3) weeks.

I don't believe that has come out. But I was there for only three (3) weeks or approximately three (3) weeks.

But I learned because it was common knowledge among the other guys in the barracks, that he had made trips in the past.

And I think he was gone for a couple days. I think he made one (1) while I was there.

But I had heard from the other guys and I guess from him, that he had made trips to Japan.

Q. Now you indicated that there came a time that the CP, Rear, and Division CP were consolidated?

A. Right. Uh-huh.

Q. Was that approximately in mid November, to the best of your recollection?

A. Right. Because I got there around the

middle of October.   And my impression is we were
there for only three (3) weeks.

          And   then   at   that   point,   the
establishment,   the   Marine establishment at Masan,
was abolished.

          And   the   Division,   Rear,   was merged
into the main -- or the Rear CP was merged into the
Main CP. And all personnel that had been stationed
at Masan   in these Rear Sections were combined with
the other part of their Sections in the Main CP.

          So Ed   Ganes and   I, who   had been the
only officers assigned   to   the   Board of Awards,
Rear, went up to the Main CP and   were part   of the
staff of   the one   and only Board of Awards Section
in the Main CP. Of   course, which   is now   the one
and only CP.

          Q.   Now did Mr. Robertson accompany you to
the Division CP that November as well?

          A.   Right.   And Pat Robertson also went up
there and went to the S & C Files of the Main CP.

          Q.   When you   were at the Division CP from
mid November on, did   you   have   an   opportunity to
meet or   talk with Pat Robertson during that period
of time?

          A.   Yes, I did. Not   as   often.   But Ed

Ganes frequently visited him. He lived in the S & C tent and Ed Ganes would visit him fairly often down there.

He didn't visit us, because they had a better setup down there and, well, if you visited him, sometimes you could get beer, where you couldn't get any beer if you visited us.

Q. How was that?

A. Well, I don't know. But they always had, or they frequently had beer. And we usually don't.

So Ed would frequently visit him. And sometimes, I would go along with Ed. So I guess I went about half the time or maybe a little more than half the time, that Ed did. Ed went fairly often down there. And so we sat around and talked.

Q. Did you have an occasion to observe or take note of the fact that Mr. Robertson made any trips to Japan during the period of time that he was assigned to the Division CP from mid November on?

A. That I cannot answer. Well, I can't. I would say, no. I didn't notice that he did.

Q. Now let me just ask you a few questions to sort of wrap up your Marine career.

1   Am I correct then that you stayed in

2 Korea until some time in 1952, is that correct?

3   A.   Right.   March of '52.   Ed Ganes and

4 Pat Robertson left on rotation before I did.   I

5 would say December or January.

6   And I remained until March.   And then

7 I was rotated back to the States in March, all the

8 time still assigned to the Board of Awards.

9   Q.   Now after you came back to the United

10 States, would you just briefly describe for me your

11 career and what you've done over the last thirty

12 (30) years so we can have a little background for

13 the record?

14   A.   Do you want me to wind up the Marine

15 Corps too?

16   Q.   Yes, please.

17   A.   Well, I, of course, got about a

18 month's leave.

19   And then I went to Headquarters of

20 Fleet Marine Force, Atlantic, for my next

21 assignment.

22   And I was in the Operations Subsection

23 of the G-3 Section of the Fleet Marine Force,

24 Atlantic, in Norfolk from, I guess April -- well,

25 no, I guess maybe the first of May.

Because I killed much of March getting home. And then I got thirty- (30) day's leave plus travel time from sometime in May until September.

At that point, my obligated service ended. I entered the Marine Corps through the NROTC under the Holloway plan.

And in the first year of the Holloway plan, those who went through it were obligated upon getting their commission, to serve fifteen (15) months.

After that, they made it two (2) years. And then, of course, it's longer now. So I was obligated to serve fifteen (15) months when I got out, when I got my commission.

But then, of course, President Truman added twelve (12) and made it twenty-seven (27) months at some point early in the Korean War.

And so in September of '52, my twenty-seven (27) ended and I was free to switch to the Reserves and go off of active duty.

And it was kind of touch and go because I wanted to go to graduate school at the University of North Carolina in linguistics. And the graduate school started in September of '52.

But I got out just in time to get to

Chapel Hill and start graduate school. And then I attended graduate school at Chapel Hill for four (4) years, got a PhD in Comparative Linguistics in June of 1956 from the University of North Carolina.

I got a job teaching at North Texas State University. For all practical purposes, I have never taught Comparative Linguistics. I've always taught foreign languages because I never got a job at a fancy enough school that they had a Comparative Linguistics program. So I made my living teaching foreign languages. I got a job teaching foreign languages at North Texas State College, it was then, in Denton, Texas. I was there two (2) years.

Then I left and came to New Orleans in 1958 when they founded LSU in New Orleans which is now called University of New Orleans. And I joined the original faculty of the University of New Orleans -- well, that's what they call it now -- in '58, taught there for seven (7) years and then in 1965, went to Tulane University, moved to Tulane University, taught there for quite a few years and then in nineteen -- I guess it actually was 1979, I retired from Tulane.

And I've been retired since.

Q.   Now have you ever spoken to Mr. Paul McCloskey over the last two (2) years?

A.   I've never spoken to Paul McCloskey at all, as far as I know.

Q.   Do you recall meeting Paul McCloskey in the Marine Corps in 1951?

A.   No.   I'm not supposed to, am I?

Q.   I don't know.

A.   I don't know.   If they were in the fifth or sixth draft, he was at a special basic, he was in a special basic class, I guess one of the first ones.   So he and I were at Quantico together.

I was at Beech Island (Phonetically spelled) because an NROTC graduate was at the basic school and which was original intended to be the one-and-only basic program going on then because we were assigned to it as peace-time officers.

And he was in one of the numerous special basic classes that came through Quantico at that time.

Q.   You don't have any recollection or ever meeting Paul McCloskey or talking to him?

A.   No.   I'm sure I have not met him.

MR. LEHNER: I have no further questions at this time.

EXAMINATION BY MR. LEISING:

Q. Did you want a glass of water or anything?

A. Oh, no. No thanks.

Q. Mr. Brosman, when did you first talk to Mr. Lehner?

A. Well, I guesss, about a week before I spoke to you. Well, not more than two (2) weeks or more than two (2) or three (3) days.

Q. Had you spoken to anyone prior to that time, about this case?

A. No one other than my wife. Of course, when this appeared in the paper, I told my wife "Why, heck, I know about this." And I told her about it then. That's all.

Q. Then you have not spoken with either John Gerhart, Ed Ganes or this Lieutenant Dennis?

A. No, not since -- oh, I started to say not since Korea. But I have spoken to Ed Ganes once, but not about this.

I spoke to him once when he was a graduate student of Virginia and I was a graduate student of Carolina, but not about this.

Q. Did Mr. Lehner provide you with any materials prior to today's deposition?

A.   No.

Q.   No newspaper articles, no depositions or anything like that?

A.   No, oh, no.   I've read two (2) or three (3) of them, newspaper articles that appeared in the Times-Picayune.

Q.   To your knowledge, is Lieutenant Dennis still alive?

A.   I don't know.

Q.   Do you know what Mr. McCloskey has alleged, and what is the basis of this lawsuit?

A.   I think I have a general idea of what he has alleged.

Q.   What is that?

A.   He alleged that -- well, essentially, what I said Dennis and Ed Ganes said took place. He alleged that Pat Robertson's father got him out of serving in combat in Korea.

And then, of course, that's contradictory to what Pat Robinson has claimed in his resumes and stuff since.

Q.   Did Ed Ganes ever tell you that Pat Robertson had requested his father to intervene on his behalf?

A.   No, I don't believe he did.   I'm sure

I cannot say that he did.

Q.   Let me ask you this. Do you think that Ed Ganes is a truthful person?

A.   Yes.

Q.   Mr. Ganes' deposition was taken in this matter on December 2, 1986. And I have a couple portions from his transcript of that.

And let me go through a couple of the passages here and ask you questions on these various passages.

First question, "Did Pat Robertson ever discuss with you" -- Mr. Ganes -- "any attempt for him to avoid serving in Korea?" The answer by Mr. Ganes "Oh, no."

That's on Page 11 of the transcript.

Do you have any reason to believe that that was not a truthful answer?

A.   Well, of course, this is all just opinion of mine.

But, yeah, I would say Ed Ganes is an honest person, generally.

But like me, he knew at this point, I'm sure, since from the newspapers, what was going on. And he might try to cover up for Pat.

I don't know what their relationship

is now. I mean if his relationship is now or has been recently, what it was -- if his relationship with Pat Robertson is now what it was back when they were in their twenties, he might try to cover up for Pat.

Q. Isn't it true that the only thing, these rumors that you've heard, the speculation, the only thing you've heard was the fact that --

MR. LEHNER: I'm going to object to your characterization as "Rumors and speculation."

He testified that Ed Ganes told him with firsthand knowledge as to what had happened to him. That's more than a rumor and speculation.'

EXAMINATION BY MR. LEISING: (Resuming)

Q. Isn't it true that what Ed Ganes told you was that Senator Robertson had somehow intervened on Pat's behalf?

A. Yes.

Q. Ed Ganes never told you that Pat Robertson ever requested assistance, is that correct?

A. I believe that's correct.

Q. Isn't it also correct that Ed Ganes told you that he did not know for a fact whether or not Senator Robertson had intervened. But that there was speculation to that effect, that it might have been what happened, and how they ended up at Otsu, Japan?

A.   No.   I don't believe Ed told me-- see, we weren't considering this from this point of view.   I don't believe Ed told me that Pat -- I don't think he went into great detail about whether Pat knew it or not because I assumed he did.

But I have to admit that's an assumption.

But we weren't concerned about what Pat knew and when he knew it because we weren't anticipating this trial.

Q.   How did Mr. Ganes explain to you that the senator was able to accomplish this intervention?

A.   He didn't.

Q.   Did you ask him?

A.   No, I don't believe I did.   I just assumed that senators can do things like that.

Q.   And Mr. Ganes didn't volunteer any idea as to how this was brought about?

A.   I don't believe he did.   I mean such as identifying the persons he contacted or something like that, I don't believe he did.

Q.   Did Mr. Ganes ever tell you that Pat Robertson had called home from Japan when they were enroute to Korea to request a change in orders?

A.   No. This is the phone call that's supposed to take place from the docks that I read about in the newspapers?

Q.   Yes, sir.

A.   No, that I know he didn't tell me about.

Q.   Had you ever heard about that before, prior to reading it in the newspapers?

A.   No. No, I read it in the -- I heard about it first. Then I read it in the newspaper.

Q.   So neither Lieutenant Dennis or Lieutenant Gerhart had told you about a phone call?

A.   Right.

Q.   Did Lieutenant Dennis or Lieutenant Gerhart explain to you how Senator Robertson had accomplished this intervention on behalf of his son?

A.   No, they did not.

Q.   Did you ever talk to Pat Robertson when you were with him in the military about this incident?

A.   No, I'm pretty sure I did not. I

don't think.

Q.   Let me go back to my original question here in the transcript on Page 11. Please listen carefully.

The question is "Did Pat Robertson ever discuss with you any attempt for him to avoid serving in Korea?" "Oh, no," is the answer.

Now is that consistent with your testimony today?

A.   Well, almost certainly, it's not at all consistent with the impression one would gain from my testimony.

Technically, it doesn't conflict with it. Or it doesn't conflict with it directly though because I didn't say how Ed Ganes found out about it.

But I grant you, it certainly seems to be in conflict.

Q.   Aren't you, however, just assuming that Mr. Robertson, Pat Robertson, had requested intervention by his father?

A.   Right.   I believe I said that to one of you two earlier today, that my belief that Pat Robertson asked his father to get him out, is an assumption on my part.

Q.   Mr. Brosman, are you aware that at the time Pat Robertson, Ed Ganes and John Gerhart were taken off the draft in Japan that a total of eight (8) officers and some eighty (80) enlisted men were also removed from the draft?

A.   I didn't know about the enlisted men. Robertson, Ganes, Gerhart and one (1), two (2), three (3), others or three (3) to four (4) others. The number of officers is just slightly above what I would have said I had heard about.

If it's eight (8) officers, I would have said it was six (6) or seven (7) at the outside, from the Ganes/Dennis stories.

The enlisted men, I didn't know about.

Q.   Wasn't the Ganes/Dennis story that you related earlier today, that a congressman or senator had removed or caused to have the son and a few others, three (3) or four (4) others removed from the draft?

That would make a total of four (4) or five (5), right?

A.   Well, okay. I may have said that. In that case, yes, it's four (4) or five (5).

Q.   So carrying your scenario, it would mean that if Senator Robertson had in fact done this, that some eight (8) officers and some eighty (80) enlisted men were pulled in order to cover up Pat Robertson's being lifted from the draft?

MR. LEHNER: I'm going to object to that question.

There's a factual inaccuracy in Mr. Leising's question which I would like to object to.

There's nothing in the record that suggests that eighty (80) officers and, indeed --

MR. LEISING: (Interrupting) Eighty (80) enlisted men.

MR. LEHNER: Eighty (80) enlisted men or the two (2) additional officers were removed from the draft at the same time that six (6) officers, including Mr. Robertson and Mr. Ganes, were removed.

There is nothing in the record that suggests this was done to eighty (80) persons.

MR. LEISING: Maybe not in today's record, but the record of the whole proceedings, it's clear that the day before Mr. Robertson and five (5) others were removed, two (2) other officers removed, that on the day that Robertson and others were removed, there were about eighty (80) enlisted men removed.

It's in the military files.

THE WITNESS: Well, I don't know about the eighty (80) enlisted men or such number of officers.

EXAMINATION BY MR. LEISING: (Resuming)

Q. Are you familiar with the term "Scuttlebutt"?

A. "Scuttlebutt." Yes.

Q. What does that generally mean?

A. It means a rumor.

Q. Is that something that's prevalent in the military?

A. Yes. "Scuttlebutt" is -- well, of course, "Scuttlebutt" is rumor when it takes place in the military.

Q. And while you were in the Marine Corps, did you ever have occasion to hear any "Scuttlebutt"?

A. Yes.

Q. Did you ever have an occasion to engage in "Scuttlebutt"?

A. Yes. I guess so, pass it along.

Q. Is it fair to say that as a rumor is passed along, that occasionally there's embellishment besides?

A.   Yes.

Q.   Is it also fair to say that sometimes the parties in the "Scuttlebutt" are people who are either famous in their own right or somehow related or connected to famous people?

A.   Well, rumors in general, yes. I don't know about the particulars. But rumors in general, yes.

I don't know about military "Scuttlebutt."

Q.   Is there something peculiar about military "Scuttlebutt" that would exempt it from that rule?

A.   Well, it's normally about where we're moving and it doesn't really deal with that so much.

But I'll go along with you about it.

Q.   Now you say you were talking to Lieutenant Dennis and John Gerhart around August, 1951?

A.   Right.   I didn't say much except "Hello" to Gerhart.

Q.   And what did Gerhart say?

A.   "Hello," I guess. "Glad to meet you," I suppose.

Q.   But I mean of Lieutenant Dennis'
telling of this story?

A.   Well, nothing much, except maybe he
nodded or maybe he said "Uh-huh" or something like
that.

Q.   Did Lieutenant Dennis indicate from
whom he had heard this story?

A.   My impression -- but, of course he--
to some extent, it would be Gerhart, himself."

But my impression was that he was
present at Casual Company when these things took
place.   He was assigned there.

Q.   Assigned there at what time?

A.   I don't know.   But before Gerhart and
Ed Ganes and Pat Robertson left there.

Q.   Was he there at the time that they
arrived?

A.   I don't think so.   But I don't know.
My impression is he joined it after they did.

Q.   So he wouldn't have had any firsthand
knowledge as to how they ended up there initially?

A.   No.

Q.   So Lieutenant Dennis' sources of this
story are John Gerhart and/or --

A.   (Interrupting) His observations.

Q.   His other observations?

A.   Yes.

Q.   And your sources of the story are from Lieutenant Dennis, in the first instance, and again from Lieutenant Ganes later?

A.   Right.

Q.   Now you said that Lieutenant Dennis had indicated that when one of the men approached General Shepherd at a party, that the General was surprised that the men were there, is that correct?

A.   I don't know that he was -- I didn't know that he was at a party.

But my impression is that when Gerhart informed General Shepherd about this, General Shepherd was surprised.

Q.   Why was he surprised?

A.   Well, I assume he didn't know about it.

Q.   Is that what Lieutenant Dennis or John Gerhart said?

A.   I don't -- well, I mean I don't-- again, they didn't analyze it like that.

They just said he seemed surprised and then said' "Well, if you want to go to Korea, you can go to Korea" or something like that.

Q.   But was he surprised that they were at Camp Otsu?

MR.   LEHNER: I'm going to object to this line of questioning.

The witness has no idea of knowing what was in General Shepherd's mind at the time.

He can testify as to what Dennis or Gerhart told him.

MR. LEISING: That's what I'm asking him.

MR. LEHNER: No.   You can ask him what Dennis or Gerhart told him.   But you can't ask him what General Shepherd may have had on his mind.

THE WITNESS: He was surprised at the whole story, that he had been pulled off, that he had been on a replacement draft and had been pulled out of the replacement draft and assigned to Japan.

EXAMINATION BY MR. LEISING: (Resuming)

Q.   So from your understanding of the story as related by Lieutenant Dennis with John Gerhart standing right there, General Shepherd apparently didn't know about these men being pulled from the draft?

A.   That's what you would think.   Yes.

Q.   When Lieutenant Dennis was relating

the story to you, did you or any of the other

officers around, ask how this congressman was able

to get his son pulled from the draft?

A.   No. I'm pretty sure we didn't.

Q.   About how long did this conversation

last?

A.   Well, just about as long as it would

take for me to summarize it.

Q.   And where were you at the time?

A.   We were in front of the -- I'm pretty

sure we were in front of the Company Commander's

tent at Item Company.

We were in Reserve and so we all had

tents.

Q.   You were just standing out in the yard

there, talking?

A.   I think so. Yes.

Q.   Like a five- (5) minute conversation?

A.   I don't know what we were doing. We

were standing out there, talking.

And my recollection is though that

Dennis brought Gerhart over and introduced us to

him -- introduced him to us.

And then we all said "Hello." And

then maybe a couple of other remarks were

exchanged.

And then he said "Let me tell you a funny story about this guy." And then he told the story and, I don't know, somebody must have made some little comment or something and that was about it.

Q. Isn't it correct, therefore, that you have no personal knowledge, firsthand knowledge, that Pat Robertson actually received preferential treatment?

A. Right. I have no firsthand knowledge.

Q. You also have no personal, firsthand knowledge, that Pat Robertson ever asked to be assigned duty to Camp Otsu?

A. Right.

Q. You also have no personal, firsthand knowledge, that Pat Robertson ever called home from Japan to request a change in his order?

A. Right.

Q. And you have no personal, firsthand knowledge that Senator Robertson actually intervened on Pat Robertson's behalf?

A. Right.

Q. Do you know what the duties of the S & C, the Security and Classification Officer, were?

A.   My impression is that these were the files for all documents that were generated by the CP or received by the CP that were classified, I guess "Confidential" or higher.

I don't know how much of this I know and how much of this I assumed.

But all paper work that was generated by any Section of the CP, or received by any Section of the CP, was normally kept in files by the Section that dealt with it.

For example, with the Board of Awards, we had a file with all the material that came into the Board of Awards, the recommendations and stuff and papers, you know, of what took place, what happened to it.

But that documents that were classified weren't stored by whatever Section had originated them. But they were all stored in one place devoted exclusively to that. And that was the S & C Files.

And I guess they had safes or something in there. But it didn't seem any more secure than our tent. There wasn't anybody with guns hanging around or anything.

Because, as I say, I went down there

with Ed Sanes to visit Pat Robertson.

But they stored them. I guess they were logged in or out or something if they ever left the files, unlike ours.

Q. By the way, you said that when you went "Down there to visit him." That was down to what? That was down at the Division CP or what?

A. That was in Division CP. I don't know why I used the term "Down" rather than "Up" or whatever.

But they were in a tent about, I don't know, a hundred and fifty (150) yards, two hundred (200) yards, from our tent.

Q. Now are you familiar with the term "Registered publication" in the context of S & C's duties?

A. No. It sounds vaguely familiar.

I think I probably once knew but I don't know now.

Q. Are you familiar with the fact or do you know whether it was a fact, that the S & C Officer would have to periodically go to Japan to either pick up classified documents or return classified documents?

A. No, I don't.

Q.   You don't?

A.   That's possible.   But, no, I don't.

Q.   Who referred to Pat Robertson as the "Masan Liquor Officer"?

A.   Well, I guess just about everybody in our barracks, or whatever you want to call it.

That is, I'm not sure he didn't do it himself, as I think I said earlier. But he was-- and then other, I guess.

It was just more or less general jocular reference by people there.

Q.   Did he ever buy you liquor?

A.   Oh, no.   He brought -- I had to buy my own liquor at the Officers' Club.   We had an Officers' Club at Masan.

It was that cushy a setup.   And he brought the liquor back to the Officers' Club, this is my impression.

Q.   And that impression is based on what?

A.   General talk there at Masan.

Q.   General "Scuttlebutt"?

A.   Or, well, I don't know. I think it's more in between "Scuttlebutt" and common knowledge.

Q.   Do you have any firsthand, personal knowledge that he actually brought back liquor from

Japan?

A.   Firsthand knowledge?

Q.   Yes, sir.

A.   Oh, no.

Q.   Did you ever see him with cases of liquor?

A.   No.

Q.   Did the Officers' Club have its own Mess Officer?

A.   I don't know. He may have been it. I don't know. But I don't know. I believe they did.

Q.   Now you say that when you were in Masan that Pat Robertson had made one (1) trip to Japan while you were there, as you recall?

A.   I said I thought so. But I wasn't sure of that. While I was there, I'm not sure that he did. I'm pretty sure that he did. But I hated to say with complete certainty that he did.

Q.   Did anyone tell you that he was going over to pick up liquor during that, if there was this one (1) trip from Masan?

A.   I can't recall. If my recollection is that he made the trip, then the reason I say he made the trip is that someone told me he was going to pick up liquor.

1   But, as I say, I can't say with

2 absolute certainty that he made a trip.

3   Q. So you have no idea as to whether or

4 not he was going there for official duties

5 connected with his S & C assignment?

6   A. Right. I don't even know for sure

7 that he made the trip.

8   Q. Would you say it's a correct statement

9 that Pat Robertson's major duty in Korea was to act

10 as the Division Liquor Officer?

11   A. No, I wouldn't. That was not his

12 major duty.

13   Q. How much did you socialize with Ed

14 Ganes when you were stationed together?

15   A. A relatively large amount. I mean

16 more than with anyone else.

17   Q. And what about with Pat Robertson?

18   A. Not very much unless -- not very much

19 at Masan. At the Division CP, a fair amount,

20 through Ed Ganes.

21   Q. Do you recall any specific

22 conversations you might have had with Pat

23 Robertson?

24   A. Well, yeah. He was scared to death he

25 had gonorrhea and was very relieved when he found

57

out that it was what the corpsman called "Nonspecific drip."

Of course, I've thought of that often, with his highest posturing.

Q. Well, isn't it true that this "Nonspecific drip" is not any kind of disease transmitted by sexual intercourse or anything else, that it's an infection of the urinary tract?

A. Right. But he thought he had gonorrhea. And I don't think he thought he got that from any other source.

Q. Do you recall any other conversations you might have had with him? Specifically, did you ever talk to him about his earlier duty in Japan?

A. No.

Q. Why not?

A. Well, it was -- I thought it might be a rather embarrassing subject and so -- plus, except for Ed Ganes who was already a friend of his, I was the newest guy in that barracks. Actually, I was the newest guy, but only by about a day or two (2), over Ed Ganes.

And the others never did, so I didn't.

Q. How do you recall Pat Robertson being in those days?

A.   Well, I -- it's hard to say.   I liked him a lot less than Ed Ganes.   But it's hard to say why.

One   thing   was,   he was -- well, he's more   inconsiderate,   pretty   inconsiderate   for, I mean, things like the cleaning the girl.

We had a cleaning girl who came in. It's like the story of the fraternity house and the nineteen- (19) year-old housemother.   We had cleaning   girl   who   was   nineteen (19) who was our maid in our barracks.   But   she was   a nice Korean girl.

And we had a lot of prostitutes around there, for example.   And, well,   Pat used   to fool around with   her all   the time.   That is, pinching her and carrying on.

And every   once   in   awhile,   he would chase   her   outside   the   house   and   then he would continue chasing her and   pinching her   outside the house.

That   would   terrify   her   because the Koreans would see.

And, of course, these prostitutes were dead   meat   when   we   left   because they had ruined their lives to make   money   off   of   the Americans.

But once the Americans left, they were really finished.

And she didn't want the Korean men to see her fooling around like with an American. And she'd plead with him to stop and he wouldn't stop.

And none of the rest of us would have done that.

Q.   You never saw anyone else messing around with women?

A.   Oh, not none of the -- not with that maid.

Oh, a lot of guys messed around with the prostitute's that wanted to get messed around with, including Pat.

Q.   As I understand it, that when you first met Ed Ganes, you started talking about old times that each of you had, you know, on earlier assignments?

A.   Uh-huh, yes.

Q.   And he indicated that he had been in Japan. And then you started telling him the story you'd heard from Lieutenant Dennis?

A.   Well, very soon, I recognized similarity between what Dennis had told me and what he was saying.

And so, yes, I told him. I started to tell him. I told him that I'd heard a story that was like that, and started telling him.

Q. And that story was that a congressman had intervened on behalf of his son to have his orders changed to avoid combat and has some others pulled along with him, basically as window dressing?

A. Yes. Though I believe it was specifically a senator.

And I think the window-dressing idea was always just our own explanation. I mean Dennis and Gerhart didn't know why or at least if they did, they didn't tell me.

And I just assumed it.

Q. Ganes never told you that the reason that he was pulled was for window dressing?

A. No. Ganes was pulled, I understood, was to protect Ganes. Though I don't know that Ganes knew it in advance.

But I think after, somehow or other, he found out that he had been singled out by Senator Robertson, as well as Pat.

Q. How did he find that out? From whom?

A. I don't know. But, of course, he

probably -- I always just -- I mean since it was so easy, I assumed Pat told him. But I don't know when.

Q.   He never told you that?

A.   No. I don't believe Ed did.

Q.   This is all your assumption?

A.   Right.

Q.   And so when you relayed this story to Ed Ganes, he said "Oh, yes, I was one of the group that was pulled with Gerhart"?

A.   Yes.

Q.   And what else did he say?

A.   At some point, he told me that Pat Robertson was, too, and that Pat was the senator's son.

And then, as I say, we went over the whole story that Dennis had told.

I can't say now who supplied what parts. That is, Ed supplied it and I said that agreed with what Dennis had told me, or I supplied it as what Dennis had told me, and Ed agreed that that's what happened.

But together, we just told the whole story.

Q.   Well, what other parts to the story

are there prior to Gerhart approaching General Shepherd?

A.   Well, I guess, of course, you take issue with it.

But, of course, the story begins with a senator, with Senator Robertson arranged to get Pat pulled out of the draft, and Ed Ganes and some other guys, who included Gerhart.

So that would be where it began.

And then, Gerhart's encounter with Shepherd. And then Shepherd's response to that.

Q.   So basically, there are three (3) elements to the story?

A.   And then Pat went into a tizzy when he found out what had happened.

And then, as I recall, that's when Dennis' story ends.

Q.   Now you've also said that Mr. Ganes indicated to you that Senator Robertson was able to step in again?

A.   Yes.

Q.   And how did he accomplish that?

A.   How did Senator Robertson do it?

Q.   Right.

A.   I don't know. I mean, Ed Ganes did

not attempt to tell me how, if he knew.

     Q.   You didn't ask him?

     A.   I don't think so.

     MR. LEHNER: Are you talking about the mechanics or what?

     MR. LEISING: Yes.

EXAMINATION BY MR. LEISING: (Resuming)

     Q.   You didn't ask how the senator was able to supposedly accomplish this second instance of intervention on Pat's behalf?

     A.   No, I didn't because after World War II and then Korea, I mean, there is a great deal of cynicism about that sort of thing and I just felt that way, I mean.

     If he told me -- if Ed said that a senator got his son out of combat, I didn't ask him how because I just assumed he could.

     Q.   So based upon your understanding of what might have happened in the Second World war--

     A.   (Interrupting) There were a lot of stories about the Second World War about influential people doing that, and to a slight extent in Korea.

     And, of course, this was pretty soon after the First World -- did I say First World War?

64

Q.   Perhaps. I'm not sure.

A.   This is shortly after the Second World War.

But anyway, I mean I just shared the general American cynicism that if someone told me that a senator got his son out of combat, I wouldn't ask how, how did he do it.

Q.   Could that cynicism also extend to the notion that if somebody was the son of a congressman and happened to get a better assignment that others, that perhaps "Scuttlebutt" would develop around as to how this guy got his good job?

A.   It could happen. Of course, the statistics are pretty wierd, I guess.

Q.   What statistics?

A.   Well, the percentages of the eight (8) people including a senator's son, when one thinks of the number of officers in a draft.

I think we were a Battalion or a Regiment even of the draft.

Q.   Are you aware that after General Shepherd was approached by Gerhart, how quickly do you think, is your understanding, that Gerhart and Ganes left Camp Otsu, after the General come through?

A.   I would guess, two (2) or three (3) weeks. I would have -- I don't believe Ed told me but I don't know why he wouldn't have. But I would guess two (2) or three (3) weeks.   But that's a guess.

Q.   Why do you characterize it then as sort of a "Sudden emergency" and that Senator Robertson supposedly was not able to do anything for Ed Ganes at that point?

A.   Well, of course, the two (2) or three (3) weeks included the orders and everything. And so, unless one is going to -- on this one, I've got to fall back on not knowing the mechanics of getting people out of combat.

But that was the time it would take for General Shepherd to follow his evidence, make his decision.

And then, I don't know. I suppose the senator would have to go through Washington channels and then intervene in Fleet Marine Corps, Pacific, affairs.

And I suppose the General was going to take care of it between his headquarters and Korea and not via Washington.   So it would be a little more complicated procedure, I suppose.

But really, I guess I can't just say where it happened.

Q.   Did Ganes ever tell you that -- here, I'll quote from Page 26 of his transcript where he says "I know that within a week or two (2) we received orders.   This was after the General had come through.   But before the orders went into effect, Gerhart and I were given a week, ten- (10) days or maybe two- (2) weeks' leave to take.   It wouldn't be R and R but a vacation.   We went to Fugi."

A.   No, I don't know anything about that.

Q.   He didn't tell you about that?

A.   No.

Q.   Did Ed Ganes ever tell you that when he arrived in Japan, that when his ship first docked on Japan, that he'd received orders to Korea?

A.   No -- well, no.   I'd have to say no. I was just trying to think what my orders said.

Q.   By the way, did you stop in Japan on the way over?

A.   Yes.

Q.   Where did you stop?

A.   Yokosuka.

Q.   Was that the only port?

A.   No, because we stopped at Yokohama coming back.

Q.   But I mean that's the only port that you stopped at on the way over?

A.   Oh, yes.

Q.   How long did you stay there?

A.   About two (2), three (3) days.

Q.   What did you do while you were there?

A.   We got one (1) -- everybody got one (1) day and night, one (1) day liberty, up to late at night, and then -- I guess we were there two (2) days, one (1) day liberty and one (1) day confined to the ship.

Q.   So he never indicated to you that when he and Pat Robertson arrived in Japan, that they had orders to Korea and that either they or Pat alone called home to try to get the orders changed?

A.   He didn't indicate that. I believe-- no, he didn't indicate that.

But I think, if you're in a replacement draft, you have orders to Korea because I was in one.

But the phone call, I know nothing about. I've read that in the paper. But I didn't know anything about it.

Q.   Did you leave from San Diego?

A.   Yes.

Q.   And as best you recall, you had orders to Korea when you boarded the ship in San Diego?

A.   I think I was supposed to go to report to the First Marine. I think I was ordered to the First Marine Division.

But I didn't have to read them because I was in the replacement. I was in the ninth replacement draft.

And if you're in a replacement draft, you know where you're going.   I mean it's assumed that you're going to Korea.

But I think it actually says so too.

Q.   By the way, who is the Commanding Officer there when you were at the Rear CP?

A.   Colonel Bigfoot Brown was.   That was a sort of a camp-like thing. And I believe Colonel Bigfoot Brown was the Commanding Officer.

Q.   Okay. What about at Masan?

A.   Oh, I'm sorry.   I had Masan in mind when I answered that.

The   Commanding   Officer   of   the Division?

Q.   Well, you were basically in the Adjutant Section, weren't you?

A.   I guess I was. I don't know.

Q.   All right. Well, do you recall who the Adjutant was when you were in Masan?

A.   Where?

Q.   Let's go over Masan first.

A.   Who the Adjutant at Masan was?

Q.   Yes.

A.   No.

Q.   Or if there was an Adjutant at Masan?

A.   Well, right. I think there was but I don't know who he was.

I probably passed through his office on the way. I mean, I guess I passed. If he existed, I must have passed through his office on the way to the Board of Awards.

Q.   Who was your immediate supervisor?

A.   At Masan?

Q.   Yes.

A.   Nobody. Ed Ganes and I were the only two (2) officers assigned to the Board of Awards, Rear.

One of us, was a citation writer and the other one was the assistant recorder of the

Board of Awards in charge of the Board of Awards,
Rear.

And it took us the three (3) weeks to
find out which of us was which.

Apparently, it turns out, I was the--
at least after I got there, it turns out that I was
officially considered to be assistant recorder of
the Board of Awards in charge of the Rear because
I'm senior to him by a few hundred file numbers.

My serial number is oh, five, oh,
five, four, nine (050549) and I'm a little higher
than he is because we have the same -- we're both
second lieutenants and we have the same rank, the
same date of rank, so only the fact that my name
begins with "B" and his with "G" and that put me,
of all the guys who got commissioned that day, that
put me a few hundred numbers ahead of him and that
makes me senior to him.

And so nominally, it turned out
finally that I was supposed to be in charge of the
Board of Awards, Rear, and he was a citation
writer.

But who my immediate superior was, I
don't know. I think, like in one respect, my
immediate superior was the recorder of the Board of

Awards was a Lieutenant Dibble (Phonetically) back at the main CP.

Of course, we're kind of divided up like that. And we're together at Masan only for housekeeping purposes.

And if I had a superior at Masan, I didn't know who he was. Nobody ever checked up on us.

We were fairly conscientious. And I actually -- Ed and I worked a fair amount at Masan, which puts us in a minority.

MR. LEISING: I think I'm about done. I think that's all.

EXAMINATION BY MR. LEHNER:

Q. Let me just ask you a couple of follow-up questions.

I believe in response to a question that Mr. Leising asked, you testified that you believe you may have heard Mr. Robertson refer to himself as the "Liquor Officer," is that correct?

A. Yes, jollily, of course.

Q. Did you ever have an occasion to learn or did you know that Mr. Robertson, during the period of time you were at Masan, was assigned to the billet as the Area Assistant Exchange Officer?

A.   No -- well, I have a vague
recollection, I believe I told you, that he might
have been connected with the Officers' Club. But I
had a vague idea that he is -- I have a vague idea
that he was involved somehow with that sort of
thing, whether it's the Post Exchange or the
Officers' Club or something for the Enlisted-Man's
Club.

But I can't specify what it is and it
could be that it's not even correct.

Q.   Now you recall that there was an
Officers' Club in Masan?

A.   Oh, yes, indeed.

Q.   And do you recall whether there was an
Exchange, a Post Exchange, at Masan as well?

A.   I don't know. I suppose there was.
Of course, there was an Enlisted-Man's
Club and I understand they at least got beer or
something for those guys, too.

But I guess there was a Post Exchange.

Q.   Now you spent a number of weeks at
Masan.

Were those days that you would
consider as being in combat?

A.   Oh, no, quite the reverse. Of course,

I was very sorry when those three (3) weeks -- of course, I knew I wasn't going back to combat because at the CP in a war, being at the Main CP in a war like Korea is not being in combat though, of course, it officially counts as a combat zone.

But I was sorry to leave Masan because I knew I wasn't going into combat in the Main CP but I was leading a very cushy life for living in the tent, living in tents.

Q.   And I guess that that would be true then of the months that you spent at the Division CP?

Would you consider that to have been days in combat?

A.   No, though if I got a medal for meritorious citation writing at the Division CP which, of course, is not inconceivable, it would have been the Combat V because we were officially in the combat zone.

Q.   Do you recall a fellow named Bifred Bar (Phonetically spelled)?

A.   That sounds familiar but I don't know.

Though I cannot put the name to any particular face, there were a couple of people, according to Ed that   -- and he may have shown me this written down somewhere. There were a couple of people who were nominally assigned to the Board of Awards, Board of Awards, Rear, who never came by.

And for some reason, Ed and I were expected to write citations. These guys didn't.

Q. Would you describe for me briefly your duties in the Board of Awards? Specifically, were you in charge of recommending people for Bronze Stars?

A. Well, no, we didn't do that. We process, we processed the paperwork connected with that.

In other words, somebody down-- though, of course, Generals took care of favorite sergeants right there in the CP and got them Meritorious Awards for service.

But typical awards, some guy down in a Company gets recommended for an award. It comes up through his Battalion, through his Regiment, to the Division CP. The recommendation stating what he did and all sorts of supporting documentation and so on, a recommendation that he receive some particular award.

And the Board of Awards -- do you want

me to go into all of the steps for an award?

Q. Well, I'm specifically interested in if you have any knowledge as to how were the mechanics or what role you may have played in awarding the Bronze Stars to people who received it during the course of the War.

Do you have any recollection of that?

A. What we did?

Q. Yes.

A. Well, if it's a Bronze -- well, if the guy is recommended for anything, the recommendation comes to the Board of Awards -- the First Marine Division from the Regiment, who's gotten it from Battalion and so on. And it comes to the Board of Awards' Office.

We take everything they've got, stick a buck tag on it and start sending it around to members of the Board of Awards.

Now the Board of Awards consists of all the Field-Grade Officers who are serving in the CP for any reason.

The Chairman of the Board of Award, ex officio, is the Assistant Division Commander. It was General Faley (Phonetically spelled).

And then the Recorder of the Board of

Awards, or like a secretary, is the guy who is in charge of the staff of the Board of Awards. And he is actually a member of the Board of Awards, too.

But otherwise, it's all Field-Grade Officers.

But they never meet. The Board never meets. It's just an empty title.

And what happens is that then we stick a buck tag on the recommendation and then one of the guys in our office, which we'd build up a stack of them.

And one of the guys in our office runs it to one (1) of the members of the Board of Awards and he votes for it.

If the guy is recommended for a Bronze Star, he doesn't vote yes or no. He could write down "Bronze Star" or he could bump it to "Silver Star" or he could bring it down to "Letter of Commendation" or no award.

He says what he thinks the guy ought to get and signs the buck tag to the right of that.

We take it to five (5) guys like that. And then, of course, we take it to another five (5) to try to keep the work load with these officers, all of whom have other duties, even.

And when five (5) of them have voted, we bring it back. If it's clear cut what they want, we write a citation for it. If it's not, we send it to a sixth or a seventh until we get a majority.

And then our office, I or Ed Ganes or somebody like that, if we're all there together, we write up a citation based on what the fellow did because his recommendation states that.

And we draft a covering letter for the General to sign, General Thomas, the Commanding General of the Division. And the we sent the whole thing. Then, of 'course, we type it with numerous copies.

And then the whole thing is taken up to General Whaley (Phonetically spelled). And if he objects to it in some way, well, he sends it back to us and we write it up the way he said, not the way the five (5) guys said.

If, as in most cases, he approves it, he gives it to the General to sign and then the fellow gets the award.

We handled everything up through Silver Star and Legion of Merit. They're the same level. One is meritorious service and one is heroic.

And then, above that, the Commanding General of the Division can't award it. He can only recommend.

So we just send a recommendation to Washington for a Navy Cross or Distinguished-Service Metal.

Q. One other question concerning any conversation you had with Ed Ganes.

Did he describe to you in any of your conversations, what his duties were when he was at Camp Otsu?

A. No, he didn't. I don't know. I don't know what they did.

I don't think they did much of anything but I don't know what it was.

Q. You don't remember discussing what he may have done with him?

A. No.

MR. LEHNER: I have no further questions.

MR. LEISING: I have no questions.

(Whereupon, the taking of the witness' testimony was concluded.)

C E R T I F I C A T E

I, Goldie F. Kinchen, Certified Shorthand Reporter, State of Louisiana, do hereby certify that PAUL WILLIAM BROSMAN, JR., who, after having been first duly sworn to testify to the truth, the whole truth, and nothing but the truth, did testify as hereinbefore set forth in the foregoing seventy-eight (78) pages;

That the testimony was reported by me in shorthand and transcribed under my personal direction and supervision, and is a true and correct transcript, to the best of my ability and understanding;

That I am not of Counsel, not related to Counsel, nor to the parties hereto, and am in no way interested in the outcome of this event.

Goldie F. Kinchen, CSR, RPR

Goldie F. Kinchen,
Certified Shorthand Reporter,
Registered Professional Reporter

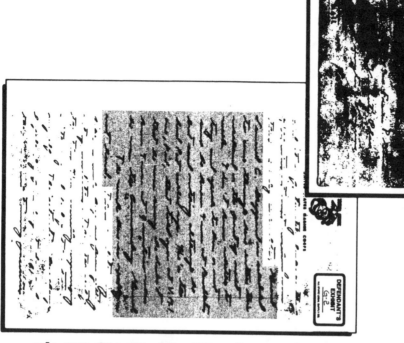

General Lemuel C. Shepherd is scheduled to come through here either this weekend or the first of next week. I don't know whether to try and speak to him or not since he knew I was at Pendleton but said nothing although he had Pat called up. He's the one, Did, that told you at V.M.I. that he was sorry he didn't know I was at Quantico when he was the Commanding General.

The work here is really not hard.

Letter of Edwin M. Gaines
March 6, 1951

Today I'm Officer of the day again. Yesterday General General Shepherd came through for the day. We had spent a week preparing, including all day Sunday, and were gratified with his apparently extreme satisfaction with what he saw. From his remarks I presume I'll be here for a month or two at least. I was introduced to him, but it was not until later when Pat told him I was Lexington that he saw any connections. Then he came over and chatted with me, complimenting you highly, Did.

Letter of Edwin M. Gaines
May 19, 1951

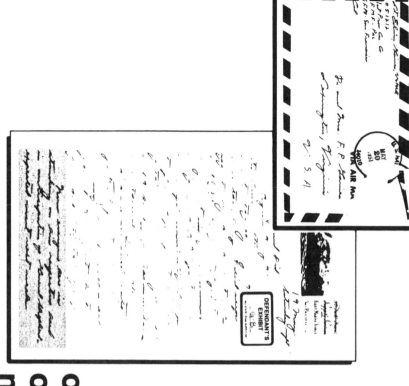

Now everyone here is standing on his respective head in anticipation of General Shepherd's expected visit next week sometime, It's sorta of a work and relax cycle now between generals' visits. At least it gives me a feeling of being an old hand now to be able to greet the general again.

Letter of Edwin M. Gaines
June 1, 1951

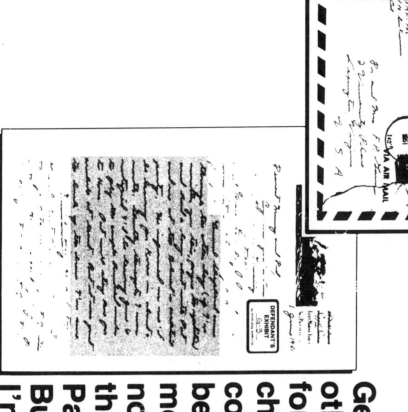

General Shepherd came through the other day (if I've written you this, forgive the repetition) and had a long chat with Pat and me at the Colonel's cocktail party. He informed us we'd be leaving for Korea in about a month. Shortly thereafter I was notified I'd be leaving June 6 to ply the couple hundred miles to Korea. Pat will stay here for awhile at least. But it was just the luck of the draw I'm sure.

Letter of Edwin M. Gaines
October 3, 1951

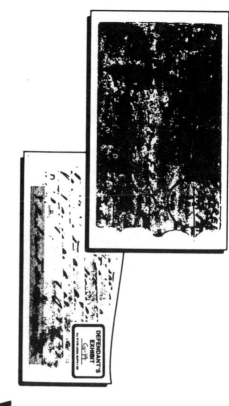

I had sent a message to Pat in Wonsan, about forty miles from here, that I was here. And he came to see me. It was really good to see the old reprobate. He was genuinely anxious to do all he could for me and brought a present. He's now courrier between Wonsan and Japan, flying back and forth with three to five days of every every week in Japan.

Letter of Edwin M. Gaines
November 3, 1951

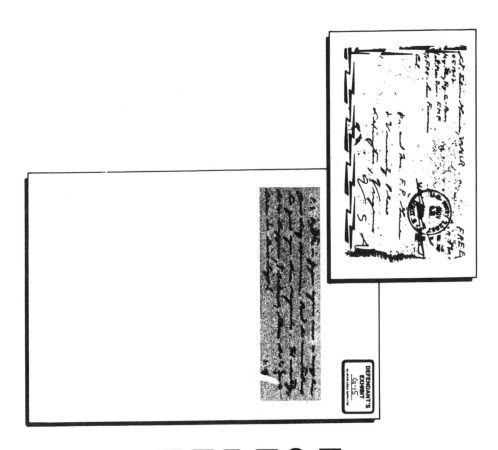

P.S. Pat's in Japan again now on one of his five day excursions. But he wanted me to give you his regards. Honestly, he's happier, I believe, than he's ever been in his life!

Appendix F

The official biography of a career professional Marine officer is placed here simply as an example of typical assignments a regular Marine officer might have in 35 years of service in the Corps during the decades of the '40s, '50s, '60s and '70s.

Colonel Robert Schening, now in his 70s, remains active as a volunteer Red Cross worker during periods of flood, hurricanes and other disasters.

COLONEL RICHARD JOHN SCHENING, USMC

Enlisting in the U.S. Marine Corps as a private in September, 1940, Colonel Schening attended basic training (Boot Camp) at PARRIS ISLAND, SOUTH CAROLINA. Upon completing Boot Camp in December, 1940, he was assigned to the 5th Marine Regiment, First Marine Brigade, Fleet Marine Force, on duty at GUANTANAMO BAY, CUBA. While in CUBA, the Marines of the Brigade were involved in testing and perfecting many new innovations in amphibious warfare which would soon be applied in combat during WORLD WAR II. In February, 1941, the Marine Corps formed the First Marine Division. The formation of the First Marine Division marked the first time the Marine Corps had its own unit of Division size and the first integrated amphibious striking force of such size ever formed in the United States Armed Forces.

Returning from CUBA in May, 1941, Colonel Schening was initially stationed at PARRIS ISLAND, SOUTH CAROLINA with the 1st Marine Regiment. In August of that year, he was transferred to CAMP LEJEUNE (New River), NORTH CAROLINA, the new home of the First Marine Division. With the outbreak of WORLD WAR II in December, 1941 (The Attack on PEARL HARBOR), the Division began deploying units to the PACIFIC. On May 20, 1942, Colonel Schening, again assigned to the 5th Marines and other elements of the Division sailed from NORFOLK, VIRGINIA, via the PANAMA CANAL to WELLINGTON, NEW ZEALAND, arriving there on June 20th.

Taking part in the first American ground offensive action of WORLD WAR II, in the PACIFIC, Colonel Schening participated in the amphibious assault of TULAGI/GUADALCANAL, BRITISH SOLOMON ISLANDS, on August 7, 1942. He also participated in combat operations in MILNE and ORO BAY, NEW GUINEA; CAPE GLOUCHESTER, TALESEA and CAPE HOSKINS, NEW BRITAIN ISLAND, and on PELELIU, PALAU ISLANDS. Wounded twice during these operations and reaching the rank of Sergeant, he was awarded a "Battlefield" Commission as a Second Lieutenant during the battle for PELELIU ISLAND.

During the period of June, 1945 to June, 1950, he held various assignments at the Marine Barracks, New York Naval Shipyard, BROOKLYN, NEW YORK; with the Marine Detachment aboard the Battleship "USS IOWA" (BB-61), in the PACIFIC and again with the 5th Marines, First Division at CAMP PENDLETON, OCEANSIDE, CALIFORNIA. While assigned to the 5th Marines, Colonel Schening held assignments as an Infantry Platoon Leader, Assistant Battalion S-3 (Operations), Company Commander and as a Battalion S-2 (Intelligence) Officer.

With the outbreak of the KOREAN WAR in June, 1950, the First Marine Division was again called upon to be one of the first units committed to the war. Colonel Schening, then a First Lieutenant and the Executive Officer of "C" Company, 1st Battalion, 5th Marines, sailed from SAN DIEGO, CALIFORNIA on July 25, 1950, for PUSAN, KOREA. During the ten (10) months he spent in KOREA, Colonel Schening participated in combat operations in the PUSAN PERIMETER; INCHON LANDING; BATTLE for SEOUL, CHOSIN RESERVOIR and in CENTRAL, KOREA. Wounded for the third time, in CENTRAL, KOREA on May 29, 1951, while commanding "C" Company, 1st Battalion, 5th Marines, he was medically evacuated to the U.S. Naval Hospital, YOKOSUKA, JAPAN. He remained hospitalized until his return to the UNITED STATES in July, 1951.

His first assignment on return from KOREA was with the Marine Corps Organized Reserve Program as an Inspector-Instructor. This assignment included reactivating the 2nd Rifle Company, USMCR in NEW ROCHELL, NEW YORK, whose previous members were still serving in KOREA. A second task was to act as a "Casualty Assistance" Officer who made "Home Visits" to the families of wounded or deceased Marines of the KOREAN WAR and resided in the area. During this period, Colonel Schening was promoted to Captain.

Between 1953-1956, Colonel Schening was assigned to the U.S. Naval Retraining Command, PORTSMOUTH, NEW HAMPSHIRE, where he was assigned as the Assistant Custody Officer and In-Service Training Officer. As the Assistant Custody Officer, he assisted the Custody Officer (Major), in providing safety and security for over 3000 military prisoners and 400 civilian and military staff. As the In-Service Training Officer, he was responsible for the orientation and training of all military and civilian personnel assigned to the Command in the prior handling, control and training of the prisoners. While at PORTSMOUTH, Colonel Schening attended a three month "Correctional Administration" Course conducted at George Washington University, WASHINGTON, DC. In July of 1955, Colonel Schening was promoted to Major.

In December of 1956, Colonel Schening was assigned to attend the U.S. Army's "Anti-Aircraft/Guided Missile School" at FORT BLISS, EL PASO, TEXAS. There he studied the Administration, Supply, Operations and Defense functions of Anti-Aircraft/Guided Missile Units. Upon completing this four month course, he was further assigned for duty with the 2nd Anti-Aircraft, Automatic Weapons Battalion (Self-Propelled) at the Marine Corps Base, TWENTY-NINE PALMS, CALIFORNIA. While with the Battalion, Colonel Schening's assignments included those of Battalion S-3 (Operations) and as Battalion Executive Officer.

In October, 1958, Colonel Schening was ordered to duty with the U.S. Marine Component, U.S. Naval Advisory Group, SOEUL, KOREA. Prior to departing the UNITED STATES, he attended a month long course at the U.S. Military Assistance School in ARLINGTON, VIRGINIA. Arriving in SEOUL, KOREA on the 7th of November, 1958, he was assigned duties as the G-2/G-3 (Intelligence/Operations) Advisor to The Republic of Korea Marine Corps Headquarters, SEOUL, KOREA. During the last five months of his stay, he was assigned as the Senior Advisor to the 1st Republic of Korea Marine Division stationed at POHANG, KOREA. While in KOREA, Colonel Schening attended many Security Defense Conferences in JAPAN, TAIWAN, OKINAWA and the PHILIPPINES as a representative of the United States and United Nations Commands.

Returning to the UNITED STATES in November, 1959, Colonel Schening reported for duty at the Marine Corps Schools, QUANTICO, VIRGINIA, where he was assigned as an Instructor/Writer at the Marine Corps Education Center's "Extension School." After two and a half years in that assignment, he attended the nine month "Senior Amphibious Warfare College," Class of 1962-63. While a student at QUANTICO, he was promoted to Lieutenant Colonel.

Leaving QUANTICO in June, 1963, Colonel Schening reported to Headquarters, U.S. Marine Corps, WASHINGTON, DC. Initially assigned as a writer, then Head of the Marine Corps Historical Branch, he was reassigned after six months to the Plan Branch, G-3 Division., For the next two and a half years Colonel Schening performed duties as an "Action" Officer in the Joint Planning Group under the Deputy Chief of Staff (Plans & Programs). In that assignment, he was responsible for Marine Corps action papers to the Joint Chiefs of Staff. His specific area of responsibility covered Plans, Programs and Policies of concern to the Marine Corps, regarding Europe, NATO and Berlin. In connection with these responsibilities, Colonel Schening attended numerous European, NATO and Berlin defense conferences in ENGLAND and FRANCE. Included in these was a two week NATO Strategy Seminar held at St. James College, OXFORD, ENGLAND.

In August, 1966, Colonel Schening was transferred to the Second Marine Division, CAMP LEJEUNE, NORTH CAROLINA. He was assigned the duties of Assistant G-4 (Logistics) and later as the Assistant Chief of Staff, G-4, of the 16th Marine Expeditionary Brigade which conducted operations in the CARIBBEAN area from October, 1966 to March, 1967.

In June, 1967, Colonel Schening departed for combat duty in the REPUBLIC of VIETNAM. Assigned as the Commanding Officer of the 1st Battalion, 9th Marines, Third Marine Division, he joined the Battalion then operating in the "DEMILITARIZED

ZONE" between NORTH and SOUTH VIETNAM. He and the Battalion participated in combat operations around "CON-THIEN, THE ROCK PILE, CAMP CARROLL, CAM-LO and DONG-HA."

During the period that the Battalion was at CON-THIEN and under continuous mortar and artillery fire, Colonel Schening earned his fourth "Purple Heart." The second half of duty in VIET NAM, Colonel Schening was assigned as the III Marine Amphibious Force, Liaison Officer, to the Second Republic of Korea Brigade. The Brigade (known as the "Blue" Dragon Brigade), was one of the Free World Forces supporting the South Vietnamese Government. During the period he was assigned to the ROK Marines, the Brigade conducted combat operations in the CHUI-LAI and HOI-AN/DANANG area. While at HOI-AN, the Brigade was involved in the January, 1968, North Vietnamese "TET" Offensive.

Returning to the UNITED STATES in July, 1968, Colonel Schening was initially assigned to the National Security Agency, FORT MEADE, MARYLAND, but in being promoted to Colonel in September, he was reassigned to Headquarters, U.S. Marine Corps, WASHINGTON, DC. Assigned to the Plans and Operations Branch of the G-4 Division (Logistics), his duties were those of Logistic Planner representing the Marine Corps to the Joint Chiefs of Staff. In that position, he was responsible to the Commandant of the Marine Corps, for all Marine Corps logistic action and strategic mobility papers concerning plans, programs and policies being considered by the Joint Chiefs of Staff.

In May, 1970, Colonel Schening attended The Defense Management Systems Course at the Naval Post Graduate School, MONTEREY, CALIFORNIA. On completing school in June, he was ordered to assume command of the Marine Barracks, National Security Agency (NSA). Taking command on July 2, 1970, Colonel Schening was responsible for providing the physical security forces and plans to support the National Security Agency's mission. To do this, the Barracks was staffed with 500 "Top Secret" cleared Marines. In addition to its mission to the National Security Agency, the Barracks had for eight years provided a ceremonial detail to perform the "Tatoo" Ceremony at the National Historic Shrine at FORT McHENRY, BALTIMORE, MARYLAND. This ceremony which was reenacted once a week during the summer months, was put on in conjunction with the City of Baltimore and the National Park Service. A National Freedom Foundation Medal was presented to the Marine Barracks, Fort Meade for this effort.

In September, 1973, Colonel Schening was ordered to duty with Headquarters, Fleet Marine Force, Atlantic, in NORFOLK, VIRGINIA. At that command, he was assigned duties as the Assistant Chief of Staff, G-1 (Personnel). He was responsible to the Commanding General for all personnel plans, programs and policies for the Force which numbered over 40,000 Marines. These Marines, making up the Second Marine Division, Second Marine Air Wing and Force Troops were Headquartered in bases on the East Coast. Elements of these units were deployed to EUROPE, MEDITERRANEAN, CARIBBEAN, in the ATLANTIC and Continental United States.

After a year in the above assignment, Colonel Schening was ordered back to WASHINGTON where he was assigned as the Marine Corps Representative to the Naval Physical Evaluation Board at the National Naval Medical Center, BETHESDA, MARYLAND. He remained in that assignment until his retirement from the Marine Corps on May 1, 1975, after serving over 34-1/2 years.

AWARDS AND DECORATIONS

Silver Star Medal
Legion of Merit w/Combat "V"
Meritorious Service Medal
Joint Service Commendation Medal
Purple Heart w/3 Gold Stars
Combat Action Ribbon
Presidential Unit Citation w/7
    Bronze Stars
Navy Unit Commendation w/1 Star
Marine Corps Good COnduct Medal
American Defense Medal w/1 Star
American Theater Medal

Asiatic Pacific Service Medal
    w/5 Bronze Stars
World War II Victory Medal
National Defense Medal w/1 Star
Korean Service Medal w/1 Silver Star
Vietnamese Campaign Medal w/3 Stars
United Nations Service Medal
Korean Order of Military Merit
Korean Presidential Citation
Vietnamese Service Medal
Vietnamese Cross of Gallantry
    w/Palm & Frame

PROMOTIONS

Private-Sergeant	1940-43	Captain	June -1952
Second Lieutenant	December-1944	Major	July-1955
First Lieutenant	June-1946	Lieutenant Colonel	February-1963

Colonel-September-1968

Reviewed June 1977

Colonel Richard J. Schening, USMC (Ret)

Retiring from the U.S. Marine Corps on May 1, 1975, I accepted a position at the Arlington Hospital, Arlington, Virginia, as the Director, Safety, Security & Communications.

My over-all responsibilities consisted of Organizing, Training and Managing the Security Force and Communications Office and Operators. The Communications function included the total management of the Telephone System for the Hospital and Patients, the In-house and Medical Radio Paging System, the Security and Emergency Radio System, the Emergency Alarm, and Paging System.

As Director, Safety-Security, I was responsible for Loss Prevention, Accident and Theft Investigation, Parking, Identification System and Vehicle Registration, the Safety Program, Orientation Training of all Hospital Employees, the Security Force, and writing and exercising all Hospital Emergency Plans. These included:

> Disaster Plan
> Safety plan
> Radiological Safety Plan
> Bomb Threat Plan
> Security Plan
> Fire Plan
> Emergency Evacuation Plan
> Handicap Access Plan
> Emergency Communications Plan

After ten (10) years at the Hospital, I again elected to retire in order to be able to spend more time in my volunteer work with the American Red Cross. This work actually started in 1980 while I was employed by the Hospital. Sometime in the Spring of 1980, I was asked to assist the local Chapter of the American Red Cross in developing their Disaster Plan. I did and found myself appointed as the Chairman of the Disaster Committee. As a Volunteer with the Arlington County Chapter, ARC for the past 11-12 years I have held the following positions. Chairman, Disaster Committee; Chairman,

Building and Grounds Committee; Six (6) years on the Chapter's Board of Directors and Executive Committee, and as a "Disaster Specialist" in The Disaster Services Human Resource System (DSHRS). This System is organized to provide qualified and trained personnel to respond to National Disasters. To date, I have participated (since 1988), in six (6) National Disasters.

In addition to my work at the Chapter and with the DSHRS, I volunteer two days a week at the Red Cross Eastern Operations Headquarters located in Alexandria, Virginia. I work for Disaster Services and assist in coordination of the Emergency Response Vehicle (ERV's) Fleet on the East Coast. (70 ERV's).

I also volunteer as a "Disaster Specialist" to the Potomac Tri-State Territory Field Office also in Alexandria, Virginia. In this position, I cover eight (8) Counties in Maryland and Virginia assisting small territorial Chapters in Disaster Training, Planning and Preparedness.

I'm married, wife; Mary Patricia (McCarthy). We have seven (7) children—Ages 25 to 36 and six (6) Grandchildren.

Sorry, I cannot admit to any exotic educational background.

Charlie Company's defense perimeter the night of June 1 →

Pete and Helen McCloskey, Hill 610, Korea 1987

About the Author

Paul N. "Pete" McCloskey, Jr. is a 4th generation Californian, born in Loma Linda, California in 1927. His great-grandfather was orphaned during the potato famine in Ireland in the 1840s and emigrated to the United States at the age of eight, becoming a farmer in Merced County, California. Both grandfathers and his father practiced law in California, as McCloskey does today, specializing in condemnation and other civil litigation in Menlo Park, California.

McCloskey attended grammar school and high school in South Pasadena, California, and after 19 months service as an enlisted man in the U.S. Navy, entered Stanford University in 1947, receiving a bachelor's degree in 1950 and a Doctor of Jurisprudence degree from Stanford law School in 1953. McCloskey enlisted in the Marine Corps Platoon Leaders Class (PLC) program in 1948 and was commissioned as a Second Lieutenant in the Marine Corps Reserve just prior to the North Korean attack on South Korea in June, 1950. He served nine months with the Fifth Marine Regiment, in Korea in 1951, and was awarded the Navy Cross, Silver Star and two Purple Hearts for wounds received on May 29 and June 11, 1951. Upon returning to civilian life he commanded a Marine Reserve Rifle Company until 1960.

McCloskey served as a Deputy District Attorney in Alameda County from 1953 to 1955, thereafter practicing law in Palo Alto until 1967, during which time he was a founding partner of McCloskey, Wilson & Mosher, now Wilson, Sonsini, Goodrich & Rosati, as well as a partner in California's first environmental law firm, Butler & McCloskey.

He was elected to Congress in 1967, defeating the Honorable Shirley Temple Black, and after being reelected to the House seven times, was defeated in the U.S. Senate primary in California in 1982 by now Governor Pete Wilson.

He received the National Park Association 1970 award for his service as National Co-Chairman of the first Earth Day.

In 1972 McCloskey challenged President Richard Nixon's Viet Nam War policy in the Republican presidential primary in New Hampshire and seven other states, receiving one delegate to the Republican convention from New Mexico.

He is married to the former Helen Hooper of Woodside, California, who served as his press secretary while in Congress. The McCloskeys were married in 1982 at Fall River Mills, California. Mrs. McCloskey edited, designed and published this book.

McCloskey has four children, Nancy, a public health administrator in Washington, D.C., Peter, a trial lawyer with the Civil Rights Division of the U.S. Justice Department, John, manager of the family farm in Rumsey, California, and Kathleen, a veterinarian of Waynesboro, Pennsylvania.

McCloskey currently serves as Chairman of the Commission on National and Community Service, created by the National and Community Service Act of 1990, and teaches one course a year at Santa Clara University.

McCloskey is the author of two books: an 8th grade text, *The U.S. Constitution*, Behavioral Research Laboratories, 1961, and *Truth and Untruth, Political Deceit in America*, Simon and Shuster, 1972. As President of the Conference of Barristers he also edited Guides to Professional Conduct for New California Practitioners, California State Bar, 1961.

He and Mrs. McCloskey reside at 580 Mountain Home Rd., Woodside, California 94062, and any corrections to these essays may be sent to him at that address.